THE
ADDRESS
BOOK

Other Books by Michael Levine

The Corporate Address Book

The Music Address Book

The Environmental Address Book

The Kid's Address Book

Guerrilla PR

Lessons at the Halfway Point

Take It from Me: Practical and Inspiring
Advice from the Celebrated and the Successful

Selling Goodness

The Health Address Book

The Princess and the Package

How to Raise Your Social IQ

THE ADDRESS BOOK

How to Reach Anyone Who *Is* Anyone

MICHAEL LEVINE

A Perigee Book

Every effort has been made to provide the most current mailing addresses. Addresses, however, do change, and neither the publisher nor the author is responsible for misdirected or returned mail.

A Perigee Book
Published by The Berkley Publishing Group
A division of Penguin Putnam Inc.
375 Hudson Street
New York, New York 10014

First printing of the tenth edition: April 2001

ISBN 0-399-52667-6
ISSN 1090-0101

Published simultaneously in Canada.

The Penguin Putnam Inc. World Wide Web site address is
http://www.penguinputnam.com

Printed in the United States of America

10 9 8 7 6 5 4 3

Acknowledgments

I'm lucky. I get to say publicly to the special people in my life how much they mean to me. To each of them, my appreciation for their help with this book and, most of all, their unwavering friendship and love.

My literary agent, Alice Martell.

My friends at Putnam, where I have been published since 1984.

My father, Arthur O. Levine, stepmother, Marilyn, and sister, Patty.

My special friends Adam Christing, Richard Imprescia, Karen Karsian, Richard Lawson, Nancy Mager, John McKillop, Cable Neuhaus, and Alyse Reynolds.

Special thanks to Joe Kaufmann for commitment to excellence in the researching of this book.

To my work associates Jim Erickson, Rebecca Gallegos, Phil Kass, Mark Lowen, Steve Wagner.

Interns interested in working in Mr. Levine's Los Angeles office should contact:

Intern Coordinator
Levine Communications Office
5750 Wilshire Blvd.
Suite 555
Los Angeles, CA 90036
Action@levinepr.com

Introduction

A couple of years ago, I proudly accepted an invitation to deliver a speech at the Harvard Business School. Never having visited an Ivy League school, I wasn't quite sure what to expect.

The audience of America's best and brightest took me completely by surprise—and damn near gave the faculty a collective heart attack—when they stood and cheered my concluding observation: "Some ideas are so stupid, only intellectuals can believe them."

I came to appreciate this truism about twelve years ago when I first approached New York's publishing elite with my admittedly simple idea to create a series of address books. One by one, they peered down from their thrones, rejecting the idea as "far too simple," and suggesting that in this hurry-up world, only fools would be naive enough to write to people they didn't know.

Finally, Putnam saw its worth, and today, it is estimated over 4,000,000 letters have been successfully delivered, thanks to this best-selling series of address books.

I've heard from desperate medical patients who have received help from blood donors thanks to the book, from lost loves reunited, from consumers battling and beating corporate villains, and, of course, from fans hearing from their heroes.

By the way, a few years ago I visited the White House, and never in my life did I feel prouder than when I saw *The Address Book* on the desks in several executive offices.

Yes, the address book was a simple idea; an idea that works. But, how can you make it work for you?

*How can you make sure the notable receives your letter? The number-one reason mail to notables is left unanswered is that it is addressed improperly and never reaches its intended destination. A letter addressed simply to "Barbra Streisand, Hollywood, California" will find its way only to the dead-letter file of the post office. The complete, accurate addresses in this book will get your mail to the offices, agents, studios, managers, or even homes of the addressees, and I have been unable to find one notable, no matter how busy or important, who doesn't personally read some of his or her mail—even the President of the United States. That doesn't mean notables read and answer every single piece, but it should offer encouragement to people who write to them.

*Politicians have a standard rule of thumb: for every letter they receive, they estimate that one hundred people who didn't take the time to write are thinking the same thought as the letter expresses. So you can calculate the effect of your single letter by multiplying it by one hundred! And all entertainment figures keep a close watch on their mail. It is a real indication of what people are thinking and feeling. Often, the notable is surrounded by a small group of associates who tend to isolate the star from the public. Your letter helps break down this barrier. Amazing things have been accomplished with letters as long as they have the proper mailing address.

*Here are several important things to remember in writing notables: Always include a self-addressed stamped envelope. This is the single most important factor in writing a letter if you want a response. Because of the unusually high volume of mail notable people receive, anything you can do to make it easier for them to respond is going to work in your favor. Keep your letters short and to the point. Notables are usually extremely busy people, and long letters tend to be set aside for "future" consideration. For instance, if you want an autographed picture of your favorite TV personality, don't write three pages of prose to explain your request.

*Make your letters as easy to read as possible. This means type it or, at the very least, handwrite it very neatly. Avoid crayons, markers, or even pencils. And don't forget to leave some margins on the paper.

*Be sure to include your name and address (even on all materials that you include with your letter) in the event the materials are separated from your letter. You would be amazed how many people write letters without return addresses and then wonder why they never hear from the person to whom they wrote.

*Never send food to notables. Due to spoilage and security matters, it cannot be eaten anyway. (Would you eat a box of homemade brownies given to you by a total stranger?) If you send gifts, don't wrap them in large boxes with yards of paper, string, and tape around them. (They may not have a crowbar on hand.) Again, don't forget to include your name and address on all material you send. Of course, don't send—or ask for—money.

*In writing to corporation heads, remember most of them rose to their lofty positions because they were better problem-solvers than their company peers. Good corporation heads are zealous about finding solutions to written complaints (especially if you have sent copies of your complaint letters to appropriate consumer organizations). A recent survey of corporation heads showed that 88 percent of all letters of complaint were resolved. Therefore, the old adage, "When you have a problem, go to the top," appears to be accurate. Likewise, corporation executives greatly appreciate hearing good news (satisfaction, extra service, helpful employees, and so forth).

But nowhere is it written that mail should only be filled with praise and congratulations. You may enjoy shaking a fist at your favorite villain, so I have included infamous people in my book.

Most people are usually very kind and sincere in their letters. They write what they would say or ask if they had the opportunity to do so in person. This is especially true of children, who are extremely honest. On the other hand, infamous people and others who are out of favor with the public predictably receive hostile and angry letters.

Most of the people, famous and infamous, listed in *The Address Book* are movers and shakers, and thus highly transient, changing their addresses far more often than the average person. Their mail is usually forwarded to them, but occasionally a letter may be returned to the sender. If this should happen to your letter, first check to make sure that you have copied the address correctly. If you wish to locate another address for the person to whom you are writing, begin your search by writing to him or her in care of the company or association with which they may have been most recently associated. For example, if a musician or singer has last recorded an album with a specific record company, write in care of that company; a sports figure might be contacted through the last team he or she was associated with; an author through his or her most recent publisher; and so forth.

According to 1987 statistics, about 90 million pieces of mail land in the dead-letter pile because the carrier couldn't make out the address, so write clearly.

Remember, *a person who writes to another makes more impact than ten thousand who are silent.*

—Michael Levine
Los Angeles, CA
levinepr@earthlink.net

And none will hear the postman's knock without a quickening of the heart. For who can bear to feel himself forgotten?

—W. H. AUDEN, from "Night Mail"

Aadland, Beverly
PO Box 1115
Canyon Country, CA 91350
Actress

Aaron, Hank
PO Box 4064
Atlanta, GA 30302
Former baseball player

Aaron, Tommy
PO Drawer 545
Buford, GA 30518
Golfer

AARP (American Association for Retired Persons)
601 E Street NW
Washington, DC 20049
Website: http://www.aarp.org/
E-mail: member@aarp.org
Joseph S. Perkins, President
Association for senior citizens

ABBA
Postbus 3079
NL4700 GB
Roosendaal
The Netherlands
Pop group

Abbot Laboratories
100 Abbott Park Rd.
Abbott Park, IL 60064
Website: http://www.abbott.com
Miles D. White, Chairman and CEO
Drug manufacturer

Abbott and Costello Fan Club
PO Box 2084
Toluca Lake, CA 91610

Abbott, Gregory
PO Box 68
Bergenfield, NY 07621
Singer

ABC Entertainment
2040 Ave. of the Stars
Century City, CA 90067
or
77 West 66th St., 9th Floor
New York, NY 10023
Robert F. Callahan, President, ABC Broadcast Group
Major television network

Abdul, Paula
14755 Ventura Blvd, #1-710
Sherman Oaks, CA 91403
or
12434 Wilshire Blvd., #770
Los Angeles, CA 90024
Singer, dancer, choreographer
Birthday: 6/19/62

Abdul-Jabbar, Kareem
2049 Century Park East, Suite
    1200
Century City, CA 90067

Abdullah the Butcher
1000 S. Industrial Blvd.
Dallas, TX 75207
Wrestler

Abraham, F. Murray
40 Fifth Ave. #2C
New York, NY 10011
Actor
Birthday: 10/24/39

Acker, Sharon
6310 San Vicente Blvd., #401
Los Angeles, CA 90048
Actress

Above the Line Agency
9200 Sunset Blvd., #401
Los Angeles, CA 90069
Rima Greer, agent
*Agency that handles directors,
    clients include Irvin Kershner,
    Ryan Rowe, John Hopkins,
    and others*

Abramson, Leslie Hope
4929 Wilshire Blvd., #940
Los Angeles, CA 90010
*Attorney who represented Erik
    Menendez*

**Academy of Motion Pictures
    Arts and Sciences
    (AMPAS)**
8949 Wilshire Blvd.
Beverly Hills, CA 90210
Bruce Davis,
    Executive Director
Website: www.oscar.org
E-mail: ampas@oscar.org
*Film organization, awards the
    Oscars*

**Academy of Television Arts
    and Sciences (ATAS)**
5220 Lankershim Blvd.
North Hollywood, CA 91601
or
111 West 57th St. Suite 1050
New York, NY 10019
Website: http://
    www.emmyonline.org/
*TV organization; awards the
    Emmy*

Acadiana Symphony Assoc.
412 Travis St.
Lafayette, LA 70503
Website: http://
    cust.iamerica.net/
    symphony/
E-mail: symphony@iamerica.net
Maestro Xiao-Lu Li, Conductor
orchestra

Accuracy in Media, Inc.
4455 Connecticut Ave., #330
Washington, DC 20008
Reed Irvine, chairman
Website: http://www.aim.org/
*Group concerned with fairness,
    balance, and accuracy in
    news reporting*

AC/DC
46 Kensington Ct. St.
London W8 5DP
England
Rock group

Ace Hardware
2200 Kensington Ct.
Oak Brook, IL 60523
David F. Hodnik, President
    and CEO
Website: http://www.
acehardware.com
Wholesalers

**Action on Smoking and Health
    (ASH)**
2013 H St. NW
Washington, DC 20006
Website: http://www.ash.org/
John F. Banzhaf III, Executive
    Director
*The nation's oldest and largest
    antismoking organization and
    the only one which regularly
    takes legal action to fight
    smoking and protect the rights
    of nonsmokers*

Actors and Others for Animals
11523 Burbank Blvd.
North Hollywood, CA 91601
Website: http://
    www.actorsandothers.com/
E-mail:
    info@actorsandothers.com
Cathy Singleton, Executive
    Director
*Protection group for the welfare of
    animals*

Actor's Equity Association
165 W. 46th St.
New York, NY 10036
Website: http://
    www.actorsequity.org/
Patrick Quinn, President
Stage actors' union

Acuff, Roy
Grand Ole Opry
2804 Opryland Dr.
Nashville, TN 37214
Country music singer

Adair, Deborah
PO Box 1980
Studio City, CA 91614
Actress
Birthday: 5/23/52

Adair, Red
PO Box 747
Bellville, TX 77418
*Owns company that puts out oil
    well fires*

Adam, HRH Prince Hans
Schloss Vaduz
Liechenstein

Adams, Bryan
406–68 Water St.
Vancouver BC V6B 14A
Canada
Website: http://
    www.bryanadams.com/
Singer/songwriter
Birthday: 11/5/59

Adams, Cecil
Website: http://
    www.straightdope.com/
E-mail:
    cecil@chicagoreader.com
Columnist

Adams, Don
2160 Century Park East
Los Angeles, CA 90067
Actor, writer, director
Birthday: 4/19/?

Adams, Douglas
76206.2507@compuserve.com
  or adamsd@cerf.net
*Author, The Hitchhiker's Guide to
  the Galaxy*

Adams, Joey
8942 Wilshire Blvd.
Beverly Hills, CA 90211
Actor, writer, director
Birthday: 1/06/11

Adams, Maude
11901 Sunset Blvd., #214
Los Angeles, CA 90049
or
1939 Century Park W, #403
Los Angeles, CA 90067
Model/actress
Birthday: 2/12/45

Adams, Dr. Patch
PO Box 268
Hillsboro, WV 24946
*Doctor portrayed by Robin
  Williams in the movie
  Patch Adams*

Adams, Scott
Website: http://
  www.unitedemedia.com/
  comics/dilbert/
E-mail: scottadam@aol.com
Cartoonist, creator of Dilbert

ADC Band
17397 Santa Barbara
Detroit, MI 48221
Music group

Ad Council
261 Madison Ave., 11th Floor
New York, NY
Website: http://
  www.adcouncil.org/
Lpeggy Conlon, President
E-mail:
  editor@marketingclick.com
*Nonprofit volunteer organization
  that conducts public service
  advertising*

Trace Adkins Fan Club
PO Box 121889
Nashville, TN 37212

Adler, Margot
% National Public Radio
2025 M Street N.W.
Washington, DC 20036
News correspondent

Adrian Symphony Orchestra
Cornelius House
110 S. Madison
Adrian, MI 49221
Website: http://www.aso.org/
E-mail: aso@lni.net
David Katz, Conductor

Advocacy Institute
1629 K St., NW, Suite 200
Washington, DC 20006
Website: http://
  wwww.advocacy.org/
E-mail: info@advocacy.org
*Dedicated to strengthening the
  capacity of public interest/
  social and economic justice
  advocates to influence and
  change public policy*

Advocates for Highway and Auto Safety
750 First St. NE, #901
Washington, DC 20002
Website: http://wwww.saferoads.org/
Joan Claybrook, Consumer Co-Chair
Dedicated to traffic safety

Advocates for Self-Government
1202 N. Tennessee St., Suite 202
Cartersville, GA 30120
Website: http://www.self-gov.org/
E-mail: Advocates@self-gov.org
Marshall Fritz, Founder
Encourages people to encounter, evaluate, and embrace the ideas of liberty and improve communications

Advocates for Youth
1025 Vermont Ave. NW, #200
Washington, DC 20005
Website: http://www.advocatesforyouth.org/
E-mail: info@advocatesforyouth.org
James Wagoner, President
Creates programs and promotes policies which help young people make informed and responsible decisions about their sexual and reproductive health

Aerosmith
PO Box 4668
San Francisco, CA 94101
or
584 Broadway, #1009
New York, NY 10012
Rock group

Aetna
151 Farmington Ave.
Hartford, CT 06156
Website: http://www.aetna.com
William Donaldson, Chairman, President and CEO
Health and life insurance

Affleck, Ben
405 S. Beverly Dr., #500
Beverly Hills, CA 90212
Actor
Birthday: 8/15/72

AFLAC
1932 Wynnton Rd.
Columbus, GA 31999
Website: http://www.aflac.com
Paul S. Amos, CEO
Life and health insurance

The Africa-America Institute
Chanin Building
380 Lexington Ave.
New York, NY 10168
or
1625 Massachusetts Ave., N.W., Suite 400
Washington, DC 20036
Website: http://www.aaionline.org/
Roger Wilkins, Chairman
A nonprofit, multi-racial, multi-ethnic organization whose mission is to promote African development, primarily through education and training

Agassi, Andre
ATP Tour North America
200 ATP Tour Blvd.
Ponte Vedra Beach, FL 32082
Tennis player
Birthday: 4/29/70

AGCO
4205 River Green Pkwy.
Duluth, GA 30096
Website: http://
    www.agcocorp.com
Robert J. Ratliff, Chairman
*Distributor of agricultural
    equipment*

Agee, Marilyn
8641 Sugar Gum Rd.
Riverside, CA 92508
Website: http://www.kiwi.net/
    ~mjagee/
Biblical prophecy author

Agony Column
Cosmopolitan
224 W. 54th St.
New York, NY 10019
Attn: Irma Kurtz
Magazine advice column

Aid Association for Lutherans
4321 N. Ballard Rd.
Appleton, WI 54919
John O. Gilbert, President and
    CEO
*Life and health insurance
    (mutual)*

Aikman, Troy
PO Box 630227
Irving, TX 75063
Football player
Birthday: 1/21/66

Ailes, Roger
440 Park Ave. South
New York, NY 10016
Producer, director

Ainge, Danny
2910 North Central
Phoenix, AZ 95012
Basketball player

Air Products and Chemicals
7201 Hamilton Blvd.
Allentown, PA 18195
Website: http://
    www.airproducts.com
Harold A. Wagner, Chairman
    and CEO
Chemicals

Air Supply
9200 Sunset Blvd.
Los Angeles, CA 90069
Music group

Airborne Freight
3101 Western Ave.
Seattle, WA 98121
Website: http://www.airborne-
    express.com
Robert S. Cline, Chairman and
    CEO
Mail, package, freight delivery

Alabama
PO Box 529
Ft. Payne, AL 35967
Country music group

**Al-Anon Family Group
    Headquarters, Inc.**
1600 Corporate Landing Pkwy.
Virginia Beach, VA 23454
Website: http://www.al-
    anon.alateen.org/
E-mail: WSO@al-anon.org
*Support group for families of
    alcoholics*

Alateen
Al-Anon Family Group
    Headquarters, Inc.
1600 Corporate Landing Pkwy.
Virginia Beach, VA 23454
Website: http://www.al-
    anon.alateen.org/alalist_
    usa.html
E-mail: WSO@al-anon.org
*Alateen is for young people whose
    lives have been affected by
    someone else's drinking*

Albano, Capt. Lou
16 Mechanic St.
Carmel, NY 10512
Wrestler, manager

Albee, Edward
PO Box 697
Montauk, NY 11954
Playwright

Albert, Eddie
1930 Century Park West, #403
Los Angeles, CA 90067
Actor
Birthday: 4/22/09

Albertsons
250 Parkcenter Blvd.
Boise, ID 83706
Website: www.albertsons.com
Gary G. Michael, Chairman
    and CEO
Food & drug stores

Albright, Lola
PO Box 250070
Glendale, CA 91225
Actress
Birthday: 7/20/24

Albright, Madeleine
1318 34th St. NW
Washington, DC 20007
Secretary of State

Alcoa
201 Isabella St. at 7th St.
    Bridge
Pittsburgh, PA 15212
Website: http://
    www.shareholder.com/
    alcoa
Paul H. O'Neill, Chairman
Alain J. P. Belda, President and
    CEO
Metals

Alcoholics Anonymous
307 Seventh Ave., 2nd Floor
New York, NY 10001
Website: http://www.alcoholics-
    anonymous.org/
Support group for alcoholics

Alda, Alan
1122 S. Robertson Blvd. #15
Los Angeles, CA 90035
Actor
Birthday: 1/28/36

Aldrin, Buzz Dr.
838 N. Doheny Dr. #1407
W. Hollywood, CA 90069
Former astronaut

Alexander, Daniele
PO Box 23362
Nashville, TN 37202
Country music singer

Alexander, Denise
270 N. Danon Dr., #1199
Beverly Hills, CA 90210
Actress

Alexander, Jane
1325 Ave. of the Americas
New York, NY 10019
Actress

Alexander, Jason (Jay Scott
        Greenspan)
405 S. Beverly Dr., #500
Beverly Hills, CA 90212
Actor
Birthday: 9/23/59

Alexander, Lamar
1109 Owen Pl. NE
Washington, DC 20008
Politician

Alexander, Shana
156 Fifth Ave. #617
New York, NY 10010
News correspondent

Alexandria Symphony
        Orchestra
PO 11014
Alexandria, VA 22312
Website: http://www.cais.com/
        webweave/symphony.htm
Kim Allen Kluge, Music
        Director/Conductor
Marcia N. Speck, Executive
        Director

Alexis, Kim
343 N. Maple Dr., #185
Beverly Hills, CA 90210
Supermodel

Alfonso, Kristian
10061 Riverside Dr., #798
Toluca Lake, CA 91602
Soap opera star

Ali, Muhammad (Cassius Clay)
5456 Wilshire Blvd.
Los Angeles, CA 90036
Boxing champion
Birthday: 1/17/42

Alice in Chains
207 1/2 First Ave. So. #300
Seattle, WA 98104
Music group

Allard, J.
E-mail: jallard@microsoft.com
Microsoft TCP/IP specialist

Allegheny Technologies
        Incorporated
1000 Six PPG Place
Pittsburgh, PA 15222
Thomas A. Corcoran,
        Chairman, President, and
        CEO
Specialty metals

Allegiance
1430 Waukegan Rd.
McGaw Park, IL 60085
Website: http://
        www.allegiance.net
Joseph F. Damico Healthcare,
        Group President; EVP,
        Cardinal Health

Allen, Corey
8642 Hollywood Blvd.
Los Angeles, CA 90069
Actor, writer, director

Deborah Allen's Front Row
        Friends
PO Box 120849
Nashville, TN 37212
Fan club

Allen, Elizabeth
PO Box 243
Lake Peekskill, NY 10537
Actress

Allen, Joan
40 W. 57th St.
New York, NY 10019
Actress

Allen, Jonelle
8730 Sunset Blvd., #480
Los Angeles, CA 90069
Actress, singer

Allen, Karen
PO Box 237
Monterey, MA 01245
or
PO Box 5617
Beverly Hills, CA 90212
Actress
Birthday: 10/05/51

Allen, Marty
5750 Wilshire Blvd., #580
Los Angeles, CA 90036
Comedian

Allen, Nancy
8154 Muholland Terr.
Los Angeles, CA 90046
Actress
Birthday: 6/24/50

Allen, Rex Jr.
PO Box 120501
Nashville, TN 37212
Country music singer

Allen, Rex Sr.
Box 430
Sonoita, AZ 85637
Country music singer

Allen, Robert
32 Ave. of the Americas
New York, NY 10013
Business leader

Allen, Tim (Tim Allen Dick)
7920 Sunset Blvd., #400
Los Angeles, CA 90046
or
1122 S. Robertson Blvd., #15
Los Angeles, CA 90035
E-mail:
      HI.Tim@refuge.cuug.ab.ca
Actor
Birthday: 6/13/53

Allen, Woody
930 Fifth Ave.
New York, NY 10018
Actor, comedian, director
Birthday: 12/01/35

Alley, Kirstie
132 S. Rodeo Dr., #300
Beverly Hills, CA 90212
Actress
Birthday: 1/12/55

All 4 One
11693 San Vicente Blvd., #550
Los Angeles, CA 90049
Website: http://www.otb1.com/
      all-4-one/
Music group

Alliance for Aging Research
2021 K St. NW, #305
Washington, DC 20006
Website:
      www.agingresearch.org
John L. Steffens, National
      Chairman
*Organization promoting medical
      research on aging*

Alliance for Justice
2000 P St., N.W., Suite 712
Washington, DC 20036
Website: http://www.afj.org/
E-mail: alliance@afj.org
*National association of
environmental, civil rights,
mental health, women's,
children's, and consumer
advocacy organizations*

Alliance to Save Energy
1200 18th St., NW Suite 900
Washington, DC 20036
Website: http://www.ase.org/
Senator Jeff Bingaman (D-
N.M.), Chairman of the
Board
*A nonprofit coalition of business,
government, environmental,
and consumer leaders
promoting efficient use of
energy*

Allman Brothers
40 West 57th St.
New York, NY 10019
Music group

Allman, Greg
40 West 57th St.
New York, NY 10019
Musician
Birthday: 12/07/47

Allmerica Financial
440 Lincoln St.
Worcester, MA 01653
Website: http://
www.allmerica.com
John F. O'Brien, President and
CEO
Henry St. Cyr, Vice President,
Investor Relations
P & C insurance

Allred, Gloria
6300 Wilshire Blvd., #1500
Los Angeles, CA
Attorney

Allstate
Allstate Plaza
2775 Sanders Rd.
Northbrook, IL 60062
Website: http://
www.allstate.com
Edward M. Liddy, Chairman,
President, and CEO,
Allstate Corporation and
Allstate Insurance
Insurance

Alltel
1 Allied Dr.
Little Rock, AR 72202
Website: http://www.alltel.com
Joe T. Ford, Chairman and
CEO
Telecommunications

Alpert, Hollis
PO Box 142
Shelter Island, NY 11964
Writer

Alpert, Dr. Richard
Box 1558
Boulder, CO 80306
Psychologist

Alt, Carol
4526 Wilshire Blvd.
Los Angeles, CA 90010
Supermodel

Altman, Robert
9200 Harrington Dr.
Potomac, MD 20854
Financier

Altman, Robert
502 Park Ave., #15G
New York, NY 10022
Writer, producer, director

Alva, Luigi
via Moscova 46/3
Mailand 20121
Italy
Tenor

Alvin and the Chipmunks
122 E. 57th St., #400
New York, NY 10003
Animated singing group

Amanpour, Christiane
2 Stephen St., #100
London W1p 2PL
England
Broadcast journalist

Amazing Rhythm Aces
1010 16th St. So.
Nashville, TN 37212
Music group

Ambrosia
245 E. 54th St.
New York, NY 10022
Music group

Amerada, Hess
1185 Ave. of the Americas
New York, NY 10036
Website: www.hew.com
John B. Hess, Chairman and
    CEO
Petroleum refining

Ameren
1901 Chouteau Ave.
St. Louis, MO 63103
Website: www.ameren.com
Charles W. Mueller, Chairman,
    President, and CEO
Utilities, gas, and electric

America
345 N. Maple Dr., #300
Beverly Hills, CA 90210
Music group

**American Association of
    English Handbell Ringers**
1055 East Centerville Station
    Rd.
Dayton, OH 45459
Vic Kostenko, Executive
    Director
Website: http://www.agehr.org/
E-mail: TheAGEHR@aol.com

**American Association of
    University Women (AAUW)**
1111 16th St. NW
Washington, DC 20036
Website: http://www.aauw.org/
E-mail: info@mail.aauw.org
*Promotes education and equity for
    women and girls through
    research; fellowships and
    grants; activism; voter
    education; and support for sex
    discrimination lawsuits*

American Bear Association
PO Box 55
Franklin, NC 28744
E-mail: bears@dnet.net
Bill Lea, President
Promotes the welfare of the black
bear though a better
understanding

American Cancer Society
1599 Clifton Rd. NE
Atlanta, GA 30203
Website: http://www.cancer.
org/frames.html
John R. Seffrin, Ph.D., CEO

American Cinematographer
PO Box 2230
Hollywood, CA 90078
Website: http://
www.cinematographer.com/
magazine/
Jim McCullaugh, Publisher
E-mail: Jim@theasc.com
Magazine for cinematographers
and editors

American Civil Liberties Union
(ACLU)
125 Broad St.
New York, NY 10004
Website: http://www.aclu.org/
E-mail: aclu@aclu.org
Ira Glasser, Executive Director
Advocate of individual rights

American Conservative Union
(ACU)
1007 Cameron St.
Alexandria, VA 22314
Website: http://
www.conservative.org/
E-mail: acu@conservative.org
David A. Keene, Chairman
Thomas R. Katina, Executive
Director
The nation's oldest conservative
lobbying organization, its
purpose is to effectively
communicate and advance the
goals and principles of
conservatism

American Council for Capital
Formation
1750 K St. NW, #400
Washington, DC 20006
Website: http://www.accf.org/
E-mail:
awilkes@mindspring.com
Dr. Charls E. Walker,
Chairman and Founder;
former Deputy Secretary of
the Treasury
A nonprofit, nonpartisan
organization dedicated to the
advocacy of tax and
environmental policies that
encourage saving and
investment

American Council on
Education (ACE)
One Dupont Circle #800
Washington, DC 20036
Website: http://
www.ACENET.edu/
Stanley O. Ikenberry, President
ACE is dedicated to the belief that
equal education opportunity
and a strong higher education
system are essential
cornerstones of a democratic
society

American Council on Science and Health (ACSH)

1995 Broadway, 16th Fl.
New York, NY 10023
Website: http://www.acsh.org/
Elizabeth M. Whelan, Sc.D.,
M.P.H. President
E-mail: whelan@acsh.org
A. Alan Moghissi, Ph.D.,
Chairman of the Board

A consumer education consortium concerned with issues related to food, nutrition, chemicals, pharmaceuticals, lifestyles, the environment, and health.

American Dietetic Association

216 West Jackson Blvd.
Chicago, IL 60606
Website: http://
www.eatright.org/
E-mail: infocenter@eatright.org
Polly Fitz, Chairman

American Enterprise Institute for Public Policy Research

1150 17th St. NW
Washington, DC 20036
Website: http://www.aei.org/
E-mail: info@aei.org
Christopher C. DeMuth,
President

Dedicated to preserving and strengthening the foundations of freedom—limited government, private enterprise, vital cultural and political institutions, and a strong foreign policy and national defense—through scholarly research, open debate, and publications

American Farm Bureau Federation

225 Touhy Ave.
Park Ridge, IL 60068
or
600 Maryland Ave. SW, #800
Washington, DC 20024
Website: http://www.fb.com/
Bob Stallman, President
E-mail: bstallman@fb.org
The voice of agriculture

American Federation of Government Employees

80 F St. NW
Washington, DC 20001
Website: http://www.afge.org/
splash/splash.htm
Bobby L. Harnage, National
President

The largest federal employee union representing some 600,000 federal and D.C. government workers nationwide

American Federation of State, County and Municipal Employees (AFSCME)

1625 L St. NW
Washington, DC 20036
Website: http://www.afscme.org/
E-mail: webmaster@afscme.org
Gerald W. McEntee,
International President

The nation's largest public employee and health care workers union

American Foreign Policy Council

1521 16th St., NW
Washington, DC 20036
Website: http://www.afpc.org/
Sandy Bostian, Program
Director
A nonprofit organization dedicated to bringing information to those who make or influence the foreign policy of the United States and to assisting world leaders with building democracies and market economies

American Gas Association

1515 Wilson Blvd.
Arlington, VA 22209
Website: http://www.aga.com/
Lennart Selander, President
The American Gas Association (AGA) represents 181 local natural gas utilities that deliver gas to 54 million homes and businesses in all 50 states

American Jewish Congress

2027 Massachusetts Ave. NW
Washington, DC 20036
Website: http://
www.ajcongress.org/
E-mail: washrep@ajcongress.org
Jack Rosen, President
Considered the legal voice of the American Jewish community

American League of Lobbyists

PO Box 30005
Alexandria, VA 22310
Website: http://www.alldc.org/
E-mail: info@alldc.org
Kenneth E. Feltman, President
A national organization founded in 1979 dedicated to serving government relations and public affairs professionals

American Legislative Exchange Council

910 17th St. NW, 5th Floor
Washington, DC 20006
Website: http://www.alec.org/
main.cfm
E-mail: info@alec.org
Duane Parde, Executive
Director
E-mail: dparde@alec.org
The nation's largest bipartisan, individual membership association of state legislators, with nearly 2,400 members across America

American Library Association

50 E. Huron St.
Chicago, IL 60611
Website: http://www.ala.org/
E-mail: ala@ala.org
Sarah Long, President
E-mail: sarahl@nslsilus.org
The oldest, largest, and most influential library association in the world, for more than a century, it has been a leader in defending intellectual freedom and promoting the highest quality library and information services

American Medical Association (AMA)

515 N. State St.
Chicago, IL 60610
Website: http://www.ama-assn.org
Percy Wootton, M.D. President
Dedicated to promoting the art and science of medicine and the betterment of public health

American Postal Workers Union
1300 L St. NW
Washington, DC 20005
Website: http://www.apwu.org/
Moe Biller, APWU President
The largest postal union representing 366,000 union members in the United States

American Public Health Association
800 I St., NW
Washington, DC 20001
Website: http://www.apha.org/
E-mail: comments@apha.org
Mohammad N. Akhter, M.D., MPH, Executive Director
The oldest and largest organization of public health professionals in the world, representing more than 50,000 members from over 50 occupations of public health

American Rivers
1025 Vermont Ave., #720
Washington, DC 20005
Website: http://www.amrivers.org/
E-mail: amrivers@amrivers.org
Rebecca R. Wodder, President
Amy Butler, Associate Director of Foundation Relations
National river-conservation organization whose mission is to protect and restore America's river systems and to foster a river stewardship ethic

American Security Council
1155 15th St. NW, #1101
Washington, DC 20005

American Tort Reform Association
1850 M St., NW Suite 1095
Washington, DC 20036
Website: http://www.atra.org/
Sherman Joyce, President
E-mail: sjoyce@atra.org
Founded in 1986, it is a broad based, bipartisan coalition of more than 300 businesses, corporations, municipalities, associations, and professional firms who support civil justice reform

American Veterinary Medical Association
1931 North Meacham Rd., Suite 100
Schaumburg, IL 60173
Website: http://www.avma.org/
E-mail: help@atlahq.org
Dr. Joseph Kinnarney, Vice President
The objective of the Association is to advance the science and art of veterinary medicine, including its relationship to public health, biological science, and agriculture

American-Arab Anti-Discrimination Committee (ADC)
4201 Connecticut Ave. NW, #500
Washington, DC 20008
Website: http://www.adc.org/
E-mail: adc@adc.org
Hala Maksoud, President
E-mail: hmaksoud@adc.org
Civil rights organization committed to defending the rights of people of Arab descent and promoting their rich cultural heritage

Americans for Democratic Action (ADA)
1625 K St. NW #210
Washington, DC 20006
Website: http://adaction.org/
E-mail:
    adaction@Ix.netcom.com
The nation's oldest independent liberal political organization, it pioneered the development and promotion of a national liberal agenda of public policy formulation and action

Americans for Indian Opportunity
681 Juniper Hill Rd.
Bernalillo, NM 87004
Website: http://
    Indiannet.indian.com/
    aio.html
E-mail: lharris@unm.edu

AmeriSource Health
300 Chester Field Pkwy.
Malvern, PA 19355
Website: http://
    www.amerisource.com
R. David Yost, President and CEO
Wholesale pharmecuticals

American Electric Power
1 Riverside Plaza
Columbus, OH 43215
Website: http://www.aep.com
E. Linn Draper, Jr., Chairman, President, and CEO
Gas and electric utilities

American Express
200 Vesey St.
New York, NY 10285
Website: http://
    www.americanexpress.com
Harvey Golub, Chairman and CEO
Diversified financials

American Family Insurance Group
6000 American Pkwy.
Madison, WI 53783
Website: www.amfam.com
Dale F. Mathwich, Chairman and CEO
Insurance

American Financial Group
1 E. Fourth St.
Cincinnati, OH 45202
Website: http://www.amfnl.com
Carl H. Lindner, CEO
Insurance

American General
2929 Allen Pkwy.
Houston, TX 77019
Website: http://www.agc.com
Robert M. Devlin, Chairman, President and CEO
Life and health Insurance

American Home Products
5 Giralda Farms
Madison, NJ 07940
Website: http://www.ahp.com
John R. Stafford, Chairman, President, and CEO
Pharmaceuticals

American International Group
70 Pine St.
New York, NY 10270
Website: http://www.aig.com
Maurice R. "Hank" Greenberg,
    Chairman and CEO;
    Chairman, Transatlantic
    Holdings; President and
    CEO, C. V. Starr
P & C insurance

American Society of
    Composers, Authors and
    Publishers (ASCAP), New
    York
One Lincoln Plaza
New York, NY 10023
Website: http://
    www.ascap.com/
Marilyn Bergman, ASCAP
    President and Chairman of
    the Board
The only performing rights
    licensing organization in the
    United States whose Board of
    Directors is made up entirely
    of writers and music
    publishers elected by and from
    its membership

American Society of
    Cinematographers (ASC)
PO Box 2230
Hollywood, CA 90078
Website: http://
    www.cinematographer.com/
Stephen Pizzello, editor
E-mail: editor@theasc.com

American Society of
    Composers, Authors and
    Publishers (ASCAP),
    London
8 Cork St.
London W1X1PB
England
Website: http://www.ascap.com

American Society of
    Composers, Authors and
    Publishers (ASCAP), Los
    Angeles
7920 Sunset Blvd., Suite 300
Los Angeles, CA 90046
Website: http://www.ascap.com/

American Society of
    Composers, Authors and
    Publishers (ASCAP),
    Atlanta
ASCAP Membership, Atlanta
PMB 400
541 10th St. NW
Atlanta, GA 30318
Website: http://www.ascap.com/

American Society of
    Composers, Authors and
    Publishers (ASCAP), Miami
844 Alton Rd., Suite 1
Miami Beach, FL 33139
Website: http://www.ascap.com

**American Society of
    Composers, Authors and
    Publishers (ASCAP),
    Nashville**
Two Music Square West
Nashville, TN 37203
Website: http://www.ascap.com/

**American Society of
    Composers, Authors and
    Publishers (ASCAP),
    Midwest**
1608 W. Belmont Ave., Suite
    200
Chicago, IL 60657
Website: http://www.ascap.com/

**American Society of
    Composers, Authors and
    Publishers (ASCAP),
    Puerto Rico**
1519 Ponce de Leon Ave.,
    Suite 505
Santurce, PR 00909
Website: http://www.ascap.com/

American Standard
1 Centennial Ave.
Piscataway, NJ 08855
Website: http://
    www.americanstandard.com
Frederic M. Poses, Chairman
    and CEO
Industrial and farm equiptment

Ameritech
2000 West Ameritech Center
    Dr.
Hoffman Estates, IL 60195
Website: http://
    www.ameritech.com
Walt Catlow, CEO
Telecommunications

Ames, Trey
15760 Ventura Blvd., #1730
Encino, CA 91436
Actor

Amgen, Inc.
1 Amgen Center Dr.
Thousand Oaks, CA 91320
Website: http://
    www.amgen.com
George B. Rathmann,
    Chairman Emeritus,
    Chairman, and President
*One of the world's largest
    biotechnology companies*

Amick, Madchen
8840 Wilshire Blvd.
Beverly Hills, CA 90212
Actress

Amin, Idi
Box 8948
Jidda 21492
Saudi Arabia
Former dictator of Uganda
Birthday: 1/1/25

Amnesty International, USA
322 8th Ave.
New York, NY 10001
Website: http://www.amnesty-
usa.org/
E-mail: aimember@aiusa.org
*Founded in 1961, Amnesty
International is a grassroots
activist organization whose
one-million strong members are
dedicated to freeing prisoners
of conscience; to gaining fair
trials for political prisoners; to
ending torture, political
killings, and
"disappearances," and to
abolishing the death penalty
throughout the world. Amnesty
International USA (AIUSA) is
the U.S. Section of this
international human rights
movement.*

Amos, Deborah
% National Public Radio,
2025 M Street NW
Washington, DC 20036
News correspondent

Amos, John
PO Box 18764
Encino CA 91416
or
Box 587
Califon, NJ 07830
Actor
Birthday: 12/27/41

Amos, Tori (Myra Ellen Amos)
9830 Wilshire Blvd.
Beverly Hills, CA 90212
Singer, songwriter
Birthday: 8/22/64

Amos, Wally (Famous)
PO Box 897
Kailua, HI 96734
Entrepreneur

AMR
4333 Amon Carter Blvd.
Fort Worth, TX 76155
Website: http://
www.amrcorp.com
Donald J. Carty, Chairman,
President, and CEO
Airline

Anderson, Barbara
PO Box 10118
Santa Fe, NM 87504
Actress

Anderson, Bill
PO Box 888
Hermitage, TN 37076
Country music singer

Anderson, Gillian
% The X-Files
20th Century Fox
10201 Pico Blvd.
Los Angeles, CA 90035
Actress
Birthday: 8/9/68

Anderson, John B.
Nova University Law Center
Ft. Lauderdale, FL 33314-7796
Former Representative

Anderson, John
PO Box 810
Smithville, TN 37166
Country music singer

Anderson, Louie
2756 N. Green Valley Parkway,
 #449
Las Vegas, NV 89014
Comedian, game show host

Anderson, Lynn
PO Box EE
Taos, NM 87571
Singer
Birthday: 9/26/47

Anderson, Richard Dean
1122 S. Robertson Blvd., #15
Los Angeles, CA 90035
Actor
Birthday: 1/23/50

Anderson-Lee, Pamela
151 El Camino Dr.
Beverly Hills, CA 90212
Actress

Anderson, Terry
50 Rockefeller Plaza
New York, NY 10020
News correspondent

Andress, Ursula
Via Francesco Siacci 38
Rome 1-00197
Italy
Actress
Birthday: 3/19/36

Andretti, John
PO Box 2104
Davidson, NC 28036
Race car driver

Andretti, Mario
53 Victory Lane
Nazareth, PA 18604
or
% Andretti Signature Line
3310 Airport Rd.
Allentown, PA 18103
Race car driver
Birthday: 2/28/40

Andrew, HRH Prince
Suninghill Park
Windsor
England
Son of Queen Elizabeth
Birthday: 2/19/60

Andrews, Julie
PO Box 491668
Los Angeles CA 90049
Actress/singer
Birthday: 10/1/35

**Angelou, Maya (Margueritte
 Anne Johnson)**
104 B Wingate Hall
PO Box 7314
Winston-Salem, NC 27109
Website: http://www.educeth.ch
 /english/readinglist/
 angeloum/index.html
Poet
Birthday: 4/4/28

Angle, Jim
% National Public Radio
2025 M St., N.W.
Washington, DC 20036
News Correspondent

Anheuser-Busch
1 Busch Place
St. Louis, MO 63118
Website: http://www.anheuser-
busch.com
August A. Busch III, Chairman
and President; Chairman
and CEO
Beverages

Aniston, Jennifer
% Creative Artists Agency
9830 Wilshire Blvd.
Beverly Hills, CA 90212
or
1122 S. Robertson Blvd. #15
Los Angeles, CA 90035
Actress
Birthday: 2/11/69

Anixter
4711 Golf Rd.
Skokie, IL 60637
Website: http://
www.anixter.com
Samuel Zell, Chairman
Robert W. Grubbs, Jr.,
President and CEO
Wire and cable wholesalers

Anka, Paul
433 N. Camden Dr.
Beverly Hills, CA 90210
Singer/songwriter
Birthday: 7/30/41

Annan, Secy. Gen. Kofi
799 United Nations Plaza
New York, NY 10017
Secretary General of the U.N.

Anne, HRH Princess
Gatcombe Park
Glouchestershire
England
Daughter of Queen Elizabeth

**Ann-Margret (Ann-Margret
Olson)**
5664 Cahuenga Blvd. #336
North Hollywood, CA 91601
Actress
Birthday: 4/28/41

Anthem Insurance
120 Monument Circle
Indianapolis, IN 46204
L. Ben Lytle, Chairman,
President, and CEO
Life and health insurance

Anthrax
15 Haldane Crescent
Piners Health
Wakefield Heath
Wakefield WF1 4TE
England
Heavy metal group

Anti-Defamation League (ADL)
823 United Nations Plaza
New York, NY 10017
Website: http://www.adl.org/
E-mail: webmaster@adl.org
Abraham H. Foxman, National
Director
*Fights anti-Semitism through
programs and services that
counteract hatred, prejudice,
and bigotry*

Anton, Susan
40 W. 57th St.
New York, NY 10019
Actress
Birthday: 10/12/50

Anwar, Gabrielle
253 26th St. #A-203
Santa Monica, CA 90402
Actress
Birthday: 2/4/70

Aoki, Rocky
8685 N.W. 53rd Terrace
Miami, FL 3155
Food entrepreneur

Aon
123 N. Wacker Dr.
Chicago, IL 60606
Website: http://www.aon.com
Patrick G. Ryan, Chairman and
  CEO
Diversified financials

Apple Computer
1 Infinite Loop
Cupertino, CA 95014
Website: http://www.apple.com
Steven P. Jobs, CEO
Computers, office equipment

Applegate, Christina
% International Creative
  Management
8942 Wilshire Blvd.
Beverly Hills, CA 90211
Actress
Birthday: 11/25/72

Applied Materials
3050 Bowers Ave.
Santa Clara, CA 95054
Website: http://
  www.appliedmaterials.com
James C. Morgan, Chairman
  and CEO
Electronics, semiconductors

Aquino, Ex-President Corazon
% Pius XVI Center
UN Manila
Philippines
Former president of the Philippines

Arab American Institute
1600 K St., NW, Suite 601
Washington, DC 20006
Website: http://www.aaiusa.org/
James Zogby, President
E-mail: jzoby@aaiusa.org
*The Arab American Institute was
  organized in 1985 to represent
  Arab American interests in
  government and politics*

Aramark
1101 Market St.
Philadelphia, PA 19107
Joseph Neubauer, Chairman
  and CEO
*Food and support services,
  uniforms, and child care*

Archer Daniel's Midland
4666 Faries Pkwy.
Decatur, IL 62526
Website: http://
  www.admworld.com
Dwayne O. Andreas, Chairman
  Emeritus
Allen Andreas, Chairman and
  CEO
*One of the world's largest
  processors of oilseeds, corn,
  and wheat*

Archer, Anne
% Ilene Feldman Agency
8730 Sunset Blvd., #490
Los Angeles, CA 90069
Actress
Birthday: 10/25/50

Archerd, Army
% *Daily Variety*
5700 Wilshire Blvd., #120
Los Angeles, CA 90036
Columnist

Arens, Moshe
49 Hagderat Savyon
Israel
Politician

Arias, Ex-President Oscar
AFP Apdo 8-6410-1000
San Jose
Costa Rica
*Former president of Costa Rica
and Nobel Peace Prize winner*

Arinze, Francis Cardinal
Piazza San Calisto 16
00153 Rome
Italy
Cardinal

Arkin, Adam
2372 Veteran Ave. #102
Los Angeles, CA 90064
Actor

Arkin, Alan
21 E. 40th St. #1705
New York, NY 10016
or
% William Morris Agency
151 S. El Camino Dr.
Beverly Hills, CA 90212
Actor
Birthday: 3/26/34

Arledge, Roone
778 Park Ave. #15
New York, NY 10021
*Sports TV innovator of live events,
    anthology shows, Olympic
    coverage, and* Monday Night
    Football
Birthday: 7/8/31

Armani, Giorgio
Palazzo Durini 24
Milan 1-20122
Italy
or
650 Fifth Ave.
New York, NY 10019
Fashion designer
Birthday: 7/11/34

Armatrading, Joan
2 Ramillies St.
London W1V 1DF
England
Singer/guitarist
Birthday: 12/9/50

Armstrong, Anne
Armstrong Ranch
Armstrong, TX 78338
Politician

Arness, James (James Aurness)
PO Box 49599
Los Angeles, CA 90049
Actor
Birthday: 5/26/23

Arnold, Eddy
PO Box 97
Brentwood, TN 37024
Country music singer

Arnold, Tom
1122 S. Robertson Blvd. #15
Los Angeles, CA 90035
or
151 El Camino Dr.
Beverly Hills, CA 90212
Actor/comedian/producer
Birthday: 3/6/59

Arquette, Patricia
1122 S. Robertson Blvd. #15
Los Angeles, CA 90035
Actress
Birthday: 4/8/68

Arrested Development
9380 SW 72nd St. #B-220
Miami, FL 33174
Musical group

Arrow Electronics
25 Hub Dr.
Melville, NY 11747
Website: http://www.arrow.com
Stephen P. Kaufman, CEO
Wholesale electronics

Art of Noise, The
Box 119
London W11 4AN
England
Music group

Arts and Entertainment
235 East 45th Street
New York, NY 10017
Cable network

Ash, Mary Kay
16251 Dallas Pkwy.
Dallas, TX 75248
Cosmetics executive

Ashdown, Paddy
House of Commons
London SW1A AA
England
Politician

Asheville Symphony Orchestra
PO Box 2852
Asheville, NC 28802
Website: http://
    www.ashevillesymphony.org/
George M. Bilbrey, M.D.,
    President
Robert Hart Baker, Music
    Director

Ashford and Simpson
254 W. 72nd St. #1A
New York, NY 10023
Musical group

**Asian American Journalists
    Association**
1182 Market St. Suite 320
San Francisco, CA 94102
Website: http://www.aaja.org/
E-mail: National@aaja.org
Rene Astudillo, Executive
    Director
*Seeks to increase employment of
    Asian American print and
    broadcast journalist, assist
    high school and college
    students pursuing journalism
    careers, encourage fair,
    sensitive and accurate news
    coverage of Asian American
    issues, provide support for
    Asian American journalists*

Asleep at the Wheel
PO Box 463
Austin, TX 78767
Country music group

Asner, Ed
3556 Mound View Ave.
Studio City, CA 91604
E-mail: 72726.357@
    compuserve.com
Actor
Birthday: 11/15/29

Assante, Armand
367 Windsor Hwy.
New Windsor, NY 12553
Actor
Birthday: 10/4/49

**Associated Builders and
    Contractors**
1300 N. 17th St., 8th Floor
Roslyn, VA 22209
Website: http://www.abc.org
Robert P. Hepner, Executive
    Vice President
*A national trade association
    representing over 21,000
    contractors, subcontractors,
    material suppliers, and related
    firms from across the country
    and from all specialties in the
    construction industry*

**Association for Community
    Based Education (ACBE)**
1805 Florida Ave. NW
Washington, DC 20009
*The ABCE's membership is
    comprised of community
    activist organizations,
    including many that operate
    literacy projects*

**Association for the
    Advancement of Mexican
    Americans**
204 Clifton
Houston, TX 77083
Website: http://
    www.neosoft.com/~aama/
E-mail: aama@neosoft.com
Matt Miller, President
*Committed to advancing at-risk
    and disadvantaged youth and
    families with an array of
    innovative programs of
    excellence that provide
    alternative education, social
    services, and community
    development*

**Association of Independent
    Commercial Producers
    (AICP)**
11 East 22nd St. 4th Floor
New York, NY 10010
Website: http://www.aicp.com/
Matt Miller, President
E-mail: mattm@aicp.com
*Represents commercial production
    companies*

Astin, John
PO Box 49698
Los Angeles CA 90049
Actor/writer/director
Birthday: 3/30/30

Astin, Sean
% Samantha Crisp
William Morris Agency
151 S. El Camino Dr.
Beverly Hills, CA 90212
Actor
Birthday: 2/25/71

AT&T
32 Ave. of the Americas
New York, NY 10013
Web site: http://www.att.com
C. Michael Armstrong,
    Chairman and CEO
Telecommunications company

Atkins, Chet
1013 17th Ave. So.
Nashville, TN 37212
Guitarist
Birthday: 6/20/24

Atkinson, Rowan
PBJ Management Ltd.
5 Soho Square
London
W1V 5DE
England
Actor—Bean

AtomFilms
80 S. Washington St., Suite 303
Seattle, WA 98014
Website: www.atomfilms.com
E-mail: info@atomfilms.com
Mika Salmi, CEO and Founder
Web content provider

Atomic Pop
1447 Cloverfield Blvd., Suite
    201
Santa Monica, CA 90404
Website: www.atomicpop.com
E-mail: ateller@atomicpop.com
Al Teller, CEO and Founder
E-commerce

Attenborough, Lord Richard
5 Park Rd.
Richmond Surrey
England
Writer, producer
Birthday: 8/29/23

Auberjonois, Rene
8428 C Melrose Pl.
Los Angeles, CA 90069
Actor
Birthday: 7/1/40

Auermann, Nadja
% Elite Models
111 East 22nd St.
New York, NY 10010
Supermodel
Birthday: 1971

Autobytel.com
18872 MacArthur Blvd.
Irvine, CA 92612
Website: www.autobytel.com
E-mail: markl@autobytel.com
Mark Lorimer, President and
    CEO
E-commerce

Avery Dennison
150 N. Orange Grove Blvd.
Pasadena, CA 91103
Website: http://
    www.averydennison.com
Philip M. Neal, Chairman and
    CEO
Labels, office supplies

Avon
1345 Ave. of the Americas
New York, NY 10105
Website: http://www.avon.com
Stanley C. Gaul, Chairman
Cosmetics and soaps

Aykroyd, Dan
8271 Melrose Ave. #110
Los Angeles, CA 90046
or
9830 Wilshire Blvd.
Beverly Hills, CA 90212
Actor/writer
Birthday: 7/1/52

Ayn Rand Institute
The Center for the
    Advancement of
    Objectivism
4640 Admiralty Way, Suite 406
Marina del Rey, CA 90292
Website: http://
    www.aynrand.org/
E-mail: mail@aynrand.org
Leonard Peikoff, Founder
*Seeks to promote and expound
    Rand's philosophy
    (Objectivism) with various
    resources and activities*

Aznavour, Charles
76–78 ave. des Champs Elysses
Paris F75008
France
*Singer, called the "Frank Sinatra
    of France"*
Birthday: 5/22/24

B

If you want to know your true opinion of someone, watch the effect produced in you by the first sight of a letter from him.

—SCHOPENHAUER

B-52's, The
947 N. La Cienega Blvd. #G
Los Angeles, CA 90069
Music group

Babbitt, Bruce
Secretary of the Interior
5169 Watson St., N.W.
Washington, DC 20016

Babock, Barbara
10100 Santa Monica Blvd.
#2500
Los Angeles, CA 90067
Actress

Babyface (Kenneth Edmonds)
10231 Charing Cross Rd.
Los Angeles, CA 90024
Singer, songwriter, producer
Birthday: 1958

Bacall, Lauren (Betty Perske)
1 W. 72nd St., #43
New York, NY 10023
or
151 El Camino Dr.
Beverly Hills, CA 90212
Actress
Birthday: 9/16/24

Bachman Turner Overdrive
1505 W. 2nd Ave., #299
Vancouver BC V6h 3Y4
Canada
Music group

Bach Week Festival in Evanston
PO Box 466
Deerfield, IL 60015-0466
Website: http://
www.bachweek.org/
E-mail: bachwk@aol.com
Mr. Richard Webster, Music
Director
Bach Week has earned the reputation as one of the Midwest's most highly regarded and respected concert series

Backstage West
779 Broadway
New York, NY 10003
Website: http://
www.backstage.com/
E-mail:
backstage@backstage.com
Steve Elish, Publisher
E-mail: Selish@backstage.com
Magazine for actors

Backstreet Boys
7380 Sand Lake Rd., #350
Orlando, FL 32819
Music group

Bacon, Kevin
9830 Wilshire Blvd.
Beverly Hills, CA 90212
or
Box 668
Sharon, CT 06069
Actor
Birthday: 7/8/58

Bader, Dietrich
% *The Drew Carey Show*
4000 Warner Blvd.
Burbank, CA 91522
Actor

Badham, John
% Elkins and Elkins
16830 Ventura Blvd., #300
Encino, CA 91436
Movie director

Baer, Max, Jr.
PO Box 1831
Zephyr Cove, NV 89448
Actor

Baez, Joan
PO Box 1026
Menlo Park, CA 94026
Singer
Birthday: 1/9/41

Bailey, F. Lee
1400 Centre Park Blvd., #909
West Palm Beach, FL 33401
Attorney
Birthday: 6/10/33

Baillie and the Boys
PO Box 121185
Arlington, TX 76012
or
% The Bobby Roberts
    Company
PO Box 1547
Goodlettsville, TN 37070
Country music group

Bailey, Razzy
Box 62
Geneva, NE 68361
or
% Marilyn Schultze, President
PO Box 11950
Nashville, TN 37222
E-mail: razzypres@hotmail.com
Fan club for country music singer

Baio, Scott
4333 Forman Ave.
Toluca Lake, CA 91602
Actor
Birthday: 9/22/61

Baker, Hughes
3900 Essex Lane
PO Box 4740
Houston, TX 77027
Website: http://
    www.bakerhughes.com
Joe B. Foster, Chairman,
    President, and CEO
*Provides products and services for
    the global petroleum market*

Baker, Carrol
PO Box 480589
Los Angeles, CA 90048
Actress
Birthday: 11/15/25

Baker, Howard, Jr.
PO Box 8
Huntsville, TN 37756
Former senator
Birthday: 11/15/25

Baker, James A., III
1299 Pennsylvania Ave. N.W.
Washington, DC 20004
Former Secretary of State

Baker, Janet Abbott
450 Edgeware Road
London W2
England
Mezzo-soprano

Bakker, Jim (James O.)
15948 Lancaster Hwy.
Charlotte, NC 28277
TV evangelist in PTL scandal
Birthday: 1/2/40

Baker, Lisa
% Playboy Ent.
9242 Beverly Blvd.
Beverly Hills, CA 90210
Model

Baker, Tom
PO Box 5877
Nottingham NG159JG
England
Website: http://
www.officialtombaker
website.co.uk/
Actor known as 'Dr. Who'
Birthday: 1/20/34

Bakula, Scott
9560 Wilshire Blvd., #500
Beverly Hills, CA 90212
or
15300 Ventura Blvd., #315
Sherman Oaks, CA 91403
Actor
Birthday: 10/9/55

Baldwin, William
25 Music Sq. E.
Nashville, TN 37203
or
955 S. Carrillo Dr., #200
Beverly Hills, CA 90212
Actor
Birthday: 1963

Ballard, Kaye
PO Box 922
Rancho Mirage, CA 92270
Singer
Birthday: 11/20/26

Ballard, Roger
PO Box 46305
Baton Rouge, LA 70895
or
25 Music Square E.
Nashville, TN 37203
Country music singer

Baltimore Gas and Electric
PO Box 1475
Baltimore, MD 21203
Website: http://www.bge.com
Christian H. Poindexter,
    President and CEO
Gas and electric utilities

Bama Band
% Rob Battle, Ent. Artists
819 18th Ave. So.
Nashville, TN 37203
Country music group

Banc One Corp.
100 E. Broad St.
Columbus, OH 43271
Website: http://
    www.bankone.com
John B. McCoy, CEO
Commercial Banks

Bancroft, Anne (Anna Maria
    Italiano)
% 20th Century Fox
Box 900
Beverly Hills, CA 90213
Actress

BankAmerica Corp.
100 N. Tryon St., 18th Floor
Charlotte, NC 28255
Website: http://
    www.bankamerica.com
Hugh L. McColl, Jr., Chairman
    and CEO
Commercial banks

Bank of New York Company
48 Wall St.
New York, NY 10286
Website: http://
    www.bankofny.com
Thomas A. Renyi, Chairman
    and CEO, The Bank of
    New York Company and
    The Bank of New York
Commercial bank

Band, The
121 N. San Vicente Blvd.
Beverly Hills, CA 90211
Musical group

Bandar, Prince Sultan-al-saud
601 New Hampshire NW
Washington, DC 20037
Saudi Arabia's ambassador to the
    United States

Banderas, Antonio
3110 Main St., #205
Santa Monica, CA 90405
Actor
Birthday: 1960

Bando, Saul
% Milwaukee Brewers
Milwaukee County Stadium
Milwaukee, WI 53214
Baseball player

Bandy, Moe
2802 Covington Pl.
Nashville, TN 37204
Musician

Bani Sadr, Abol Hassan
Auvers-sur-Oise
France
Former president of Iran

Banks, Ernie
% Chicago Cubs
1060 W. Addison St.
Chicago, IL 60613
Baseball player

Banks, Tyra
1999 Ave. of the Stars, #2850
Los Angeles, CA 90067
Actress/model
Birthday: 12/3/73

Barbeau, Adrienne
PO Box 1839
Studio City, CA 91614
or
9255 Sunset Blvd., #515
Los Angeles, CA 90069
Actress
Birthday: 6/11/45

Barbiera, Paula
PO Box 20483
Panama City, FL 32411
Model, O. J. Simpson's ex-girlfriend

Bardot, Brigette
La Madrague F-83990
St. Tropez
France
Actress
Birthday: 9/28/34

Barker, Bob (Robert William Barker)
5750 Wilshire Blvd., #475
Los Angeles, CA 90036
Host of The Price Is Right
Birthday: 12/12/23

Barker, Clive
PO Box 691885
West Hollywood, CA 90069
Author

Barkin, Ellen
% Creative Artists Agency
9830 Wilshire Blvd.
Beverly Hills, CA 90212
Actress
Birthday: 4/16/54

Barkley, Charles
10 Greenway Plaza E
Houston, TX 77277
Basketball player

Barnard, Dr. Christian
Box 6143, Weigemoed 7538
Capetown
South Africa
Heart surgeon

Barnes, Priscilla
8428-C Melrose Pl.
West Hollywood, CA 90069
Actress
Birthday: 12/7/56

Barnes & Noble
122 Fifth Ave.
New York, NY 10011
Website: http://
    www.BarnesandNoble.com
Leonard Riggio, Chairman and
    CEO; Chairman,
    barnesandnoble.com
Bookseller

Barney
300 E. Beethany Rd.
Box 8000
Allen, TX 75002
Dinosaur

Baros, Dana
151 Merrimac St., 4th Floor
Boston, MA. 02114
*Boston Celtics guard (height
    5'11")*
Birthday: 4/13/67

Barr, Julie
420 Madison Ave., #1400
New York, NY 10017
Actress

Barris, Chuck
17 E. 76th St.
New York, NY 10021
TV producer

Barrows, Sydney Biddle
210 W. 70th St.
New York, NY 10023
Alleged madam

Barry, Dave
1 Herald Plaza
Miami, FL 33101
E-mail: 733314.722@
compuserve.com
Humorist/columnist

Barry, Gene
151 El Camino Dr.
Beverly Hills, CA 90212
Actor
Birthday: 6/14/22

Barry, Mayor Marion
161 Raleigh St. SE
Washington, DC 20032
Mayor of Washington, D.C.
Birthday: 3/6/36

Barrymore, Drew
1122 S. Robertson Blvd., #15
Los Angeles, CA 90035
Actress
Birthday: 2/22/75

Baryshnikov, Mikhail
157 W. 57th. St., #502
New York, NY 10019
Ballet dancer, actor
Birthday: 1/28/48

Basinger, Kim
9830 Wilshire Blvd.
Beverly Hills, CA 90212
Birthday: 12/8/53

Bassey, Shirley
24 Ave. Princess Grace #1200
Monte Carlo
Monaco
Singer
Birthday: 1/8/37

Bateman, Jason
2628 2nd St.
Santa Monica, CA 90405
Actor
Birthday: 1/14/69

Bateman Justine
2628 2nd St.
Santa Monica, CA 90405
Actress
Birthday: 2/19/66

**Bates, Kathy (Kathleen Doyle
Bates)**
121 N. San Vicente Blvd.
Beverly Hills, CA 90211
Actress
Birthday: 6/28/48

Battle, Kathleen
165 W. 57th St.
New York, NY 10019
Opera singer
Birthday: 8/13/48

Baxter, Meredith
2049 Century Park E., #2500
Los Angeles, CA 90067
Actress
Birthday: 6/21/47

Baxter International
1 Baxter Pkwy.
Deerfield, IL 60015
Website: http://
www.baxter.com
William B. Graham, Chairman
Emeritus
Harry M. Jansen Kraemer, Jr.,
Chairman and CEO,
Baxter International,
Baxter World Trade
Corporation, and Baxter
Healthcare Corporation
*Scientific, photo, control, and
medical equipment*

Bay City Rollers
21a Clifftown Rd.
Southend-on-Sea
Essex SSL 1AB
England
Rock band

Bayh, Birch
1575 I St., #1025
Washington, DC 20005
Former senator

"Baywatch Hawaii"
The Baywatch Production Co.
510 18th Ave.
Honolulu, HI 96816
Website: http://
    www.baywatch.com/
    baywatchhawaii/start2.htm
TV series

**Bazelon Center for Mental
    Health Law**
1101 15th St. NW, #1212
Washington, DC 20005
Website: http://
    www.bazelon.org/
E-mail: bazelon@nicom.com
Lee Carty, Communications
    Director
*Legal advocacy for the civil rights
    and human dignity of people
    with mental disabilities*

Beach Boys, The
8942 Wilshire Blvd.
Beverly Hills, CA 90211
Music group

Beals, Jennifer
14755 Ventura Blvd., #710
Sherman Oaks, CA 91403
Actress
Birthday: 12/19/63

Beard, Amanda
1 Olympic Plaza
Colorado Springs, CO 80909
Olympic gold medal swimmer

Bear Stearns
245 Park Ave.
New York, NY 10167
Website: http://
    www.bearstearns.com
Alan C. Greenberg, Chairman,
    Bear Stearns Companies
    and Bear, Stearns & Co.
Securities

Beastie Boys
% EMI
1290 Ave. of the Americas
New York, NY 10104
Rap group

Beatrix, HM Queen
Kasteel Drakestijn
Lage Vuursche 3744 BA
Holland
Queen of Holland

**Beatty, Warren (Henry Warren
    Beaty)**
9830 Wilshire Blvd.
Beverly Hills, Ca. 90212
*Actor, Shirley MacLaine's brother,
    married to Annette Bening*
Birthday: 3/30/37

Beavis & Butt-Head
1515 Broadway, #400
New York, NY 10036
Animated characters

Beck
17835 Ventura Blvd., #310
Encino, CA 91316
Musician

Beck, Jeff
11 Old Sq. Lincoln's Inn
London WC2
England
Musican

Beck, Marilyn
PO Box 11079
Beverly Hills, CA 90210
Columnist, critic
Birthday: 12/17/28

Becker, Boris
Nusslocher Str. 51
69181 Leimen
Germany
Professional tennis player
Birthday: 11/22/67

Becton, Dickinson
1 Becton Dr.
Franklin Lakes, NJ 07417
Website: http://www.bd.com
Clateo Castellini, Chairman
*Scientific, photo, and control
    equipment and medical and
    bio systems*

Bedelia, Bonnie
% ICM
8942 Wilshire Blvd.
Beverly Hills, CA 90211
Actress

Bed and Breakfast
% Live Music and Ent.
Rothenbaumchaussee 209
20149 Hamburg
Germany
Music group

The Bee Gees
20505 US Hwy 19 North, #12-
    290
Clearwater, FL 33764
Web: http://www.beegees.net
Email: beegees@beegees.net

Beene, Geoffrey
550 7th Ave.
New York, NY 10018
Clothes designer

Begley, Ed, Jr.
Sterling/Winters Company
1900 Ave. of the Stars, #1640
Los Angeles, CA 90067
Birthday: 9/16/49

Bell, Archie
PO Box 11669
Knoxville, TN 37939
Singer

Bell, Wendell
Yale University
PO Box 208265
New Haven, CT 06520
E-mail: wendell.bell@yale.edu
*Professor emeritus of sociology at
    Yale University, and author of*
    Foundations of Futures
    Studies, Volumes 1 and 2

Bellamy Brothers
PO Box #801
San Antonio, FL 33576
or
13917 Restless Lane
Dade City, FL 33525
Country music group

Bellamy, Bill
9830 Wilshire Blvd.
Beverly Hills, CA 90212
Musician

Bell Atlantic
1095 Sixth Ave.
New York, NY 10036
Website: http://
    www.bellatlantic.com
Charles R. Lee, Chairman and
    Co-CEO
Ivan G. Seidenberg, President
    and Co-CEO
Telecommunications

Belle, Albert
% Chicago White Sox
324 W. 35th St.
Chicago, IL 60616
Baseball player

BellSouth
1155 Peachtree St. N.E.
Atlanta, GA 30309
Website: http://
    www.bellsouthcorp.com
F. Duane Ackerman, Chairman
    and CEO
Telecommunications

Belmundo, Jean-Paul
9 rue des Sts.-Peres
Paris F-75006
France
Actor
4/9/?

Belushi, Jim
8271 Melrose Ave., #110
Los Angeles, CA 90046
Actor

Belzer, Richard
9000 Sunset Blvd., #122200
Los Angeles, CA 90069
Comedian, actor

Benatar, Pat
584 N. Larchmont Blvd.
Los Angeles, CA 90004
Singer
Birthday: 1/19/52

Benedict, Dirk
4605 Lankershim Blvd., #305
North Hollywood, CA 91602
Actor
Birthday: 1/01/45

Beneficial
301 N. Walnut St.
Wilmington, DE 19801
Website: http://
    www.beneficial.com/
Finn M. W. Caspersen, CEO
Financial corporation

Ben Folds Five
PO Box 1028
Chapel Hill, NC 27514
website: http://www.bffweb.com
E-mail: bffmail@aol.com
Music group

Bening, Annette
13671 Muholland Dr.
Beverly Hills, CA 90210
Actress, married to Warren Beatty
Birthday: 5/29/58

Benji
242 N. Canon Dr.
Beverly Hills, CA 90210
Acting dog

Bennett, Bill
1776 I St., NW, #890,
Washington, DC 20006
Author

Bennett, Cornelius
% Buffalo Bills
One Bills Dr.
Orchard Park, NY 14127
Football player

Benson, George
Turner Management Group
3500 W. Olive Ave., #900
Burbank, CA 91505
Singer
Birthday: 3/2/43

Benson, Jodi
% Special Artists Agency
Attn: Marcia Hurwitz
345 N. Maple Dr., #302
Beverly Hills, CA 90210
Actress

Benson, Joe
PO Box 12464
La Crescenta, CA 91224
Website: http://
    www.unclejoe.com
E-mail: unclejoe@unclejoe.com
Los Angeles radio personality

Benson, Robby (Robby Segal)
PO Box 1305
Woodland Hills, CA 91364
Actor, writer, director
Birthday: 1/21/55

Bentsen, Hon. Lloyd
901 15th. St. NW, #700
Washington, DC 20005
*Former vice-presidential candidate,
    former senator*

Berenson, Marisa
80 Av. Charles de Gaulle
F92200 Neully
France
Actress
Birthday: 2/15/47

Berenger, Tom
PO Box 1842
Beaufort, SC 29901
Actor
Birthday: 5/31/50

Berg, Matraca
% Susan Hackney
2100 West End Ave., #1000
Nashville, TN 37203
Country music duo

Bergen, Candice
1122 S. Robertson Blvd., #15
Los Angeles, CA 90035
Actress
Birthday: 5/9/46

Bergen Brunswick
4000 Metropolitan Dr.
Orange, CA 92868
Website: http://
    www.bergenbrunswig.com
Robert E. Martini, Chairman,
    Interim President, and
    Interim CEO
*Pharmaceuticals, healthcare
    supplier*

Berkeley, Elizabeth
12400 Ventura Blvd., #122
Studio City, CA 91604
Actress

Berkowitz, David
#78A1976
Sullivan Corr. Fac., Box AG
Fallsburg, NY 12733
Convicted killer, "Son of Sam"
Birthday: 6/1/53

Berkshire Hathaway
1440 Kiewit Plaza
Omaha, NE 68131
Website:
    www.bershirehathaway.com
Warren E. Buffett, Chairman
    and CEO
P & C insurance (stock)

Berle, Milton
10490 Wilshire Blvd., #1603
Los Angeles, CA 90024
Comedian, actor
Birthday: 7/12/08

Bernard, Crystal
9830 Wilshire Blvd.
Beverly Hills, CA 90212
Actress

Bernhard, Sandra
26500 W. Agoura Rd.
Calabasas, CA 91302
Actress, comediene
Birthday: 6/16/?

Bernsen, Corbin
11075 Santa Monica Blvd.,
    #150
Los Angeles, CA 90025
Actor
Birthday: 9/07/54

Berra, Yogi
PO Box 462
Caldwell, NJ 07006
Former baseball player

Berry, Chuck
Berry Park
Buckner Rd.
Wentzville, MO 63385
Singer, songwriter
Birthday: 10/18/26

Berry, Halle
1122 S. Robertson Blvd., #15
Los Angeles, CA 90035
Actress

Berry, John
1211 16th St. S.
Nashville, TN 37212
Country music singer

John Berry's Pack
1807 N. Dixie, Suite 116
Elizabethtown, KY 42701
Country music fan club

Berry, Ken
4704 Cahuenga Blvd.
North Hollywood, CA 91602
Actor
Birthday: 11/3/33

Bertinelli, Valerie
151 El Camino Dr.
Beverly Hills, CA 90212
Actress
Birthday: 4/23/60

Besson, Luc
76 Oxford St.
London W1N 0AX
England
Film director
Birthday: 3/18/59

Best, Pete
#8 Hyman's Green
W. Derby
Liverpool 12
England
Former Beatle
Birthday: 11/24/41

Best Buy
7075 Flying Cloud Dr.
Eden Prairie, MN 55344
Website: http://
    www.bestbuy.com
Richard M. Schulze, Chairman
    and CEO
Specialist electronics retailers

Best Foods
International Plaza
700 Sylvan Ave.
Englewood Cliffs, NJ 07632
Website: http://
    www.bestfoods.com
Charles R. Shoemate, CEO
Food producer

Bethlehem Steel
1170 Eighth Ave.
Bethlehem, PA 18016
Website: http://
    www.bethsteel.com
Curtis H. Barnette, Chairman
    and CEO
Metals

Beverly Enterprises
1000 Beverly Way
Fort Smith, AR 72919
Website: http://
    www.beverlynet.com
David R. Banks, Chairman and
    CEO
Health care, nursing homes

Beverly Hills Hotel, The
9641 Sunset Blvd.
Beverly Hills, CA 90210
Website: http://www.thebeverly
    hillshotel.com/home.htm
E-mail: Concierge@BeverlyHills
Hotel.com or Reservations@
BeverlyHillsHotel.com
*Famous hotel is renowned for its
    celebrity clientele and home of
    the world famous Polo
    Lounge, the hotel was built in
    1912, magnificently renovated
    in 1995*

B. F. Goodrich
Four Coliseum Centre
2730 W. Tyvola Rd.
Charlotte, NC 28217
Website: http://
    www.bfgoodrich.com
David L. Burner, Chairman,
    President and CEO
*Aerospace systems and services and
    specialty chemicals*

B. G. Prince of Rap
℅ Allstars Music
Hundshager Weg 30
68623 Hofheim
Germany
Rap artist

Biafra, Jello (Eric Boucher)
PO Box 419092
San Francisco, CA 94141
*Former lead singer of the punk
    rock band Dead Kennedys*

Bialik, Mayim
1529 N. Cahuenga Blvd., #19
Los Angeles, CA 90028
Actress
Birthday: 12/12/75

Biffi, Giacomo Cardinal
ArchivesCovado
Via Altabella 6
Bologna 40126
Italy

Biggs-Dawsen, Rozann
1630 Ft. Campbell Blvd. #9143
Clarksville, TN 37042
Lt. B'Elanna Torres on Star Trek:
    Voyager

Bijan
699 5th Ave.
New York, NY 10022
Designer

Billingsley, Barbara
PO Box 1588
Pacific Palisades, CA 9072
Actress, played Beaver's mother on
    Leave It to Beaver
Birthday: 12/22/22

Bindley Western
8909 Purdue Rd.
Indianapolis, IN 46268
Website: http://
    www.bindley.com
William E. Bindley, Chairman,
    President and CEO
*Wholesale distributors of
    pharmaceuticals, health and
    beauty care products, and
    home health care products in
    the United States*

Bingham, Traci
2029 Century Park E. 3250
Los Angeles, CA 90067
Actress on Baywatch

Bird, Larry
RR #1 Box 77A
West Baden Springs, IN 47469
*Former Indiana Pacers basketball
    coach*
Birthday: 12/7/56

Birney, David
20 Ocean Park Blvd. #11
Santa Monica, CA 90405
Actor
Birthday: 4/23/39

Bishop, Stephen
% Miles Hymes
18321 Ventura Bl. #580
Tarzana, CA 91356
Musician

Bisset, Jacqueline
10 av. George V
F-75008 Paris
France
or
Guttman Assoc
118 S Beverly Dr.
Beverly Hills, CA 90212
Actress
Birthday: 9/13/44

BizRate
4053 Redwood Ave.
Los Angeles, CA 90066
Website: www.bizrate.com
E-mail: farhad@bizrate.com
Farhad Mohit, CEO and
    President
E-commerce

B. J.'s Wholesale Club
1 Mercer Rd.
Natick, MA 01760
Website: http://
    www.bjswholesale.com
Herbert J. Zarkin, Chairman
John J. Nugent, President and
    CEO
Membership food and drug stores

Black Crowes, The
888 7th. Ave., #602
New York, NY 10107
Music group

Black Oak Arkansas
1487 Red Run Fox
Liburn, GA 30247
Music group

Black, Clint
8489 W. Third St., #200
Los Angeles, CA 90048
Country singer/songwriter
Birthday: 2/4/62

Black, Karen (Karen Ziegler)
3500 W. Olive Ave., #1400
Burbank, CA 91505
Actress
Birthday: 7/1/42

Black & Decker
701 E. Joppa Rd.
Towson, MD 21286
Website: http://
    www.blackanddecker.com
Nolan D. Archibald, Chairman,
    President and CEO
*Tools and industrial and farm
    equipment*

Blackstone, Harry, Jr.
11075 Santa Monica Blvd.,
    #275
Los Angeles, CA 90025
Magician

Blackwood, Nina
% Angelwood
23705 Vanowen St., #111
West Hills, CA 91307
Singer

Blair, Linda
15821 Ventura Blvd., #235
Encino, CA 91436
Actress
Birthday: 1/22/59

Blakely, Susan
8436 W. Third St., #740
Los Angeles, CA 90048
Actress
Birthday: 9/7/50

Blakley, Ronee
8033 Sunset Blvd., #693
Los Angeles, CA 90046
Actress, singer

Bland, Bobby "Blue"
1995 Broadway, #501
New York, NY 10023
Singer

Blanda, George
PO Box 1153
LaQuinta, CA 92253
Former football player

Blass, Bill
550 7th Ave.
New York, NY 10018
Fashion designer
Birthday: 6/22/22

Blasters, The
555 Chorro St., #A-1
San Luis Obispo, CA 93401
Rock band

Bledsoe, Drew
% New England Patriots
Route 1
Foxboro, MA 02035
Football player

Bledsoe, Tempestt
10100 Santa Monica Blvd.,
    #3480
Los Angeles, CA 90067
Actress
Birthday: 8/1/73

Blind Melon
9229 Sunset Blvd. #607
Los Angeles, CA 90069
Alternative band

Blood, Sweat and Tears
43 Washington St.
Groveland, MA 01834
Musical group

Bloodsworth-Thomason, Linda
4024 Radford Ave. Bldg. 5,
    #104
Studio City, CA 91604
Film and TV producer

Blount, Lisa
5750 Wilshire Blvd., #580
Los Angeles, CA 90036
Actress

Blount, Mel
RD 1 Box 91
Claysville, PA 15323
Former football player

Blue, Vida
PO Box 1449
Pleasonton, CA 94566
*Former baseball player; charges $9
    for trading card, $5 for 3 ×
    5*

Blues Traveler
PO Box 1128
New York, NY 10101
Website: http://
    www.bluestraveler.com
E-mail: blackcatz@earthlink.net
Rock band

Blume, Judy
40 E. 48th St., #100
New York, NY 10017
Author
Birthday: 2/12/38

Blur
20 Manchester Sq.
London W1A 1ES
England
Music group

Blyth, Ann
Box 9754
Rancho Santa Fe, CA 92067
Actress
Birthday: 8/16/28

Boaz, David
Cato Institute
1000 Massachusetts Ave., N.W.
Washington, DC 20001
E-mail: dboaz@cato.org
*Author and executive vice
    president of the Cato Institute*

Bobek, Nicole
PO Box 4534
Tequesta, FL 33469
Figure skater

Bocho, Steven
694 Amalfi Dr.
Pacific Palisades, CA 90272
Producer, screenwriter
Birthday: 12/16/43

Boeing
7755 E. Marginal Way S.
Seattle, WA 98108
Website: http://
    www.boeing.com
Philip M. Condit, Chairman
    and CEO
Aerospace

Bogguss, Suzy
1207 17th Ave., #101
Nashville, TN 37212
Country music singer

Bogues, Mugsy
% Golden State Warriors
Oakland Coliseum Arena
7000 Coliseum Way
Oakland, CA 94621
Basketball player

Boice, Dr. James
1935 Pine St.
Philadelphia, PA 19103
Theologian

Boise Cascade
1111 W. Jefferson St.
Boise, ID 83702
Website: http://www.bc.com
George J. Harad, Chairman
    and CEO; Chairman Boise
    Cascade Office Products
*Forest and paper products and
    office supplies*

Bologna, Joseph
16830 Ventura Blvd., #326
Encino, CA 91436
Actor, writer, director
Birthday: 12/30/38

Bolton, Michael
PO Box 679
Branford, CT 06516
Singer

Bon Jovi
248 W. 17th. St., #502
New York, NY 10107
Rock group

Bon Jovi, Jon (Jon Bongiovi)
248 W. 17th St. #502
New York, NY 10107
Rock singer
Birthday: 5/10/60

Bonaduce, Danny
651 Washington St.
New York, NY 10014
Actor, talk show host

Bonds, Bary
9595 Wilshire Blvd., #711
Beverly Hills, CA 90212
Baseball player

**Bonds, Gary "U.S." (Gary
    Anderson)**
875 Ave. of the Americas,
    #1906
New York, NY 10001
Singer
Birthday: 6/6/39

Bone Thugs and Harmony
8942 Wilshire Blvd.
Beverly Hills, CA 90211
Music group

Bono (Paul Hewson)
4 Windmill Ln.
Dublin, 2
Ireland
Singer, songwriter
Birthday: 5/10/60

Bono, Chastity
PO Box 960
Beverly Hills, CA 90213
Sonny and Cher's daughter
Birthday: 3/4/69

Booker T and the MGs
59 Parsons St.
Newtonville, MA 02160
Music group

Boone, Larry
% Gene Ferguson
PO Box 23795
Nashville, TN 37212
Musician

Boone, Debbie
4334 Kestar Ave.
Sherman Oaks, CA 91403
Actress, singer

Boone, Pat
904 N. Beverly Dr.
Beverly Hills, CA 90210
Singer
Birthday: 6/1/34

Betty Boop, Fan Club
6024 Fullerton Ave., #2
Buena Park, CA 90621

Boosler, Elayne
584 N. Larchmont Blvd.
Los Angeles, CA 90004
Comedienne, actress

Boothe, Powers
PO Box 9242
Calabasas, CA 91372
Actor

Boothroyd, Betty
House of Commons
London SW1A 0AA
England
*First woman speaker of the House
of Commons*

Borden
180 E. Broad St.
Columbus, OH 43215
C. Robert Kidder, Chairman
*Specialty chemicals and consumer
adhesives; the company rates
as the #1 producer of
household and school glues
(Elmer's) in the U.S., and
also makes caulks and
sealants*

Borg, Bjorn
1360 E. 9th. St., #100
Cleveland, OH 44114
Tennis player
Birthday: 6/7/56

Borge, Victor
Fieldpoint Park
Greenwich, CT 06830
Pianist, comedian
Birthday: 1/3/09

Borman, Col. Frank
PO Box 1139
Fairacres, NM 88033
Astronaut

Boston
9200 Sunset Blvd, #530
Los Angeles, CA 90069
Music group

Bostwick, Barry
1640 S. Sepulveda Blvd., #218
Los Angeles, CA 90025
Actor
Birthday: 2/24/46

Boston Bruins
Fleet Center
Boston, MA 02114

**Boston Modern Orchestra
   Project**
1108 Boylston St., Suite 303
Boston, MA 02115
Website: http://
   www.bmop.org/
E-mail: bmop@bmop.org
Gil Rose, Music Director

**Boston Symphony Orchestra/
   Boston Pops Orchestra**
Symphony Hall
301 Massachusetts Ave.
Boston, MA 02115
Website: http://www.bso.org/
Seiji Ozawa, Music Director

Bottoms, Joe
1015 Gayley Ave., #300
Los Angeles, CA 90024
Actor

Boucher, Phillippe
Staples Center
1111 S. Figueroa Street
Los Angeles, CA 90015
Hockey player

Boulez, Pierre
1 Pl. Igor Stravinsky
F75004 Paris
France
Conductor, composer

Boutros-Boutros-Ghali
2 Ave. El nil
Giza
Cairo
Egypt
*Secretary-General of the United
   Nations*
Birthday: 11/14/22

Bowie, David
180–182 Tottenham Ct. Rd
London W1X 7LH
England
Musician

Bowles, Camilla Parker
Middlewick House
Nr. Corshm., Wiltshire
England
*Longstanding companion and
   confidante of Prince Charles*

Boxcar Willie
HCR 1, Box 7085
Branson, MO 65616
Country music singer

Boxleitner, Bruce
23679 Calabasas Rd., #181
Calabasas, CA 91302
Actor
Birthday: 5/12/50

Boxtops, The
2011 Ferry Ave., #U-19
Camden, NJ 08104
Music group

Boy George (George O'Dowd)
63 Grosvenor St.
London W1X 9DA
England
Singer, songwriter, author
Birthday: 6/14/61

Boy Howdy
% Club Howdy
PO Box 570784
Tarzana, CA 91357-0784
Country music group

Boyle, Peter
130 East End Ave.
New York, NY 10024
Actor
Birthday: 1/18/33

Boyz II Men
% WMA
1325 Ave. of the Americas
New York, NY 10019
Vocal group

Bozo the Clown
% WGN Television
2501 Bradley Place
Chicago, IL 60618

BP Amoco p.l.c.
Britannic House
1 Finsbury Circus
London EC2M 7BA
United Kingdom
Website: bpamoco.com
Peter D. Sutherland, Chairman
Petroleum refining

Bracco, Lorraine
18 E. 53rd. St., #1400
New York, NY 10022
Actress
Birthday: 11/30/54

Bradford, Barbara Taylor
450 Park Ave., #1903
New York, NY 10022
Author

Brady, Marsha
Maureen McCormick Fan Club
22817 Pera Rd.
Woodland Hills, CA 91364

Branagh, Kenneth
Shepperton Studios
Studios Rd.
Shepperton
TW170QD
England
Actor
Birthday: 12/10/60

Bradlee, Benjamin
3014 N St. NW
Washington, DC 20007
Journalist

Bradley, Ed
% *60 Minutes*
555 W. 57th St.
New York, NY 10019
News correspondent

Bradshaw, John
2412 South Blvd.
Houston, TX 77098
*Lecturer and author of self-
improvement books*

Brady, James
1255 I St., #1100
Washington, DC 20005
Former Whitehouse Press Secretary

Brady, Sarah
1255 I St., #1100
Washington, DC 20005
Gun control advocate

Brando, Marlon
13828 Weddington
Van Nuys, CA 91401
Actor
Birthday: 4/03/24

Brands X
17171 Roscoe Blvd., #104
Northridge, CA 91325
Music group

Brandy (Norwood)
22817 Ventura Blvd., #432
Woodland Hills, CA 91364
Actress

Branigan, Laura
1501 Broadway, #1301
New York, NY 10036
Singer

Braxton, Toni
9255 Sunset Blvd., #610
Los Angeles, CA 90069
Singer
Birthday: 1968

Breeders, The
3575 Cahuenga Blvd., W. #450
Los Angeles, CA 90068
Music group

Breedlove, Craig
200 N. Front St.
Rio Vista, CA 94571
Land speed record setter

Bread for the World/BFW Institute
1100 Wayne Ave., #1000
Silver Spring, MD 20910
Website: http://www.bread.org/
Citizens' movement seeking "justice" for the world's hungry people by lobbying our nation's decision makers

Brechner Center for Freedom of Information
PO Box 118400
3208 Weimer Hall
University of Florida
Gainesville, FL 32611
Website: http://www.jou.ufl. edu/brechner/brochure. htm
E-mail: bchamber@jou.ufl.edu
Sandra F. Chance Director
A unit of the College of Journalism and Communications at the University of Florida which is relied upon by media organizations nationwide for information about media law developments in Florida

Brennan, Eileen
10110 Emperian Way, #304
Los Angeles, CA 90067
Actress
Birthday: 9/03/35

Brenneman, Amy
9830 Wilshire Blvd.
Beverly Hills, CA 90212
Actress
Birthday: 2/4/45

Brenner, David
17 E. 16th St., #3
New York, NY 10003
Comedian
Birthday: 2/4/45

Breslin, Jimmy
Newsday
Park Ave.
New York, NY 10016
Author, columnist

Brett, George
PO Box 419969
Kansas City, MO 64141
Former baseball player

Bridges, Beau
5525 N. Jed Smith Rd.
Hidden Hills, CA 91302
Actor
Birthday: 12/09/41

Bridges, Elisa
1560 Broadway, #1308
New York, NY 10036
Model

Bridges, Jeff
% Creative Artists Agency
9830 Wilshire Blvd.
Beverly Hills, CA 90212
or
5525 N. Jed Smith Rd.
Hidden Hills, CA 91302
Actor
Birthday: 12/4/49

Bridges, Todd
3518 Cahuenga Blvd., W. #216
Los Angeles, CA 90068
Actor
Birthday: 5/27/65

Bright, Dr. Bill
515 North Cabrillo Park Dr.,
     #225
Santa Ana, CA 9270
or
1111 W. Sunset Blvd., Suite
     600
Los Angeles, CA 90012
Evangelist

Brightman, Sarah
1 Sussex Pl., #1421
London W6 9XT
England
Website: http://www.sarah-
     brightman.com/
*Singer, Lord Lloyd Webber created
     the role of Christine in*
     Phantom of the Opera
     especially for her

Brillstein, Bernie
Brillstein-Grey Enterprises
9150 Wilshire Blvd.
Beverly Hills, CA 90212
Theatrical/literary agent

Brinkley, Christie
1122 S. Robertson Blvd., #15
Los Angeles, CA 90035
Model/actress
Birthday: 2/2/54

Bristol-Meyers Squibb
345 Park Ave.
New York, NY 10154
Website: http://www.bms.com
Charles A. Heimbold, Jr.,
     Chairman and CEO
Pharmaceutical manufacturer

Broadcast Music, Inc. (BMI)
London
84 Harley House
Marylebone Rd.
London NW1 5HN
ENGLAND
Website: http://www.bmi.com/
Music licensing organization

Broadcast Music, Inc. (BMI)
8730 Sunset Blvd., 3rd Floor
West Los Angeles, CA 90046
Website: http://www.bmi.com/
E-mail: infotech@bmi.com
Robert Barone, Vice President,
    Operations and
    Information Technology
Music licensing organization

Broadcast Music, Inc. (BMI)
Nashville
10 Music Square East
Nashville, TN 37203
Website: http://www.bmi.com/
Music licensing organization

Broadcast Music, Inc. (BMI)
New York
320 West 57th St.
New York, NY 10019
Website: http://www.bmi.com/
Music licensing organization

Broderick, Matthew
PO Box 69646
Los Angeles, CA 90069
Actor
Birthday: 3/21/62

**Brokaw, Tom (Thomas John
    Brokaw)**
NBC News
30 Rockefeller Plaza
New York, NY 10112
E-mail: nightly@nbc.com
*Television broadcast executive,
    correspondent*
Birthday: 2/06/40

Brolin, James
PO Box 56927
Sherman Oaks, CA 91413
Actor
Birthday: 7/18/40

Bronson, Charles
PO Box 2644
Malibu, CA 90265
Actor
Birthday: 11/03/22

Brooklyn Bridge
PO Box 63
Cliffwood, NJ 07721
Music group

Brooks and Dunn
PO 120669
Nashville, TN 37212
Country music group

**Brooks, Albert (Albert
    Einstein)**
1880 Century Park East, #900
Los Angeles, CA 90067
Actor, writer, director
Birthday: 7/22/47

**Brooks, Garth (Troyal Garth
    Brooks)**
1111 17th. Ave. S.
Nashville, TN 37212
Country music singer
Birthday: 2/7/62

Brooks, James L.
8942 Wilshire Blvd.
Beverly Hills, CA 90211
Producer, director, screenwriter
Birthday: 5/9/40

Brosnan, Pierce
PO Box 982
Malibu, CA 90265
Actor
Birthday: 5/15/53

Brother, Phelps
PO Box 849
Goodlettsville, TN 37070
Country singer

Brothers Four, The
300 Vine St., #314
Seattle, WA 98121
Music group

Brothers, Dr. Joyce
235 E. 45th St.
New York, NY 10017
TV personality, psychologist
Birthday: 10/20/28

Brown, Bryan
110 Queen St.
Woollahra NSW 2025
Australia
Actor
Birthday: 6/23/47

Brown, Denise
PO Box 380
Monarch Bay, CA 92629
Nicole Brown-Simpson's sister

Brown, Georg Stanford
% International Artists
8033 Sunset Blvd., #1800
Los Angeles, CA 90046
Actor

Brown, Helen Gurley
1 W 81st St., #220
New York, NY 10024
Magazine editor

Brown, Jim
1851 Sunset Plaza Dr.
Los Angeles, CA 90069
Actor, former football player
Birthday: 2/17/36

Brown, Jim Ed
PO Box 121089
Nashville, TN 37212
Country music singer

Brown, "Downtown" Julie
250 W. 57th. St., #821
New York, NY 10107
Actress

Brown, Junior
PO Box 180763
Utica, MI 48318
Country music singer

Brown, Olivia
% David Shapira & Assoc.
15301 Ventural Blvd., Suite 345
Sherman Oaks, CA 91403
Actress

Brown, T. Graham
PO Box 50337
Nashville, TN 37205
Country music singer

Brown, Mayor Willie, Jr.
401 Van Ness Ave., #336
San Francisco, CA 94102
Email: DaMayor@ci.sf.ca.us
Mayor of San Francisco

Browne, Sylvia
35 Dillon Ave.
Campbell, CA 95008
Pyschic

Browning, Kurt
11160 River Valley Rd., #3189
Edmonton
Alberta, T5J 2G7
Canada
Ice skater

**Browning Ferris Industries
    (now a subsidiary of Allied
    Waste Industries)**
757 N. Eldridge Rd.
Houston, TX 77079
Website: http://www.bfi.com
Donald W. Slager, President
    and CEO; VP Operations,
    Allied Waste Industries
Waste management

Bruce, Ed
PO Box 120428
Nashville, TN 37212
Country music singer

Brunswick
1 N. Field Court
Lake Forest, IL 60045
George W. Buckley, Chairman
    and CEO
Transportation equipment

Buchanan, James M.
George Mason University
4400 University Dr.
Fairfax, VA 22030
Nobel Prize winner in *Economic
    Science, 1986; best known for
    such works as* Fiscal Theory
    and Political Economy,
    The Calculus of Consent,
    The Limits of Liberty,
    Democracy in Deficit, The
    Power to Tax, *and* The
    Reason of Rules

Buchanan, Pat
6862 Elm St., #210
McLean, VA 22101
Website: http://
    www.gopatgo2000.org/
Presidential candidate

Buckinghams, The
620 16th Ave.
So. Hopkins, MN 55343
Musical group

Buckley, Betty
420 Madison Ave., #1400
New York, NY 10017
Actress
Birthday: 7/3/47

Buckley, William F., Jr.
150 E. 35th St.
New York, NY 10016
Author, editor
Birthday: 11/24/25

Buffett, Jimmy
540 S. Ocean Blvd.
Palm Beach, FL 33480
or
550-B Duval St.
Key West, FL 33040
*Pop singer, his fans are called
    Parrot Heads.*

Bullock, Sandra
PO Box 161090
Austin, TX 78716
Actress

Bunning, Jim
% Baseball Hall of Fame
PO Box 590
Cooperstown, NY 13326
Baseball player

Bure, Pavel
% Vancouver Canucks
100 N. Renfrew St.
Vancouver, BC V5K 3N7
Canada
Hockey player

Burghoff, Gary
13834 Magnolia Blvd.
Encino, CA 91423
Actor
Birthday: 5/25/40

Burke, Delta
1012 Royal St.
New Orleans, LA 70116
Actress
Birthday: 7/30/56

Burlington Northern Santa FE
2650 Lou Menk Dr.
Fort Worth, TX 76131
Website: http://www.bnsf.com
Robert D. Krebs, Chairman
    and CEO
Railroads

Burnette, Billy
1025 16th Ave. So., Suite 401
Nashville, TN 37212
Country music singer

Burnett, Carol
7800 Beverly Blvd.
Los Angeles, CA 90036
Actress/comedian
Birthday: 4/26/33

Burns, Ken
Maple Grove Rd.
Walpole, NH 03608
Documentary maker
Birthday: 7/29/53

Burstyn, Ellen
PO Box 217
Palisades, NY 10964
Actress

Burton, LeVar
13601 Ventura Blvd., #209
Sherman Oaks, CA 91423
Actor
Birthday: 2/16/57

Burton, Tim
445 Redondo Ave., #7
Long Beach, CA 90814
Director

Bush
285 W. Broadway, #230
New York, NY 10013
Music group

Bush, George and Barbara
9 W. Oak Dr.
Houston, TX 77056
Former President and First Lady
Birthday: Barbara Bush:
    1/28/25
Birthday: George Bush:
    1/12/24

Bush, President George W.
The White House
1600 Pennsylvania Avenue
Washington, D.C. 20500

Bush, Jeb
The Capitol
Tallahassee, FL 32399
Governor of Florida, son of former
    President George Bush

**Business-Industry Political
Action Committee (BIPAC)**
888 Sixteenth St. NW
Washington, DC 20006
Website: http://
   www.bipac.org/
E-mail: info@bipac.org
*An independent, bipartisan
   organization, founded in
   1963. Through its Political
   Action Fund, BIPAC works to
   elect pro-business candidates to
   Congress. BIPAC's Business
   Institute for Political Analysis
   carries out extensive programs
   of political analysis, research,
   and communication on
   campaigns and elections, and
   fosters business participation
   in the political process*

Busey, Gary
12424 Wilshire Blvd., #840
Los Angeles, CA 90025
or
18424 Coastline Dr.
Malibu, CA 90265
Actor
Birthday: 6/29/44

Butler, Brett
8942 Wilshire Blvd.
Beverly Hills, CA 90211
Comedienne

Robert Butler
% William Morris Agency
151 El Camino Dr.
Beverly Hills, CA 90212
Film director

Buzzi, Ruth
% Sesame Street (CTW)
1 Lincoln Plaza
New York, NY 10023
Comedian
Birthday: 7/24/36

Byner, Jon
1 S. Ocean Blvd., #316
Boca Raton, FL 33432
Comedian

Tracy Byrd Fan Club
"Byrd Watchers"
PO Box 7703
Beaumont, TX 77726
Country music fan club

The Byrds
PO Box 106
Rochdale, ON16 4HW
England
Music group

Byrnes, Ed
PO 1623
Beverly Hills, CA 90213
Played Kookie on 77 Sunset Strip
Actor

A telephone call from a friend is joy—unless you're in the middle of a meal, having a bath or on the point of going out to an engagement for which you are already late. A letter in effect is saying, "I am setting aside some of my time for you alone; I'm thinking of you. This is more important to me than anything that I am doing."

—JOHN GREENALL, *Daily Telegraph*

C&C Music Factory
250 W. 57th. St., #821
New York, NY 10107
Music group

Caan, James
PO Box 6646
Denver, CO 80206
Actor
Birthday: 3/25/39

Caballe, Montserrat
Caball
Via Augusta 59
Barcelona, 08006 Spain
Opera singer

Cage, Nicolas (Nicholas Coppola)
1122 S. Robertson Blvd., #15
Los Angeles, CA 90035
Actor
Birthday: 1/7/64

Cain, Dean
1122 S. Robertson Blvd., #15
Los Angeles, CA 90035
Actor, Host of Ripley's Believe It or Not!

Caine, Michael
Rectory Farm House
North Stoke
GB-Oxfordshire
England
or
% International Creative Management
8942 Wilshire Blvd.
Beverly Hills, CA 90211
Actor
Birthday: 3/14/33

Calley, Lt. William
% V. V. Vicks
Cross Country Plaza
Columbus, GA 31906
Involved in the Mi Lai Massacre

Camacho, Hector "Macho"
4751 Yardarm Ln.
Boynton Beach, FL 33436
Prizefighter

Cameron, Candace
PO Box 8665
Calabasas, CA 91372
Actress

Cameron, James
3500 W. Olive Ave., #1400
Burbank, CA 91505
or
919 Santa Monica Blvd.
Santa Monica, CA 90401
Director

Cameron, Kirk
PO Box 8665
Calabasas, CA 91372
Actor
Birthday: 10/12/70

Campbell Soup
Campbell Place
Camden, NJ 08103
Website: http://
     www.campbellsoups.com
Dale F. Morrisson, CEO
Food manufacturer

Bruce Campbell
14431 Ventura Blvd., #120
Sherman Oaks, CA 91423
Actor

Campbell, Kim
Canadian Consulate
550 S. Hope St.
Los Angeles, CA 90071
Former Canadian Prime Minister

Campbell, Glen
10351 Santa Monica Blvd.,
     #300
Los Angeles, CA 90025
Singer, songwriter
Birthday: 4/22/36

Campbell, Naomi
Ford Model Management
344 E. 59th St.
New York, NY 10022
or
% Elite Model Management
111 East 22nd St.
New York, NY 10010
Supermodel

Campbell, Neve
% Creative Artists Agency
9830 Wilshire Blvd.
Beverly Hills, CA 90212
Actress, dancer
Birthday: 10/3/73

Campbell, Stacy Dean
1105-C 16th. Ave. So.
Nashville, TN 37212
Country singer

**Campaign for an Effective
     Crime Policy**
514 Tenth St., NW
Washington, DC 20004
Website: www.crimepolicy.org
E-mail: staf@crimepolicy.org
*Launched in 1992 by a
     nonpartisan group of criminal
     justice leaders; encourages a
     less politicized, more informed
     date about one, our nations
     most difficult problems*

Campaign for U.N. Reform
420 7th St. SE, Suite C
Washington, DC 20003
Website: http://www.cunr.org/
E-mail: CUNR@cunr.org

Candiotti, Tom
% Los Angeles Dodgers
1000 Elysian Park Ave.
Los Angeles, CA 90012
Baseball player

Canned Heat
PO Box 3773
San Rafael, CA 94912
Music group

Cannell, Steven J.
7083 Hollywood Blvd.
Hollywood, CA 90028
Website: http://
    www.cannell.com/
Author/TV producer

Cannon, Dyan
8033 Sunset Blvd., #254
Los Angeles, CA 90046
Actress
Birthday: 1/04/39

Cannon, J. D.
45 W. 60th. St., #10J
New York, NY 10023
Actor

Canyon
Encore Entertainment
PO Box 1259
Dallas, TX 75065
Country music group

Capshaw, Kate
PO Box 869
Pacific Palisades, CA 90272
Actress

Captain and Tennille
17530 Ventura Blvd., #108
Encino, CA 91316
Singing duo

Cara, Irene
8033 Sunset Blvd. #735
Los Angeles, CA 90046
Actress
Birthday: 3/18/59

Cardin, Pierre
59 Rue du Foubourg
St. Honore
F-75008 Paris
France
Fashion designer
Birthday: 7/7/22

Cardinal Health
7000 Cardinal Place
Dublin, OH 43017
Website: http://www.cardinal-
    health.com
Robert D. Walter, Chairman
    and CEO
Wholesaler

CARE
151 Ellis St.
Atlanta, GA 30303
Website: http://www.care.org/
E-mail: Doherty@care.org or
    info@care.org
*Works to affirm the dignity and
    worth of individuals and
    families in some of the poorest
    communities of the world*

Carey, Drew
955 S. Carillo Dr., #100
Los Angeles, CA 90048
Actor

Carey, Harry, Jr.
PO Box 3256
Durango, CO 81302
Actor

Carey, Mariah
345 N. Maple Dr., #300
Beverly Hills, CA 90210
Singer
Birthday: 3/26/70

Carey, Ron
419 N. Larchmont Blvd.
Los Angeles, CA 90004
Actor

Carey, Ron
25 Louisiana Ave., N.W.
Washington, DC 20001
Teamster president

Carli, Claudio
V. Aldo Banzi, 66
Rome 00128
Italy

Carlin, George
11911 San Vicente Blvd., #348
Los Angeles, CA 90049
Comedian, actor
Birthday: 5/12/?

Carlson, Paulette
1906 Chet Atkins Pl., #502
Nashville, TN 37212
Country singer

Carlton, Steve
555 S. Camino Del Rio, #B2
Durango, CO 81301
Former baseball player

Caroline, Princess
Villa Le Clos
St. Pierre Ave.
Saint Martin
Monte Carlo
Monaco
Birthday: 1/23/57

Carney, Art
RR #20 Box 911
Westbrook, CT 06498
Actor
Birthday: 11/14/18

Caron, Leslie
10 av. George V
F-75116 Paris
France
Actress
Birthday: 7/01/31

Carpenter, Mary Chapin
15030 Ventura Blvd., #1–710
Sherman Oaks, CA 91403
Country singer

Carpenter, Richard
PO Box 1084
Downey, CA 90240
Singer

Carpenter, Lt. Cmdr. Scott
55 E. 87th St., #4A
New York, NY 10128
Astronaut

Carr, Vikki
PO Box 780968
San Antonio, TX 78278
Singer
Birthday: 7/19/41

Carradine, David
628 S. San Fernando Rd., #C
Burbank, CA 91505
Actor
Birthday: 12/08/36

Carradine, Keith
PO Box 460
Placerville, CO 81430
Actor
Birthday: 8/8/49

Carrera, Barbara
PO Box 7631
Beverly Hills, CA 90212
Actress, "Bond" girl
Birthday: 12/31/45

Carrere, Tia
8228 Sunset Blvd., #300
Los Angeles, CA 90048
Actress
Birthday: 1/6/67

Jim Carrey
% United Talent Agency
9560 Wilshire Blvd., Suite. 500
Beverly Hills, CA 90212
or
PO Box 57593
Sherman Oaks, CA 91403
Actor, comedian
Birthday: 1/17/62

Carroll, Diahann
PO Box 2999
Beverly Hills, CA 90213
Actress
Birthday: 7/17/35

Carrot Top
% Carrot Top, Inc.
Disney-MGM Studios
Lake Buena Vista, FL 32830
Comedian

Carson, Jeff
1002 18th Ave. S.
Nashville, TN 37212
Country music singer

The Carter Center
453 Freedom Parkway
Atlanta, GA 30307
Website: http://www.carter
    center.org/home.html
John Hardman, M.D.,
    Executive Director
*In partnership with Emory
    University, it is guided by a
    fundamental commitment to
    human rights, wages peace by
    bringing warring parties to the
    negotiating table, monitoring
    elections, safeguarding human
    rights, and building strong
    democracies through economic
    development*

Carter, Carlene
PO Box 120845
Nashville, TN 37212
Country music singer

Carter, Dixie
10635 Santa Monica Blvd.,
    #130
Los Angeles, CA 90025
Actress

Carter, Jimmy
1 Woodlawn Dr.
Plains, GA 31780
Website: http://
    www.cartercenter.org/
    home.html
Former President

Carter-Cash, June
700 E. Main St.
Henderson, TN 37075
Country singer
Birthday: 6/22/29

Carter, Lynda
9200 Harrington Dr.
Potomac, MD 20854
Actress
Birthday: 7/24/51

Carter, Nell
8484 Wilshire Blvd., #500
Beverly Hills, CA 90211
Actress, singer

Carter, Rosalyn
1 Woodlawn Dr.
Plains, GA 31780
Former First Lady

Carter, Rubin "Hurricane"
PO Box 295
College Park, MD 20741
Former boxer, subject of film
    Hurricane

Cartwright, Angela
10143 Riverside Dr.
Toluca Lake, CA 91602
Actress

Cartwright, Lionel
27 Music Square E., #182
Nashville, TN 37203
Country singer

Caruso, David
270 N. Canon Dr., #1058
Beverly Hills, CA 90210
Actor

Carville, James
209 Pennsylvania Ave. SE, #800
Washington, DC 20003
Political commentator

Casaroli, Agostino Cardinal
00120 Vatican City State
Vatican
Cardinal

Case
700 State St.
Racine, WI 53404
Website: http://
    www.casecorp.com
Jean-Pierre Rosso, CEO
Industrial and farm equipment

Case, Steve
22000 AOL Way
Dulles, VA 20166
Website: http://
    www.hometown.aol.com/
    stevecase/index.html
E-mail: SteveCase@aol.com/
Chairman and CEO of America
    Online

Cash, Johnny
700 E. Main St.
Hendersonville, TN 37045
Country music singer
Birthday: 2/26/32

Cash, Rosalind
PO Box 1605
Topanga, CA 90290
Actress

Cash, Rosanne
326 Carlton Ave., #3
Brooklyn, NY 11205
Country music singer
Birthday: 5/24/55

Casals, Rosie
PO Box 537
Sausalito, CA 94966
Tennis player

Casper, Billy
PO Box 210010
Chula Vista, CA 91921
Professional golfer
Birthday: 6/4/31

Cassidy, David
3799 Las Vegas Blvd. S.
Las Vegas, NV 89109
Actor, singer
Birthday: 4/12/50

Cassidy, Shaun
8484 Wilshire Blvd., #500
Beverly Hills, CA 90212
Actor, singer
Birthday: 9/27/58

Caterpillar
100 N.E. Adams St.
Peoria, IL 61629
Website: http://
    www.caterpillar.com
Glen A. Barton, Chairman and
    CEO
Industrial and farm equipment

Cates, Phoebe
1636 3rd Ave., #309
New York, NY 10128
Actress
Birthday: 7/16/63

Cato Institute
1000 Massachusetts Ave. NW
Washington, DC 20001
Website: http://www.cato.org/
E-mail: cato@cato.org
Edward H. Crane, President
    and CEO
*Promoting public policy based on
    limited government, free
    markets, individual liberty,
    and peace*

Cavett, Dick
109 E. 79th St., #2C
New York, NY 10021
TV host
Birthday: 11/19/36

CBS
7800 Beverly Blvd.
Los Angeles, CA 90036
or
51 W. 52 St.
New York, NY 10019
Website: http://www.cbs.com
E-mail: marketing@cbs.com
Leslie Moonves, President and
    CEO
Television network

Cendant
9 W. 57th St.
New York, NY 10019
Website: http://
    www.cendant.com
Henry R. Silverman, Chairman,
    President and CEO
Advertising, marketing

**Center for Democracy and
    Technology**
1634 Eye Street NW, Suite
    1100
Washington, DC 20006
Website: http://www.cdt.org/
E-mail: webmaster@cdt.org
Jerry Berman, Executive
    Director
E-mail: jberman@cdt.org
*A non-profit public interest
    organization based in
    Washington, D.C.; works for
    public policies that advance
    civil liberties and democratic
    values in new computer and
    communications technologies*

Center for Defense Information

1779 Massachusetts Ave., NW
Washington, DC 20036
Website: http://www.cdi.org
E-mail: info@cdi.org
Eugene J. Carroll, Jr., USN
(Ret.), Deputy Director:
Rear Admiral

*A private, nongovernmental,
research organization which
believes that strong social,
economic, political, and
military components and a
healthy environment contribute
equally to the nation's security*

Center for Democratic Renewal and Education, Inc.

PO Box 50469
Atlanta, GA 30302
E-mail: cdr@igc.apc.org

*Founded in 1979 as the National
Anti-Klan Network, the Center
for Democratic Renewal and
Education is a multiracial
organization that advances
the vision of a democratic,
diverse and just society free of
racism and bigotry; it helps
communities combat groups,
movements, and government
practices that promote hatred
and bigotry and is committed
to public policies based on
equity and justice*

Center for Ethics, Capital Markets, Political Economy

P.O. Box 1845 University
Station
Charlottesville, VA 22903
Website: http://
www.iath.virginia.edu/
cecmpe/
E-mail: cecmpe@jefferson.
village.virginia.edu
E. N. Weaver, Jr., M.D., Sr.
Amata Miller, OP, Ph.D.,
John D. Feldmann,
Directors

*A nonprofit organization
established in 1994 to provide
a discussion forum and
information resource for
persons who believe that moral
concerns should be taken into
account in economic and
political thinking*

Center for Governmental Studies

California Commission on
Campaign Financing
10951 W. Pico Blvd. #206
Los Angeles, CA 90064
Website: http://www.cgs.org/
E-mail: center@cgs.org

*Its goal is to enhance the quality
and quantity of governmental
information available to
citizens through the use of
modern communications
technologies and expand the
opportunities of citizens to
participate in the elective and
governmental processes*

Center for Law and Social Policy
1616 P Street NW, #150
Washington, DC 20036
Website: http://www.cgs.org/
E-mail: info@clasp.org
Education, policy research, and advocacy organization seeking to improve the economic conditions of low-income families and secure access for the poor to our civil justice system

Center for Policy Alternatives
1875 Connecticut Ave. NW, #710
Washington, DC 20009
Website: http://www.cfpa.org/
Linda Tarr-Whelan, President and Chair
A nonprofit, nonpartisan public policy and leadership development center devoted to community-based solutions that strengthen families and communities

Center for Research on Women
Wellesley College
106 Central St.
Wellesley, MA 02181-8259
Website: http://www.wellesley.edu/WCW/crwsub.html
Pamela Baker-Webber
E-mail: pbaker@wellesley.edu
An interdisciplinary community of scholars are engaged in research, programs, and publications which examine the lives of women, men, and children in a changing world

Center for Responsive Politics
1101 14th St., NW, Suite 1030
Washington, DC 20005
Website: http://www.opensecrets.org/
E-mail: info@crp.org
Paul Hoff, Chairman
A nonprofit, nonpartisan organization that specializes in the study of Congress and particularly the role that money plays in its elections and actions

Center for Science in the Public Interest
1875 Connecticut Ave. NW, #300
Washington, DC 20009
Website: http://www.cspinet.org/
E-mail: cspi@cspinet.org/
Michael F. Jacobson, Executive Director
A nonprofit education and advocacy organization that focuses on improving the safety and nutritional quality of our food supply

Center for Strategic and Budgetary Assessments
1730 Rhode Island Ave., NW, Suite 912
Washington, DC 20036
Website: http://www.csbaonline.org/
E-mail: info@csbaonline.org
James G. Roche, Chair
An independent research institute established to promote innovative thinking about defense planning and investment for the 21st century

Center for the New West
600 World Trade Center
1625 Broadway, #600
Denver, CO 80202
Website: http://
    www.newwest.org/
Kara Steele, Executive Director
E-mail: ksteele@newwest.org
Policy research institute focusing
    on trade, technology,
    education, and the enterprise
    economy

Center for the Study of
    Popular Culture
PO Box 67398
Los Angeles, CA 90067
Website: http://www.cspc.org/
E-mail: info@cspc.org
Peter Collier and David
    Horowitz, founders
Nationally known writers, editors,
    and political commentators
    whose intellectual development
    has evolved from early,
    influential support for the
    New Left and Black Panther
    movements to the forefront of
    neoconservatism

Center for Voting and
    Democracy
6930 Carroll Ave., Suite 901
Takoma Park, MD 20912
Website: http://www.igc.apc.
    org/cvd/
E-mail:
    FairVote@compuserve.com
Robert Richie, Executive
    Director
John B. Anderson, President
Nonprofit organization based in
    Washington D.C., educates
    the public about the impact of
    different voting systems on
    voter turnout, representation,
    accountability, and the
    influence of money in elections

Center for Women's Policy
    Studies
1211 Connecticut. Ave, NW,
    Suite 312
Washington, D.C. 20036
Website: http://www.center
    women policy.org/
E-mail: tchin@
centerwomenpolicy.org
Kathleen Stoll, Policy Analyst
A national nonprofit, multiethnic
    and multicultural feminist
    policy research and advocacy
    institution; addresses cutting-
    edge issues that have
    significant future implications
    for women

Center on Budget and Policy
    Priorities
820 First St. NE, Suite 510
Washington, DC 20002
Website: http://www.cbpp.org/
E-mail: bazie@cbpp.org
Robert Greenstein Founder
    and Executive Director
Conducts research and analysis on
    a range of government policies
    and programs with an
    emphasis on those affecting
    low- and moderate-income
    people

Center on Children and
    Families (CC+F)
295 Lafayette St., Suite 920
New York, NY 10012
Website: http://
    www.kidsuccess.com/
Beverly Brooks, Executive
    Director
Founded in 1919 with a mission
    to protect children from abuse
    and neglect, CC+F has
    evolved to encompass a broad
    array of programs designed to
    promote "kid success;" a
    dedicated staff of 200, CC+F
    serves over 16,000 children
    and families each year

Centex
2728 North Harwood
Dallas, TX 75201
Website: http://
   www.centex.com
Laurence E. Hirsch, Chairman
   and CEO
Engineering, construction

Cetera, Peter
8900 Wilshire Blvd., #300
Beverly Hills, CA 90211
Singer, musician
Birthday: 9/13/44

Chan, Jackie
303-305 Austin Tower, #400
Tsimsatsui
Austin Kowloon
China
Actor
Birthday: 4/7/54

Chance, Jeff
PO Box 2977
Hendersonville, TN 37077
Country music singer

Chaplin, Ben
2-4 Noel St.
GB-London
W1V 3RB
England
Actor

Chaplin, Charlie Fan Club
300 S. Topanga Canyon
Topanga, CA 90290

Chapman, Cee Cee
PO Box 1422
Franklin, TN 37065
Country music singer

Chapman, Mark David
#81 A 3860
Box 149
Attica Correctional Facility
Attica, NY 14011
John Lennon's assassin

Chapman, Tracy
120 W. 44th. St., #704
New York, NY 10036
Singer
Birthday: 3/20/64

Charisse, Cyd
10724 Wilshire Blvd., #1406
Los Angeles, CA 90024
Actress
Birthday: 3/3/23

**Charles, Ray (Ray Charles
   Robinson)**
2107 W. Washington Blvd.,
   #200
Los Angeles, CA 90018
Singer, songwriter
Birthday: 3/23/30

Charleson, Leslie
% *General Hospital*
ABC-TV
4151 Prospect Ave.
Los Angeles, CA 90027
Soap opera star

Charo
532 Portlock Rd.
Honolulu, HI 96825
or
% Reef Towers
227 Lewers St.
Honolulu, HI 96814
Actress, guitarist
Birthday: 1/15/51

Chase, Chevy (Cornelius Crane Chase)
955 S. Carillo Dr, #200
Los Angeles, CA 90048
Actor, comedian
Birthday: 10/8/43

Chase Manhattan Corp.
270 Park Ave.
New York, NY 10017
Website: http://www.chase.com
William B. Harrison, Jr.,
   Chairman, President, and
   CEO, Chase Manhattan
   and Chase Bank
Commercial bank

Chateau Marmont
8221 Sunset Blvd.
Los Angeles, CA 90046
John Belushi died here in 1982

HRH Charles, Prince of Wales (Charles Philip Arthur George Windsor)
Highgrove House
Doughton
Tetbury GL8 8TN
England
Heir to the Throne of Great Britain
Birthday: 11/14/48

Cheap Trick
3805 Country Rd.
Middleton, WI 53262
Music group

CheckOut.com
345 North Maple Dr.
Beverly Hills, CA 90210
Website: www.checkout.com
E-mail: pr@checkout.com
Richard Wolpert, Co-founder
   and CEO
E-commerce

Cheney, Dick
500 N. Akard St., #3600
Dallas, TX 75201
Business leader, former head of the Department of Defense

Cher (Cherilyn Sarkisian La Piere)
% William Morris Agency
151 El Camino Dr.
Beverly Hills, CA 90212
or
PO Box 2425
Milford, CT 06460
Actress, director, singer
Birthday 5/20/46.

Cherokee Nation
PO Box 948, Highway 62
Tahlequah, OK 74465
Website: http://
   www.cherokee.org/
E-mail: Public_Affairs@
   cherokee.org
Chad Smith, Principal Chief
E-mail: csmith@cherokee.org

Cherry Poppin Daddies
PO Box 10494
Eugene, OR 97440
Music group

Chesnutt, Mark
PO Box 120544
Nashville, TN 37212
Country music singer

Chevron
575 Market St.
San Francisco, CA 94105
Website: http://
    www.chevron.com
David J. O'Reilly, Chairman
    and CEO
Petroleum refining

Chiao, Leroy
% NASA
Johnson Space Center
Astronaut Office/Mail Code
    CB
2101 NASA Road 1
Houston, TX 77058
Astronaut

Chicago
8900 Wilshire Blvd., #300
Beverly Hills, CA 90211
Music group

Chiffons, The
1650 Broadway, #508
New York, NY 10019
Music group

Childs, Andy
PO Box 24563
Nashville, TN 37202
Country music singer

**Child Welfare League of
    America**
440 1st St. NW, #310
Washington, DC 20001
Website: http://www.cwla.org/
E-mail: webweaver@cwla.org
Richard H. Fleming, President
*Membership association of public
    and private nonprofit agencies
    that serve and advocate for
    abused, neglected, and
    otherwise vulnerable children*

Chong, Rae Daun
% Metropolitan Talent Agency
4526 Wilshire Blvd.
Los Angeles, CA 90010
Actress
Birthday: 2/28/61

Chordettes, The
150 E. Olive Ave., #109
Burbank, CA 91502
Music group

Chow, Amy
% West Valley Gymnastics
    School
1190 Del Ave. #1
Campbell, CA 95008
or
% US Gymnastics Fed.
201 S. Capitol Ave., Suite 300
Indianapolis, IN 46225
Gymnast

CHS Electronics
2000 NW 84th Ave.
Miami, FL 33122
Website: http://www.chse.com
Surinder Khurana, Chief
    Information Officer
Electronics wholesaler

Christensen, Helena
% Marilyn Gaulthiar Agence
62 boulevard Sebastopol
F-75003 Paris
France
Supermodel

Chubb
15 Mountain View Rd.
Warren, NJ 07061
Website: http://
    www.chubb.com
Dean R. O'Hare, CEO
Insurance P & C (stock)

Chuck Wagon Gang
PO Box 140571
Nashville, TN 37214
Musical group

Chumbawamba
43 Brook Green
London W6 7EF
England
Musical group

Chung, Connie
1 W. 72nd St.
New York, NY 10023
Newscaster
Birthday: 8/20/46

Cigna
1 Liberty Place
Philadelphia, PA 19192
Website: http://www.cigna.com
Wilson H. Taylor, CEO
Life and health insurance (stock)

Cinergy
139 E. Fourth St.
Cincinnati, OH 45202
Website: http://
    www.cinergy.com
Jackson H. Randolph,
    Chairman
James E. Rogers, VC,
    President, and CEO
Gas and electric utilities

Circuit City
9950 Maryland Dr.
Richmond, VA 23233
Website: http://
    www.circuitcity.com
Richard L. Sharp, President
    and CEO
*The #2 U.S. retailer of major
    appliances and consumer
    electronics*

Cisco Systems
170 W. Tasman Dr.
San Jose, CA 95134
Website: http://www.cisco.com
John P. Morgridge, Chairman
*Electronics, network
    communications*

Citicorp
153 E. 53rd St.
New York, NY 10043
Website: http://
    www.citibank.com
Sanford I. Weill, Chairman
    and CEO
Multinational bank

Citizen Action
1750 Rhode Island Ave. NW,
    #403
Washington, DC 20036
Website: http://www.fas.org/
    pub/gen/ggg/citizen.html
*A nationwide consumer and
    environmental organization*

Citizens Against Government Waste
1301 Connecticut Ave. NW, #400
Washington, DC 20036
Website: http://www.cagw.org/
E-mail: webmaster@cagw.org
Thomas A. Schatz, President
A private, nonpartisan, nonprofit organization dedicated to educating Americans about the waste, mismanagement, and inefficiency in the federal government

Citizens Committee for the Right to Keep and Bear Arms
600 Pennsylvania Ave. SE, #205
Washington, DC 20003
Website:http://www.ccrkba.org/
E-mail: info@ccrkba.org
Alan Gottlieb
Organization dedicated to preserving and protecting the Second Amendment

Citizens for a Sound Economy
1250 H St. NW, #700
Washington, DC 20005-3908
Website: http://www.cse.org/cse
Paul Beckner, President
Fights for lower taxes and less regulation

Citizens for Tax Justice
1311 L Street NW, #400
Washington, DC 20005
Website: http://www.ctj.org/
E-mail: mattg@ctj.org
Robert S. McIntyre, Director
A nonpartisan research and advocacy organization working for a fair, progressive tax system

Citizen Information Center
380 A Ave., PO Box 369
Lake Oswego, OR 97034
Website: http://www.ci.oswego.or.us/citizen/citizen.htm
E-mail: webmistress@ci.oswego.or.us
Organization which helps citizens of Lake Oswego, Oregon, solve city-related problems

Citizens' Commission on Civil Rights
2000 M St. NW, #400
Washington, DC 20036
Website: http://www.cccr.org/
E-mail: citizens@cccr.org
Corrine M. Yu, Director and Counsel
Established to monitor civil rights policies and practices of the federal government and seek ways to accelerate progress in the area of civil rights

Claiborne, Liz
650 Fifth Ave.
New York, NY 10019
Fashion designer

Clancy, Tom
PO Box 800
Huntington, MD 20639
Author

Clapton, Eric
46 Kensington Ct.
London W8 5DP
England
Musician
Birthday: 3/30/45

Clark, Dick
3003 W. Olive Ave.
Burbank, CA 91505
TV host, producer
Birthday: 11/30/29

Clark, Joe
707 7th Ave. SW #1300
Calgary, Alb
T2P 3H6
Canada
Former Prime Minister of Canada
Birthday: 1939

Clark, Marcia
151 El Camino Dr.
Beverly Hills, CA 90212
*Prosecutor in the O. J. Simpson
    criminal trial*

Clark, Roy
1800 Forest Blvd.
Tulsa, OK 74114
Musician
Birthday: 8/16/33

Clark, Susan
Georgian Bay Productions
3815 W. Olive Ave., #202
Burbank, CA 91505
Actress
Birthday: 3/08/44

Clarke, Arthur C.
4715 Gregory Rd.
Colombo
Sri Lanka
Science-fiction author
Birthday: 12/16/17

Clash, The
268 Camden Rd.
London NW1
England
Music group

Clay, Andrew Dice
836 N. La Cienega Blvd., #202
Los Angeles, CA 90069
Comedian, actor

Clayburgh, Jill
P.O. Box 18
Lakeville, CT 06039
Actress
Birthday: 4/30/44

Claydermann, Richard
% Delphine Records
150 bd. Haussmann
75008 Paris
France
Musician
Birthday: 12/28/53

Clean Air Trust
1625 K Street NW, #725
Washington, DC 20006
The Hon. Robert T. Stafford,
    Honorary Co-Chairman
Website: http://
    www.cleanairtrust.org/
E-mail: frank@cleanairtrust.org
Environmental organization

Clean Water Action
4455 Connecticut Ave. NW,
    Suite A300
Washington, DC 20008
Website: http://
    www.cleanwateraction.org/
E-mail: cwa@cleanwater.org
David Zwick, President
*Organizes strong grassroots groups,
    coalitions, and campaigns to
    protect our environment,
    health, economic well-being,
    and community quality of life*

Cleese, John
82 Ladbroke Rd.
London W11 3NU
England
Comedian, actor
Birthday: 10/27/39

Clemens, Roger
% Toronto Blue Jays
The Skydome, 1 Blue Jays Way
Toronto
Ontario M5V 1J1
Canada
Baseball player
Birthday: 8/4/62

Cline, Patsy, Fan Club
Box 244
Dorchester, MA 02125

Always Patsy Cline
PO Box 2236
Winchester, VA 22604
Patsy Cline fan club

Clinton, Chelsea
Stanford University
Wilbur Hall
Palo Alto, CA 94305
Bill and Hillary's daughter

Cloke, Kirsten
% The Gersh Agency
PO Box 5617
Beverly Hills, CA 90210
Actress

Clooney, George
4000 Warner Blvd. #B81-117
Burbank, CA 91522
Actor, nephew of Rosemary Clooney
Birthday: 5/6/61

Close, Glenn
9830 Wilshire Blvd.
Beverly Hills, CA 90212
Actress
Birthday: 3/19/47

CMS Energy
Fairlane Plaza South, Suite
    1100
330 Town Center Dr.
Dearborn, MI 48126
Website: http://
    www.cmsenergy.com
William T. McCormick, Jr.,
    CEO
Gas and electric utilities

CNF Inc.
3240 Hillview Ave.
Palo Alto, CA 94304
Website: http://www.cnf.com
Donald E. Moffitt, CEO
Trucking

**Coalition on Human Needs
    (CHN)**
1700 K St., NW, Suite 1150
Washington, DC 20006
Website: http://www.chn.org/
Stuart P. Campbell, Executive
    Director
*An alliance of over 100 national
    organizations working together
    to promote public policies
    which address the needs of low-
    income and other vulnerable
    populations*

Costal
9 Greenway Plaza
Houston, TX 77046
Website: http://
    www.coastalcorp.com
David A. Arledge Chairman,
    President, and CEO
Petroleum refining

Coasters, The
2756 N. Green Valley Pkwy.,
    #449
Las Vegas, NV 89014
Music group

Coca, Imogene
PO Box 5151
Westport, CT 06881
Actress
Birthday: 11/18/1908

Coca-Cola
1 Coca-Cola Plaza
Atlanta, GA 30313
Website: http://
    www.cocacola.com
Douglas N. Daft, Chairman
    and CEO
Beverages

Coca-Cola Enterprises
2500 Windy Ridge Pkwy.
Atlanta, GA 30339
Website: http://
    www.cokecce.com
Summerfield K. Johnston, Jr.,
    Chairman and CEO
Beverages

Cochran, Johnnie L.
2373 Hobart Blvd.
Los Angeles, CA 90027
Lawyer in O. J. Simpson trial

Cocker, Joe
16830 Ventura Blvd., #501
Encino, CA 91436
Singer
Birthday: 5/20/42

Coe, David Allan
PO Box 270188
Nashville, TN 37227-0188
Country music singer

Coen, Joel
% United Talent Agency
9560 Wilshire Blvd., Suite 516
Beverly Hills, CA 90212
Film director, writer
Birthday: 11/29/54

Cohen, William
The Pentagon
Rm. 2E777 #1400
Washington, DC 20201
Secretary of Defense

Cohn, Mindy
9300 Wilshire Blvd., #400
Beverly Hills, CA 90212
Actress
Birthday: 5/20/66

Cole, Natalie
955 S. Carillo Dr., #200
Los Angeles, CA 90048
Singer
Birthday: 2/08/50

Colgate-Palmolive
300 Park Ave.
New York, NY 10022
Website: http://
    www.colgate.com
Reuben Mark, CEO
Soaps, cosmetics

Collie, Mark
3322 West End Ave., #520
Nashville, TN 37203
Country music singer

Collins, Eileen
2101 NASA Rd.
Houston, TX 77058
*Astronaut. First female space
    shuttle pilot and the first
    woman in the U.S. to
    command a space shuttle
    mission*

Collins, Jackie
PO Box 5473
Glendale, CA 91221
Author
Birthday: 10/4/41

Collins, Phil
30 Ives St.
London SW3 2nd
England
Musician
Birthday: 1/30/?

Columbia Energy Group
13880 Dulles Corner Ln.
Herndon, VA 20171
Website: http://
    www.columbiaenergy.com
Oliver G. Richard III,
    Chairman, President, and
    CEO
Gas and electric utilities

Columbia/HCA Healthcare
1 Park Plaza
Nashville, TN 37203
Website: http://
    www.columbia.net
Thomas F. Frist, Jr., Chairman
    and CEO
Health care

Colvin, Shawn
30 West 21st St., 7th Floor
New York, NY 10010
Website: http://
    www.shawncolvin.com/
    flashsplash.html
Musician
Birthday: 1/10/58

Combs, Sean "Puff Daddy"
8436 W. 3rd St., #650
Los Angeles, CA 90048
Musician
Birthday: 11/9/69

Comcast
1500 Market St.
Philadelphia, PA 19102
Website: http://
    www.comcast.com
Ralph J. Roberts, Chairman
Telecommunications

Comdisco
6111 N. River Rd.
Rosemont, IL 60018
Website: http://
    www.comdisco.com
Nicholas K. Pontikes, President
    and CEO
Computer and data services

Comerica
Comerica Tower at Detroit
    Center 500
Woodward Ave., MC 3391
Detroit, MI 48226
Website: http://
    www.comerica.com
Eugene A. Miller, Chairman,
    President, and CEO
Commercial banks

Commission on Presidential Debates

1200 New Hampshire, NW
Box 445
Washington, DC 20036
Website: http://
www.debates.org/
Frank J. Fahrenkopf, Jr., and
Paul G. Kirk, Jr., Co-
Chairmen
Established in 1987 to ensure that debates, as a permanent part of every general election, provide the best possible information to viewers and listeners; its primary purpose is to sponsor and produce debates for the United States presidential and vice presidential candidates and to undertake research and educational activities relating to the debates

Committee for a Responsible Federal Budget

220 1/2 E St. NE
Washington, DC 20002
Website: http://www.network-
democracy.org/social-
security/bb/whc/crfb.html
E-mail: crfb@aol.com
Bill Frenzel and Timothy
Penny, Co-Chairmen
A bipartisan, nonprofit educational organization committed to educating the public regarding the budget process and particular issues that have significant fiscal policy impact

Committee for Children

2203 Airport Way S., #500
Seattle, WA 98134
Website: http://
www.cfchildren.org/
E-mail:
webmatron@cfchildren.org
A nonprofit organization dedicated to the prevention of child abuse and youth violence through the development of educational curricula and original research

Committee for Study of the American Electorate

421 New Jersey Ave. SE
Washington, DC 20003
Website: http://tap.epn.org/
csae/
Maurice Rosenblatt, President
A Washington-based, nonpartisan, nonprofit tax exempt research institution with a primary focus on issues surrounding citizen engagement in politics

Committee to Advocate Texas Sovereignty (CATS)

5303 Allum Rd.
Houston, TX 77045
Website: http://
www.texassovereignty.org/
intro.html
Jim Davidson
E-mail: JDavidson@cbjd.net
Organization that believes that Texas should be sovereign and independent of the United States

Commodores, The

1920 Benson Ave.
St. Paul, MN 55116
Music group

Common Cause
1250 Connecticut Ave., NW
Washington, DC 20036
Website: http://
    www.commoncause.org/
John Gardner, Founder
A nonprofit, nonpartisan citizen's
    lobbying organization
    promoting open, honest, and
    accountable government

Community Nutrition Institute
910 17th St. NW, #413
Washington, DC 20006
Website: http://
    www.unidial.com/~cni/
Rodney E. Leonard, Executive
    Director and Founder
E-mail: relcni@ecenet.com
A leading advocate for consumer
    protection food program
    development and management
    and sound federal diet and
    health policies

Compaq Computer
20555 State Hwy. 249
Houston, TX 77070
Website: http://
    www.compaq.com
Michael D. Capellas, President
    and CEO
Computers and office equipment

Compassion in Dying
PMB 415, 6312 SW Capitol
    Hwy.
Portland, OR 97201
Website: http://
    www.Compassion
    InDying.org
E-mail: info@compassion
    indying.org
Barbara Coombs Lee, PA, FNP,
    JD, Executive Director
An organization which believes in
    the right to die with dignity

**Competitive Enterprise
    Institute**
1001 Connecticut Ave. NW,
    #1250
Washington, DC 20036
Website: http://www.cei.org/
E-mail: info@cei.org
Emily Duke, Director of
    Development
E-mail: eduke@cei.org
A pro-market, public policy group
    committed to advancing the
    principles of free enterprise
    and limited government

Council on Competiveness
1500 K St. NW, Suite 850
Washington, DC 20005
Website: http://
    www.compete.org/
John Yochelson, President
Shapes the national debate on
    competitiveness by
    concentrating on a few critical
    issues, including technological
    innovation, workforce
    development, and the
    benchmarking of U.S.
    economic performance against
    other countries

CompUSA
14951 N. Dallas Pkwy.
Dallas, TX 75240
Website: http://
    www.compusa.com
Carlos Slim Domit, Chairman
Harold F. Compton, CEO
Computer retailers

**Computer Associates
    International**
1 Computer Associates Plaza
Islandia, NY 11788
Website: http://www.cai.com
Charles B. Wang, Chairman
    and CEO
Computer software

**Computer Professionals for
 Social Responsibility**
PO Box 717
Palo Alto, CA 94302
Website: http://www.cpsr.org/
E-mail: cpsr@cpsr.org or
 webmaster@cpsr.org
*A public-interest alliance of
 computer scientists and others
 concerned about the impact of
 computer technology on society*

Computer Sciences
2100 E. Grand Ave.
El Segundo, CA 90245
Website: http://www.csc.com
Van B. Honeycutt, Chairman,
 President, and CEO
Computer and data services

ConAgra
1 ConAgra Dr.
Omaha, NE 68102
Website: http://
 www.conagra.com
Bruce Rohde, Chairman,
 President, and CEO
Food producer

**Concerned Women for
 America**
1015 Fifteenth St., NW, Suite
 1100
Washington, DC 20005
Website: http://www.cwfa.org/
Beverly LaHaye, Chairman and
 Founder
*A national politically active
 women's organization
 promoting Christian values
 and morality in family life
 and public policy*

Concord Coalition
1819 H Street, NW, Suite 800
Washington, DC 20006
Website:http://
 www.concordcoalition.org
E-mail: concord@
 concordcoalition.org
*A nonprofit, charitable
 organization. Nearly 200,000
 citizens nationwide have
 joined Concord's movement for
 a strong economic future for
 all generations. They are
 changing the political calculus
 by standing up for the general
 interest—for an end to federal
 budget deficits, for equitable
 Social Security and Medicare
 reform, for stronger long-term
 economic growth, and for a
 higher standard of living for
 future generations of
 Americans*

Confederate Railroad
118 16th. Ave. S., #201
Nashville, TN 37203
Country music group

Conlee, John
38 Music Sq. E., #117
Nashville, TN 37203
Country music singer

Conley, Earl Thomas
657 Baker Rd.
Smyrna, TN 37167
Country music singer

Congressional Accountability Project
Connecticut Ave. NW, Suite #3A
Washington, DC 20009
Website: http://www.essential.org/orgs/CAP/CAP.html
E-mail: cap@essential.org
Gary Ruskin, Director
Congressional watchdog organization

Congressional Budget Office
U.S. Congress
2nd and D Streets SW
Washington, DC 20515
Website: http://www.cbo.gov/
Danniel L. Crippen, Director
Created by the Congressional Budget and Impoundment Control Act of 1974, CBO's mission is to provide the Congress with objective, timely, nonpartisan analyses needed for economic and budget decisions and with the information and estimates required for the Congressional budget process

Congressional Quarterly, Inc.
1414 22nd St. NW
Washington, DC 20037
Website: http://www.cq.com/
E-mail: webmaster@cq.com
Andrew Barnes, Chairman
A world-class provider of information on government, politics, and public policy

Conn, Didi
1901 Ave. of the Stars, #1450
Los Angeles, CA 90067
Actress
Birthday: 7/13/57

Connery, Jason
% Joy Jameson Ltd.
The Plaza
535 Kings Rd. #19
London SW10 OSZ
England
Actor, son of Sean Connery
Birthday: 1/11/63

Connery, Sean
% Creative Artists Agency
9830 Wilshire Blvd.
Beverly Hills, CA 90212
Actor
Birthday: 8/25/30

Conrad (Hefner), Kimberly
% Playmate Promotions
9492 Beverly Blvd.
Beverly Hills, CA 90210
Hugh Hefner's former wife

Conrad, Robert
PO Box 5067
Bear Valley, CA 95223
Actor
Birthday: 3/1/35

Conseco
11825 N. Pennsylvania St.
Carmel, IN 46032
Website: http://www.conseco.com
Gary C. Wendt, Chairman and CEO
Life and health insurance (stock)

Conservative Caucus
450 Maple Ave. East
Vienna, VA 22180
Website: http://
    www.conservativeusa.org
E-mail: webmaster@
conservativeusa.org
Howard Phillips, Founder and
    Chairman
*Dedicated to educating citizens
    about how we must take
    action to restore America to its
    Constitutionaly limited
    government*

Consolidated Edison
4 Irving Place
New York, NY 10003
Website: http://www.coned.com
Eugene R. McGrath,
    Chairman, President, and
    CEO
Gas and electric utilities

Consolidated Stores
300 Phillipi Rd.
Columbus, OH 43228
Website: http://
    www.cnstores.com
William G. Kelley, CEO
*Specialist retailers, KB Stores, Big
    Lot/Odd/Lot Stores*

Constantine, Kevin
% Pittsburgh Penguins
Civic Arena, Gate 9
Pittsburgh, PA 15219
Website: http://www.pittsburgh
    penguins.com/
E-mail: coaches@mail.
pittsburgpenguins.com
*Head coach of the Pittsburgh
    Penguins*

Constantine, Michael
1800 Ave. of the Stars, #400
Los Angeles, CA 90067
Actor
Birthday: 5/22/27

Constitution Society, The
1731 Howe Ave., #370
Sacramento, CA 95825
or
6900 San Pedro #147-230
San Antonio, TX 78216
Website: http://
    www.constitution.org/
*A private nonprofit organization
    dedicated to research and
    public education on the
    principles of constitutional
    republican government. It
    publishes documentation,
    engages in litigation, and
    organizes local citizens groups
    to work for reform. This
    organization was founded in
    response to the growing
    concern that noncompliance
    with the U.S. Constitution
    and most state constitutions is
    creating a crisis of legitimacy
    that threatens freedom and
    civil rights.*

**Consumer Energy Council of
    America Research
    Foundation**
2000 L St. NW, #802
Washington, DC 20036
Website: www.cecarf.org
*CECA is committed to constructive
    involvement of government
    and private organizations in
    broad educational initiatives
    and in the creation of self-
    sustaining and socially
    responsible markets for
    essential services*

Consumer Federation of America
1424 16th Street NW, #604
Washington, DC 20036
Website: http://
    www.stateandlocal.org/
Founded in 1972 as a private,
    nonprofit, 501(c)(3) research
    and education organization to
    complement the work of
    Consumer Federation of
    America. The Foundation has
    a threefold mission: to assist
    state and local organizations,
    to provide information to the
    public on consumer issues,
    and to conduct consumer
    research projects.

Consumers Union
101 Truman Ave.
Yonkers, NY 10703
Website: http://
    www.consumersunion.org/
Naomi Meyer, Fellow for
    Economic Justice
Its mission has been to test
    products, inform the public,
    and protect consumers

Continental Airlines
1600 Smith St., Dept. HQSEO
Houston, TX 77002
Website: http://
    www.continental.com
Gordon M. Bethune,
    Chairman and CEO
Airline

Conway, Tim
PO Box 17047
Encino, CA 91416
Actor
Birthday: 11/14/33

Coolio
6733 Sepulveda Blvd., #270
Los Angeles, CA 90045
Rap artist
Birthday: 8/1/63

Cooper Industries
600 Travis St., Suite 5800
Houston, TX 77002
Website: http://
    www.cooperindustries.com
H. John Riley, Jr., Chairman,
    President, and CEO
Electronics and electrical
    equipment

Copperfield, David (David Kotkin)
1122 S. Robertson Blvd., #15
Los Angeles, CA 90035
or
515 Post Oak Blvd., #300
Houston, TX 77027
Website: http://
    www.dcopperfield.com
Magician
Birthday: 9/15/56

CoreStates Financial Corp.
One First Union Center,
301 South College St., Suite
    4000
Charlotte, NC 28288
Website: http://
    www.corestates.com
G. Alex Bernhardt, Sr.,
    Chairman and CEO
Commercial bank

Corgan, Billy
9830 Wilshire Blvd.
Beverly Hills, CA 90212
Musician, lead singer of Smashing
    Pumpkins
Birthday: 3/17/67

The Official Danielle Cormack Fan Club
Ephiny of the Amazons
PO Box 459
Hermosa Beach, CA 90254
Website: http://
    members.aol.com/
    dancorfans/index.html
E-mail: DanCorFans@aol.com

Corman, Roger
11611 San Vicente Blvd.
Los Angeles, CA 90049
Film producer

Cornelius, Helen
PO Box 121089
Nashville, TN 37212
Country music singer

Corning
1 Riverfront Plaza
Corning, NY 14831
Website: http://
    www.corning.com
Roger G. Ackerman, Chairman
    and CEO
Building materials, glass

Corporate Express
1 Environmental Way
Broomfield, CO 80021
Website: http://www.corporate-
    express.com
Robert L. King, President and
    CEO; President and CEO,
    North American
    Operations
Specialist retailers, office products

Cort, Bud
955 S. Carillo Dr., #300
Los Angeles, CA 90048
Actor

Cosby, Bill
Box 88
Greenfield, MA 01301
Comedian, actor
Birthday: 7/11/37

Cossette, Pierre
8899 Bevelry Blvd., #100
Los Angeles, CA 90036
Producer

Costco
999 Lake Dr.
Issaquah, WA 98027
Website: http://www.costco.com
Jeffrey H. Brotman, Chairman
James D. Sinegal, President
    and CEO
Specialist retailers, warehouse store

Costello, Elvis (Declan Patrick McManus)
9028 Gr. Guest Rd.
Middlesex TW8 9EW
England
Musician
Birthday: 8/25/54

Costner, Kevin
PO Box 275
Montrose, CA 91021
Actor, director, producer
Birthday: 1/18/55

David Coulthard
% McLaren Int'l Ltd.
Woking Business Park
Albert Dr.
Woking
GB-Surrey GU21 5JS
Professional Formula-1 driver

Council on Competiveness
1500 K St., NW, Suite 850
Washington, DC 20005
Website: http://
    www.compete.org/
John Yochelson, President
Shapes the national debate on
    competitiveness by
    concentrating on a few critical
    issues, including technological
    innovation, workforce
    development, and the
    benchmarking of U.S.
    economic performance against
    other countries

Council of State Governments
2760 Research Park Dr.
PO Box 11910
Lexington, KY 40578
Website: http://www.csg.org
E-mail: info@csg.org
Governor Paul Patton,
    President
Founded on the premise that the
    states are the best sources of
    insight and innovation, CSG
    provides a network for
    identifying and sharing ideas
    with state leaders

Council on Foreign Relations
The Harold Pratt House
58 East 68th St.
New York, NY 10021
Website: http://www.cfr.org
E-mail: ppappachan@cfr.org
Peter G. Peterson Chairman of
    the Board
Founded in 1921 by businessmen,
    bankers, and lawyers
    determined to keep the United
    States engaged in the world,
    today the Council is composed
    of men and women from all
    walks of international life and
    from all parts of America,
    dedicated to the belief that the
    nation's peace and prosperity
    are firmly linked to that of the
    rest of the world

Counting Crows
947 N. La Cienega Blvd., #G
Los Angeles, CA 90069
Music group

Couric, Katie
NBC
30 Rockefeller Plaza
New York, NY 10122
Broadcast journalist
Birthday: 1/7/57

Courier, Jim
% IMG
1 Erieview Plaza, #1300
Cleveland, OH 44114
Professional tennis player
Birthday: 8/17/70

Cowsills, The
22647 Ventura Blvd., #416
Woodland Hills, CA 91364
Music group

Cox-Arquette, Courtney
1122 S. Robertson Blvd., #15
Los Angeles, CA 90035
Actress
Birthday: 6/15/64

Cox, DeAnna
818 18th Ave. S.
Nashville, TN 37203
Country music singer

Cox Family, The
PO Box 787
Cotton Valley, LA 71018
Country music group

CP&L Energy Inc
411 Fayetteville St.
Raleigh, NC 27602
Website: http://www.cplc.com
William Cavanaugh III,
    Chairman, President, and
    CEO
Gas and electric utilities

Craddock, Billy "Crash"
21 Laconwood Dr.
Springfield, IL 62707
Country music singer

Craig, Jenny
PO Box 387190
La Jolla, CA 92038
Diet company founder

Cranberries, The
9255 Sunset Blvd., #200
Los Angeles, CA 90069
Music group

Crash Test Dummies
1505 W. 2nd St., #200
Vancouver, BC
V6H 3Y4
Canada
Music group

Craven, Wes
8491 Sunset Blvd., #375
West Hollywood, CA 90069
Film director
Birthday: 8/2/39

Crawford, Cindy
1122 S. Robertson Blvd., #15
Los Angeles, CA 90035
Model, actress
Birthday: 2/20/66

Crawford, Michael
10 Argyle St.
London
W1V 1AB
England
Singer
Birthday: 1/19/52

Cray, Robert
Box 170429
San Francisco, CA 94117
Musician

Creedence Clearwater Revival
40 W. 57th St.
New York, NY 10019
Music group

Creme, Benjamin
59 Darmouth Park Rd.
London
NW5 1SL
England
New Age speaker, author

Creole, Kid
42 Molyneaux St.
London
W1
England
Musician

Crenna, Richard
% Creative Artists Agency
9830 Wilshire Blvd.
Beverly Hills, CA 90212
Actor
Birthday: 11/30/27

Cronenberg, David
217 Avenue Rd.
Toronto, Ont
M5R 2J3
Canada
Film director
Birthday: 3/15/43

Cronkite, Walter
51 W. 52nd. St. #1934
New York, NY 10019
News broadcaster
Birthday: 11/4/16

Crook, Lorianne
% Jim Owens Assoc.
1515 McGavock
Nashville, TN 37203
TV host

Crosby, Bing, Fan Club
% W. Martin
435 S. Holmes Ave.
Kirkwood, MO 63122

**Crosby, Bing, Historical
  Society**
P.O. Box 216
Tacoma, WA 98403

Crosby, David
PO Box 9008
Solvang, CA 93464
Musician
Birthday: 8/14/41

Crosby, Norm
% Jono Productions, Inc.
5750 Wilshire Blvd., #580
Los Angeles, CA 90036
Comedian
Birthday: 9/15/27

Crosby, Rob
PO Box 121551
Nashville, TN 37212
Country musician

Cross, Christopher
PO Box 5156
Santa Barbara, CA 93150
Website: http://
    www.christophercross.com/
Singer
Birthday: 5/12/48

Crosby, Stills & Nash
9830 Wilshire Blvd.
Beverly Hills, CA 9022
Music group

Crow, Sheryl
10345 W. Olympic Blvd., #200
Los Angeles, CA 90064
Singer, songwriter

Crowe, Cameron
9830 Wilshire Blvd.
Beverly Hills, CA 90212
Director
Birthday: 7/13/?

Crowell, Rodney
1514 South St., #100
Nashville, TN 37212
Musician
Birthday: 8/17/50

Crown, Cork and Seal
1 Crown Way
Philadelphia, PA 19106
Website: http://
     www.crowncork.com
William J. Avery, Chairman
     and CEO
Metal products

Cruise, Tom
955 S. Carillo Dr., #200
Los Angeles, CA 90048
Actor
Birthday: 7/3/62

Cryner, Bobbie
PO Box 2147
Hendersonville, TN 37077
Country music singer

Crystal, Billy
9830 Wilshire Blvd., #500
Beverly Hills, CA 90212
Actor comedian, director, producer
Birthday: 3/14/47

Csupo, Gabor
6353 Sunset Blvd.
Hollywood, CA 90028
Website: http://
     www.klaskycsupo.com
E-mail: recruitment@
klaskycsupo.com
Creator of Rugrats

CSX
James Center
901 E. Cary St.
Richmond, VA 23219
Website: http://www.csx.com
John W. Snow, CEO
Railroads

**Culinary Institute of America
     at Greystone**
2555 Main St.
St. Helena, CA 94574
E-mail: www.ciachef.edu
Roger Riccardi, Managing
     Director
*Offers continuing education and
     career development classes for
     food and wine professionals in
     highly focused formats.
     Courses vary in length from
     three days to a 30-week
     Baking and Pastry Arts
     Certification Program, with
     the average class lasting one
     week and an average student
     stay of three weeks.*

Culinary Arts Institute of Louisiana
427 Lafayette St.
Baton Rouge, LA 70802
Website: http://www.caila.com/
Vi Harrington, Founder and owner
An associate degree–granting institute located in the deep South in an old hotel overlooking the beautiful Mississippi River. Several riverboat casinos are located very nearby. It is unique in that 50 percent of the culinary student's time is spent cooking and running a white linen, full service restaurant. Because of this, a two-year program can be completed in 15 months. The institute participates in exchange programs with Le Cordon Bleu, in Paris, France, and the University of Hawaii.

Culkin, Macaulay
9560 Wilshire. Blvd., #516
Beverly Hills, CA 90212
Actor
Birthday: 8/26/80

Culture Club
63 Grosvenor St.
London W1X 9DA
England
Music group

Cumberland Gap, The
159 Madison Ave., #2G
New York, NY 10016
Music group

Cummins Engine
500 Jackson St.
Columbus, IN 47202
Website: http://www.cummins.com
Theodore M. Solso, Chairman and CEO
Industrial and farm equipment

Cuomo, Mario
50 Sutton Pl S. #11-G
New York, NY 10022
Former governor of New York
Birthday: 6/15/?

Cure, The
% Levine & Schneider PR
8730 Sunset Blvd., #600
Los Angeles, CA 90069
Music group

Curtin, Jane
PO Box 1070
Sharon, CT 06069
Actress
Birthday: 9/06/47

Curtis, Jamie Lee
% Creative Artists Agency
9830 Wilshire Blvd.
Beverly Hills, CA 90212
Actress, author
Birthday: 11/22/58

Cusack, John
% William Morris Agency
151 S. El Camino Dr.
Beverly Hills, CA 90212
Actor, producer, stage director
Birthday: 6/28/66

CVS
One CVS Dr.
Woonsocket, RI 02895
Website: http://www.cvs.com
Thomas M. Ryan Chairman,
      President, and CEO
Food and drug stores

Cypress Hill
151 El Camino Dr.
Beverly Hills, CA 90212
Music group

Cyrus, Billy Ray
PO Box 1206
Franklin, TN 37115
Country music singer
Birthday: 8/25/61

D

A letter is a conversation you can hold.

—NANCY BUNNING

D'Abo, Maryam
9255 Sunset Blvd. #515
Los Angeles, CA 90069
Actress

D'Abo, Olivia
1122 S. Robertson Blvd #15
Los Angeles, CA 90035
Actress
Birthday: 1/22/67

Dahl, Arlene
% Dahlmark Prod.
PO Box 116
Sparkill, NY 10976
Actress
Birthday: 8/11/28

Daimler Chrysler
Epplestrasse 225
70546 Stuttgart
Germany
Website: http://
    www.daimlerchrysler.com
Hilmar Kopper, Board
    Chairman, Supervisory
Motor vehicles

Dallas Cowboy Cheerleaders
1 Cowboys Parkway
Irving, TX 75063

Dalton, Abby
PO Box 100
Mammoth Lakes, CA 03546
Actress
Birthday: 8/11/27

Dalton, Lacy J.
820 Cartwright Rd.
Reno, NV 89511
Country music singer

Daltry, Roger
18/21 Jermyn St., #300
London SW1Y 6hP
England
Musician
Birthday: 3/1/45

Daly, Carson
% MTV
1515 Broadway
New York, NY 10036
MTV VJ

Dana
4500 Dorr St., PO Box 1000
Toledo, OH 43697
Website: http://www.dana.com
Joseph M. Magliochetti,
    Chairman, President, and
    CEO
Motor vehicles and parts

Dana, Bill
PO Box 1792
Santa Monica, CA 90406
Comedian, actor

Dangerfield, Rodney
10580 Wilshire Blvd., #21-NE
Los Angles, CA 90024
Website: http://
   www.rodney.com/
Comedian

Daniel, Davis
PO Box 120186
Nashville, TN 37212
Country music singer

Daniels, Charlie
17060 Central Pike
Lebanon, TN 37087
Country music singer

Danza, Tony
10202 W. Washington Blvd.
David Lean Bldg.
Culver City, CA 90232
Actor
Birthday: 4/21/51

Darden Restaurants
5900 Lake Ellenor Dr.
Orlando, FL 32809
Joe R. Lee, Chairman and
   CEO
Food services

Dark Shadows Fan Club
PO Box 69A04
West Hollywood, CA 90069

Darren, James
PO Box 1088
Beverly Hills, CA 90213
Actor
Birthday: 6/9/36

Dateline NBC
30 Rockefeller Plaza
New York, NY 10112
E-mail: dateline@news.nbc.com
TV series

Davis, Daniel
% TriStar (*The Nanny*)
9336 W. Washington Blvd.
Culver City, CA 90232
Actor

Davis, Josie
10635 Santa Monica, Blvd.,
   #130
Los Angeles, CA 90025
Actress

Davis, Linda
2100 West End Ave., #1000
Nashville, TN 37203
Musician

Davis, Skeeter
PO Box 1288
Brentwood, TN 37209
Country music singer

Davis, Stephanie
PO Box 121495
Nashville, TN 37212
Country music singer

Dawson, Marco
% PGA Tour
112 TPC Blvd.
Ponte Vedra Beach, FL 32082
Golfer

**Day, Doris (Doris von
   Kappelhoff)**
PO Box 223163
Carmel, CA 93922
Actress
Birthday: 4/1/24

Day, Lee
278 Aspen Ct., Bldg. 15
Stanhope, NJ 07874
*Pet hairstylist, pet entertainer,
    creator of the pet
    "barkmitzvah"*

Day-Lewis, Daniel
46 Albemarie St.
London W1X 4PP
England
Actor
Birthday: 4/20/58

De Niro, Robert
9830 Wilshire Blvd.
Beverly Hills, CA 90212
Actor
Birthday: 8/17/43

Dean, Billy
3310 West End Ave., #500
Nashville, TN 37203
Country music singer

Dean, Jimmy
8000 Centerview Pkwy., #400
Cordova, TN 38018
Country music singer

Dean Foods
600 N. River Rd.
Franklin Park, IL 60131
Website: http://
    www.deanfoods.com
Howard M. Dean, CEO
Food producer

DeAngelis, Barbara
15332 Antioch St., #504
Pacific Palisades, CA 90272
Actress

DeBakey, Dr. Michael
One Baylor Plaza, #A-902
Houston, TX 77030
Heart surgeon

**Death with Dignity Education
    Center**
1818 N Street, NW Suite 450
Washington, DC 20036
Website:http//
    www.deathwithdignity.org/
E-mail: admin@deathwith
    dignity.org
Estelle Rogers, Executive
    Director
*Promotes a comprehensive,
    humane, responsive system of
    care for terminally ill patients*

Dee, Sandra
% Mr. Larry Martindale
    Agency
18915 Nordhoff St., Suite 5
Northridge, CA 91324
Actress
Birthday: 4/23/42

Deep Purple
Box 254
Sheffield S61DF
England
Music group

Deere
1 John Deere Place
Moline, IL 61265
Website: http://www.deere.com
Hans W. Becherer, Chairman
Robert Lane, President and
    CEO
Industrial and farm equipment

Defenders of Wildlife
1101 14th Street NW, #1400
Washington, DC 20005
Website: http://
    www.defenders.org/
E-mail:
    webmaster@defenders.org
Alan R. Pilkington, Chairman
    of Board of Directors
*Dedicated to the protection of all
    native wild animals and
    plants in their natural
    communities*

Dees, Rick
3400 Riverside Dr., #800
Burbank, CA 91505
Radio personality

Def Leppard
72 Chancellor's Rd.
London W6 9 QB
England
Music group

DeGeneres, Ellen
9465 Wilshire Blvd., #444
Beverly Hills, CA 90211
Actress, comedian
Birthday: 1/26/98

DeKlerk, Frederik W.
120 Plain St.
Priv. Bag X-999
Capetown 8000
Republic of South Africa
*Former South African president
    and Nobel laureate*

Dell Computer
1 Dell Way
Round Rock, TX 78682
Website: http://www.dell.com
Michael S. Dell, CEO
Computers, office equipment

Del Ray, Martin
% Sherry Halton
1223 17th Ave. So.
Nashville, TN 37212
Country music singer

Delta Airlines
1030 Delta Blvd.
Atlanta, GA 30320
Website: http://www.delta-
    air.com
Leo F. Mullin, Chairman,
    President, and CEO
Airline

De Luise, Dom
% Page and Ma Business
    Management
11661 San Vicente Blvd., #910
Los Angeles, CA 90049
Actor

**Democratic Congressional
    Campaign Committee**
430 S. Capitol St. SE
Washington, DC 20003
Website: http://www.dccc.org/
Patrick Kennedy, Chairman
*Devoted to electing a Democratic
    majority in the House of
    Representatives*

Democratic Freedom Caucus
PO Box 9466
Baltimore, MD 21228
Website: http://
    www.progress.org/dfc/
E-mail: romike@crosslink.net
*A "progressive libertarian" group
    within the Democratic Party*

**Democratic National
    Committee**
430 S. Capitol St. SE
Washington, DC 20003
Website: http://
    www.democrats.org/
    index.html
Joe Andrew, National Chair
*The national party organization
    for the Democratic Party of the
    United States*

**Democratic Senatorial
    Campaign Committee**
430 S. Capitol St. SE
Washington, DC 20003
Website: http://www.dscc.org/
E-mail: info@dscc.org
Senator Robert Torricelli,
    Chairman
*A national party committee formed
    by the Democratic members of
    the U.S. Senate to raise funds
    for Democratic U.S. Senate
    candidates throughout the
    country*

DeMornay, Rebecca
1122 S. Robertson Blvd., #15
Los Angeles, CA 90035
Actress

Dench, Dame Judith
% Julien Belfrage and Assoc.
46 Albemarle Street
GB-
London W1X 4PP
England
Actress

Dennehy, Brian
121 N. San Vicente Blvd.
Beverly Hills, CA 90211
Actor

Denver, Bob
PO Box 269
Princeton, WV 24740
Actor

DePalma, Brian
9830 Wilshire Blvd.
Beverly Hills, CA 90212
Director

Depeche Mode
PO Box 1281
London N1 9UX
England
Music group

Depp, Johnny
% United Talent Agency
9560 Wilshire Blvd. Suite 500
Beverly Hills, CA 90212
or
2049 Century Park East, #2500
Los Angeles, CA 90067
*Actor, director, musician,
    screenwriter*
Birthday: 6/9/63

Dern, Bruce
PO Box 1581
Santa Monica, CA 90406
Actor

Dern, Laura
2401 S. Main St.
Santa Monica, CA 90405
Actress
Birthday: 2/10/67

Dershowitz, Alan
1563 Massachusetts Ave.
Cambridge, MA 02138
Attorney

Deukmejian, George
555 W. 5th St.
Los Angeles, CA 90013
Former governor of California

DeVito, Danny
PO Box 491246
Los Angeles, CA 90049
Actor

Devo
PO Box 6868
Burbank, CA 91410
Music group

DeWitt, Joyce
101 Ocean Ave., #L-4
Santa Monica, CA 90402
Actress
Birthday: 4/7/?

Dey, Susan
10390 Santa Monica Blvd.,
    #300
Los Angeles, CA 90025
Actress
Birthday: 12/10/52

Diamond Rio
33 Music Square W., #110
Nashville, TN 37203
Website: http://
    www.diamondrio.com
Country music group

**Diana, Princess of Wales
    Memorial Fund**
P.O. Box 1
London WC1B 5HW
England

Diaz, Cameron
955 S. Carrillo Dr., #300
Los Angeles, CA 90048
Actress, model
Birthday: 8/30/72

Dicaprio, Leonardo
955 S. Carrillo Dr., #300
Los Angeles, CA 90048
Website: http://
    www.dicaprio.com
E-mail: webmaster@
pde.paramount.com
Actor
Birthday: 11/11/74

**Dickens, Little Jimmy (James
    Cecil Dickens)**
Grand Ole Opry
PO Box 131
Nashville, TN 37214
Country musician

Diffie, Joe
50 Music Square W., #300
Nashville, TN 37203
Country music singer

Digital Entertainment Network
2230 Broadway
Santa Monica, CA 90404
David Neuman, President and
    Director
Website: www.de.net
E-mail: dneuman@den.net
Web content provider

Dillards
1600 Cantrell Rd.
Little Rock, AR 72201
Website: http://
    www.dillards.com
William Dillard, Chairman
William Dillard II, CEO
*General merchandisers, department
    stores*

Diller, Phyllis
11365 Ventura Blvd., #100
Studio City, CA. 91604
Comedian

Dillon, Dean
PO Box 935
Round Rock, TX 78680
Country music singer

Dillon, Matt
9465 Wilshire Blvd., #419
Beverly Hills, CA 90212
Actor
Birthday: 2/18/64

Diniz, Pedro
% Arrows/TWR Formula One
    Ltd.
Leafield Technical Centre
Leafield
Whitney
GB-Oxon OX8 5PF
Professional Formula-1 driver

Dinkins, David
625 Madison Ave.
New York, NY 10022
Former mayor of New York

Dion, Céline
4 Place Laval #500
Laval PQ H7N
Canada
or
9830 Wilshire Blvd.
Beverly Hills, CA 90212
Singer
Birthday: 3/30/68

Dior, Christian
St. Anna Platz 2
80538 Munich
Germany
Designer

Dire Straits
72 Chancellor's Rd.
London W6 9RS
England
Music group

Dirt Band
PO Box 1915
Aspen, CO 81611
Music group

Disney, Roy E.
% Shamrock Broadcasting Co.
4444 Lakeside Dr.
Burbank, CA 91505
or
500 S. Buena Vista St.
Burbank, CA 91521
Broadcasting executive

Dixiana
PO Box 3569
Greenville, SC 29608
Country music group

Dixie Chicks
68 Lindsley Ave.
Nashville, TN 37210
Country music group

Dixie Cups, The
7200 France Ave., #300
Edina, MN 55435
Music group

Dixieland Rhythym Kings, The
PO Box 12403
Atlanta, GA 30355
Music group

Doherty, Shannen
9560 Wilshire Blvd., #516
Beverly Hills, CA 90212
Actress
Birthday: 4/12/71

Dole Foods
1365 Oak Crest Dr.
Westlake Village, CA 91361
Website: http://www.dole.com
David H. Murdock, Chairman
    and CEO
Food producer

Dole, Bob
700 New Hampshire Ave. NW
Washington, DC 20037
or
810 First St, NE, #300
Washington, DC 20002
Former senator from Kansas,
    senate majority leader, and
    1996 presidential candidate

Dole, Elizabeth
700 New Hampshire Ave. NW
Washington, DC 20037
Former head of the American Red
    Cross, former Secretary of
    Transportation

Dolenz, Mickey
9200 Sunset Blvd., #1200
Los Angeles, CA 90069
Musician, Member of The Monkees
Birthday: 3/19/45

Domingo, Placido
157 W. 57th St., #502
New York, NY 10019
Tenor
Birthday: 1/21/41

Dominion Resources Black
    Warrior Trust
Bank of America Plaza
901 Main St., 17th Fl.
Dallas, TX 75202
Website: http://
    www.domres.com
Ron E. Hooper, VP and
    Administrator
Gas and electric, utilities

Domino's Pizza LLC
30 Frank Lloyd Wright Dr.
PO Box 997
Ann Arbor, MI 48106
Website: www.dominos.com
David Brandon, Chairman and
    CEO

Donahue, Elinor
400 S. Beverly Dr., #101
Beverly Hills, CA 90212
Actress
Birthday: 4/19/37

Donahue, Phil
420 E. 54th. St. #22F
New York, NY 10022
Former talk show host
Birthday: 12/31/35

Doobie Brothers
15140 Sonoma Hwy.
Glen Ellen, CA 95442
Music group

Doodie.com
PO Box 93757
Los Angeles, CA 90093
Tom Winkler, Creator
Website:www.doodie.com
E-mail:
    tommyswan@earthlink.net
Internet content provider

Doors, The
8033 Sunset Blvd., #76
Los Angeles, CA 90046
Music group

Dorn, Michael
% Agency for the Performing
    Arts
9000 Sunset Blvd., Suite 1200
Los Angeles, CA 90069
Actor
Birthday: 12/19/52

Douglas, Donna
PO Box 1511
Huntington Beach, CA 92647
Actress
Birthday: 9/26/39

Dover
280 Park Ave.
New York, NY 10017
Website: http://
    www.dovercorporation.com
Thomas L. Reece, Chairman,
    President, and CEO
Industrial and farm equipment

Dow Chemical
2030 Dow Center
Midland, MI 48674
Website: http://www.dow.com
Frank P. Popoff, Chairman
William S. Stavropoulos,
    President and CEO
Chemicals

Dow, Tony
13317 Ventura Blvd., #1
Sherman Oaks, CA 91423
Actor

Downey, Robert, Jr.
20 Waterside Plaza, #28D
New York, NY 10010
Actor
Birthday: 4/4/65

Dre, Dr.
10900 Wilshire Blvd., #1230
Los Angeles, CA 90024
Musician, rapper, record producer
Birthday: 2/18/66

Dr. Hook
PO Box 398
Flagler Beach, FL 32136
Music group

Dramalogue
PO Box 38771
Hollywood, CA 90038
Newspaper for actors

Drapper, John T. a.k.a Cap'n Crunch
Website: http://
  webcrunchers.woz.org/
  crunch/
E-mail:
  crunch@webcruncher.com
*Famous pioneer hacker used
  whistle out of Cap'n Crunch
  cereal box to hack long
  distance calls*

Dresser Industries
10077 Grogans Mill Rd., Suite
  500
The Woodlands, TX 77380
Website: http://
  www.dresser.com
David Norton, President and
  CEO
Industrial and farm equipment

Louis-Dreyfus, Julia
% William Morris Agency
151 El Camino Dr.
Beverly Hills, CA 90212
Actress
Birthday: 1/13/61

Dreyfus, Richard
% Addis-Weschler and Assoc.
955 S. Carillo Dr., #300
Los Angeles, CA 90048
Actor
Birthday: 10/29/47

Driever, Klaus
Medienallee 4
85774 Unterföhring
Germany
Inventor
Birthday: 12/10/70

Driver, Minnie
1122 S. Robertson Blvd., #15
Los Angeles, CA 90035
or
9701 Wilshire Blvd., 10th.
  Floor
Beverly Hills, CA 90212
Actress
Birthday: 1/31/71

Drug Policy Foundation
925 Ninth Ave.
New York, NY 10019
Website: http://
  www.drugpolicy.org/
E-mail: webfeedback@dpf.org
Ethan Nadelmann, Director
E-mail:
  enadelmann@sorosny.org/
*An independent, nonprofit
  organization with over 20,000
  members that publicizes
  alternatives to current drug
  strategies, believes that the
  drug war is not working*

Dryer, Fred
1122 S. Robertson Blvd., #15
Los Angeles, CA 90035
Website: http://
  www.fdprods.com/
Actor, producer

DTE Energy
2000 Second Ave.
Detroit, MI 48226
Website: http://
  www.dteenergy.com
Anthony F. Earley, Jr.,
  Chairman, President, CEO,
  and COO, DTE Energy
  and Detroit Edison
Gas and electric utilities

Duchovny, David
10201 W. Pico Blvd.
Los Angeles, CA 90035
Actor
Birthday: 8/7/60

Duffy, Julia
9255 Sunset Blvd., #1010
Los Angeles, CA 90069
Actress

Duffy, Patrick
PO Box D
Tarzana, CA 91356
Actor
Birthday: 3/19/49

Duke, David
PO Box 577
Metairie, LA 70004
or
Box 188
Mandeville, LA 70470
Website: www.davidduke.org
E-mail:
davidduke@davidduke.net
*Former Ku Klux-Klan leader
turned politician*

Dukes of Dixieland
PO Box 56757
New Orleans, LA 70156
Music group

Duke Energy
422 S. Church St.
Charlotte, NC 28202
Website: http://www.duke-
energy.com
Richard B. Priory, CEO
Gas and electric utilities

Dunaway, Faye
2311 W. Victory Blvd., #384
Burbank, CA 91506
Actress

Dunn, Holly
209 10th. Ave. South, #347
Nashville, TN 37203
Singer

Dunne, Dominick
155 E. 49th St.
New York, NY 10017
Author

Dunne, Griffin
1501 Broadway, #2600
New York, NY 10036
Actor
Birthday: 6/8/55

Duran Duran
9255 Sunset Blvd., #200
Los Angeles, CA 90069
Music group

Duvall, Robert
1122 S. Robertson Blvd., #15
Los Angeles, CA 90035
Actor
Birthday: 1/15/31

Duvall, Shelley
Rt. #1 Box 377-A
Blanco, TX 78606
Actress, producer

Dylan, Bob
PO Box 870
Cooper Station
New York, NY 10276
Singer/songwriter
Birthday: 5/24/41

Dylan, Jakob
H.K. Management
8900 Wilshire Blvd.
Beverly Hills, CA 90211
Singer

E

A letter is the mind alone without corporeal friend.

Eagles, The
9200 Sunset Blvd., #1000
Los Angeles, CA 90069
Music group

Eagle Forum
316 Pennsylvania Ave., Suite 203
Washington, DC 20003
Website: http://
    www.eagleforum.org/
E-mail: eagle@eagleforum.org
Phyllis Schlafly, President
Stands for the fundamental right of parents to guide the education of their own children

Eagleton Institute on Politics
Rutgers University
191 Ryders Ln.
New Brunswick, NJ 08901
Website: http://
    www.rci.rutgers.edu/
    ~eagleton/
E-mail:
    eagleton@rci.rutgers.edu
Ruth B. Mandel, Director
E-mail:
    rmandel@rci.rutgers.edu

Develops new knowledge and understanding of emerging topics and themes in American politics and government in order to encourage more responsive and effective leadership

Eakin, Thomas C.
2728 Shelley Rd.
Shaker Heights, OH 44122
Sports promotion executive
Birthday: 12/16/33

Earl, Steve
1815 Division St., #295
Nashville, TN 37203
Country music singer

Earth Wind and Fire
9169 Sunset Blvd.
Los Angeles, CA 90069
Music group

Eastman Chemical
100 N. Eastman Rd.
Kingsport, TN 37660
Website: http://
    www.eastman.com
Earnest W. Deavenport, Jr.,
    CEO
Chemicals

Eastman Kodak
343 State St.
Rochester, NY 14650
Website: http://www.kodak.com
George M. C. Fisher, CEO
Daniel A. Carp, President,
    CEO, and COO
*Scientific, photography, and
    control equipment*

Easton, Sheena
7095 Hollywood Blvd., #469
Hollywood, CA 90028
Website: http://
    www.sheenaeaston.com/
Singer, actress
Birthday: 4/29/59

East-West Center
1601 East-West Rd.
Honolulu, HI 96848
Website: http://
    www.ewc.hawaii.edu/
E-mail: ewcinfo@EastWest
    Center.org
Daniel Berman, President, East-
    West Center Association
*An internationally recognized
    education and research
    organization established by the
    U.S. Congress to strengthen
    understanding and relations
    between the United States and
    the countries of the Asia
    Pacific region, Asia, and the
    Pacific*

Eastwood, Clint
4000 Warner Blvd., #16
Burbank, CA 91522
Actor
Birthday: 5/29/30

Eaton
Eaton Center
Cleveland, OH 44114
Website: http://www.eaton.com
Alexander M. "Sandy" Cutler
    Chairman, President, and
    CEO
*Electrical power distribution and
    control equipment, truck
    drivetrain systems, engine
    components, and hydraulic
    products for the aerospace,
    automotive, and marine
    industries*

Eban, Abba
PO Box 394
Hertzelia
Israel
*Israel politician and foreign
    minister*

Ebert, Roger
PO Box 146366
Chicago, IL 60614
Movie critic
Birthday: 6/18/42

Ebsen, Buddy
PO Box 2069
Palos Verdes Peninsula, CA
    90274
Actor
Birthday: 4/2/1908

Eckersley, Dennis
% St. Louis Cardinals
Busch Stadium
250 Stadium Plaza
St. Louis, MO 63126
Baseball player

Economic Policy Institute
1660 L Street NW, Suite 1200
Washington, DC 20036
Website: http://epinet.org/
E-mail: epi@epinet.org
Jeff Faux, President
E-mail: jfaux@epinet.org
A nonprofit, nonpartisan think
tank that seeks to broaden the
public debate about strategies
to achieve a prosperous and
fair economy

Eden, Barbara
PO Box 5556
Sherman Oaks, CA 91403
Actress
Birthday: 8/22/34

Edison International
2244 Walnut Grove Ave.
Rosemead, CA 91770
Website: http://
    www.edisonx.com
John E. Bryson, Chairman,
    President, and CEO
Gas and electric utilities

Educators for Social
    Responsibility
23 Garden St.
Cambridge, MA 02138
Website: http://
    www.esrnational.org/
E-mail:
    educators@esrnational.org
A national nonprofit organization
    dedicated to helping young
    people develop the convictions
    and skills to build a safe,
    sustainable, and just world

Edwards, Anthony
15260 Ventura Blvd., #1420
Sherman Oaks, CA 91403
Actor

Edwards, Blake
PO Box 491668
Los Angeles, CA 90049
Producer

Eggar, Samantha
12304 Santa Monica Blvd.,
    #104
Los Angeles, CA 90025
Actress

Eggert, Nicole
% William Caroll Agency
120 S. Victory Blvd.
Burbank, CA 91502
Supermodel

Eichhorn, Lisa
1501 Broadway, #2600
New York, NY 10036
Actress
Birthday: 2/4/52

E. I. du Pont de Nemours
1007 Market St.
Wilmington, DE 19898
Website: http://
    www.dupont.com
Charles O. Holliday, Jr.,
    Chairman and CEO
The largest chemical company in
    the United States

Eisner, Michael
500 S. Buena Vista St.
Burbank, CA 91521
Entertainment executive
Birthday: 4/21/26

Ekland, Britt
280 S. Beverly Dr., #300
Beverly Hills, CA 90212
Actress

Electra, Carmen
1122 S. Robertson Blvd., #15
Los Angeles, CA 90035
Actress

Electronic Frontier Foundation
1550 Bryant, #725
San Francisco, CA 94117
Website: http://www.eff.org
E-mail: eff@eff.org or
    info@eff.org
Shari Steele, Executive
    Director and President
E-mail: ssteele@eff.org
*A nonprofit, nonpartisan
    organization working in the
    public interest to protect
    fundamental civil liberties,
    including privacy and freedom
    of expression in the arena of
    computers and the Internet*

Electric Light Orchestra
297-101 Kinderkamack Rd.,
    #128
Oradell, NJ 07649
Music group

Elfman, Danny
345 N. Maple Dr., #385
Beverly Hills, CA 90210
Musician, composer

Elfman, Jenna
7920 Sunset Blvd., #401
Los Angeles, CA 90069
Actress
Birthday: 9/30/71

Eli Lilly
Lilly Corporate Center
Indianapolis, IN 46285
Website: http://www.lilly.com
Sidney Taurel, Chairman,
    President, and CEO
*Pharmaceuticals, makes Prozac,
    the world's best-selling
    antidepressant*

Elizabeth, HRH Queen II
Buckingham Palace
London SW1
England

Elizabeth, HRH Queen Mother
Clarence House
London SW1
England

Elizondo, Hector
15030 Ventura Blvd., #751
Sherman Oaks, CA 91403
Actor

Elliot, Chris
151 El Camino Dr.
Beverly Hills, CA 90212
Actor

Elliott, Sam
151 El Camino Dr.
Beverly Hills, CA 90212
Actor

Ellison, Harlan
PO Box 55548
Sherman Oaks, CA 91423
Science fiction author

El Paso Natural Gas
1001 Louisiana St.
Houston, TX 77002
Website: http://www.epng.com
William A. Wise, Chairman,
    President, and CEO
Pipelines

Electronic Data Systems
5400 Legacy Dr.
Plano, TX 75024
Website: http://www.eds.com
Richard H. Brown, Chairman
    and CEO
Computer and data services

Elvira (Cassandra Peterson)
PO Box 38246
Los Angeles, CA 90038
Web: http://www.elvira.com
Television personality

Ely, Joe
% Campfire Nightmares
7101 Hwy. 71W., Suite A 9
Austin, TX 78735
Country music singer

Ely, Ron
151 El Camino Dr.
Beverly Hills, CA 90212
Actor

Embery, Joan
San Diego Zoo
Park Blvd.
San Diego, CA 92104
*Animal expert, television
    personality*

EMC
35 Parkwood Dr.
Hopkinton, MA 01748
Website: http://www.emc.com
Richard J. Egan, Chairman
Michael C. Ruettgers, CEO
Computer peripherals

Emerson Electric
8000 W. Florissant Ave.
St. Louis, MO 63136
Website: http://
    www.emersonelectric.com
Charles F. Knight, Chairman
    and CEO
Electronics, electrical equipment

Emerson Lake and Palmer
370 City Rd.
Islingon
London EC1V 2QA
England
Music group

Emery, Ralph
PO Box 916
Hendersonville, TN 37033
*Television personality, Nashville
    Network talk show host*

Emilio
209 10th Ave. #347
Nashville, TN 37077
Country music singer

Empower America
1701 Pennsylvania Ave. NW,
    Suite 900
Washington, DC 20006
Website: http://
    www.empower.org/
E-mail:
    empower1@empower.org
William J. Bennett, Co-Director
E-mail: jeffk@empower.org
Jack Kemp, Co-Director
E-mail: jfkemp@empower.org
Josette Shiner, President
*Encourages public policy solutions
    that maximize free markets
    and individual responsibility*

En Vogue
9255 Sunset Blvd., #200
Los Angeles, CA 90069
Music group

Endometriosis Alliance of New York, The
PO Box 326
Cooper Station
New York, NY 10276
Website: http://
    www.monmouth.com/
    ~mkatzman/
healing/endo.htm
A mutual self-help, nonprofit organization providing accurate, current, and independent information about endometriosis

Endometriosis Association, The
8585 North 76th Place
Milwaukee, WI 53223
Website: http://
    www.EndometriosisAssn.org/
E-mail: endo@endo
    metriosisassn.org
A nonprofit organization that provides support to women and girls, educates the public and medical community, and conducts and promotes research related to endometriosis

Energizer Bunny, The
800 Chouteau Ave.
St. Louis, MO 63164

Energizer Holdings, Inc.
800 Chouteau Ave.
St. Louis, MO 63164
Website: http://
    www.energizer.com
William P. Stiritz, Chairman
J. Patrick Mulcahy, CEO
#2 battery maker in the United States

Engelhard
101 Wood Ave.
Iselin, NJ 08830
Website: http://
    www.engelhard.com
Orin R. Smith, Chairman and
    CEO
Chemicals

Engels, Marty
11365 Ventura Blvd., #100
Studio City, CA 91604
Comedian

England, Ty
3322 West End Ave., #520
Nashville, TN 37213
Musician

Ty England Fan Club
PO Box 120964
Nashville, TN 37212

Eno, Brian
330 Harrow Rd.
London W9
England
Musician

Enron
1400 Smith St.
Houston, TX 77002
Website: http://www.enron.com
Kenneth L. Lay, CEO
*The #1 buyer and seller of natural
gas and the top wholesale
power marketer in the United
States*

Entergy
639 Loyola Ave.
New Orleans, LA 70113
Website: http://
www.entergy.com
Robert Luft, Chairman
J. Wayne Leonard, CEO
Donald C. Hintz, President
Gas and electric utilities

**Entertainment Media Ventures
LLC**
828 Moraga Dr., 2nd Floor
Los Angeles, CA 90049
Website: http://
www.emventures.com
Sanford R. Climan, Founder
E-mail: sandy@emventures.com
Venture capital

Entwhistle, John
PO Box 241
Lake Peekskill, NY 10537
Musician

Environmental Defense Fund
257 Park Ave. South
New York, NY 10010
Website: http://www.edf.org/
E-mail: Contact@
environmentaldefense.org
Fred Krupp, Executive Director
*Representing 300,000 members,
combines science, economics,
and law to find economically
sustainable solutions to
environmental problems*

**Environmental Health Center—
Dallas**
8345 Walnut Hill Lane, Suite
220
Dallas, TX 75231
Website: http://www.ehcd.com/
E-mail: cg@ehcd.com
*Diagnosis/treatment for
individuals with allergy and
environmental-related illnesses*

Environmental Law Institute
1616 P St. NW #200
Washington, DC 20036
Website: http://www.eli.org/
J. William Futrell, President
*Working to advance environmental
protection by improving law,
policy, and management*

Erving, Julius
PO Box 914100
Longwood, FL 32791
Basketball player

Estefan, Gloria
151 El Camino Dr.
Beverly Hills, CA 90212
Musician, singer
Birthday: 9/1/57

Estee Lauder
767 Fifth Ave.
New York, NY 10153
Website: http://
www.elcompanies.com
Leonard A. Lauder, CEO
Soaps, cosmetics

Estevez, Emilio
PO Box 4041
Malibu, CA 90264
Actor
Birthday: 5/12/62

Eszterhas, Joe
8942 Wilshire Blvd.
Beverly Hills, CA 90211
Screenwriter

Etheridge, Melissa
4425 Riverside Dr., #102
Burbank, CA 91505
Singer
Birthday: 5/29/61

**Ethics and Public Policy
   Center**
1015 15th St. NW, #900
Washington, DC 20005
Website: http://www.eppc.org/
E-mail: ethics@eppc.org
Elliott Abrams, President
*Studies the interconnections
   between religious faith,
   political practice, and social
   values*

EToys
3100 Ocean Park Blvd., Suite
   300
Santa Monica, CA 90405
Website: http://www.etoys.com
Toby Link, President and CEO
E-mail: toby@etoys.com
E-commerce

Eubanks, Bob
11365 Ventura Blvd., #100
Studio City, CA 91604
TV game show host
Birthday: 1/8/38

Eubanks, Kevin
% Tonight Show
NBC Entertainment
3000 W. Alameda Ave.
Burbank, CA 91527
Jay Leno's bandleader

Eure, Wesley
PO Box 69405
Los Angeles, CA 90069
Actor

Eurythmics
Box 245
London N8 9QG
England
Music group

**Euthanasia Research and
   Guidance Organization
   (ERGO!)**
24829 Norris Lane
Junction City, OR 97448
Website: http://
   www.FinalExit.org
E-mail: ergo@efn.org
Derek Humphry, Founder and
   President
*Organization that believes in the
   right to die*

Evangeline
Lafayette Square Station
PO Box 2700
New Orleans, LA 70176
or
Music Square East
Nashville, TN 37203
Country music group

Evans, Dale
15650 Senneca Rd.
Victorville, CA 92392
Actress, queen of the cowboys
Birthday: 10/31/12

Everett, Jim
PO Box 609609
San Diego, CA 92160
Football player

Everly Brothers
PO Box 56
Dunmore, KY 42339
Music duo

Ewing, Skip
PO Box 17254
Nashville, TN 37217
Country music singer

Exxon Mobil Corporation
5959 Las Colinas Blvd.
Irving, TX 75039
Website: http://
   www.exxon.mobil.com
Lee R. Raymond, Chairman,
   President, and CEO

F

A letter is a cozy quilt, hand-stitched with the thread of friendship.

—FARN BULLINGTON

Fabares, Shelly (Michelle Marie Fabares)
PO Box 6010-909
Sherman Oaks, CA 91413
Actress
Birthday: 1/19/42

Fahey, Jeff
8942 Wilshire Blvd.
Beverly Hills, CA 90211
Actor

Fairchild, Barbara
1078 Skyview Dr.
Branson, MO 65616
Country music singer

FAIR/Fairness and Accuracy in Reporting
130 W. 25th St.
New York, NY 10001
Website: http://www.fair.org/fair/
E-mail: fair@fair.org
Jeff Cohen, Executive Director
Has been offering documented criticism of media bias and censorship since 1986

Fairchild, Morgan (Patsy McClenny)
PO Box 57593
Sherman Oaks, CA 91403
Actress
Birthday: 2/30/50

Falk, Peter
100 Universal City Plaza
Universal City, CA 91608
Actor
Birthday: 9/26/27

Falwell, Rev. Jerry
PO Box 6004
Forest, VA 24551
Minister, founder of the Moral Majority and Liberty University

Families and Work Institute
330 Seventh Ave., 14th Floor
New York, NY 10001
Website: http://www.familiesandworkinst.org/
E-mail: ebrownfield@familiesandworkinst.org
Ellen Galinsky, President
A nonprofit organization that addresses the changing nature of work and family life

Families USA Foundation
1334 G St. NW, #300
Washington, DC 20005
Website: http://
    www.familiesusa.org/
E-mail: info@familiesusa.org
Philippe Villers, President and
    Co-Founder
*A national nonprofit, nonpartisan
    organization dedicated to the
    achievement of high-quality,
    affordable health and long-
    term care for all Americans*

Family Violence Prevention
    Fund
383 Rhode Island St., #304
San Francisco, CA 94103
Website: http://www.fvpf.org/
E-mail: fund@fvpf.org
Esta Soler, Executive Director
*A national nonprofit organization
    that focuses on domestic
    violence education, prevention,
    and public policy reform*

Fannie Mae
3900 Wisconsin Ave. NW
Washington, DC 20016
Website: http://
    www.fanniemae.com
E-mail:
    webmaster@fanniemae.com
Franklin D. Raines, Chairman,
    and CEO
*The world's largest diversified
    financial company and source
    of home mortagage funds*

Fargo, Donna
P.O. Box 233
Crescent, GA 31304
Country music singer
Birthday: 11/10/45

Farina, Dennis
955 S. Carrillo Dr., #300
Los Angeles, CA 90048
Actor

Farmland Industries
3315 N. Farmland Trffcwy.
Kansas City, MO 64116
Website: http://
    www.farmland.com
Albert J. Shivley, Chairman
Food producer

Farrakhan, Rev. Louis
4855 S. Woodlawn Ave.
Chicago, IL 60615
or
734 W 79th St.
Chicago, IL 60620
Spokesman for the Nation of Islam

Farell, Mike
MSC 826 PO Box 6010
Sherman Oaks, CA 91413-6010
Actor
Birthday: 2/6/39

Farrell, Sharon (Sharon
    Forthman)
360 S. Doheny Dr.
Beverly Hills, CA 90211
Actress
Birthday: 12/24/46

Farrell, Shea (Edward Leo
    Farrell III)
10000 Santa Monica Blvd.,
    #305
Los Angeles, CA 90067
Actor
Birthday: 10/21/57

Farrell, Terry
6500 Wilshire Blvd., #2200
Los Angeles, CA 90048
Actress
Birthday: 11/19/63

Farve, Brett
% Green Bay Packers
PO Box 10628
Green Bay, WI 54307
Football player

FasTV
5670 Wilshire Blvd., Suite 1550
Los Angeles, CA 90036
Prince Khaled Al-Nehyen,
    Chairman
William Wegles, President and
    COO
Website: http://www.fastv.com
E-mail: bswegles@fastv.com
Interactive TV

Fat Boy
250 W. 57th. St., #1723
New York, NY 10107
Music group

Faustino, David
11350 Ventura Blvd., #206
Studio City, CA 91604
Actor
Birthday: 3/7/74

FedEx
6075 Poplar Ave., Suite. 300
Memphis, TN 38119
Website: http://
    www.fedexcorp.com
Frederick W. Smith, Chairman,
    President, and CEO
Mail, package, and freight delivery

F.E.A.R. Foundation
PO Box 33985
Washington, DC 20033
Website: http://www.fear.org/
E-mail: powerhit@fli.net
Robert Bauman, member of
    board of directors
*Forfeiture Endangers American
    Rights is a national nonprofit
    organization dedicated to the
    reform of federal and state
    asset forfeiture laws to restore
    due process and protect the
    property rights of innocent
    citizens*

**Federal Bureau of
    Investigation (FBI)**
J. Edgar Hoover Building
935 Pennsylvania Ave., NW
Washington, DC 20535
Website: http://www.fbi.gov
Louis J. Freeh, Director of the
    FBI

**Federal Election Commission
    (FEC)**
999 E St. NW
Washington, DC 20463
Website: http://www.fec.gov/
E-mail: webmaster@fec.gov
Lynne A. McFarland, Inspector
    General
*Administers and enforces the
    Federal Election Campaign
    Act (FECA)*

Federal Home Loan Mortgage
8200 Jones Branch Dr.
McLean, VA 22102
Website: http://
    www.freddiemac.com
Leland C. Brendsel, Chairman
    and CEO

A *stockholder-owned corporation chartered by Congress in 1970 to create a continuous flow of funds to mortgage lenders in support of homeownership and rental housing.*

The Federalist Society
1015 18th St. NW, Suite 425
Washington, DC 20036
Website: http://www.fed-soc.org/
E-mail: fedsoc@radix.net
Steven G. Calabresi, National Co-Chairman
David M. McIntosh, National Co-Chairman
Eugene B. Meyer, Executive Director
E-mail: ebmeyer@fed-soc.org
A group of conservatives and libertarians interested in the current state of the legal order.

Federated Department Stores
7 W. Seventh St.
Cincinnati, OH 45202
Website: http://www.federated-fds.com
James M. Zimmerman, Chairman and CEO
General merchandisers; Federated runs nine regional chains: Bloomingdale's, Macy's, Lazarus, The Bon Marche, Burdines, Stern's, Rich's, Goldsmith's, and Fingerhut companies

Federation for American Immigration Reform
1666 Connecticut Ave. NW, #400
Washington, DC 20009
Website: http://www.fairus.org/
E-mail: info@fairus.org

Sharon Barnes, Chairman, Board of Directors
A national, membership-based, educational organization with 70,000 members across the country, working to help the American public convince Congress that our nation's immigration laws must be reformed

Feelgood, Dr.
3 E. 54th. St.
New York, NY 10022
Website: http://www.drfeelgood.de/index.htm
Music group

Feiffer, Jules
RR #1 Box 440
Vineyard Haven, MA 02568
Political cartoonist

Feldman, Corey
10960 Wilshire Blvd., #1100
Los Angeles, CA 90024
Actor
Birthday: 3/16/71

Feldon, Barbara
14 East 74th. St.
New York, NY 10021
Actress
Birthday: 3/12/??

Felix the Cat
12020 Chandler Blvd., #200
North Hollywood, CA 91607
Cartoon cat

Fender, Freddie
PO Box 530
Bel Aire, OH 43906
Country music singer
Birthday: 6/4/37

Ferguson, Marilyn
PO Box 42211
Los Angeles, CA 90042
New Age author

Ferguson, Tom
PO Box 50249
Austin, TX 78763
Website: http://
    www.doctom.com/
E-mail doctom@doctom.com
*Author of Health Online (Addison-
    Wesley) and editor and
    publisher of The Ferguson
    Report: The Newsletter of
    Consumer Health Informatics
    and Online Health*

Ferraro, Chris
% Pittsburgh Penguins
Civic Arena
66 Mario Lemieux Pl.
Pittsburg, PA 15219
Hockey player

Ferrigno, Lou
PO Box 1671
Santa Monica, CA 90402
Actor/bodybuilder
Birthday: 11/9/51

Field, Sally
9830 Wilshire Blvd.
Beverly Hills, CA 90212
Actress
Birthday: 11/6/46

Fierstein, Harvey
232 N. Canon Dr.
Beverly Hills, CA 90210
Actor

Fifth Dimension
1900 Ave. of the Stars, #1640
Los Angeles, CA 90067
Music group

Fiorentino, Linda
% C.A.A.
9830 Wilshire Blvd.
Beverly Hills, CA 90212
Actress
Birthday: 3/9/30

First Data
5660 New Northside Dr., Suite
    1400
Atlanta, GA 30328
Website: http://
    www.firstdatacorp.com
Henry C. "Ric" Duques,
    Chairman and CEO
Computer and data services

First Union Corp.
1 First Union Center
Charlotte, NC 28288
Website: http://
    www.firstunion.com
G. Kennedy "Ken" Thompson,
    CEO G.
Commercial bank

FirstEnergy
76 S. Main St.
Akron, OH 44308
Website: http://
    www.firstenergycorp.com
H. Peter Burg, Chairman and
    CEO
Anthony J. Alexander,
    President
Gas and electric utilities

Fishburne, Laurence
% Paradigm
10100 Santa Monica Blvd.,
    25th Floor
Los Angeles, CA 90067
Actor, playwright, screenwriter,
    stage director
Birthday: 7/30/61

Fisher, Carrie
1700 Coldwater Canyon
Beverly Hills, CA 90210
or
9830 Wilshire Blvd.
Beverly Hills, CA 90212
Actress, author, daughter of Eddie
    Fisher and Debbie Reynolds
Birthday: 1/1/56

Fisher, Joely
9485 Wilshire Blvd., #430
Beverly Hills, CA 90212
Actress, singer, half-sister of Carrie
    Fisher

Fishel, Danielle
% *Boy Meets World*
ABC-TV
2040 Ave. of the Stars
Los Angeles, CA 90064
Actress
Birthday: 5/5/81

Fisher, Frances
7920 Sunset Blvd., #401
Los Angeles, CA 90046
Actress

Fisichella, Giancarlo
% Jordan Formula One Ltd.
Silverstone Circuit
Towcester
GB-Northhamptonshire NN12
    8TN
England
Professional Formula-1 driver

Fixx, The
6255 Sunset Blvd., 2nd Floor
Los Angeles, CA 90028
Music group

Flack, Roberta
1 W. 72nd St.
New York, NY 10022
Singer
Birthday: 2/10/39

Flaming Lips, The
PO Box 75995
Oklahoma City, OK 73147
Music group

Flanery, Sean Patrick
3500 W. Olive Ave., #920
Burbank, CA 91505
Actor

Flatt, Lester
PO Box 647
Hendersonville, TN 37215
Musician

Fleet Boston Financial Group
1 Federal St.
Boston, MA 02110
Website: http://www.fleet.com
Terrence Murray, Chairman
    and CEO
Commercial bank

Fleetwood Enterprises
3125 Myers St.
Riverside, CA 92503
Website: http://
    www.fleetwood.com
Glenn F. Kummer, Chairman
    and CEO
Engineering, construction

Fleetwood Mac
4905 S. Atlantic Ave.
Daytona Beach, FL 32127
Music group

Fleetwood, Mick
4905 S. Atlantic Ave.
Daytona Beach, FL 32127
Musician

Fleming
6301 Waterford Blvd.
Oklahoma City, OK 73126
Website: http://
    www.fleming.com
Mark S. Hansen, Chairman
    and CEO
Wholesalers, food products

Fleming, Peggy
% Studio Fan Mail
1122 S. Robertson Blvd., Suite
    15
Los Angeles, CA 90035
Actress, ice skater
Birthday: 7/27/48

Fletcher, Louise
PO Box 64656
Los Angeles, CA 90064
Actress

Flintones, The
3400 Cahuenga Blvd.
Los Angeles, CA 90068
A modern stone-age family

Flockhart, Calista
PO Box 5617
Beverly Hills, CA 90210
Actress
Birthday: 11/11/64

Florida Progress
1 Progress Plaza
St. Petersburg, FL 33701
Website: http://www.fpc.com
Richard Korpan, Chairman,
    President, and CEO
Gas and electric utilities

Fluor
1 Enterprise Dr.
Aliso Viejo, CA 92656
Website: http://www.fluor.com
Philip J. Carroll, Jr., Chairman
    and CEO
Engineering, construction

FMC
200 E. Randolph Dr.
Chicago, IL 60601
Website: http://www.fmc.com
Robert N. Burt, Chairman and
    CEO
Chemicals

**Foch, Nina (Nina Consuelo
    Maud Fock)**
PO Box 1884
Beverly Hills, CA 90213
Actress
Birthday: 4/20/24

Fogelberg, Dan
PO Box 2399
Pagosa Springs, CO 81147
Singer
Birthday: 8/31/51

Fogerty, John
PO Box 375
Granada Hills, CA 91364
Singer, songwriter
Birthday: 5/28/45

Foley, David
% NBC
3000 W. Alameda Ave.
Burbank, CA 91523
Actor
Birthday: 1/4/63

Fonda, Bridget
9560 Wilshire Blvd., #516
Beverly Hills, CA 90212
Actress, Jane Fonda's niece
Birthday: 1/27/64

Fonda, Jane
9830 Wilshire Blvd.
Beverly Hills, CA 90212
Actress
Birthday: 12/21/37

Fonda, Peter (Peter Seymour Fonda)
Rt. 38 Box 2024
Livingston, MT 59047
Actor, Bridget's father, Jane's brother

Fontaine, Joan
PO Box 222600
Carmel, CA 93922
Actress

Food Research and Action Center
1875 Connecticut Ave. NW, #540
Washington, DC 20009
Website: http://www.frac.org/
E-mail: webmaster@frac.org
Matthew E. Melmed, Chair, Board of Directors
Working to improve public policies to eradicate hunger and undernutrition in the United States

Foo Fighters
370 City Rd.
Islington
London EC1 V2QA
England
Music group

Forbes, Malcome, Jr. (Steve)
60 Fifth Ave.
New York, NY 10011
Magazine publisher, presidential candidate

Force, John
% John Force Racing
23253 East LaPalma Ave.
Yorba Linda, CA 92687
Website: http://www.johnforceracing.com/splash1.htm
Race car driver

John Force Fan Club
1480 South Hohokam Dr.
Tempe, AZ 85281

Ford, Betty
1801 Ave. of the Stars, #902
Los Angeles, CA 90067
Former first lady

Ford, Chris
% Milwaukee Bucks
1001 N. 4th St.
Milwaukee, WI 53203
Basketball player

"Ford Model Name"
% Ford Model Mgmt.
344 E. 59th St.
New York, NY 10022
Address to write to Ford Models

Ford, Faith
9460 Wilshire Blvd., #7
Beverly Hills, CA 90212
Actress
Birthday: 9/14/64

Ford, Gerald R.
40365 San Dune Rd.
Rancho Mirage, CA 92270
or
PO Box 927
Rancho Mirage, CA
Former president
Birthday: 7/14/13

Ford, Harrison
% United Talent Agency
9560 Wilshire Blvd., Suite 500
Beverly Hills, CA 90212
Actor
Birthday: 7/13/42

Ford, Patricia
% Playmate Promotions
9242 Beverly Blvd.
Beverly Hills, CA 90210
Model

Ford, Whitey
38 Schoolhouse Ln.
Lake Success, NY 11020
Former baseball player

Ford Foundation
320 East 43rd St.
New York, NY 10017
Website: http://
    www.fordfound.org
Paul A. Allaire, Chairman,
    Board of Trustees
*Grant organization that supports
    activities that strengthen
    democratic values, reduce
    poverty and injustice, promote
    international cooperation and
    advance human achievement*

Ford Motor Company
One American Rd.
Dearborn, MI 48126
Website: http://www.ford.com
William C. Ford, Jr., Chairman
Jacques A. Nasser, President
    and CEO
Autos and trucks

Forester Sisters
PO Box 1456
Trenton, GA 30752
Country music group

Foreigner
9830 Wilshire Blvd.
Beverly Hills, CA 90212
Music group

Forman, Milos
150 Central Park So.
New York, NY 10019
Director

Fort James Corp.
1650 Lake Cook Rd.
Deerfield, IL 60015
Website: http://
    www.fortjames.com
Miles L. Marsh, Chairman and
    CEO
Forest and paper products

Forte, Fabian
6671 Sunset Blvd., #1502
Los Angeles, CA 90028
Singer

Fortune Brands
300 Tower Pkwy.
Lincolnshire, IL 60069
Website: http://
    www.fortunebrands.com
Norman H. Wesley, Chairman
    and CEO
*Leading U.S. producer of distilled
    spirits (Jim Beam, DeKuyper,
    and Ronrico) and golf
    equipment (Titleist, Cobra,
    FootJoy, and Pinnacle).
    Fortune also makes home
    products (Moen faucets,
    Aristokraft and Schrock
    cabinets, and Master Lock
    padlocks) as well as office
    products (ACCO, Day-Timers,
    and Swingline)*

Foss, General Joe
PO Box 566
Scottsdale, AZ 85252
*The first American to tie Eddie
    Rickenbacker's World War I
    record of 26 aerial combat
    victories; he was the World
    War II Marine Corp Ace of
    Aces, Congressional Medal of
    Honor winner, and former
    governor of South Dakota*

Foster, Jodie
8942 Wilshire Blvd.
Beverly Hills, CA 90211
Actress, director, producer
Birthday: 11/19/62

Foster, Meg
606 N. Larchmont Blvd., #309
Los Angeles, CA 90004
Actress

Foster, Radney
1908 Wedgewood
Nashville, TN 37212
Country music singer

Foster, Wheeler
Perryville Corporate Park
Clinton, NJ 08809
Website: http://www.fwc.com
Richard J. Swift, Chairman,
    President and CEO
Engineering, construction

**Foundation for Biomedical
    Research**
818 Connecticut Ave. NW,
    #303
Washington, DC 20006
Website: http://
    www.fbresearch.org/
E-mail: info@fbresearch.org
Frankie Trull, President
*A nonprofit organization that
    focuses on the proper use of
    animals in medical research*

Foundation for Economic Education (FEE)
30 S. Broadway
Irvington-on-Hudson, NY 10533
Website: http://www.fee.org/
E-mail: freeman@fee.org
Dr. Donald J. Boudreaux, President
Nonpolitical, educational champion of private property, the free-market, and limited government

Foundation Health Systems
21600 Oxnard St.
Woodland Hills, CA 91367
Website: http://www.fhs.com
Richard W. Hanselman, Chairman
Jay M. Gellert, President and CEO
Health Care

Fountain, Pete
237 N. Peters St., #400
New Orleans, LA 71030
Musician

Four Aces, The
11761 E. Speedway Blvd.
Tucson, AZ 85748
Music group

Four Freshman, The
PO Box 93534
Las Vegas, NV 89193
Music group

Four Lads, The
11761 E. Speedway Blvd.
Tucson, AZ 85748
Music group

Four Preps, The
15760 Ventura Blvd., #1206
Encino, CA 91436
Music group

Four Seasons, The
PO Box 262
Carteret, NJ 07008
Music group

Four Tops
40 W. 57th St.
New York, NY 10019
Music group

Fox Brothers
Rt.6
Bending Chestnut
Franklin, TN 37064
Country music group

Foxx, Jamie
15445 Ventura Blvd., #790
Sherman Oaks, CA 91403
Actor

Foxworthy, Jeff
8380 Melrose Ave., #310
Los Angeles, CA 90069
Comedian, actor

Fox, Michael J.
% Creative Artists Agency
9830 Wilshire Blvd.
Beverly Hills, CA 90212
Website: www.michaeljfox.org/
Actor
Birthday: 6/9/61

FPL Group
700 Universe Blvd.
Juno Beach, FL 33408
Website: http://
    www.fplgroup.com
James L. Broadhead, Chairman
    and CEO
Gas and electric utilities

Francis, Cleve
PO Box 15258
Alexandria, VA 22309
Country music singer

Francis, Ron
% Pittsburgh Penguins
66 Mario Lemieux Place
Pittsburgh, PA 15219
Hockey player

Franken, Al
345 N. Maple Dr., #302
Beverly Hills, CA 90210
Actor, writer

Franklin, Bonnie
10635 Santa Monica Blvd.,
    #130
Los Angeles, CA 90025
Actress

Franz, Dennis
2300 Century Hill, #75
Los Angeles, CA 90067
Actor

Fraser, Brendan
2118 Wilshire Blvd., #513
Santa Monica, CA 90403
Actor

Freberg, Stan
10450 Wilshire Blvd., #1A
Los Angeles, CA 90024
Writer, comedian

Fred Meyer, Inc.
3800 SE 22nd Ave.
Portland, OR 97202
Website: http://
    www.fredmeyer.com
Ronald W. Burkle, Chairman
Food and drug stores

Freddie and the Dreamers
9 Ridge Rd.
Emerson, NJ 07630
Music group

Free-PC
74 North Pasadena Ave., 8th
    Floor
Pasadena, CA 91103
Don Lavigne, CEO
Website: http://www.free-
    pc.com
E-mail: don@free-pc.com
E-commerce

Freedom Forum
1101 Wilson Blvd.
Arlington, VA 22209
Website: http://
    www.freedomforum.org/
E-mail:
    news@freedomforum.org
Charles L. Overby, Chairman
    and CEO
*A nonpartisan, international
    foundation dedicated to free
    press, free speech, and free
    spirit for all people. Its
    mission is to help the public
    and the news media
    understand one another better.*

Freedom Forum Media Studies Center
580 Madison Ave., 42nd Floor
New York, NY 10022
Website: http://
www.freedomforum.org/
whoweare/media.asp
E-mail:
mfitzsi@mediastudies.org
Robert H. Giles, Director
The Media Studies Center is
the nation's premier media
think tank devoted to
improving understanding
of media issues by the
press and the public

Freeh, Louis
FBI
9th and Pennsylvania Ave. NW
Washington, DC 20035
Director of the FBI

Frentzen, Heinz-Harald
% Williams GP Engineering
Ltd.
Grove
Wantage
GB Oxfordshire OX12 0DQ
England
Professional Formula-1 driver

Frey, Glenn
8900 Wilshire Blvd., #300
Beverly Hills, CA 90211
Musician

Fricke, Janie
PO Box 798
Lancaster, TX 75146
Country music singer

Friedman, Milton
Hoover Institute
Stanford University
Palo Alto, CA 94305
Economist, Nobel Prize winner

Friends
% Warner Bros.
4000 Warner Blvd.
Burbank, CA 91522
TV series

Friends Committee on National Legislation
245 2nd St., NE
Washington, DC 20002
Website: www.fcnl.org
E-mail: fcnl@fcnl.org
Joe Volk, Executive Secretary
*A nationwide network of
thousands of Quakers Lobby
bringing the testimonies of
Friends to bear on a wide
range of national legislation
regarding peace and social
justice issues*

Friends of the Earth
1025 Vermont Ave., NW
Washington, DC 20005
Website: http://www.foe.org
E-mail: foe@foe.org
Charles Secrett, Executive
Director
*The largest international network
of environmental groups in
the world, represented in 52
countries*

Frizzell, David
% Christina Frazer
PO Box 120964
Nashville, TN 37212
Country music singer

Fuel Cells 2000
1625 K St. NW, Suite 725
Washington, DC 20006
Website: http://
    www.fuelcells.org/
E-mail:
    webmaster@fuelcells.org
Bernadette Geyer, Director
*A private, nonprofit, educational
    organization providing
    information to policy makers,
    the media, and the public and
    supporting the early
    utilization of fuel cells by such
    means as pilot projects and
    government purchases*

Fujita, Dr. Yoshio
6-21-7 Renkojl
Tama-shi 206
Japan
Astronomer

**Fully Informed Jury
    Association (FIJA)**
PO Box 59
Helmville, MT 59843
Website: http://www.fija.org
E-mail: WebForeman@fija.org
*A nonprofit association dedicated
    to education of all Americans
    about their rights, powers, and
    responsibilities as trial jurors*

Fund for Animals
200 W. 57th St.
New York, NY 10019
Website: http://www.fund.org/
    home/
E-mail: fundinfo@fund.org
Cleveland Amory, Founder and
    President
Michael Markarian, Executive
    Vice President
E-mail: mmarkarian@fund.org
Animal activist organization

Fuhrman, Mark
PO Box 141
Sandpoint, ID 83864
*Police witness in O. J. Simpson
    trial*

Future of Freedom Foundation
11350 Random Hills Rd., Suite
    800
Fairfax, VA 22030
Website: http://www.fff.org
E-mail: freedom@fff.org
Jacob G. Hornberger,
    President
*Advances the libertarian
    philosophy by providing an
    uncompromising moral and
    economic case for individual
    liberty, free markets, private
    property, and limited
    government*

G

A letter sings of love and hope, still warm from the hug of an envelope.

—VICKI RENTZ

G., Kenny
9830 Wilshire Blvd.
Beverly Hills, CA 90212
Musician
Birthday: 6/5/?

Gabriel, Peter
Box 35
Corsham
Wiltshire, London SW13 8SZ
England
Musician

Gagne, Greg
℅ Los Angeles Dodgers
1000 Elysian Park Ave.
Los Angeles, CA 90012
Baseball player

Gail, Max
PO Box 4160
Malibu, CA 90265
Actor

Galbraith, John Kenneth
Department of Economics
Littauer Center, Room 206
Harvard University
Cambridge, MA 02138
Economist; please contact by mail

Gallagher, Danny
49 Crouch Hill,
Finsbury Park
London N4
ENGLAND
Healer

Galloway, Joey
℅ Dallas Cowboys
One Cowboys Parkway
Irving, TX 75063
Football player

Game Show Network
510202 W. Washington Blvd.
Culver City, CA 90232
Michael Fleming, President
E-mail: michael_
       fleming@spe.sony.com

Gannett
1100 Wilson Blvd.
Arlington, VA 22234
Website: http://
       www.gannett.com
John J. Curley, CEO
Douglas H. McCorkindale,
       President and CEO
Publishing, printing

Gantner, Jim
% Milwaukee Brewers
Milwaukee County Stadium
Milwaukee, WI 53214
Baseball player

Gantin, Bernardin Cardinal
Piazza S. Calisto 16
00153 Rome
Italy

Gap
1 Harrison St.
San Francisco, CA 94105
Website: http://www.gap.com
Donald G. Fisher, Chairman
Millard S. "Mickey" Dre,
    President and CEO
Clothing retailer

Garcia, Andy
% Paradigm
10100 Santa Monica Blvd. 25th
    Floor
Los Angeles, CA 90067
Actor
Birthday: 4/12/56

Garofalo, Jeanene
1122 S. Robertson Blvd., #15
Los Angeles, CA 90035
Actress

Garr, Terri
9200 Sunset Blvd., #428
Los Angeles, CA 90069
or
9150 Wilshire Blvd., #350
Beverly Hills, CA 90212-3427
Actress
Birthday: 12/11/45

Garrison, David
9229 Sunset Blvd., #710
Los Angeles, CA 90069
Actor

Gates, Bill
1 Microsoft Way
Redmond, WA 98052
Founder of Microsoft
Birthday: 10/28/55

Gateway
4545 Towne Centre Ct.
San Diego, CA 92121
Website: http://
    www.gateway.com
Theodore W. Waitt, Chairman
David J. Robino, Vice
    Chairman
Jeffrey Weitzen, President and
    CEO
Computers, office equipment

Gatlin Brothers
207 Westpoint Rd., #202
Kansas City, MO 64111
Country music group

Gatlin, Larry
Fantasy Harbour
Waccamaw
Myrtle Beach, SC 29577
Musician

Gayle, Crystal
51 Music Square East
Nashville, TN 37203
Country music singer
Birthday: 1/9/51

Gaynor, Gloria
% Cliffside Music
PO Box 374
Fairview, NJ 07010
or
Longford Ave.
Southall
Middlesex UB1 3QT
England
Singer
Birthday: 9/7/48

Geary, Tony
% *General Hospital*
ABC-TV
4151 Prospect Ave.
Los Angeles, CA 90027
Soap opera star

Geffen, David
100 Universal Plaza
Lakeridge Bldg., #601
Universal City, CA 91608
*Founder of Geffen Records, Co-
Founder of Dreamworks
Studios*

Geldof, Sir Bob
Davington Priory
Priory Rd.
Faversham ME13 7EJ
England
Musician

Gellar, Sarah Michelle
% *Buffy the Vampire Slayer*
% The Warner Brothers
Television Network
4000 Warner Blvd.
Burbank, CA 91522
or
1122 S. Robertson Blvd., #15
Los Angeles, CA 90035
Actress, model
Birthday: 4/14/77

Geller, Uri
Sonning-on-Thames
Berkshire
England
Psychic

GenAmerica Corporation
700 Market St.
St. Louis, MO 63101
Richard A. Liddy, Chairman,
President and CEO
Life and health insurance (stock)

General Dynamics
3190 Fairview Park Dr.
Falls Church, VA 22042
Website: http://www.gdeb.com/
pr/corp_info
Nicholas D. Chabraja,
Chairman and CEO
Aerospace

General Electric
3135 Easton Turnpike
Fairfield, CT 06431
Website: http://www.ge.com
Mr. John F. "Jack" Welch, Jr.,
Chairman and CEO
Electrical equipment company

General Mills
1 General Mills Blvd.
Minneapolis, MN 55426
Website: http://
www.generalmills.com
Stephen W. Sanger, Chairman
and CEO
Food producer

General Motors
300 Renaissance Center
Detroit, MI 48265
Website: http://www.gm.com
John F. Smith, Jr., CEO
*World's #1 maker of cars and
    trucks*

Genesis
9200 Sunset Blvd., #900
Los Angeles, CA 90069
Music group

Gentry, Bobbie
269 S. Beverly Dr., #368
Beverly Hills, CA 90212
Singer

Genuine Parts
2999 Circle 75 Pkwy.
Atlanta, GA 30339
Website: http://www.genpt.com
Larry L. Prince, Chairman and
    CEO
Wholesalers, automobile parts

George, Wally
14155 Magnolia Blvd., #127
Sherman Oaks, CA 91423
TV talk show host

Georgia-Pacific
133 Peachtree St. NE
Atlanta, GA 30303
Website: http://www.gp.com
A. D. Correll, Chairman,
    President, and CEO
Forest and paper products

Gerard, Gil
23679 Calabasas Rd., #325
Calabasas, CA 91302
Actor

Gere, Richard
22 W. 15th St.
New York, NY 10011
Actor

Germond, Jack
1627 K St., NW #1100
Washington, DC 20006
Newspaper columnist

Gerry and the Pacemakers
6 Ridge Rd.
Emerson, NJ 07630
Musical group

GeRue, Gene "Bumpy"
HC78, Box 1105
Zanoni, MO 65784
Website: http://
    www.ruralize.com
E-mail:
    genegerue@ruralize.com
Author of the books How to Find
    Your Ideal Country Home,
    Ruralize Your Dream

Getty, Estelle
10960 Wilshire Blvd., #2050
Los Angeles, CA 90024
Actress

International Ghost Hunters Society
12885 SW North Rim Rd.
Crooked River Ranch, OR 97760
Website: http://www.ghostweb.com/
E-mail: ghostweb@ghostweb.com
Rev. Dave Oester and Rev. Sharon Gill, Ghost Hunters
A worldwide paranormal research organization dedicated to the study of ghosts and poltergeists phenomena known as the spirits of the dead

Giant Food
6300 Sheriff Rd.
Landover, MD 20785
Richard Baird, Chairman, President, and CEO
Food and drug stores

Gibb, Barry
20505 US 19 North #12-290
Clearwater, FL 33624
Musician

Gibb, Maurice and Robin
20505 US 19 North #12-290
Clearwater, FL 33624
Musicians

Gibbons, Leeza
PO Box 4321
Los Angeles, CA 90068
Talk show host

Gibson, Don
PO Box 50474
Nashville, TN 37205
Country music singer

Gibson, Mel
4000 Warner Blvd., #139-17
Burbank, CA 91522
Actor
Birthday: 1/7/56

Gibson Miller Band
% Sherry Halton
PO Box 120964
Nashville, TN 37212
Country music group

Gifford, Frank
625 Madison Ave., #1200
New York, NY 10022
Sportscaster, four-time All Pro (1955–57, 59), NFL MVP in 1956; led NY Giants to three NFL title games, married to Kathy Lee Gifford
Birthday: 8/16/30

Gifford, Kathy Lee
625 Madison Ave., #1200
New York, NY 10022
TV host, married to Frank Gifford
Birthday: 8/16/53

Gilbert, Melissa
PO Box 57593
Sherman Oaks, CA 91403
Actress
Birthday: 5/8/64

Gill, Vince
PO Box 1407
White House, TN 37188
Country music singer
Birthday: 4/12/57

Gillette
Prudential Tower Building
Boston, MA 02199
Michael C. Hawley, Chairman
    and CEO
Edward F. DeGraan, President
    and COO
Metal products

Gilley, Mickey
PO Box 1242
Pasadena, TX 77501
Country music singer
Birthday: 3/9/36

Gilliam, Terry
The Old Hall
South Grove
Highgate
London N6
England
Comedian, actor, director
Birthday: 1/22/40

Gilmore, Jimmie Dale
% Main Grand Stand Prom.
122 Longwood Ave.
Austin, TX 78734
Country music singer.

Gimble, Johnny
PO Box 347
Dripping Springs, TX 78620
Country music singer

Gin Blossom
151 El Camino Dr.
Beverly Hills, CA 90212
Music group

Ginger Spice
35 Parkgate Rd., #32
Ransome Dock
London SW11 4NP
England
Singer, member of the Spice Girls

Ginsberg, Ruth Bader
700 New Hampshire Ave. NW
Washington, DC 20037
Supreme Court Justice

Ginsburg, Att. William
10100 Santa Monica Blvd.,
    #800
Los Angeles, CA 90067
*Former attorney for Monica
    Lewinsky*

Gipsy Kings
1460 4th. St. #205
Santa Monica, CA 90401
Music group

Girls Against Boys
PO Box 020426
Brooklyn, NY 11202
Music group

Givens, Robin
PO Box 118
Stone Ridge, NY 12484
*Actress, talk show host, former wife
    of Mike Tyson*

Goen, Bob
5555 Melrose Ave., #1
Los Angeles, CA 90038
Co-host of Entertainment Tonight

Goldberg, Whoopi
9171 Wilshire Blvd., #300
Beverly Hills, CA 90210
Comedian, actress, producer

Goldblum, Jeff
955 S. Carrillo Dr., #399
Los Angeles, CA 90048
Actor

Golden, William Lee
RR 2 Saundersville Rd.
Hendersonville, TN 37075
Country music singer

Goldens, The
PO Box 1795
Hendersonville, TN 37077
Country music group

Golden West Financial Corp.
1901 Harrison St.
Oakland, CA 94612
Herbert M. Sandler, Co-
    Chairman and Co-CEO
Marion Sandler, Co-Chairman
    and Co-CEO
Savings institution

Goldsboro, Bobby
PO Box 5250
Ocala, FL 32678
Country music singer

Goldwait, Bobcat
10061 Riverside Dr., #760
Toluca Lake, CA 91602
Comedian

Gonzales, Juan
% Texas Rangers
1000 Ballpark Way
Arlington, TX 76011
Baseball player

Goo Goo Dolls
129 Park St.
London W1Y 3SA
England
Music group

Goodall, Jane
PO Box 14890
Silver Spring, MD 20911
or
PO Box 41720
Tucson, AZ 85717
Website: http://
    www.janegoodall.org/
*Scientist known for her study of
    chimpanzies*
Birthday: 4/3/34

Gooding, Cuba, Jr.
1122 S. Robertson Blvd., #15
Los Angeles, CA 90035
Actor
Birthday: 1/2/68

Goodman, John
619 Amalfi Dr.
Pacific Palisades, CA 90272
Actor

Goodrich, Gail
% Basketball Hall of Fame
1150 W. Columbus Ave.
Springfield, MA 01101
Basketball player

Goodyear Tire and Rubber
1144 E. Market St.
Akron, OH 44316
Website: http://
    www.goodyear.com
Samir G. Gibara, Chairman,
    President and CEO
Rubber and plastic products

Gorbachev, Mikhail
49 Leningradsky prospekt 209
Moscow
Russia
Former head of the Soviet Union
Birthday: 3/2/31

Gore, Al
Admiral House
34th and Massachusetts Streets
Washington, DC 20005
Website: http://
    www.whitehouse.gov/WH/
    EOP/OVP/
    index-plain.html
E-mail: vice.president@
    whitehouse.gov
*Former Vice President of United
    States*
Birthday: 3/31/48

Gore, Tipper
Admiral House
34th and Massachusetts Streets
Washington, DC 20005
Website: http://
    www.whitehouse.gov/WH/
    EOP/VP-Wife/
*Wife of former Vice President Al
    Gore*
Birthday: 8/19/48

Gordeeva, Ekaterina
% Intl. Skating Ctr.
1375 Hopmeadow St.
Simsbury, CT 06070
Figure skater

Gorme, Eydie
10560 Wilshire Blvd., #601
Los Angeles, CA 90024
Singer

Gorshin, Frank
% Gor Publications
PO Box 17731
West Haven, CT 06516
or
11365 Ventura Blvd., #100
Studio City, CA 91604
Actor
Birthday: 4/5/34

Gosdin, Vern
2509 W. Marquette Ave.
Tampa, FL 33614
Country music singer

Gossett, Lou
8306 Wilshire Blvd., #438
Beverly Hills, CA 90211

GoTo.com
140 West Union St.
Pasadena, CA 91103
Jeffrey Brewer, CEO
Website: www.goto.com
E-mail: info@goto.com
Web portal

Gottfried, Gilbert
1350 Ave. of the Americas
New York, NY 10019
Comedian

Gotti, John
18261-053
Rt. 5
PO Box 2000
Marion, IL 62959
*"The Teflon Don"; convicted of
    murdering Paul Castellano,
    alleged boss of the Gambino
    Family and his driver,
    Thomas Bilotti*
Birthday: 10/27/40

Gowdy, Curt
Box 559
Salisbury, NC 28144
Sportscaster
Birthday: 7/31/19

GPU
300 Madison Ave.
Morristown, NJ 07962
Website: http://www.gpu.com
Fred D. Hafer, Chairman,
    President and CEO
Gas and electric utilities

Graceland
3765 Elvis Presley Blvd.
Memphis, TN 38116
or
PO Box 16508
Memphis, TN 38186
Website: http://www.elvis-
    presley.com/
E-mail: graceland@ixl
    memphis.com
Former home of Elvis Presley

Graf, Steffi
Mallaustr. 75
68219 Mannheim
Germany
Tennis player

Graham, Rev. Billy
PO Box 779
Minneapolis, MN 55440
Evangelist
Birthday: 11/7/18

Graham, Gerrit
8730 Sunset Blvd., #480
Los Angeles, CA 90069
Actor

Graham, Heather
9839 Wilshire Blvd.
Beverly Hills, CA 90212
Actress, model
Birthday: 1/29/70

Grammer, Kelsey
9560 Wilshire Blvd., #516
Beverly Hills, CA 90212
Actor
Birthday: 2/20/55

Grand Funk Railraod
1229 17th. Ave. South
Nashville, TN 37212
Music group

Granger, Farley
15 W. 72nd St.
New York, NY 10023
Actor
Birthday: 7/1/25

Grant, Amy
25 Music Square W.
Nashville, TN 37203
Singer
Birthday: 11/25/60

Grant, Hugh
76 Oxford St.
London W1N OAX
England
Actor

Grateful Dead
PO Box 1073-C
San Rafael, CA 94915
Music group

Graves, Peter
1122 S. Robertson Blvd., #15
Los Angeles, CA 90035
Actor

Gray, Erin
11288 Ventura Blvd.
Studio City, CA 91604
Actress

Gray, Linda
1680 N. Vine St., #617
Hollywood, CA 90028
Actress
Birthday: 9/12/41

Graybar Electric
34 N. Meramec Ave.
St. Louis, MO 63105
Carl L. Hall, President and
    CEO
Wholesaler

Gray Panthers
733 15th St. NW, Suite 437
Washington, DC 20005
Website: http://
    www.graypanthers.org/
E-mail: info@graypanthers.org
*Founded in 1970 by social activist
    Maggie Kuhn, Gray Panthers
    believe that all Americans
    should benefit from our
    country's abundance*

Great Plains
PO Box 2411
Murfreesboro, TN 37133
Country music group

Green Bay Packers, Inc.
Lombardi Ave.
Green Bay, WI 54304
Robert E. Harlan, President
    and CEO
Ron Wolf, EVP and General
    Manager
*A publically owned nonprofit
    corporation unlike any other
    football team*

Green, Al
PO Box 456
Millington, TN 38083
Singer, minister

Green Day
5337 College Ave., #555
Oakland, CA 94618
Music group

Greenpeace
702 H St. NW
Washington, DC 20001
Website: http://
    www.greenpeaceusa.org/
E-mail:
    info@wdc.greenpeace.org
Craig Culp, Greenpeace Media
    Coordinator
E-mail: Craig.Culp@wdc.
    greenpeace.org
Worldwide environmental group

The Greens/Green Party USA
PO Box 1134
Lawrence, MA 01842
Website: http://
    www.greenparty.org/
    page3.html
E-mail: andyg@greens.org
Tamara Trejo, Clearinghouse
    Coordinator
Environmental political party

Greenwood, Lee
PO Box 6537
Sevierville, TN 37864
Country music singer

Greer, Germaine
29 Fernshaw Rd.
London SW10 0TG
England
Feminist author
Birthday: 1/29/39

Gregg, Ricky Lynn
PO Box 8924
Bossier City, LA 71113
Country music singer

Gregory, Clinton
PO Box 707
Hermitage, TN 37076
Country music singer

Gretzky, Wayne
9100 Wilshire Blvd., #10000W
Beverly Hills, CA 90212
*Hockey player, 10-time NHL
    scoring champion; 9-time
    regular season MVP (1979–
    87, 89) and 9-time All-NHL
    first team*
Birthday: 1/26/61

Grey, Jennifer
91 Fifth Ave.
New York, NY 10003
Actress

Grey, Joel
141 Fifth Ave., #300
New York, NY 10011
Actor
Birthday: 4/11/32

Griese, Bob
% Pro Football Hall of Fame
2121 George Halas Dr. NW
Canton, OH 44708
Football player

Griffey, Ken, Jr.
PO Box 4100
Seattle, WA 98104
Baseball player

Griffin, Merv
9876 Wilshire Blvd.
Beverly Hills, CA 90210

Griffith, Andy
PO Box 1968
Manteo, NC 27954
or
9 Music Square S., #146
Nashville, TN 37203
Actor
Birthday: 6/2/26

Griffith, Melanie
3110 St., #205
Santa Monica, CA 90405
Actress
Birthday: 8/9/57

Griffith, Nanci
PO Box 128037
Nashville, TN 37212
Singer

Grimes, Dorothy
128 Roberts Rd.
Aston, PA 19014
Healer

Grisham, John
PO Box 1780
Oxford, MS 38655
Author

Gritz, Bo
% Talk America Radio
    Network
1455 East Tropicana, Suite 700
Las Vegas, NV 89119
*America's most decorated Green
    Beret*

Grizzard, Lewis
2951 Piedmont Rd. NE, #100
Atlanta, GA 30305
Country music singer

Groening, Matt
10201 West Pico Blvd.
Los Angeles, CA 90035
Creator and developer of The
      Simpsons
Birthday: 2/15/54

Gross, Michael
9200 Sunset Blvd., #900
Los Angeles, CA 90069
Actor

Guardian Life Insurance Co.
      of America
7 Hanover Sq.
New York, NY 10004
Joseph D. Sargent, President
      and CEO
Website: http://www.glic.com
Life and health insurance
      (mutual)

Guccione, Bob
2776 Park Ave.
New York, NY 10017
Magazine publisher

Guerrero, Roberto
PO Box 381
Clay, KY 42404
Race car driver

Guess Who
31 Hemlock Pl.
Winnepeg, Man
R2H 1LB
Canada
Music group

Guest, Christopher
PO Box 2358
Running Springs, CA 92382
or
9830 Wilshire Blvd.
Beverly Hills, CA 90212
Actor

Guidry, Ron
PO Box 278
Scott, LA 70583
Baseball player
Birthday: 8/28/50

Guisewite, Cathy
4900 Main St.
Kansas City, MO 64112
Comic strip creator

Gumbel, Bryant
524 W. 57th St.
New York, NY 10019
TV show host
Birthday: 9/29/48

Gumbel, Greg
524 W. 57th St.
New York, NY 10019
TV show host

Gun Owners of America
8001 Forbes Pl., Suite 102
Springfield, VA 22151
Website: http://
      www.gunowners.org/
E-mail:
      goamail@gunowners.org
Larry Pratt, Executive Director
Group devoted to protecting the
      Second Amendment

Guns N' Roses
83 Riverside Dr.
New York, NY 10024
Music group

Guthrie, Arlo
The Farm
Washington, MA 01223
Singer, songwriter
Birthday: 7/10/47

Guy, Jasmine
21243 Ventura Blvd., #101
Woodland Hills, CA 91364
Actress, dancer
Birthday: 3/10/64

Gwynn, Tony
% San Diego Padres
PO Box 2000
San Diego, CA 92112
Baseball player

News from home is best carried in a letter, and so much can be written on a little piece of paper. Inside the envelope can be sunshine or dark dismal days.

—HANS CHRISTIAN ANDERSON

Haas, Lukas
10683 Santa Monica Blvd.
Los Angeles, CA 90025
Actor
Birthday: 4/16/76

Hackman, Gene
118 S. Beverly Dr., #1201
Beverly Hills, CA 90212
Actor
Birthday: 1/30/30

Hagar, Sammy
Box 5395
Novato, CA 94948
Musician
Birthday: 10/13/47

Haggard, Merle
3009 Easy St.
Sevierville, TN 37862
Country music singer

Haig, Gen. Alexander M., Jr.
1155 15th St., NW, #800
Washington, DC 20005
Former Secretary of State

Haim, Corey
150 Carlton St., 2nd Floor
Toronto, Ontario
M5A 2K1 Canada
Actor
Birthday: 12/23/72

Häkkinen, Mika
% McLaren Int'l. Ltd.
Woking Business Park
Albert Dr.
Woking
GB-Surrey GU21 5JS
Professional Formula-1 driver
Birthday: 9/28/68

Halal, William E.
Dept. of Management Science
School of Business and Public
    Management
George Washington University
Washington, DC 20052
Website: http://
    gwis2.circ.gwu.edu/~halal/
E-mail: halal@gwu.edu
*Professor of management in the
    Department of Management
    Science at George Washington
    University*

Hale, Alan Spencer
5476 St. Paul Rd.
Morristown, TN 37813
Country music singer

Hale, Barbara
PO Box 6061-261
Sherman Oaks, CA 91413
Actress
Birthday: 2/18/21

Hall and Oates
9830 Wilshire Blvd.
Beverly Hills, CA 90212
Musical group

Hall, Arsenio
9560 Wilshire Blvd., #516
Beverly Hills, CA 90212
Actor, comedian

Hall, Monty
519 North Arden Dr.
Beverly Hills, CA 90210
TV game show host
Birthday: 8/25/24

Hall, Tom T.
PO Box 1246
Franklin, TN 37065
Country music singer

Halliburton
3600 Lincoln Plaza
Dallas, TX 75201
Website: http://
    www.halliburton.com
Richard B. Cheney, CEO
David J. Lesar, President and
    COO
*The world's number-one provider of
    oil field services*

Hamil, Dorothy
PO Box 16286
Baltimore, MD 21210
Former figure skater

Hamill, Mark
PO Box 55
Malibu, CA 90265
Actor
Birthday: 9/25/51

Hamilton, George
139 S. Beverly Dr., #330
Beverly Hills, CA 90212
Actor

Hamilton, George, IV
203 SW Third Ave.
Gainesville, FL 32601
Country music singer

Hamilton, Scott
20 First St.
Colorado Springs, CO 80909
Figure skater, sports commentator

Handgun Control, Inc.
1225 Eye St. NW, Suite 1100
Washington, DC 20005
Website: http://
    www.handguncontrol.org/
Sarah Brady, Chairman
Gun control organization

Hanks, Tom
PO Box 900
Beverly Hills, CA 90213
Actor

Hanna, William
4000 Warner Blvd.
Burbank, CA 91522
Animation executive

Hannaford Bros.
145 Pleasant Hill Rd.
Scarborough, ME 04074
Website: http://
     www.hannaford.com
Walter J. Salmon, Chairman
Hugh G. Farrington, President
     and CEO
Food and Drug Stores

Hannigan, Alyson
% *Buffy the Vampire Slayer*
4000 Warner Blvd.
Bldg. #34R
Burbank, CA 91522

Hanson Brothers
1045 W. 78th St.
Tulsa, OK 74132
Pop group brothers
Clarke Isaac Hanson
Birthday: 11/17/80
Jordan Taylor Hanson
Birthday: 3/14/83
Zachary Walker Hanson
Birthday: 10/22/85

Harcourt General
27 Boylston St.
Chestnut Hill, MA 02167
Website: http://
     www.harcourtgeneral.com
Richard A. Smith, CEO
Brian J. Knez, President and
     Co-CEO
General merchandisers

Hardaway, Anfernee
% Orlando Magic
One Magic Pl.
Orlando, FL 32801
Basketball player

Harding, Tonya
5113 NE 39th Ave.
Vancouver, WA 98661
Figure skater
Birthday: 11/12/70

Hargitay, Mariska
7920 Sunset Blvd., #400
Los Angeles, CA 90046
Actress

Harlem Globe Trotters
1000 S. Fremont Ave.
Alhambra, CA 91803
Basketball team

Harling, Keith
PO Box 1304
Goodlettsville, TN 37070
E-mail:
     fanclub@keithharling.com
Country music singer

Harmon, Angie
Pier 62
Hudson River and W. 23rd St.
New York, NY 10011
Actress

Harnischfeger Industries
3600 S. Lake Dr.
St. Francis, WI 53235
Website: http://
     www.harnischfeger.com
Robert B. Hoffman, Chairman
John N. Hanson, VC, CEO,
     President, and COO
Industrial and Farm Equipment

Harper, Tess
8484 Wilshire Blvd., #500
Beverly Hills, CA 90211
Actress
Birthday: 11/30/51

Harper, Valerie
PO Box 7187
Beverly Hills, CA 90212
Actress

Harrelson, Woody
16133 Ventura Blvd., #560
Encino, CA 91436
Actor

Harris
1025 W. NASA Blvd.
Melbourne, FL 32919
Website: http://www.harris.com
Phillip W. Farmer, Chairman,
    President, and CEO
Electronics, electrical equipment

Harris, Emmylou
PO Box 159007
Nashville, TN 37215
Singer
Birthday: 4/2/48

Harris, Mel
6300 Wilshire Blvd., #2110
Los Angeles, CA 90048
Actress

Harris, Neal Patrick
1122 S. Robertson Blvd., #15
Los Angeles, CA 90035
Actor
Birthday: 6/15/73

Harrison, A. J.
% Romaha Records
PO Box 823
Snellville, Georgia 30078
Website: http://www.aj-
    harrison.com/
E-mail: fan-mail@aj-
    harrison.com
Singer, actor, writer

Harrison, George
5 Park Rd.
Henley-on-Thames
RG9 1DB
England
Musician, former Beatle

Harry, Deborah
% William Morris Agency
1325 Avenue of the Americas
New York, NY 10019
Singer

Harry, HRH Prince
Highgrove House
Gloucestershire
England
Son of Prince Charles

Hart, Gary
950 17th St., #2050
Denver, CO 80202
*Former senator, former presidential
    candidate*

Freddie Hart and Heartbeats
% Tessier March Talent, Inc.
505 Canton Pass
Madison, TN 37115
Country music group

Hart, Mary
9000 Sunset Blvd., #16
Los Angeles, CA 90069
TV hostess
Birthday: 11/8/51

Hart, Melissa Joan
10880 Wilshire Blvd., #1101
Los Angeles, CA 90024
Actress

Hartford Financial Services
Hartford Plaza
Hartford, CT 06115
Website: http://
    www.thehartford.com
Ramani Ayer, CEO
P & C insurance (stock)

Harvey, Steve
9100 Wilshire Blvd., #700 E.
    Tower
Beverly Hills, CA 90212
Actor

Hasbro
1027 Newport Ave.
Pawtucket, RI 02862
Website: http://
    www.hasbro.com
Alan G. Hassenfeld, Chairman
    and CEO
*The number-two toy maker in the
    United States*

Hatch, Richard
3349 Cahuenga Blvd. W
Los Angeles, CA 90068
Actor

Hatcher, Teri
10100 Santa Monica Blvd.,
    #410
Los Angeles, CA 90067
Actress

Hauer, Rutger
9560 Wilshire Blvd., #516
Beverly Hills, CA 90212
Actor

Haven, Annette
PO Box 1244
Sausalito, CA 94966
Porn star

Havens, Ritchie
223 E 48th St.
New York, NY 10017
Musician

Hawking, Professor Stephen
University of Cambridge
Applied Math Department
Cambridge
CB3 9EW
England
E-mail S. W.Hawking@
    damtp.cam.ac.uk
*Stephen Hawking is perhaps best
    known for his discovery, in
    1974, that black holes emit
    radiation. Stephen Hawking
    has two popular books
    published; his best-seller* A
    Brief History of Time, *and
    his later book,* Black Holes
    and Baby Universes and
    Other Essays
Birthday: 1/8/42

Hawn, Goldie
955 S. Carrillo Dr., #200
Los Angeles, CA 90048
Actress
Birthday: 11/2/45

Hayden, Tom
10951 W. Pico Blvd., #202
Los Angeles, CA 90064
Politican

Hayek, Salma
PO Box 57593
Sherman Oaks, CA 91403
Actress

Hayes, Isaac
2635 Griffith Park Blvd.
Los Angeles, CA 90039
Singer
Birthday: 8/20/42

Hayes, Wade
PO Box 128546
Nashville, TN 37212

Rita Hayworth Fan Club
3943 York Ave. South
Minneapolis, MN 55410

Heft, Bob
PO Box 131
Napoleon, OH 43545
Designed the 50-star U.S. flag

H. J. Heinz
600 Grant St.
Pittsburgh, PA 15219
Anthony J. F. O'Reilly, CEO
William R. Johnson, President
   and CEO
Food producer

**The H. John Heinz III Center
   for Science, Economics,
   and the Environment**
1001 Pennsylvania Ave., NW
   Suite 735 South
Washington, DC 20004
Website: http://
   www.heinzctr.org/
E-mail: info@heinzctr.org
G. William Miller, Chairman,
   Board of Trustees
*Nonprofit organization devoted to
   collaborative research on
   environmental problems, its
   mission is to create and
   disseminate nonpartisan policy
   options for solving
   environmental problems*

**Health Care Finance
   Administration**
7500 Security Blvd.
Baltimore, MD 21244
Website: http://www.hcfa.gov/
E-mail: Question@hcfa.gov
Nancy-Ann Min DeParle,
   Administrator
*The federal agency that
   administers the Medicare,
   Medicaid and Child Health
   Insurance Programs*

**Health Insurance Association
   of America**
555 13th St. NW #600E
Washington, DC 20004
Website: http://www.hiaa.org/
E-mail: webmaster@hiaa.org
Charles N. Kahn, President
*A national trade association based
   in Washington, DC, its more
   than 250 members are
   insurers and managed care
   companies that serve tens of
   millions of Americans*

HealthSouth
1 HealthSouth Pkwy.
Birmingham, AL 35243
Website: http://
   www.healthsouth.com
E-mail: info@healthsouth.net
Richard M. Scrushy, Chairman
   and CEO
Health Care

Heart
9220 Sunset Blvd., #900
Los Angeles, CA 90069
Music group

Heche, Anne
10960 Wilshire Blvd., #1100
Los Angeles, CA 90024
Actress

Hedren, Tippi
Box 189
Acton, CA 93510
Actress, animal activist

Hee Haw
PO Box 140400
Nashville, TN 38214
Television show

Hefner, Christie
680 N. Lake Shore Dr.
Chicago, IL 60611
*Chairman and CEO of Playboy
    Enterprises*

Hefner, Hugh
680 N. Lake Shore Dr.
Chicago, IL 60611
*Founder, Chairman Emeritus, and
    Editor-in-Chief of Playboy
    magazine*

Helm, Levon
315 S. Beverly Dr., #206
Beverly Hills, CA 90212
Musician

Helms, Bobby
% Tessier March Talent, Inc.
505 Canton Pass
Madison, TN 37115
Country music singer

Heloise
PO Box 795000
San Antonio, TX 78279
Newspaper columnist, author

Hemingway, Mariel
Box 2249
Ketchum, ID 83340
*Actress, grandaughter of Ernest
    Hemingway*

Hemlock Society USA
PO Box 101810
Denver, CO 80250
Website: http://
    www.hemlock.org/hemlock/
E-mail: hemlock@privatei.com
Faye Girsh, President
A right-to-die organization

Hemsley, Sherman
PO Box 5344
Sherman Oaks, CA 91413
Actor

Henderson, Florence
Box 11295
Marina del Rey, CA 90295
Actress

Henderson, Tareva
PO Box 17303
Nashville, TN 37217
Country music singer

Hendricks, Ted
% Pro Football Hall of Fame
2121 George Halas Dr. NW
Canton, OH 44708
Football player

Henley, Don
3500 W. Olive Ave., #1400
Burbank, CA 91505
Musician

Henry, Buckl
117 E. 57th St.
New York, NY 10019
Actor, writer

Herman, Pee Wee
PO 29373
Los Angeles, CA 90029
Actor, comedian

Herman's Hermits
11761 E. Speedway Blvd.
Tucson, AZ 85748
Music group

Herndon and Friends, Ty
% Leigh Ritsema
PO Box 120658
Nashville, TN 37212
Country music group

Hershey, Barbara
% CAA
9830 Wilshire Blvd.
Beverly Hills, CA 90212
Actress
Birthday: 2/5/48

Hershey Foods
100 Crystal A Dr.
Hershey, PA 17033
Website: http://
    www.hersheys.com
Kenneth L. Wolfe, Chairman
    and CEO
*Food producer, chocolate maker,
    and the market leader in the
    U.S. candy business*

Herzigova, Eva
20 West 20th St., #600
New York, NY 10011
Supermodel
Birthday: 3/10/73

Hewitt, Jennifer Love
151 El Camino Dr.
Beverly Hills, CA 90212
Actress, dancer, singer
Birthday: 2/21/79

Hewlett Packard
3000 Hanover St.
Palo Alto, CA 94304
Website: http://www.hp.com
Richard A. Hackborn,
    Chairman
Carleton S. "Carly" Fiorina
    CEO and President
Computers, office equipment

Heyerdahl, Thor
E-38500 Guimar
Tenerife
Spain
Anthropologist, adventurer, author
Birthday: 10/6/14

H. F. Amhanson
225 S. Main Ave.
Sioux Falls, SD 57104
Website: http://
    www.homesavings.com/
Curtis L. Hage, Chairman,
    President, and CEO
Savings institution

Hickman, Dwayne
PO Box 3352
Santa Monica, CA 90403
Website: http://
    www.dobietv.com/
E-mail: dwayne@dobieart.com
Actor, artist, author

Hicks, Catherine
1122 S. Robertson Blvd., #15
Los Angeles, CA 90035
Actress

High Frontier, Inc.
2800 Shirlington Rd., #405A
Arlington, VA 22206
Website: http://
    www.highfrontier.org/
E-mail: hifront@erols.com
Ambassador Henry F. (Hank)
    Cooper, Chairman of the
    Board
*Its mission is "to ensure the nation
    is protected against ballistic
    missile attack"*

Highway 101
PO Box 1547
Goodlettsville, TN 37050
Country music group

Hilfiger, Tommy
25 W. 39th. St., #1300
New York, NY 10018
Website: http: //
    www.tommypr.com/
    index1.jhtml
Fashion designer
Birthday: 1952

Hill, Dr. Anita
300 Timberdell Rd.
Norman, OK 73109
*Attorney, author, witness in the
    Thomas Clarence confirmation
    hearings*

**Hill, Faith (Audrey Faith Perry
    Hill)**
3310 West End Ave., #500
Nashville, TN 37203
Website: http://www.faith-
    hill.com/
Singer
Birthday: 9/21/67

Hill, Kim
% Blanton Harrell
2910 Poston Ave.
Nashville, TN 37203
Country music singer

Hill, Lauryn
151 El Camino Dr.
Beverly Hills, CA 90212
Singer

Hillary, Sir Edmund (Percival)
278A Remuera Rd.
Auckland SE 2
New Zealand
*Mountain climber and Antarctic
    explorer, who, with Tenzing
    Norgay, a Sherpa from Nepal,
    was the first to reach the
    summit of Mount Everest, the
    world's highest peak*
Birthday: 7/20/19

Hillerman, John
PO Box 218
Blue Jay, CA 92317
Actor

Hilton Hotels
9336 Civic Center Dr.
Beverly Hills, CA 90210
Website: http://www.hilton.com
Barron Hilton, Chairman
Stephen F. Bollenbach,
    President and CEO
Hotels, casinos, resorts

Hinckley, John, Jr.
2700 Martin Luther King Ave.
Washington, DC 20005
*Attempted to assassinate President
    Ronald Reagan*
Birthday: 5/29/55

Hines, Gregory
377 W. 11th St., #PH-4
New York, NY 10014
or
4009 Ocean Front Walk
Venice, CA 90292
Dancer, actor
Birthday: 2/14/46

Hiroshima
1460 4th. St., #205
Santa Monica, CA 90401
Music group

Hirsch, Judd
137 W. 12th St.
New York, NY 10011
Actor

Hirschfield, Al
122 E. 95th. St.
New York, NY 10028
Caricaturist who always hides his
daughter's name, Nina, in his
drawings. You can usually
find NINA in the subject's
hair or sleeves.
Birthday: 6/21/03

Hispanic Policy Development
Project
1001 Connecticut Ave., NW,
Suite 310
Washington, DC 20036
E-mail: jlgar@erols.com
Mildred Garcia, Vice President,
Training and
Administration
Seeks to correct what the project
calls the long-standing neglect
of the Hispanic population;
address and arouse public
interest in Hispanic concerns
including employment and
secondary education; improve
communications among
Hispanics and non-Hispanics

Hite, Shere
PO Box 1037
New York, NY 10028
Author

Hobbs, Becky
PO Box 121974
Nashville, TN 37212
Country music singer

Hockney, David
2029 Century Park E., #300
Los Angeles, CA 90067
Artist

Hogan, Paul
515 N. Robertson Blvd.
Los Angeles, CA 90048
Actor

Holbrook, Hal
9200 Sunset Blvd., #1130
Los Angeles, CA 90069
Actor

Holden, Rebecca
PO Box 23504
Nashville, TN 37202
Country music singer

William Holden Wildlife
Foundation
PO Box 67981
Los Angeles, CA 90067
Website: http://www.whwf.org/
E-mail: mail@whwf.org
Goal is to awaken an awareness
and understanding of the
balance of nature and the
vital role the animals play in
the environmental network

Hole
955 S. Carrillo Dr., #200
Los Angeles, CA 90048
Music group

Hollander, Xaviera
Stadionweg 17
1077 RU Amsterdam
Holland
Website: http://
    www.xaviera.com/
"The Happy Hooker"

Holly, Buddy, Memorial
    Society
PO Box 6123
Lubbock, TX 79413

Holly, Lauren
955 S. Carrillo Dr., #300
Los Angeles, CA 90048
Actress
Birthday: 10/28/63

Holly, Mrs. Buddy (Maria
    Diaz)
PO Box 6123
Lubbock, TX 79493
Buddy Holly's widow

Hollywood Reporter
5055 Wilshire Blvd., 6th Floor
Los Angeles, CA 90036
Website: http://
www.hollywoodreporter.com/
George Christy, columnist
Trade newspaper for movie and
    television professionals

Hollywood Stock Exchange
225 Arizona Ave., #250
Santa Monica, CA 90401
Max Keiser, Co-Founder and
    Chairman
Website: www.hsx.com
E-mail: max@hsx.com
Internet content provider

Holmes, Larry
91 Larry Holmes Dr., #101
Aston, PA 18042
Boxer
Birthday: 11/3/49

Home Depot
2455 Paces Ferry Rd. NW
Atlanta, GA 30339
Website: http://
    www.homedepot.com
Arthur Blank, President and
    CEO
Specialist hardware retailers

Homestore.com
225 W. Hillcrest Dr., Suite 100
Thousand Oaks, CA 91360
Stuart H. Wolff, Chairman and
    CEO
Website: http://
    www.homestore.com
E-mail: webmaster@
    homestore.com

Honeywell
101 Columbia Rd., PO Box
    2245
Morristown, NJ 07962-2245
Website: http://
    www.honeywell.com
Michael R. Bonsignore,
Chairman and CEO
Scientific, photo, control equipment

Hooker, John Land
PO Box 170429
San Francisco, CA 94117
Musician

Hooters, Heather
536 Romance Rd. #90
Portage, MI 49002
Porn star

Hootie and the Blowfish
PO Box 5656
Columbia, SC 29250
Musical group

Hoover Institution
Stanford University,
Palo Alto, CA 94305
Website: http://www.hoover.
  org/
Peyton M. Lake, Chairman
Peter B. Bedford, Vice
  Chairman
*The principles of individual,
economic, and political
freedom; private enterprise;
and representative government
were fundamental to the
vision of the Institution's
founder. By collecting
knowledge, generating ideas,
and disseminating both, the
Institution seeks to secure and
safeguard peace, improve the
human condition, and limit
government intrusion into the
lives of individuals.*

Hope, Bob
10346 Moorpark
North Hollywood, CA 91602
Comedian, actor

Hopkins, Sir Anthony
15250 Ventura Blvd., #710
Sherman Oaks, CA 91403
Actor

Hopper, Dennis
℅ Creative Artists Agency
9830 Wilshire Blvd.
Beverly Hills, CA 90212
Actor, director

Hormel Foods
1 Hormel Place
Austin, MN 55912
Website: http://
  www.hormel.com
Joel W. Johnson, Chairman,
  President, and CEO
Food maker

Horne, Lena
23 E. 74th. St., #5A
New York, NY 100221
Singer

Hornsby, Bruce
Box 3545
Williamsburg, VA 23187
Musician

Horowitz, David
PO Box 49915
Los Angeles, CA 90049
Consumer activist

Horton, Peter
9560 Wilshire Blvd., #500
Beverly Hills, CA 90212
Actor, director, producer
Birthday: 8/20/53

Hoskins, Bob
200 Fulham Rd.
London SW10 9PN
England
Actor

Household Financial
2700 Sanders Rd.
Prospect Heights, IL 60070
Website: http://
    www.household.com
William F. Aldinger III,
    Chairman and CEO
Diversified Financials

House of Pain
151 El Camino Dr.
Beverly Hills, CA 90212
Music group

Howard, Jan
Grand Ole Opry
2804 Opryland Dr.
Nashville, TN 37214
Country music singer

Howard, Jayne
PO Box 95
Upperco, MD 21155
Author

Howard, Ron
9465 Wilshire Blvd., #700
Beverly Hills, CA 90212
Director
Birthday: 3/1/54

Huddleston, David
3518 Cahuenga Blvd. W., #216
Los Angeles, CA 90068
Actor

Hudson Brothers
151 El Camino Dr.
Beverly Hills, CA 90212
Music group

Hudson Institute
Indianapolis Headquarters
Herman Kahn Center
5395 Emerson Way
Indianapolis, IN 46226
John Clark, Ph.D., Senior
    Research Fellow and
    Director, Center for
    Central European and
    Eurasian Studies
or
Washington, DC Office
1015 18th St., NW Suite 300
Washington, DC 20036
Website: http://
    www.hudson.org/
Robert Dujarric, Research
    Fellow National Security
    Issues
*A private, not-for-profit research
    organization founded in 1961
    by the late Herman Kahn, it
    analyzes and makes
    recommendations about public
    policy for business and
    government executives and for
    the public at large*

Huffington, Arianna
1250 H St. NW #550
Washington, DC 20005
Political commentator, author

Hulce, Tom
175 5th Ave., #2409
New York, NY 10010
Actor
Birthday: 12/6/53

Human Rights Campaign
1101 14th St. NW, #200
Washington, DC 20005
Website: http://www.hrcusa.
org/
E-mail: hrc@hrc.org
Catherine Reno Brouillet,
Director
E-mail: HRCptown@mind
spring.com
*The largest full-time lobbying team
in the nation devoted to issues
of fairness for lesbian and gay
Americans*

Humana
500 W. Main St.
Louisville, KY 40201
Website: http://
www.humana.com
David A. Jones, Chairman
David A. Jones, Jr., VC
Michael B. McCallister,
President and CEO
Health Care

Humperdinck, Engelbert
PO Box 5734
Beverly Hills, CA 90209
Singer
Birthday: 5/2/36

Hunt, Dave
PO Box 7019
Bend, OR 97708
Religious author

Hunt, Helen
9830 Wilshire Blvd.
Beverly Hills, CA 90212
Actress
Birthday: 6/15/63

Hunt, Linda
% WMA
1325 Ave. of the Americas
New York, NY 10019
Actress
Birthday: 4/2/45

Hunter, Holly
9460 Wilshire Blvd. 7th. Floor
Beverly Hills, CA 90212
or
% ICM
8942 Wilshire Blvd.
Beverly Hills, CA 90211
Actress
Birthday: 3/20/58

Hunter, Rachael
1122 S. Robertson Blvd., #15
Los Angeles, CA 90035
Supermodel

Hunter, Tommy
2806 Opryland Dr.
Nashville, TN 37214
Country music singer

Hurley, Elizabeth
3 Cromwell Pl.
London SW7 2JE
England
or
% United Talent Agency
9560 Wilshire Blvd., Suite 500
Beverly Hills, CA 90212
Actress

Hurt, William
151 El Camino Dr.
Beverly Hills, CA 90212
Actor

Husky, Ferlin
38 Music Square East
Nashville, TN 37203
Country music singer
Birthday: 12/3/25

Hussein, President Saddam
Office of the President
Baghdad,
Iraq

Hussey, Olivia
PO Box 2131
Crestline, CA 92008

Hutton, Lauren
382 Lafayette St., #6
New York, NY 10003
Model, actress

Hutton, Sylvia
PO Box 158467
Nashville, TN 37215
Country music singer

Hutton, Timothy
RR #2
Box 3318
Cushman Rd.
Patterson, NY 12563
Actor

Hyland, Brian
PO Box 101
Helendale, CA 92342
Musician

Hynde, Chrissie
30 Ives St.
GB-London SW3 2ND
England
Singer
Birthday: 9/7/51

I

Persons do not become a society by living in physical proximity, any more than a man ceases to be socially influenced by being so many feet or miles removed from others. A letter may institute a more intimate association between human beings separated thousands of miles from each other than exists between dwellers under the same roof.

—JOHN DEWEY

IBP
800 Stevens Port Drive
Dakota Dunes, SD 57049
Website: http://
    www.ibpinc.com
Robert L. Peterson, Chairman
    and CEO
Richard L. Bond, President
    and COO
Food producer

Ice-T
2287 Sunset Plaza Dr.
Los Angeles, CA 90069
Rapper, actor
Birthday: 2/16/58

Idealab
130 W. Union St.
Pasadena, CA 91103
Website: www.idealab.com
E-mail: info@idealab.com
Bill Gross, Chairman and
    Founder
Venture capital

Idol, Billy
7314 Woodrow Wilson Dr.
Los Angeles, CA 90046
Singer

iFilm Network
400 Pacific Ave. 3rd. Floor
San Francisco, CA 94133
Website: www.ifilm.net
Rodger Radereman, Co-
    Chairman and Founder
E-mail: rodger@ifilm.net
Online film community

Ikon Office Solutions
70 Valley Stream Pkwy.
Valley Forge, PA 19482
Website: http://www.ikon.com
James J. Forese, Chairman,
    President, and CEO
Wholesalers

Illinois Tool Works
3600 W. Lake Ave.
Glenview, IL 60025
Website: http://www.itwinc.com
W. James Farrell, CEO
Metal products

Iman
180–182 Tottingham Ct. Rd.
London W1P9LE
England
Singer, model, wife of David Bowie
Birthday: 7/25/55

IMC Global
2100 Sanders Rd.
Northbrook, IL 60062
Website: http://
    www.imcglobal.com
Joseph P. Sullivan, Chairman
Douglas A. Pertz, President
    and CEO
Chemicals, fertilizer

Imus, Don
34-12 36th St.
Astoria, NY 11106
Radio personality

Indigo Girls
315 Ponce De Leon Ave., #755
Decatur, GA 30030
Music group

**Information Infrastructure
    Project**
Science, Technology and
    Public Policy Program
John F. Kennedy School of
    Government
Harvard University
79 John F. Kennedy St.
Cambridge, MA 02138

Ingersoll-Rand
200 Chestnut Ridge Rd.
Woodcliff Lake, NJ 07675
Website: http://www.ingersoll-
    rand.com
Herbert L. Henkel, Chairman,
    President, and CEO
Industrial and farm equipment

Ingle, John
% *General Hospital*
ABC-TV
4151 Prospect Ave.
Los Angeles, CA 90027
Soap opera star

Ingels, Marty
Suite One Prod.
8127 Melrose Ave., #1
Los Angeles, CA 90046
Actor

Ingram Micro
1600 E. St. Andrew Place
Santa Ana, CA 92705
Website: http://
    www.ingrammicro.com
Jerre L. Stead, Chairman
Kent B. Foster, President and
    CEO
*Wholesalers of computer technology
    products and service*

Ink Spots, The
5100 DuPont Blvd, #10A
Ft. Lauderdale, FL 33308
Music group

**Institute for Contemporary
    Studies**
Latham Square
1611 Telegraph Ave., Suite 902
Oakland, CA 94612
Website: http://
    www.icspress.com
Robert B. Hawkins, Jr.,
    President and CEO
*A nonprofit, nonpartisan policy
    research institute promoting
    self-governance and
    entrepreneurial ways of life*

**Institute for Food and
    Development Policy**
398 60th St.
Oakland, CA 94618
Website: http://
    www.foodfirst.org/
E-mail: foodfirst@igc.apc.org
Peter Rosset, Ph.D., Executive
    Director
*Purpose is to eliminate the
    injustices that cause hunger*

Institute for Humane Studies (IHS)
at George Mason University
3401 N. Fairfax Dr.
Arlington, VA 22201
Website: http://
osf1.gmu.edu~ihs/
Email: ihs@gmu.edu
Damon Chetson, Program
Director
Paul Edwards, Vice President
of Academic Affairs
*A unique organization that assists
undergraduate and graduate
students who have a special
interest in individual liberty*

Institute for International Economics
11 DuPont Circle NW, #620
Washington, DC 20036
Website: http://www.iie.com/
E-mail: bcoulton@iie.com,
alreeves@iie.com, or
anelson@iie.com
C. Fred Bergsten, Director
*A private, nonprofit, nonpartisan
research institution devoted to
the study of international
economic policy*

Institute for Policy Studies
733 15th St. NW, Suite 1020
Washington, DC 20005
Website: http://www.ips-dc.org/
E-mail: scott@hotsalsa.org
Richard J. Barnet, Co-Founder,
former Co-Director, and
current Fellow
E-mail: arbarnet@dwu.edu
*Nonprofit, nonpartisan research
and public education
organization dedicated to
educating the public on the
need and the means for an
orderly transfer of military
resources to civilian use*

Institute for Women's Policy Research
1707 L St., NW, Suite 750
Washington, DC 20036
Website: http://www.iwpr.org/
E-mail: iwpr@iwpr.org
Heidi Hartmann, Ph.D.,
Director and President
E-mail: hartmann@iwpr.org
*An independent, nonprofit,
scientific research organization
incorporated in the District of
Columbia, established in 1987
to rectify the limited
availability of policy relevant
research on women's lives and
to inform and stimulate debate
on issues of critical
importance for women*

Intel
2200 Mission College Blvd.
Santa Clara, CA 95052-8119
Website:www.intel.com
Gordon E. Moore, Chairman
Emeritus
Andrew S. Grove, Chairman
Craig R. Barrett, President and
CEO
*Computer peripherals and chip
maker*

International Business Machines
Old Orchard Rd.
Armonk, NY 10504
Louis V Gerstner, Chairman
and CEO
Website: http://www.ibm.com
Maker of computer systems

International Paper
2 Manhattanville Rd.
Purchase, NY 10577
Website: http://
   www.ipaper.com
John T. Dillon, Chairman and
   CEO
Forest and paper products

International Society for Individual Liberty (ISIL)
836-B Southampton Rd., #299
Benicia, CA 94510
Website: http://
   www.seventhquest.net/
   isil.org/
E-mail: isil@isil.org
Mary Lou Gutscher, ISIL 2000
   Conference Coordinator
*An association of individuals and
   organizations with members in
   over 80 countries dedicated to
   building a free and peaceful
   world, respect for individual
   rights and liberties, and an
   open and competitive economic
   system based on voluntary
   exchange and free trade*

International Society for Technology in Education (ISTE)
480 Charnelton St.
Eugene, OR 97401
Website: http://www.iste.org/
E-mail: iste@iste.org
Dr. David Moursund, Executive
   Director for Research and
   Development
*The largest teacher-based, nonprofit
   organization in the field of
   educational technology, its
   mission is to help K–12
   classroom teachers and
   administrators share effective
   methods for enhancing student
   learning through the use of
   new classroom technologies*

International Women's Health Coalition
24 E. 21st St.
New York, NY 10010
Website: http://www.iwhc.org/
E-mail: info@iwhc.org
Adrienne Germain, President
*A nonprofit organization based in
   New York City that works
   with individuals and groups
   in Africa, Asia, and Latin
   America to promote women's
   reproductive and sexual health
   and rights*

Interpublic Group
1271 Ave. of the Americas
New York, NY 10020
Website: http://
   www.interpublic.com
Philip H. Geier, Jr., Chairman
   and CEO
John J. Dooner, Jr., President
   and COO
Advertising, marketing

Interstate Bakeries
12 E. Armour Blvd.
Kansas City, MO 64111
Charles A. Sullivan, CEO
Michael D. Kafoure, President
   and COO
Food producers

Intertainer
10950 Washington Blvd.
Culver City, CA 90232
Website: www.intertainer.com
Richard Baskin, Co-Chairman
   and CEO
E-mail: rb@intertainer.com
Jonathan Taplan, Co-Chairman
   and CEP
E-mail: tap@intertainer.com
Web portal

Investigative Reporters and Editors (IRE)
UMC School of Journalism/
26A
University of Missouri
Columbia, MO 65211
Website: http://www.ire.org
E-mail: jourire@muccmail.
missouri.edu
Rosemary Armao, Executive
Director
E-mail: r2croak@aol.com
A grassroots nonprofit organization dedicated to improving the quality of investigative reporting within the field of journalism

Intervu
6815 Flanders Dr., Suite 200
San Diego, CA 92121
Harry Gruber, CEO, Co-
Founder, and Chairman
Website: www.intervu.net
E-mail: info@intervu.net
Internet technology provider

INXS
8 Hayes St., #1
Neutray Bay NSW 20891
Australia
Music group

IProNetwork
12807 Borden Ave.
Sylmar, CA 91342
Don Baarns, President
Website: www.ipronetwork.com
E-mail:
dbaarns@pronetwork.org
Internet professionals organization

Ireland, Kathy
1122 S. Robertson Blvd, #15
Los Angeles, CA 90035
Model/actress

Irish Rovers, The
179 John St., #400
Toronto
Ontario M5T 1X4
Canada

Iron Butterfly
6400 Pleasant Park Dr.
Chanhassen, MN 55317
Music group

Iron Maiden
1775 Broadway, #433
New York, NY 10019
Music group

Irons, Jeremy
200 Fulham Rd.
London SW10 9PN
England
Actor

Irving, Amy
7920 Sunset Blvd., #401
Los Angeles, CA 90046
Actress

Irwin, Tom
PO Box 5617
Beverly Hills, CA 90210
Actor and founding member of the acclaimed Chicago-based Steppenwolf Theater Company

Isley Brothers
42209 Montieth Dr.
Los Angeles, CA 90043
Music group

Ito, Judge Lance A.
Criminal Courts Building
210 W. Temple St., #M-6
Los Angeles, CA 90012
*Judge who presided over the O. J.
Simpson trial.*

ITT Industries
4 W. Red Oak Lane
White Plains, NY 10604
Website: http://www.ittind.com
D. Travis Engen, Chairman
and CEO
*Pipeline of products includes
pumps, defense systems, and
services, specialty products,
and connectors and switches*

Ivey, Judith
11500 W. Olympic Blvd., #510
Los Angeles, CA 90046
Actress
Birthday: 9/4/51

**Izaak Walton League of
America**
707 Conservation Lane
Gaithersburg, MD 20878
Website: http://www.iwla.org/
E-mail: general@iwla.org
Paul Hansen, Executive
Director
*One of the oldest conservation
organizations in the United
States*

Whatever happens to us in our lives, we find questions recurring that we would gladly discuss with some friend. Yet it is hard to find just the friend we should talk to. Often it is easier to *write* to someone whom we do not expect to ever see.

—ELEANOR ROOSEVELT

Jackson, Alan
1101 17th. Ave. So.
Nashville, TN 37212
Country music singer
Birthday: 10/17/?

Jackson, Bo
PO Box 158
Mobile, AL 36601
Professional baseball and football player

Jackson, Glenda
51 Harvey Rd.
London SE3
England
Actress
Birthday: 5/9/36

Jackson, Janet
9830 Wilshire Blvd.
Beverly Hills, CA 90212
Singer, actress
Birthday: 5/16/66

Jackson, Jeremy
% Mary Grady Agency
4444 Lankershim Blvd., #207
North Hollywood, CA 91602
Actor
Birthday: 10/16/80

Jackson, Rev. Jesse
400 I St., NW
Washington, DC 20001
Political activist
Birthday: 10/8/41

Jackson, Jonathan
9830 Wilshire Blvd.
Beverly Hills, CA 90212
Actor

Jackson, Kate
PO Box 57593
Sherman Oaks, CA 91403
Actress

Jackson, Michael
Neverland Ranch
Los Olivos, CA 93441
or
% The Firm
9100 Wilshire Blvd., Suite. 400 West
Beverly Hills, CA 90212
Singer, actor, songwriter
Birthday: 8/29/58

Jackson, Stonewall
PO Box 463
McMinnville, TN 37110
Country music singer

Jagger, Bianca
530 Park Ave., #18D
New York, NY 10021
Actress, former wife of Mick Jagger
Birthday: 5/2/45

Jagger, Mick
304 W. 81st St.
New York, NY 10024
Singer, songwriter

James, Art
11365 Ventura Blvd., #100
Studio City, CA 91604
Website: http://
        www.corpgameshow.com/
E-mail: artjames@
        corpgameshow.com
TV host

James, Brian
PO Box 1207
Pineville, WV 24874
Country music singer

James, Dalton
303 N. Buena Vista, #209
Burbank, CA 91505
Actor
Birthday: 3/19/71

James, Sonny
818 18th Ave. South
Nashville, TN 37212
Country music singer

Jan and Dean
1720 N. Ross St.
Santa Ana, CA 92706
Music duo

Jane's Addiction
532 Colorado Ave.
Santa Monica, CA 90401
Music group

**Japanese American Citizens
    League (JACL)**
1765 Sutter St.
San Francisco, CA 94065
Website: http://www.jacl.org/
E-mail: jacl@jacl.org
S. Floyd Mori, National
    President
E-mail: president@jacl.org
*Founded in 1929 to fight
    discrimination against people
    of Japanese ancestry, it is the
    largest and one of the oldest
    Asian-American organizations
    in the United States*

Jardine, Al
Box 39
Big Sur, CA 93920
Musician

Jarreau, Al
9830 Wilshire Blvd.
Beverly Hills, CA 90212
Singer

Jarrett, Keith
PO Box 2728
Bala Cynwyd, PA 19004
Musician

Jay and the Americans
1045 Pomme De Pin Dr.
New Port Ritchey, FL 34655
Music group

Jazzy Jeff and the Fresh Prince
298 Elizabeth St.
New York, NY 10012
Music group

J. C. Penney
6501 Legacy Dr.
Plano, TX 75024
Website: http://
    www.jcpenney.com
James E. Oesterreicher,
    Chairman and CEO
General merchandisers

Jean, Norma
1300 Division St.
Nashville, TN 37203
Country music singer

Jefferson Center Citizens Jury
1111 Third Ave. S., #364
Minneapolis, MN 55404
Website:http://www.jefferson_
    center.org/citizensjury.htm
E-mail: mail@jefferson-
    center.org
A comprehensive tool that allows
    decision makers to hear
    thoughtful citizen input, it is
    designed to allow decision-
    makers to hear the people's
    authentic voice

Jefferson Starship
PO Box 1821
Ojai, CA 93024
Music group

Jenner, Bruce
PO Box 11137
Beverly Hills, CA 90213
Olympic track and field medalist
Birthday: 10/28/49

Jennings, Peter
7 W. 66th St.
New York, NY 10023
News Anchor
Birthday: 7/29/38

Jennings, Waylon
824 Old Hickory Blvd.
Brentwood, TN 37027
Country music singer
Birthday: 6/15/37

Jeter, Derek
% New York Yankees
Yankee Stadium
161 St. and River Ave.
Bronx, NY 10451
Baseball player

Jethro Tull
43 Brook Green
London W6 7EF
England
Music group

Jetsons, The
3400 Cahuenga Blvd.
Los Angeles, CA 90068
Cartoon family

Jett, Joan
155 E. 55th St., #6H
New York, NY 10022
Musician

Jewel
PO Box 33494
San Diego, CA 92163
Singer

Jewish Defense League
PO Box 480370
Los Angeles, CA 90048
Website: http://www.jdl.org
E-mail: jdljdl@aol.com
Irv Rubin, National Chairman
Organization that sees the need for
a movement that is dedicated
specifically to Jewish problems
and that allocates its time,
resources, energies, and funds
to Jews

The John Birch Society, Inc.
PO Box 8040
Appleton, WI 54913
Website: http://www.jbs.org/
E-mail: jbs@jbs.org
Thomas R. Eddlem, Research
    Director
E-mail: teddlem@jbs.org
Organization devoted to the free
market system, competitive
capitalism, and private
enterprise

Jews for the Preservation of
    Firearms Ownership
PO Box 270143
Hartford, WI 53027
Website: http://www.jpfo.org/
E-mail: Against-
    Genocide@JPFO.org
Aaron Zelman, Executive
    Director
Membership in Jews for the
Preservation of Firearms
Ownership (JPFO) is open to
ALL law-abiding firearms
owners who believe that
ownership of firearms is a
civil right, not a privilege

John Paul II, Pope
Palazzo Apostolico Vaticano
1-00120 Citta del Vaticano
Italy

John, Elton Sir
Woodside
Crump Hill Rd
Old Windsor
Berkshire, England
Singer

Jillian, Ann
PO Box 57739
Sherman Oaks, CA 91413
Actress

John D. and Catherine T.
    MacArthur Foundation
140 S. Dearborn St., Suite 100
Chicago, IL 60603
Website: http://
    www.macfdn.org/
E-mail: 4answers@macfdn.org
John E. Corbally, Chairman of
    the Board
This foundation give "genius
grants"—no-strings money
awarded to people with
exceptional creative ability

Jim and Jesse
PO Box 27
Gallatin, TN 37066
Country music duo

**John Hancock Financial
    Services**
John Hancock Place
Boston, MA 02117
Stephen L. Brown, CEO
Website: http://
    www.johnhancock.com
*Insurance (including variable,
    universal, and term life, as
    well as group long-term-care),
    annuities and mutual funds,
    financial products, investment
    management, and corporate
    services*

John Locke Foundation, The
200 West Morgan St., Suite 200
Raleigh, NC 27601
Website: http://
    www.johnlocke.org/
E-mail: info@johnlocke.org
Bruce M. Babcock, Board of
    Directors
Marilyn Avila, Admimistrative
    Director
E-mail: mavila@johnlocke.org
*A nonprofit, nonpartisan policy
    institute whose purpose is to
    conduct research, disseminate
    information, and advance
    public understanding of
    society based on the principles
    of individual liberty, the
    voluntary exchanges of a free
    market economy, and limited
    government*

**John Simon Guggenheim
    Memorial Foundation**
90 Park Ave.
New York, NY 10016
Website: http://www.gf.org
E-mail: fellowships@gf.org
Joseph A. Rice, Chairman of
    the Board

*A grant foundation for arts and
    sciences and the humanities,
    except for performers. They
    will fund a choreographer, but
    not a dancer.*

Johns, Glynis
121 N. San Vicente Blvd.
Beverly Hills, CA 90211
Actress

Johnson, Beverly
8485-E Melrose Pl.
Los Angeles, CA 90046
Model

Johnson, Davey
% Baltimore Orioles
333 W. Camden St.
Baltimore, MD 21201
Baseball player

Johnson, Don
1122 S. Robertson Blvd., #15
Los Angeles, CA 90035
Actor
Birthday: 12/15/49

Johnson, Dr. Virginia
Campbell Plaza 59th and
    Arsenel
St. Louis, MO 63118
Sex researcher

Johnson, Earvin Magic
9100 Wilshire Blvd., #1060 W.
    Tower
Beverly Hills, CA 90212
or
% William Morris Agency
151 El Camino Dr.
Beverly Hills, CA 90212
Athlete, businessman
Birthday: 8/14/59

Johnson, Jimmy
Pro Player Stadium
2269 NW 199th St.
Miami, FL 33056
Head coach of the Miami Dolphins
Birthday: 7/16/43

Johnson, Keyshawn
% Tampa Bay Buccaneers
One Buccaneer Place
Tampa, FL 33607
Football player

Johnson, Lady Bird
% LBJ Presidential Library
2313 Red River St.
Austin, TX 78705
or
LBJ Ranch
Stonewall, TX 78671
Former first lady

Johnson, Michael
818 18th Ave. S., 3rd Floor
Nashville, TN 37211
Country music singer

Johnson Controls
5757 N. Green Bay Ave.
Milwaukee, WI 53209
Website: http://www.jci.com
James H. Keyes, Chairman and
    CEO
Motor vehicles and parts

Johnson & Johnson
1 J&J Plaza
New Brunswick, NJ 08933
Website: http://www.jnj.com
Ralph S. Larsen, Chairman
    and CEO
Pharmaceuticals

**Joint Center for Political and
    Economic Studies**
1090 Vermont Ave. NW, #1100
Washington, DC 20005
Website: http://
    www.jointctr.org/
Eddie N. Williams, President
Barry K. Campbell, Executive
    Vice President
*A nonprofit institution conducting
    research on political,
    economic, and social policy
    issues of concern to African
    Americans*

Jolie, Angelina
% Industry Entertainment
955 Carrillo Dr., 3rd Floor
Los Angeles, CA 90048
Actress
Birthday: 6/4/75

**Jolsoon, Al, International
    Society**
2981 Westmoore Dr.
Columbus, OH 43204

Jones, David Lynn
% Mercury
901 18th Ave. South
Nashville, TN 37203
Country music singer

Jones, Davy
PO Box 400
Beavertown, PA 17813
Musician, member of The Monkees

Jones, Dean
500 S. Buena Vista
Burbank, CA 91521
Actor

Jones, George
Rt. 3, Box 150
Murphy, NC 28906
Country music singer

Jones, James Earl
PO Box 610
Pawling, NY 12564
Actor, voice of CNN

Jones, Jenny
454 N. Columbus Dr., 4th Fl.
Chicago, IL 60611
Website: http://
    www.jennyjones.com
Talk show host

Jones, Parnelli
PO Box W
Torrance, CA 90507
Race car driver

Jones, Paula
% General Delivery
Cabot, AR 72923
*Accused President Bill Clinton of
    sexual harassment*

Jones, Quincy
Quincy Jones/David Salzman
    Entertainment
3800 Barham Blvd. #503
Los Angeles, CA 90068
Composer/musician

Jones, Randy
% San Diego Padres
PO Box 2000
San Diego, CA 92112
Baseball player

Jones, Shirley
Suite One Productions
8127 Melrose Ave., #1
Los Angeles CA 90046
or
11365 Ventura Blvd., #100
Studio City, CA 91604
Actress

Jones, Tom
10100 Santa Monica Blvd.,
    #225
Los Angeles, CA 90067
Singer

Jordan, Michael
676 Michigan Ave., #2940
Chicago, IL 60611
Website: http://
    cbs.sportsline.com/u/
    jordan/
Actor, athlete, businessman
Birthday: 2/17/63

Jordanaires, The
1300 Division St., #205
Nashville, TN 37203
Singing group

**Joseph and Edna Josephson
    Institute of Ethics**
4640 Admiralty Way, #1001
Marina del Rey, CA 90292
Website: http://www.josephson
    institute.org/
E-mail: ji@jiethics.org
Michael S. Josephson, Founder
    and President
*A public-benefit, nonpartisan,
    nonprofit membership
    organization founded by
    Michael Josephson in honor of
    his parents to improve the
    ethical quality of society by
    advocating principled
    reasoning and ethical decision-
    making*

Scott Joss Fan Club
PO Box 6208
Santa Rosa, CA 95406

Journey
63 Main St.
Cold Springs, NY 10516
Music group

J. P. Morgan
60 Wall St.
New York, NY 10260
Website: http://
    www.jpmorgan.com
Douglas A. "Sandy" Warner III,
    Chairman and CEO
Commercial banks

Judas Priest
3 E. 54th St., #1400
New York, NY 10022
Website: http://
    www.judaspriest.com/
Music group

Judd, Ashley
% William Morris Agency
151 El Camino Dr.
Beverly Hills, CA 90212
or
PO Box 680339
Franklin, TN 37068
Actress
Birthday: 4/19/68

Judd, Naomi
PO Box 682068
Nashville, TN 37217
Country music singer

Judd, Wynonna
PO Box 682068
Nashville, TN 37217
E-mail: fanclub@wynonna.com
Country music singer

As long as there are postmen, life will have zest.

—WILLIAM JAMES

Kadrey, Richard
E-mail: kadrey@well.com
Science fiction novelist

Kaelin, Brian "Kato"
6404 Wilshire Blvd., #950
Los Angeles, CA 90048
*Talk show host, actor, one time
O. J. Simpson houseguest*

Kalb, Marvin
79 John F. Kennedy St.
Cambridge, MA 02138
Broadcaster

Kanarek, Lisa
600 Preston
Forest Center,#120
Dallas, TX 75230
Author of 101 Home Office
Success Secrets

Kane, Bob
% DC Comics
1325 Ave. of Americas
New York, NY 10019
Batman creator

Kane, Big Daddy
151 El Camino Dr.
Beverly Hills, CA 90212
*Old-school rapper, whose name
stands for King Asiatic No
Equal*

Kane, Carol
8205 Santa Monica Blvd.,#1426
West Hollywood, CA 90046
Actress
Birthday: 6/18/52

Karolyi, Bela
RR #12
Box 140
Huntsville, TX 77340
Gymnastics coach

Karras, Alex
Georgian Bay Productions
3815 W. Olive Ave., #202
Burbank, CA 91505
Actor
Birthday: 7/15/35

Kasem, Casey
% Global Satellite Network
14958 Ventura Blvd.
Sherman Oaks, CA 91403
Radio and TV host

Katayama, Ukyo
% Minardi Team S.P.A.
Via Spellanzani 21
I-48018 Faenza/RA
Professional Formula-1 driver

Katzenberg, Jeffrey
100 Universal City Plaza, #10
Universal City, CA 91608
Co-founder of DreamWorks

Kauffman, David
5826 IH 10 West, Suite 101
San Antonio, TX 78201
Website: http://
    www.davidkauffman.com/
E-mail:
    david@davidkauffman.com
Christian musician

Kawasaki, Guy
PO Box 21631
Santa Barbara, CA 93121
Website: http://www.umsl.edu/
    ~sbmeade/macway/
E-mail: MacWay@aol.com
Mac guru

Kazan, Lainie
9903 Santa Monica Blvd., #283
Beverly Hills, CA 90212
Actress

Keaton, Michael
11901 Santa Monica, #547
Los Angeles, CA 90025
Actor
Birthday: 9/9/51

Keel, Howard
% Clifford Prods.
394 Red River Rd.
Palm Desert, CA 92211
Actor
Birthday: 4/13/17

Keel, John A
PO Box 351
Murray Hill Station
New York, NY 10016
UFO researcher

Keeshan, Bob
40 W. 57th St., #1600
New York, NY 10019
Captain Kangaroo
Birthday: 6/27/27

Kehoe, Brendan
Website: http//www.zen.org/
    ~brendan/
E-mail: brendan@zen.org.
Author of Zen and the Art of
    the Internet

Keillor, Garrison
45 E. 7th. St.
St. Paul, MN 55101
E-mail:
    gkeillor@madmax.mpr.org
Radio host

Keitel, Harvey
9560 Wilshire Blvd., #516
Beverly Hills, CA 90212
Actor

Keith, Toby
PO Box 8739
Rockford, IL 61126
Country music singer

Keener, Catherine
PO Box 5617
Beverly Hills, CA 90210

Keller, Marthe
5 rue Saint Dominique
75007 Paris
France
Actress
Birthday: 2/28/45

Kellner, Mark
Website: http://
    www.markkellner.com/
E-mail: mark@kellner2000.com
Writer

Kelloggs
1 Kellogg Square
Battle Creek, MI 49016
Website: http://
    www.kelloggs.com
Arnold G. Langbo, CEO
Food producer

Kelly Services
999 W. Big Beaver Rd.
Troy, MI 48084
Website: http://
    www.kellyservices.com
Terence E. Adderley,
    Chairman, President, and
    CEO
Temporary services

Kemp, Shawn
% Seattle Supersonics
190 Queen Anne Ave. N. Suite
    200
Seattle, WA 98109
Basketball player

Kendalls, The
2802 Columbine Pl.
Nashville, TN 37204
Singing group

Kennedy, Jamie
9465 Wilshire Blvd., #212
Beverly Hills, CA 90212
Actor

Kennedy, John F. Library
PO Box 8734
Boston, MA 02114

Kennedy, Ray
PO Box 158309
Nashville, TN 37215
Country music singer

**Kennedy, Senator Edward M.
    (Ted)**
2416 Tracy Pl. NW
Washington, DC 20008

Kennedy, Tom
11365 Ventura Blvd., #100
Studio City, CA 91604
*TV game show host, Jack Narz's
    Brother*
Birthday: 2/26/27

Kentucky Headhunters
209 10th Ave. So., #322
Nashville, TN 37203
Musical group

Kenzle, Leila
151 El Camino Dr.
Beverly Hills, CA 90212
Actress

Kercheval, Ken
PO Box 325
Goshen, KY 40026
Actor
Birthday: 7/15/35

Kerns, Joanna
PO Box 49216
Los Angeles, CA 90049
Actress
Birthday: 2/12/53

Kerr, Deborah
Wyherut
7250 Klosters
Grisons
Switzerland
Actress

Kerr, Graham
300 S. 1st St. #C-2
Mt. Vernon, WA 98273
The Galloping Gourmet

Kershaw, Doug
Rt. 1
Box 34285
Weld County Rd. 47
Eaton, CO 80615
Cajun singer and musician

Kershaw, Sammy
PO Box 121739
Nashville, TN 37212
Country music singer

Ketchum, Hal
1700 Hayes St., #304
Nashville, TN 37203
Country music singer

Ketchum, Hank
PO Box 1997
Monterey, CA 93942
Cartoonist

Kevorkian, Dr. Jack
4870 Lockhart St.
W. Bloomfield, MI 48323
Suicide assistance doctor

Key, Jimmy
% Baltimore Orioles
333 West Camden St.
Baltimore, MD 21201
Baseball player

KeyCorp
127 Public Square
Cleveland, OH 44114
Website: http://
    www.keybank.com
Robert W. Gillespie, Chairman
    and CEO
Commercial bank

Keyes, Dr. Alan
1030 115th St. NW, #700
Washington, DC 20005
*Presidential candidate, talk show
    host*
Birthday: 8/7/50

Keysey, Ken
Rt. 8 Box 477
Pleasant Hill, OR 97401
Author

Khan, Chaka
PO Box 16680
Beverly Hills, CA 90209
Singer
Birthday: 3/23/53

Khamani, Pres. Mohammad
The Majilis
Tehran
Iran

Khan, The Aga IV
Aga Ailemont
60270 Gouvieux
France

Khan, Prince Sadruddin Aga
CH-1245
Collonge-Bellerive
Switzerland

Khan, Princess Yasmin
146 Central Park W.
New York, NY 10023

Khruschev, Sergei
PO Box 1948
Providence, RI 02912
*Son of the former Soviet premeire
Nikita Khruschev*

Kidd, Jason
% Phoenix Suns
PO Box 1369
Phoenix, AZ 85001
Basketball player

Kidder, Margot
220 Pine Creek Rd.
Livingstone, MT 59047
Actress
Birthday: 10/17/48

Kidman, Nicole
5555 Melrose Ave.
Lucille Ball Bldg.
Los Angeles, CA 90038
or
9830 Wilshire Blvd.
Beverly Hills, CA 90212
Actress
Birthday: 6/20/67

Killebrew, Harmon
PO Box 14550
Scottsdale, AZ 85267
Former baseball player

Killy, Jean-Claude
13 Chemin ellefontaine
1223 Cologny
GE Switzerland
Olympic skier

Kilmer, Val
PO Box 362
Tesuque NM 87574
or
9830 Wilshire Blvd.
Beverly Hills, CA 90212
Actor
Birthday: 12/31/59

Kimberly-Clark
351 Phelps Dr.
Irving, TX 75038
Website: http://www.kimberly-
    clark.com
Wayne R. Sanders, Chairman
    and CEO
Forest and paper products

Kimes, Royal Wade
PO Box 128038
Nashville, TN 37212
Country music singer

King, Alan
888 7th Ave., #3800
New York, NY 10106
Comedian

King, B. B.
1414 Sixth Ave.
New York, NY 10019
Musician

King, Carole
Robinson Bar Ranch
Box 146
Stanley, ID 83278
Singer, songwriter

King, Don
% Don King Enterprises
871 W. Oakland Park Ave.
Fort Lauderdale, FL 33311
Impressario
Birthday: 8/20/31

King, Pee Wee
% CMA
1 Music Circle South
Nashville, TN 37203
Country music singer

King, Perry
1033 Gayley Ave., #201
Los Angeles, CA 90024
Actor

King, Rodney
9100 Wilshire Blvd., #250W
Beverly Hills, CA 90212
Website: http://www.rodney-
    king.com/altapazz/
    default.htm

King, Stephen
47 W. Broadway
Banfor, ME 04401
Author

Kingsley, Ben
76 Oxford St.
London, W1N OAX
England
Actor

Kingsman, The
1720 N. Ross Ave.
Santa Ana, CA 92706
Music group

Kingston Trio, The
941-0 S. 46th. St.
Phoenix, AZ 85044
Music group

Kinison, Mrs. Sam (Sherry)
PO Box 1282
Upland, CA 91785
Wife of late comedian

Kinks, The
29 Ruston Mews
London W11 1RB
England
Music group

Kinmont, Kathleen
6404 Wilshire Blvd., #950
Los Angeles, CA 90048
Actress

Kinnear, Greg
3000 W. Alameda Ave., #2908
Burbank, CA 91523
or
9150 Wilshire Blvd., #350
Beverly Hills, CA 90212
Talk show host, actor

Kinney, Kathy
10061 Riverside Dr., #777
North Hollywood, CA 91607
Actress

Kinsella, W. P.
PO Box 2162
Blaine, WA 98231
Author

Kinski, Nastassja
% William Morris Agency
151 El Camino Dr.
Beverly Hills, CA 90212
Actress, model

Kinsley, Michael
5602 Lakeview Dr., #J
Kirkland, WA 98033
Editor of Slate *Magazine*

Kirby, Durwood
PO Box 3054
N. Ft. Myers, FL 33918
Actor, announcer

Kirkconnell, Clare
Box 63
Rutherford, CA 94573
Actress

Kirkland, Sally
11300 W. Olympic Blvd., #610
Los Angeles, CA 90064
Actress
Birthday: 10/31/44

Kirsebom, Vendela
151 El Camino Dr.
Beverly Hills, CA 90212
Actress

Kiss
87730 Sunset Blvd., #175
Los Angeles, CA 90069
Music group

Kissinger, Dr. Henry
435 E. 52nd. St.
New York, NY 10022
Nobel laureate, statesman,
  Secretary of State under
  Presidents Richard M. Nixon
  and Gerald R. Ford

Klasky, Arlene
1258 N. Highland Ave.
Hollywood, CA 90038
Website: http://
  www.klaskycsupo.com
Creator of Rugrats

Klein, Calvin
205 W. 39th St.
New York, NY 10018
Fashion designer

Klemp, Cardinal Josef-Koiski
U1Miodowa 17
PL-00-583
Warsaw
Poland

Klemperer, Werner
44 W. 62nd St., 10th Floor
New York, NY 10023
Actor
Birthday: 3/29/19

Klensch, Elsa
1050 Techwood Dr. NW
Atlanta, GA 30318
Fashion commentator

Kline, Kevin
151 El Camino Dr.
Beverly Hills, CA 90212
Actor
Birthday: 10/24/47

Kline, Richard
4530 Balboa Blvd.
Encino, CA 91316
Comedian

Klum, Heidi
% Elite Model Managemt
111 East 22nd St.
New York, NY 10010
Model

K Mart
3100 W. Big Beaver Rd.
Troy, MI 48084
Website: http://www.kmart.com
Charles C. Conaway, Chairman
  of the Board and CEO
General merchandisers

Knievel, Evel
160 E. Flamingo Rd.
Las Vegas, NV 89109
Daredevil

Knight, Shirley
19528 Ventura Blvd., #559
Tarzana, CA 91356
Actress

Knight, Summer
PO Box 9786
Marina del Rey, CA 90295
Porn queen

Knight, Wayne
10061 Riverside Dr., #1043
Toluca Lake, CA 91602
Actor

Knight-Ridder
50 W. San Fernando St.
San Jose, CA 95113
Website: http://www.kri.com
P. Anthony Ridder, Chairman
    and CEO
Publishing, printing

Knotts, Don
1854 S. Beverly Glenn, #402
Los Angeles, CA 90025
Actor

Kober, Jeff
13333 Ventura Blvd., #205
Sherman Oaks, CA 91423
Actor

Koch, Edward
1290 Ave. of the Americas
New York, NY 10104
Former mayor of New York

Kodjoe, Boris
% Ford Model Agency
344 E. 59th St.
New York, NY 10022
Model

Koenig, Walter
PO Box 4395
North Hollywood, CA 91607
Actor

Kohl, Helmut
Marbacher Str. 11
D-67071 Ludwighsfen
Germany
*Former Chancellor of West
    Germany*

Kohl's
N. 56 W. 17000 Ridgewood Dr.
Menomonee Falls, WI 53051
Website: http://nt1.irin.com/
    irin/Detail.CFM/kss
William S. Kellogg, CEO
General merchandisers

Kool and the Gang
89 Fifth Ave., #700
New York, NY 10003
Music group

Kool Moe Dee
151 El Camino Dr.
Beverly Hills, CA 90212
Musician

Koontz, Dean R.
PO Box 9529
Newport Beach, CA 92658
Author

Koop, Dr. Everett
3 Ivy Point Way
Hanover, NH 03755
Former Surgeon General

Korda, Michael
1230 Ave. of the Americas
New York, NY 10019
*Author and Editor-in-chief at
Simon & Schuster*

Korn
151 E. El Camino Dr.
Beverly Hills, CA 90212
Music group

Kournikova, Anna
5500 34th St.
W. Bradenton, FL 34210
Tennis player

Kozar, Heather
PO Box 480472
Los Angeles, CA 90048
Porn star

Kozlowski, Linda
5757 Wilshire Blvd., #1
Los Angeles, CA 90036
Actress

Krakowski, Jane
8271 Melrose Ave., #110
Los Angeles, CA 90046
Actress

Kramer, Stefanie
8271 Melrose Ave., #110
Los Angeles, CA 90046
Actress

Krauss, Alison
PO Box 121711
Nashville, TN 37212
Website: http://
    www.alisonkrauss.com/
Singer

Kreskin
PO Box 1383
West Caldwell, NJ 07006
Mentalist

Kris Kross
9380 SW 72nd St., #B220
Miami, FL 33173
Music duo

Kristen, Marta
3575 Cahuenga Blvd. W., #500
Los Angeles, CA 90068
Actress

Kristofferson, Kris
PO Box 2147
Malibu, CA 90265
or
313 Lakeshore Dr.
Marietta, GA 30067
Songwriter/actor

Kroger
1014 Vine St.
Cincinnati, OH 45202
Website: http://
    www.kroger.com
Dave Dillon, President and
    COO
Food and drug stores

Kroft, Sid and Marty
7710 Woodrow Wilson Dr.
Los Angeles, CA 90046
*Producers of classic children's
    television shows*

Kruger, Hardy
Box 726
Crestline, CA 92325
Actor

Kstsulas, Andreas
% Innovative Artists
1999 Ave. of the Stars, #2850
Los Angeles, CA 90067
Commander Tomalak from Star
    Trek: The Next
    Generation

Kudrow, Lisa
1122 S. Robertson Blvd., #15
Los Angeles, CA 90035
Actress

**Kumantunga, President
    Chandrika**
President Secretariat
Columbo 1
Sri Lanka

Kurtz, Swoozie
320 Central Park W.
New York, NY 10025
Actress
Birthday: 9/6/44

Kwan, Nancy
PO Box 50747
Santa Barbara, CA 93150
Actress

People in the flesh are a lot more complicated than they appear on paper, which is both one of the attractions and one of the shortcomings of carrying on a prolonged correspondence.

—SHANA ALEXANDER

Labelle, Patti
1212 Grennox Rd.
Wynnewood, PA 19096
Singer
Birthday: 10/4/44

Labonte, Terry
PO Box 9
Harrisburg, NC 28075
Race car driver
Birthday: 11/16/56

Ladd, Cheryl
8942 Wilshire Blvd.
Beverly Hills, CA 90211
Actress
Birthday: 7/2/51

Ladd, Diane
PO Box 1859
Ojai, CA 93024
Actress, mother of Laura Dern
Birthday: 11/29/32

Laffer, Dr. Arthur
5375 Executive Square, #330
La Jolla, CA 92037
Economist

Lagerfeld, Karl
14 Blvd. De la Madeleine
F-75008 Paris
France
Fashion designer and photographer
Birthday: 1938

Lahti, Christine
1122 S. Robertson Blvd., #15
Los Angeles, CA 90035
Actress
Birthday: 4/5/50

Lai, Francis
4146 Lankershim Blvd., #401
North Hollywood, CA 91602
Website: http://www.francis-
    lai.com/
Composer

Laine, Dame Cleo
The Old Rectory
Wavendon
Milton Keynes MK17 8LT
England
Singer

Laine, Frankie
PO Box 6910
San Diego, CA 92166
Singer

Laird, Melvin
1730 Rhode Island Ave. NW
Washington, DC 20036
*American politician, U.S. Secretary
    of Defense*

Lake, Ricki
226 W. 26th. St., #400
New York, NY 10001
Actress, talk show host
Birthday: 9/21/68

Laker, Sir Freddie
138 Chapside
London Ec2V 6BL
England
Founder of original Laker Airways

Lakin, Christine
Step by Step Fan Mail
2040 Ave. of the Stars
Los Angeles, CA 90067
Actress
Birthday: 1/25/79

Lama, Dalai
Thekchen Choling
McLeod Gunji
Dharamsala
Himachal Pradesh
India
Religious leader
Birthday: 7/6/35

Lamas, Lorenzo
3727 W. Magnolia Blvd., #807
Burbank, CA 91505
Actor
Birthday: 1/20/58

Lambert, Christopher
1901 Ave. of the Stars, #1245
Los Angeles, CA 90067
Actor
Birthday: 3/29/57

Lamm, Richard
University of Denver
Center for Public Policy
Denver, CO 80208
Former governor of Colorado

Landers, Ann
435 N. Michigan Ave.
Chicago, IL 60611
Advice columnist

Landers, Audrey
4048 Las Palmas Dr.
Sarasota, FL 34238
Actress
Birthday: 7/18/59

Landers, Judy
3933 Losillas Dr.
Sarasota, FL 34238
Actress
Birthday: 10/7/61

Lando, Joe
% William Morris Agency
151 S. El Camino Dr.
Beverly Hills, CA 90212
Actor
Birthday: 12/9/61

Landry, Tom
8411 Preston Rd., Suite 720-
    LB3
Dallas, TX 75225
or
% Football Hall of Fame
2121 George Halas Dr. NW
Canton, OH 44708
Former football player

Lane, Cristy
LS Records
120 Hickory St.
Nashville, TN 37115
Country music singer

Lane, Diane
25 Sea Colony Dr.
Santa Monica, CA 90405
Actress
Birthday: 1/22/63

Lane, Nathan
PO Box 1249
White River Junction, VT
    05001
Actor

lang, k.d.
% Burnstead Prod.
PO Box 33800
Station D
Vancouver BC V6J 5C7
Canada
Singer
Birthday: 11/2/61

Lange, Hope
1801 Ave. of the Stars, #902
Los Angeles, CA 90067
Actress

Lange, Jessica
8942 Wilshire Blvd.
Beverly Hills, CA 90211
Actress

Lange, Ted
17801 Victory Blvd.
Reseda, CA 91335
Actor

Langella, Frank
151 El Camino Dr.
Beverly Hills, CA 90212
Actor
Birthday: 1/1/40

Langenkamp, Heather
9229 Sunset Blvd., #311
Los Angeles, CA 90069
Actress

Lansbury, Angela
100 Universal City Plaza Bldg.
    426
Universal City, CA 91608
Actress

LaPaglia, Anthony
955 S. Carrillo Dr., #300
Los Angeles, CA 90048
Actor

Larroquette, John
PO Box 6910
Malibu, CA 90264
Actor

Larson, Gary
Box 36A
Denver, CO 80236
Cartoonist

Larson, Nicolette
3818 Abbot Martin Rd.
Nashville, TN 37215
Singer

La Salle, Eriq
PO Box 2396
Beverly Hills, CA 90213
Actor

Lasorda, Tommy
% L.A. Dodgers
1000 Elysian Park Blvd.
Los Angeles, CA 90012
Former manager of the Dodgers

Lassie
16133 Soledad Canyon Rd.
Canyon Country, CA 91351
Acting dog

Latifah, Queen
% William Morris Agency
151 El Camino Dr.
Beverly Hills, CA 90212
Actress, singer, talk show host
Birthday: 3/18/70

Lauer, Matt
30 Rockefeller Plaza, #701
New York, NY 10112
Today *show host*

Laughlin, Tom
PO Box 25355
Los Angeles, CA 90025
Actor, director

Lauper, Cindi
826 Broadway, #400
New York, NY 10003
Singer, songwriter
Birthday: 6/20/53

Lauren, Ralph
1107 5th Ave.
New York, NY 10128
Fashion designer
Birthday: 10/14/39

Laurie, Piper
PMB 931
2118 Wilshire Blvd.
Santa Monica, CA 90403
Actress

St. Laurent, Yves
5 av. Marceau
F-75116 Paris
France
Fashion designer
Birthday: 8/4/?

Laurie, Hugh
% Hamilton Asper
     Management
Ground Floor
24 Hanway St.
London W1P 9DD
United Kingdom
Actor

Laver, Rod
Box 4798
Hilton Head Island, SC 29928
Tennis player
Birthday: 8/9/38

Lavin, Linda
PO Box 2847
Wilmington, NC 28402
Actress

Lawless, Lucy
100 Universal City Plaza, #415A
Universal City, CA 91608
Actress

The Lucy Lawless Fan Club
65 Edwin Rd.
Waltham, MA 02154

Lawrence, Martin
9560 Wilshire Blvd., #516
Beverly Hills, CA 91212
or
PO Box 7304, Suite 440
North Hollywood, CA 91603
Actor

Lawrence, Sharon
PO Box 462048
Los Angeles, CA 90046
Actress

Lawrence, Steve
10560 Wilshire Blvd., #601
Los Angeles, CA 90046
Singer

Lawrence, Tracy
2100 West End Ave., #1000
Nashville, TN 37203
Country music singer

Lawson, Dennis
21 Golden Sq.
London, W1R 3PA
England
Actor

League of Conservation Voters
1920 L Street, NW, Suite 800
Washington, DC 20036
Website: http://www.lcv.org
E-mail: lcv@lcv.org
Deb Callahan, President
*Works to create a Congress more
responsive to your
environmental concerns*

**League of United Latin
American Citizens
(LULAC)**
2000 L St., NW, Suite 610
Washington, DC 20036
Website: http://www.lulac.org/
Enrique "Rick" Dovalina,
LULAC National President
E-mail: RickDovalina@
LULAC.org
Brent Wilkes, LULAC National
Executive Director
E-mail: BWilkes@LULAC.org
*Works to bring about positive
social and economic changes
for Hispanic Americans*

**League of Women Voters of
the United States**
1730 M St. NW
Washington, DC 20036
Website: http://www.lwv.org/
Carolyn Jefferson-Jenkins,
Ph.D.
*A multi-issue organization whose
mission is to encourage the
informed and active
participation of citizens in
government*

Leach, Robin
342 Madison Ave., #950
New York, NY 10173
Television host

Leakey, Dr. Richard
PO Box 24926
Nairobi
Kenya
Paleontologist

Lear
21557 Telegraph Rd.
Southfield, MI 48086
Website: http://www.lear.com
Kenneth L. Way, CEO
Motor vehicles and parts

Lear, Norman
1999 Ave. of the Stars, #500
Los Angeles, CA 90067
TV producer

Learned, Michael
1600 N. Beverly Dr.
Beverly Hills, CA 90210
Actress

Leary, Denis
9560 Wilshire Blvd., #516
Beverly Hills, CA 90212
Comedian

Le Blanc, Matt
1122 S. Robertson Blvd., #15
Los Angeles, CA 90035
Actor

Le Brock, Kelly
PO Box 57593
Sherman Oaks, CA 91403
Website: http://
    www.kellylebrock.net/
Actress

LeDoux, Chris
PO Box 253
Sumner, IA 50674
Country music singer

**Lee, Brenda (Brenda Mae
    Tarpley)**
Brenda Lee Productions, Inc.
PO Box 101188
Nashville, TN 37210
Website: http://
    www.brendalee.com/
Singer
Birthday: 12/11/44

Lee, Christopher
21 Golden Square
GB-London W12 3PA
England
Actor

Lee, Johnny
PO Box 1644
Dickinson, TX 77539
Country music singer

Lee, Spike
40 Acres and a Mule Filmworks
124 DeKalb, 2nd Floor
Brooklyn, NY 11217
Film director

Lee, Stan
% Marvel Films
1440 S. Sepulveda, Suite 114
Los Angeles, CA 90025
or
% Marvel Comics
387 Park Ave. South
New York, NY 10016
E-mail: stanzfanz@aol.com
Publisher of Spider Man

Leggett and Platt
No. 1 Leggett Rd.
Carthage, MO 64836
Website: http://
    www.regionalstock.com/
    leg.html
Harry M. Cornell, Jr.,
    Chairman
Felix E. Wright, VC, President,
    and CEO
Furniture

Lehman Brothers Holdings
3 World Financial Center
New York, NY 10285
Website: http://
    www.lehman.com
Richard S. Fuld, Jr., Chairman
    and CEO
Securities

Leick, Hudson
PO Box 775
Fair Oaks, CA 95628
Website: http://
    www.hudsonleickfan.com
Actress

Leigh, Jennifer Jason
% International Creative
    Management
8942 Wilshire Blvd.
Beverly Hills, CA 90211
Actress
Birthday: 2/5/62

Leisure, David
8428-C Melrose Pl.
Los Angeles, CA 90046
Actor
Birthday: 11/16/50

Lemmon, Jack
955 S. Carrillo Dr., #300
Los Angeles, CA 90048
Actor
Birthday: 2/8/25

Lennon, Julian
30 Ives St.
London SW3 2nd
England
Musician

Lennox, Annie
35–37 Park Gate Rd.
Unit 2
Ransome's Docks
London SW11 4NP
England
Singer
Birthday: 12/25/54

Leno, Jay
PO Box 7885
Burbank, CA 91510
Tonight Show *host*
Birthday: 4/20/50

Leonard, Robert Sean
PO Box 103
Waldwick, NJ 07463
Actor
Birthday: 2/28/69

Leoni, Tea
2300 West Victory Blvd., #384
Burbank, CA 91506
*Actress, married to David
    Duchovny*

Leto, Jared
1999 Ave. of the Stars, Suite
    2850
Los Angeles, CA 90067
Actor

Letterman, David
1697 Broadway
New York, NY 10019
or
9830 Wilshire Blvd.
Beverly Hills, CA 90212
Comedian, talk show host
Birthday: 4/12/47

Levine, Michael
5750 Wilshire Blvd., #555
Los Angeles, CA 90036
E-mail: levinepr@earthlink.net
Author, The Address Book,
    media specialist
Birthday: 4/17/54

Lewinsky, Monica
660 Greenwich St.
New York, NY 10014
Former White House intern

Lewis, Al
612 Lighthouse Ave. #220
Pacific Grove, CA 93951
*Actor, played Grandpa on the
    Munsters*

Lewis, Carl
PO Box 571990
Houston, TX 77082
*Olympic competitor in track and
    field*

Lewis, Huey
PO Box 819
Mill Valley, CA 94942
Singer
Birthday: 7/5/50

Lewis, Jerry
3160 W. Sahara Ave #816
Las Vegas, NV 89102
or
% William Morris Agency
151 El Camino Dr.
Beverly Hills, CA 90212
Actor, comedian
Birthday: 3/16/26

Lewis, Jerry Lee
PO Box 23162
Nashville, TN 37202
Singer

Lg & E
220 W. Main St.
Louisville, KY 40232
Website: http://
    www.lgeenergy.com
Roger W. Hale, Chairman and
    CEO
Gas and electric utilities

Libertarian Party
2600 Virginia Ave. NW, #100
Washington, DC 20037
Website: http://www.lp.org/
Steve Dasbach, National
    Director
E-mail:
    Steve.Dasbach@hq.lp.org
Ron Crickenberger, Political
    Director
E-mail: Ron.Cricken
berger@hq.LP.org
*Holds that all individuals have
    the right to exercise sole
    dominion over their own lives
    and have the right to live in
    whatever manner they choose,
    so long as they do not forcibly
    interfere with the equal right
    of others to live in whatever
    manner they choose*

**Liberty Mutual Insurance
    Group**
Headquarters
175 Berkeley St.
Boston, MA 02117
Gary L. Countryman, CEO
P & C insurance (mutual)

Liddy, G. Gordon
PO Box 3649
Washington, DC 20007
Website: http://www.rtis.com/
    liddy/
E-mail: gordonliddy@aol.com
*Watergate conspirator and talk
    show host*

Lien, Jennifer
% Paramount Pictures
5555 Melrose Ave.
Los Angeles, CA 90038
Actress Kes from Star Trek:
    Voyager

Limbaugh, Rush
PO Box 2182
Palm Beach, FL 33480
or
366 Madison Ave., #700
New York, NY 10017
Website: http://
    www.rushlimbaugh.com/
    home/guest.html
E-mail: rush@eibnet.com
Radio talk show host
Birthday: 1/12/51

Limelights, The
11761 E. Speedway Blvd.
Tucson, AZ 85748
Music group

Limited
3 Limited Pkwy.
Columbus, OH 43230
Website: http://
    www.limited.com
Leslie H. Wexner, CEO
Specialist retailers

Limp Bizkit
% Interscope
10900 Wilshire Blvd.
Los Angeles, CA 90024
Music group

Lincoln National
1500 Market St., Suite 3900
Philadelphia, PA 19012
Website: http://www.lfg.com
Jon A. Boscia, President and
    CEO
Life and health insurance (stock)

Linden, Hal
9100 Sunset Blvd., #4530TE
Beverly Hills, CA 90212
Actor
Birthday: 3/20/31

Lindenberg, Udo
% Kempinski Hotel Atlantic
Am der Alster 72
D20099 Hamburg
Germany
Singer

Lindsey, George
% Avon Books
1350 Ave. of the Americas
New York, NY 10019
Country music singer

Liotta, Ray
955 S. Carrillo Dr., #300
Los Angeles, CA 90048
Actor

Lipinski, Tara
PO Box 472288
Charlotte, NC 28247
Ice skater

Lipnicki, Jonathan
% Brillstein-Greg Ent.
9150 Wilshire Blvd. #350
Beverly Hills, CA 90212
Actor
Birthday: 10/22/90

Little Texas
PO Box 709
Corsicana, TX 75151
Music group

**Little Richard (Richard Wayne
    Penniman)**
8401 Sunset Blvd.
Los Angeles, CA 90069
Singer
Birthday: 12/5/32

Litton Industries
21240 Burbank Blvd.
Woodland Hills, CA 91367
Website: http://
    www.littoncorp.com
Orion L. Hoch, Chairman
    Emeritus
Michael R. Brown, Chairman
    and CEO
Ronald Sugar, President and
    COO
Electronics, electrical equipment

Livingston, Ron
1180 S. Beverly Dr., #608
Los Angeles, CA 90035
Actor

LL Cool J
% Rush Mgmt.
298 Elizabeth St.
New York, NY 10012
Rap artist

Lloyd, Christopher
PO Box 491246
Los Angeles, CA 90049
Actor

Lloyd, Kathleen
10100 Santa Monica Blvd.,
   #2500
Los Angeles, CA 90067
Actress

Lo Bianco, Tony
15821 Ventura Blvd., #235
Encino, CA 91436
Actor

Loc, Tom
1650 Broadway, #508
New York, NY 10019
Musician

Locke, Sandra
15821 Ventura Blvd., #235
Encino, CA 91436
Actress
Birthday: 5/28/48

Lockhart, June
PO Box 3207
Santa Monica, CA 90403
Actress

Lockheed Martin
6801 Rockledge Dr.
Bethesda, MD 20817
Website: http://www.lmco.com
Robert H. Trice, Jr., Vice
   President of Corporate
   Business Development
Aerospace

Locklear, Heather
139 S. Beverly Blvd., #230
Beverly Hills, CA 90212
Actress
Birthday: 9/25/61

Loeb, Lisa
98930 Wilshire Blvd.
Beverly Hills, CA 90212
Singer, Actress

Loews
667 Madison Ave.
New York, NY 10021
Laurence A. Tisch, Co-
   Chairman
Preston R. Tisch, Co-Chairman
James S. Tisch, President and
   CEO
Website: http://www.loews.com
(stock) P and C insurance

Lollobrigida, Gina
Via Appia Antica 223
I-00179 Roma
Italy
Actress
Birthday: 7/4/27

London, Jason
151 El Camino Dr.
Beverly Hills, CA 90212
Actor

Lonestar
PO Box 128467
Nashville, TN 37212
Music group

Long, Kathy
1800 Ave. of the Stars, Suite
400
Los Angeles, CA 90067
Actress

Long, Shelley
15237 Sunset Blvd.
Pacific Palisades, CA 90272
Actress
Birthday: 8/23/49

Lopez, Jennifer
P.O. Box 57593
Sherman Oaks, CA 91403
Actress, singer
Birthday: 7/24/70

Long Island Power Authority
333 Earle Ovington Blvd
Uniondale, NY 11553
Website: http://
www.lipower.org/co.com
Richard M. Kessel, Chairman
Patrick J. Foye, Deputy
Chairman
Howard E. Steinberg, Deputy
Chairman
Gas and electric utilities

Longs Drug Stores
141 N. Civic Dr.
Walnut Creek, CA 94596
Website: http://www.longs.com
Robert M. Long, Chairman
Steve D. Roath, President and
CEO
Food and drug stores

Lopez, Mario
PO Box 4736
Chatsworth, CA 91311
Actor
Birthday: 10/10/73

Lord, Rebecca
16161 Ventura Blvd.
PMB 668
Encino, CA 91436
Website: http://
rebeccalord.com/
Adult film star

Lords, Traci (Norma Kuzma)
100 Universal City Plaza Bldg.
507, #3D
Universal City, CA 91608
Actress
Birthday: 5/7/68

**Loren, Sophia (Sophia
Scicolone)**
1151 Hidden Valley Rd.
Thousand Oaks, CA 91361
Actress
Birthday: 9/20/34

Los Lobos
2 Penn Plaza, #2600
New York, NY 10121
Music group

Louganis, Greg
PO Box 4130
Malibu, CA 90264
Olympic diver

Louis-Dreyfus, Julia
5757 Wilshire Blvd., #1
Los Angeles, CA 90036
Actress

Louise, Tina
310 E. 46th St., #18T
New York, NY 10017
Actress

Louvin, Charlie
PO Box 140324
Nashville, TN 37214
Country music singer

Love, Chesty (Cynthia S. Hess)
PO Box 66991
St. Petersburg, FL 33736
Exotic dancer

Love, Courtney
8942 Wilshire Blvd.
Beverly Hills, CA 90211
Actress, musician
Birthday: 7/9/64

Lovelace, Linda
120 Enterprise
Secaucus, NJ 07094
Former porn star

Loveless, Patty
PO Box 1423
White House, TN 37188
Country music singer

Lovett, Lyle
% General Delivery
Klein, TX 77391
Singer

Lowe, Rob
270 N. Canon Dr., #1072
Beverly Hills, CA 90210
or
% Celebrity Merchandise
PMB 710
15030 Ventura Blvd
Sherman Oaks, CA 91403
Actor
Birthday: 3/17/64

Lowell, Carey
8942 Wilshire Blvd.
Beverly Hills, CA 90211
Actress

**Low Income Housing
Information Service**
1012 14th St., #1200
Washington, DC 20005
Website: http://www.nlihc.org/
index.htm
E-mail: info@nlihc.org
Sheila Crowley, President
E-mail: sheila@nlihc.org
*The only national organization
dedicated solely to ending
America's affordable housing
crisis*

Lowe's
1605 Curtis Bridge Rd.
Wilkesboro, NC 28697
Website: http://www.lowes.com
Robert L. Tillman, Chairman,
President and CEO
Specialist retailers

LTV
200 Public Square
Cleveland, OH 44114
Website: http://
www.ltvsteel.com
Peter Kelly, Chairman,
President, and CEO
Metal producer

Lucas, George
P.O. Box 2459
San Rafael, CA 94912
Director, producer
Birthday: 5/14/44

Lucci, Susan
PO Box 621
Quogue, NY 11959
Soap opera star
Birthday: 12/23/45

Lucent Technologies
600 Mountain Ave.
Murray Hill, NJ 07974-0636
Website: http://
    www.lucent.com
Richard A. McGinn, Chairman
    and CEO
Electronics, electrical equipment

Luchsinger, Susie
PO Box 990
Atoka, OK 74525
Country music singer

**LULAC National Education
    Service Center (League of
    United Latin American
    Citizens)**
221 North Kansas, Suite 1200
El Paso, TX 79901
Website: http://www.lulac.org/
Brent Wilkes, LULAC National
    Executive Director
E-mail: BWilkes@LULAC.org
*Its mission is to advance the
    economic condition,
    educational attainment,
    political influence, health,
    and civil rights of the
    Hispanic population of the
    United States*

Lumbly, Carl
8730 Sunset Blvd. #480
Los Angeles, CA 90069
Actor

Lundgren, Dolph
1999 Ave. of the Stars, #2100
Los Angeles, CA 90067
Actor
Birthday: 10/18/59

Lundy, Jessica
151 El Camino Dr.
Beverly Hills, CA 90212
Actress

Lütgenhorst, David
% Agentur Goosmann
Fichtenstr. 33
85774 Unterföhring
Germany
Actor

Lutheran Brotherhood
625 Fourth Ave. S.
Minneapolis, MN 55415
Website: http://
    www.luthbro.com
Robert P. Gandrud, Chairman
Bruce J. Nicholson, President,
    CEO, and COO
Life insurance

Lydon, John (Johnny Rotten)
14724 Ventura Blvd., #410
Sherman Oaks, CA 91403
Musician

Lynch, David
PO Box 93624
Los Angeles, CA 90093
Director

Lynley, Carol
% Pierce and Shelly
612 Lighthouse Ave., #275
Pacific Grove, CA 93951
E-mail: carolynley@aol.com
Actress
Birthday: 2/13/42

Lynn, Amber
12400 Ventura Blvd., #329
Studio City, CA 91604
Actress

Lynn, Loretta
PO Box 120369
Nashville, TN 37212
Country music singer

Lynne, Shelby
PO Box 190
Monroeville, AL 36461
Country music singer

Lynyrd Skynyrd
6025 The Corner's Pkwy., #202
Norcross, GA 30092
Music group

Lyondell Petrochemical
Website: http://
    www.lyondell.com
William T. Butler, Chairman
Dan F. Smith, President and
    CEO
Dan F. Smith, CEO
Chemicals

Excuse me for not answering your letter sooner, but I've been so busy not answering letters that I couldn't get around to yours in time.

—GROUCHO MARX

MacDowell, Andie
939 8th. Ave., #400
New York, NY 10019
Actress
Birthday: 5/4/58

MacGraw, Ali
% Provident Financial Mgmt.
10345 W. Olympic Blvd., #200
Los Angeles, CA 90064
Actress
Birthday: 4/1/38

MacIntire, Reba
30 Music Sq. W.
Nashville, TN 37203
or
511 Fairground Ct.
Nashville, TN 37204
Country music singer

MacKenzie, Gisele
3500 W. Olive Ave., #1400
Burbank, CA 91505
Actress

Mackie, Bob
1400 Broadway
New York, NY 10018
Fashion designer

MacLaine, Shirley
25200 Old Malibu Rd., #4
Malibu, CA 90265
Actress

MacLeod, Gavin
1025 Fifth Ave.
New York, NY 10028
Actor

Macnee, Patrick
PO Box 1685
Palm Springs, CA 92263
Actor
Birthday: 2/6/22

MacPherson, Elle
414 E. 52 St. PH B
New York, NY 10022
Actress

Macy, William H.
8383 Wilshire Blvd. #550
Beverly Hills, CA 90211
Actor

Madden, John
31/32 Soho SQ
London W1V 5DG
England
Director
Birthday: 4/10/36

Madden, John
5095 Coronado Blvd.
Pleasanton, CA 94588
Sportscaster

Madigan, Amy
151 El Camino Dr.
Beverly Hills, CA 90212
Actress

Madonna
8491 Sunset Blvd. #485
Los Angeles, CA 90069
*Actress, mother of daughter
        Lourdes (born 10/14/96) and
        son Rocco Ritchie (born 8/11/
        00)*
Birthday: 8/16/58

MAD TV
5842 Sunset Blvd.
Bldg. 11, Suite 203
Attn: *MAD TV*
Hollywood, CA 90028
Television series

Mae, Vanessa
% PO Box 363
Bournmouth
Dorset
BH76LA
United Kingdom
Singer
Birthday: 10/27/78

Magnussenn, Jan
% Stewart Grand Prix Ltd.
16 Tanners Dr.
Blakelands
GB-Milton Keynes MK14 5BW
or
% Team AMG Mercedes,
Daimlerstr. 1
D-71563 Affalterbach
Professional Formula-1 driver
Birthday: 7/4/73

Mahal, Taj
PO Box 429090
San Francisco, CA 94142
Musician

Maher, Bill
% Politically Incorrect
CBS Television City
7800 Beverly Blvd.
Los Angeles, CA 90036
Host of Politically Incorrect
Actor, TV host

Mahony, Cardinal Roger
1531 W. 9th St.
Los Angeles, CA 90120

Majorino, Tina
1640 S. Sepulveda
PMB 530
Los Angeles, CA 90025
Actress

Makkena, Wendy
PO Box 5617
Beverly Hills, CA 90212
Actress

Malkovich, John
PO Box 5106
Westport, CT 06881
Actor
Birthday: 12/9/53

Mamas and The Papas
PO Box 12821
Ojai, CA 93024
Music group

Mamet, David
PO Box 381589
Cambridge, MA 02238
Director

Mancuso, Nick
3500 W. Olive Ave., #1400
Burbank, CA 91505
Actor

Mandel, Howie
8942 Wilshire Blvd.
Beverly Hills, CA 90211
Comedian, actor

Mandela, President Nelson
51 Plain St.
Johannesburg 2001
South Africa
President of South Africa

Mandela, Winnie
Orlando West
Soweto
Johannesburg
South Africa

Mandrell, Barbara
PO Box 100
Whites Creek, TN 37189
Singer

Irlene Mandrell Friend's Club
2046 Parkway
Pigeon Forge, TN 37863
Singer

Mandrell, Louise
2046 Parkway
Pigeon Forge, TN 37863
Singer

Manetti, Larry
% Epstein/Wyckoff
280 S. Beverly Dr. #400
Beverly Hills, CA 90212
Actor

Manhattan Institute
52 Vanderbilt Ave.
New York, NY, 10017
Website: http://
    www.manhattan-
    institute.org/
E-mail:
    barreiro@manhattan-
    institute.org
Lawrence Mone, President
*A think tank whose mission is to
    develop and disseminate new
    ideas that foster greater
    economic choice and
    individual responsibility*

Manhattan Transfer
8942 Wilshire Blvd.
Beverly Hills, CA 90211
Music group

Manheim Steamroller
9120 Mormon Bridge Rd.
Omaha, NE 68152
Music group

Manheim, Camryn
9057-C Nemo St.
West Hollywood, CA 90069
or
The Practice
% 20th Century Fox
10201 W. Pico Blvd.
Los Angeles, CA 90035
E-mail: camrynmail@aol.com
Actress

Mann, Michael
13746 Sunset Blvd.
Pacific Palisades, CA 90272
Director

Manners, Miss
1651 Harvard St. NW
Washington, DC 20009
Etiquette specialist

Manoff, Dinah
21244 Ventura Blvd., #101
Woodland Hills, CA 91364
Birthday: 1/25/58

Manpower
5301 N. Ironwood Rd.
Milwaukee, WI 53217
Website: http://
      www.manpower.com
John R. Walter, Chairman
Jeffrey A. Joerres, President
      and CEO
Temporary help

**Manpower Demonstration
      Research Corporation**
19th Floor
16 East 34th St.
New York, NY 10016
Website: http://www.
      mdrc.org/
E-mail: information@mdrc.org
Judith M. Gueron, President
*A nonprofit, nonpartisan research
      organization that develops
      and evaluates innovative
      approaches to moving people
      from welfare to work, building
      a stronger work force through
      training, revitalizing low-
      income communities, and
      improving education for at-
      risk youth*

Manson, Charles
#B33920
Pelican Bay Prison
Box 7000
Crescent City, CA 95531-7000
Convicted serial killer/cult leader
Birthday: 11/11/34

Manson, Marilyn
25935 Detroit Rd.
Westlake, OH 44145
Musician

Mantegna, Joe
% Peter Strain
1500 Broadway, #2001
New York, NY 10036
Actor

Manzarek, Ray
1900 Ave. of the Stars, #1040
Los Angeles, CA 90067
Actor

Maples, Marla
725 Fifth Ave.
New York, NY 10022
Donald Trump's ex-wife

Maradona, Diego
% FC Boca Juniors
Brandsen 805
1161 Capital Federal
Argentinia
Professional soccer player
Birthday: 10/30/60

Marceau, Marcel
PO Box 411197
San Francisco, CA 94141
Mime

March, Barbara
% Judy Schoen Assoc.
606 N. Larchmont Blvd., #309
Los Angeles, CA 90004
Lursa on Star Trek: The Next
    Generation *and* Star Trek:
    Deep Space Nine"

March, Jane
5 Jubilee Pl. #100
London SW3 3TD
United Kingdom
Actress

Marcos, Imelda
Leyte Providencia Dept.
Tolosa, Leyte
Philippines
Former first lady

Marcy, Dr. Geoffrey
Department of Physics and
    Astronomy
San Francisco State University
1600 Holloway
San Francisco, CA 94132

Marcy Brothers
PO Box 2502
Oroville, CA 95965
Music group

Margolin, Stuart
10000 Santa Monica Blvd.,
    #305
Los Angeles, CA 90067
Actor

Margolis, Cindy
345 N. Maple Dr., #185
Beverly Hills, CA 90212
Website: http://
    www.cindymargolis.com/
    index.cfm
Model, actress

Margulies, Julianna
405 S. Beverly Dr., #500
Beverly Hills, CA 90212
Actress

Marin, Richard (Cheech)
1122 S. Robertson Blvd., #15
Los Angeles, CA 90035
Actor

Marley, Ziggy
Jack's Hill
Kingston
Jamaica
Musician

Marriott International
10400 Fernwood Rd.
Bethesda, MD 20817
Website: http://
    www.marriott.com
J. Willard Marriott, Jr., CEO
Hotels, casinos, and resorts

Marrs, Texe
1708 Patterson Rd.
Austin, TX 78733
Religious author

Marsden, Jason
10753 Santa Monica Blvd.,
    #130
Los Angeles, CA 90025
Actor

Marshall Tucker Band
100 W. Putnam
Greenwich, CT 06830
Music group

Marshall, Penny
9465 Wilshire Blvd., #419
Beverly Hills, CA 90212
Actress, director

Marshall, Peter
11365 Ventura Blvd., #100
Studio City, CA 91604
TV game show host
Birthday: 3/20/27

Marsh and McLennan
1166 Ave., of the Americas
New York, NY 10036
Website: http://
    www.marshmac.com
Jeffrey W. Greenberg
    Chairman, President, and
    CEO
Diversified financials

Martell, Donna
PO Box 3335
Granada Hills, CA 91394
Actress

Martin, Dick
30765 Pacific Coast Hwy., #103
Malibu, CA 90265
Actor, television personality

Martin, Pamela Sue
% Pierce and Shelly
612 Lighthouse Ave., #275
Pacific Grove, CA 93951
E-mail:
    PAMSUEMART@aol.com
Actress
Birthday: 1/5/54

Martin, Ricky
% CCA
9830 Wilshire Blvd.
Beverly Hills, CA 90212
Singer
Birthday: 12/24/71

Martin, Steve
PO Box 929
Beverly Hills, CA 90213
Actor, comedian

Martindale, Wink
11365 Ventura Blvd., #100
Studio City, CA. 91604
TV game show host
Birthday: 12/4/34

Masco
21001 Van Born Rd.
Taylor, MI 48180
Website: http://www.masco.com
Richard A. Manoogian,
    Chairman and CEO
Metal Products

Masekela, Hugh
230 Park Ave., #1512
New York, NY 10169
Musician

Maske, Henry
% Sauerland Promotion
Hochstadenstr. 1–3
50674 Kön
Germany
or
% WLT Sport Int.
Römerstr. 108
54293 Trier
Germany
Former professional boxer
Birthday: 1/6/64

Mason, Marsha
320 Galiston St., #402B
Santa Fe, NM 87501
Actress
Birthday: 4/3/42

Masterson, Mary Stuart
% Constellation
PO Box 1249
White River Junction, VT
    05001
Actress

Mastrantonio, Mary Elizabeth
% Hofflund-Tolone
9465 Wilshire Blvd., #620
Beverly Hills, CA 90212
Actress
Birthday: 11/17/64

Masur, Richard
121 N. San Vicente Blvd.
Beverly Hills, CA 90211
Actor

Matchbox 20
9830 Wilshire Blvd.
Beverly Hills, CA 90212
Music group

Mathers, Jerry
30290 Rancho Viejo Rd., #122
San Juan Capistrano, CA 92675
Actor

Matheson, Tim
10290 Santa Monica Blvd.,
    #300
Los Angeles, CA 90025
Actor
Birthday: 12/31/48

Mathis, Johnny
3500 W. Olive Ave., #750
Burbank, CA 91505
Singer
Birthday: 9/30/35

Matlin, Marlee
7920 Sunset Blvd., #400
Los Angeles, CA 90046
Actress
Birthday: 8/24/65

Mattea, Kathy
900 Division St.
Nashville, TN 37203
Singer, songwriter

Mattel
333 Continental Blvd.
El Segundo, CA 90245
Website: http://
    www.barbie.com
Robert A. Eckert, Chairman
    and CEO
Toys, sporting goods

Dave Mathews Band
PO Box 1911
Charlottesville, VA 22903
Music group

Mattingly, Don
RR #5
Box 74
Evansville, IN 47711
Baseball player

Maven, Max
PO Box 3819
La Mesa, CA 92044
or
7095 Hollywood Blvd., #382
Hollywood, CA 90028
Website: http://
    www.maxmaven.com/
E-mail: MaxMaven@aol.com
Mentalist, magician

Mavericks, The
PO Box 3329
Nashville, TN 37202
Music group

Max, Peter
118 Riverside Dr.
New York, NY 10024
Artist

Maxwell
1325 Ave. of the Americas
New York, NY 10019
Website: http://
    www.sonymusic.com/artists/
    Maxwell/index2.html
R&B singer

Maxxam
5847 San Felipe
Houston, TX 77057
Charles E. Hurwitz, CEO
Metals

May, Elaine
145 Central Park West
New York, NY 10023
Actress

**The May Department Stores
    Company**
611 Olive St.
St. Louis, MO 63101
Website: http://
    www.maycompany.com
Jerome T. Loeb, Chairman
John L. Dunham, VC and CFO
Richard W. Bennet III, VC
William P. McNamara, VC
Anthony J. Torcasio, VC
General merchandisers

Mayhew, Peter
% *Star Wars* Fan Club
PO Box 111000
Aurora, CO 80042
Actor
Played Chewbacca in Star Wars

Mays, Willie
PO Box 2410
Menlo Park, CA 94026
Retired baseball player
Birthday: 5/6/31

Maytag
403 W. Fourth St. N.
Newton, IA 50208
Website: http://
    www.maytagcorp.com
Lloyd D. Ward, Chairman and
    CEO
Electronics, electrical equipment

MBNA
1100 N. King St.
Wilmington, DE 19884
Website: http://www.mbna
    international.com
Alfred Lerner, Chairman and
    CEO
Commercial bank

Mcallister, Dawson
PO Box 8123
Irving, TX 75016
Christian talk show host

McBride, Martina
406-68 Water St.
Vancouver
British Columbia
V6B 1A4
Country music singer

McBride and The Ride
PO Box 17617
Nashville, TN 37217
Music group

McCain, Senator John
1300 Crystal Dr.
Arlington, VA 22202
*Senator and former presidential
    candidate*

McCambridge, Mercedes
156 Fifth Ave., #820
New York, NY 10010
Actress

McCarter Sisters
PO Box 121551
Nashville, TN 37212
Music group

McCarthy, Andrew
8942 Wilshire Blvd.
Beverly Hills, CA 90211
Actor
Birthday: 11/29/62

McCarthy, Jenny
8424A Santa Monica Blvd.,
    #804
West Hollywood, CA 90069
1994's Playmate of the Year
Birthday: 11/2/72

McCartney, Sir Paul
1 Soho Square
London W1
England
Former Beatle

McCaughey Septuplets, The
615 N. First
Carlisle, IA 50047

McClain, Charly
PO Box 198888
Nashville, TN 37219
Country music singer

McClanahan, Rue
9454 Wilshire Blvd., #405
Beverly Hills, CA 90212
Actress
Birthday: 2/21/34

Delbert McClinton Int'l.
47 Music Square E.
Nashville, TN 37203
Country singer's fan club

McConaughey, Matthew
PO Box 1145
Malibu, CA 90265
Actor
Birthday: 11/4/69

McCord, Kent
15301 Ventura Blvd., #345
Sherman Oaks, CA 91403
Actor

McCromack, Catherine
9830 Wilshire Blvd.
Beverly Hills, CA 90212
Actress

McCormack, Mary
PO Box 67335
Los Angeles, CA 90067
Actress

McCormick, Carolyn
Box 250
Seal Beach, CA 90740
Actress

McCormick, Kelly
Box 250
Seal Beach, CA 90740
Musician

McCormick, Maureen
1925 Century Park E., #2320
Los Angeles, CA 90067
Actress (played Marsha Brady)

McCormick, Pat
23388 Mulholland Dr.
Woodland Hills, CA 91364
Comedian, writer

McCormick, Pat
Box 250
Seal Beach, CA 90740
Swimmer

McCoy, Charlie
1300 Division St., #304
Nashville, TN 37203
Musician

McCoy, Matt
4526 Wilshire Blvd.
Los Angeles, CA 90010
Actor

McCoy, Neal
3878 Oaklawn Ave., #620
Dallas, TX 75219
Country music singer

McCracken, Jeff
15760 Ventura Blvd., #1730
Encino, CA 91436
Actor

McCullough, Julie
% Pierce and Shelly
612 Lighthouse Ave., #275
Pacific Grove, CA 93951
E-mail: JulieMcCul@aol.com
Actress

McDaniel, Mel
PO Box 2285
Hendersonville, TN 37077
or
2802 Columbine Pl.
Nashville, TN 37204
Country music singer

McDermott, Dylan
PO Box 25516
Los Angeles, CA 90025
Actor

McDonald's
McDonald's Plaza
Oak Brook, IL 60523
Website: http://
www.mcdonalds.com
Jack M. Greenberg, Chairman
and CEO
Food services

McDonald, Audra
130 W. 42nd St., #1804
New York, NY 10036
Singer

McDonald, "Country" Joe
PO Box 7054
Berkeley, CA 94707
or
17337 Ventura Blvd., #208
Encino, CA 91316
Website: http://
    www.countryjoe.com/
Singer, songwriter

McDonnell, Mary
PO Box 6010-540
Sherman Oaks, CA 91413
Actress

McDormand, Frances
333 West End Ave., Suite 12-C
New York, NY 10023
Actor

McDowell, Malcolm
4 Windmill St.
London W1P 1HF
England
Actor
Birthday: 6/19/43

McDowell, Ronnie
20 Music Square W., #200
Nashville, TN 37203
Country music singer

McEntire, Reba
40 Music Square West
Nashville, TN 37203
Country music singer
Birthday: 3/28/55

McEuen, John
6044 Deal Ave.
Nashville, TN 37209
Country music singer

McFadden, Gates
% Innovative Artists
1999 Ave. of the Stars, #2850
Los Angeles, CA 90067
Actress
Played Dr. Beverly Crusher on
    Star Trek: The Next
    Generation
Birthday: 8/28/49

McFerrin, Bobby
826 Broadway, #400
New York, NY 10003
Musician

McGavin, Darren
PO Box 2939
Beverly Hills, CA 90213
Actor

McGinley, Ted
1925 Century Park E., Suite
    2320
Los Angeles, CA 90067
Actor
Birthday: 5/30/58

McGovern, Elizabeth
17319 Magnolia Blvd.
Encino, CA 91316
Actress

McGovern, George
PO Box 5591
Friendship Station
Washington, DC 20016
Former Senator

McGovern, Maureen
163 Amsterdam Ave., #174
New York, NY 10023
Website: http://www.maureen
    mcgovern.com/
Singer

McGraw, Tim
209 10th. Ave., #229
Nashville, TN 37203
Country music singer

McGraw Hill
1221 Ave. of the Americas
New York, NY 10020
Website: http://www.mcgraw-
    hill.com
Harold W. "Terry" McGraw III,
    Chairman, President, and
    CEO
Publishing, printing

McGregor, Ewan
503/504 Lotts Rd.
The Cambers
Chelsea Harbour SWIO OXF
England
Actor
Birthday: 3/31/71

McKeon, Nancy
PO Box 6778
Burbank, CA 91510
Actress
Birthday: 4/4/66

McKesson HBOC, Inc.
McKesson HBOC Plaza, One
    Post St.
San Francisco, CA 94104
Website: http://
    www.mckesson.com
Alan Seelenfreund, Chairman
John H. Hammergren, Co-
    President and Co-CEO
David L. Mahoney,
    Co-President and Co-CEO
Wholesalers

McLean, Don
450 7th. Ave., #603
New York, NY 10123
Singer, songwriter
Birthday: 10/2/45

McMurtry, Larry
Box 552
Archer City, TX 76351
Author

McMurtry, Tom
PO Box 273
Edwards AFB, CA 93523
Test pilot

McNeill, Robert Duncan
% Paramount Pictures
    Productions
·*Star Trek Voyager*
5555 Melrose Ave.
Los Angeles, CA 90038
Actor, plays Lt. Tom Paris on
    Star Trek: Voyager

McNeil, Kate
9229 Sunset Blvd., #710
Los Angeles, CA 90069
Actress

McRaney, Gerald
1012 Royal St.
New Orleans, LA 70116
Actor, married to Delta Burke
Birthday: 8/19/48

MacAnally, Mac
% T. K. Kimbrell
TKO Management
4205 Hillsboro Rd., Suite #208
Nashville, TN 37215
Country music singer

Mead
Courthouse Plaza NE
Dayton, OH 45463
Website: http://www.mead.com
Jerome F. Tatar, Chairman,
    President, and CEO
Forest and paper products

Meadows, Jayne
15201-B Burbank Blvd.
Van Nuys, CA 91411
Actress

Meara, Anne
% Innovative Artists
1999 Ave. of the Stars, #2850
Los Angeles, CA 90067
*Comedian, actress, married to Jerry
    Stiller*

Meatloaf (Marvin Lee Aday)
9255 Sunset Blvd., #200
Los Angeles, CA 90069
Singer
Birthday: 9/27/51

Media Access Project
950 18th St., NW, Suite 220
Washington, DC 20006
Website:http://
    www.mediaaccess.org/
    index.html
Andrew Jay Schwartzman,
    President and CEO
*A twenty-four-year-old nonprofit,
    public interest law firm which
    promotes the public's First
    Amendment right to hear and
    be heard on the electronic
    media of today and tomorrow*

Media Research Center
325 S. Patrick St.
Alexandria, VA 22314
Website: http://
    www.mediaresearch.org/
E-mail:
    mrc@mediaresearch.org
L. Brent Bozell III, Founder
    and Chairman
*Founded in 1987 with the mission
    of bringing political balance to
    the nation's news media and
    responsibility to the
    entertainment media, the
    Media Research Center
    (MRC) has grown into the
    nation's largest and most
    respected conservative media
    watchdog organization*

Media Studies Center
1101 Wilson Blvd.
Arlington, VA 22209
Website: http://
    www.freedomforum.org/
E-mail:
    news@freedomforum.org
Charles L. Overby, Chairman
    and CEO
*A nonpartisan, international
    foundation dedicated to free
    press, free speech, and free
    spirit for all people*

Mediascope
12711 Ventura Blvd., #280
Studio City, CA 91604
Website: http://
    www.mediascope.org/
    mediascope/index.htm
E-mail: facts@mediascope.org
Hubert D. Jessup, President
*A national, nonprofit public policy
    organization founded in 1992
    to promote constructive
    depictions of health and social
    issues in the media,
    particularly as they relate to
    children and adolescents*

**Medical Research
    Modernization Committee**
3200 Morley Rd.
Shaker Heights, OH 44122
Website: http://
    www.mrmcmed.org/
E-mail: mrmcmed@aol.com
*Works to modernize medical
    research and promote human
    health concludes that animal
    experiments take desperately
    needed money but rarely
    contribute to human health*

Mellencamp, John
Rt 1 Box 361
Nashville, IN 47448
Rock singer, songwriter, guitarist
Birthday: 10/7/51

Mellon Bank Corporation
1 Mellon Bank Center
Pittsburgh, PA 15258
Website: http://
    www.mellon.com
Commercial banks

Mellons, Ken
PO Box 756
Hermitage, TN 37076
Singer

Members of Mayday
% Low Spirit Recordings
Giesebrechtstr. 16
10629 Berlin
Germany
Music group

Men At Work
1775 Broadway, #433
New York, NY 10019
Music group

Menendez, Erik
#1878449
CSP-Sac
Box 290066
Represa, CA 95671
Convicted of killing his parents

Menendez, Lyle
#1887106
California Correctional
    Institute
CCI-Box 1031
Tehachapi, CA 93581
Convicted of killing his parents

Mensy, Tim
PO Box 128007
Nashville, TN 37212
Country music singer

Menudo
2895 Biscayne Blvd., #455
Miami, FL 33137
Music group

Mercantile Bank Corporation
216 N. Division Ave.
Grand Rapids, MI 49503
Gerald R. Johnson, Jr.,
    Chairman and CEO
Banking

Merchant, Natalie
% Creative Artists Agency
9830 Wilshire Blvd.
Beverly Hills, CA 90212
Singer, songwriter
Birthday: 10/26/63

Merisel
200 Continental Blvd.
El Segundo, CA 90245
Website: http://
www.merisel.com
David G. Sadler, President,
CEO, and COO
Computer wholesalers

Meriwether, Lee
2555 E. Colorado Blvd.
Pasadena, CA 91107
Actress, former Miss America
Birthday: 5/27/35

Merck
1 Merck Dr.
Whitehouse Station, NJ 08889
Website: http://
www.merck.com
Raymond V. Gilmartin,
Chairman and CEO
Pharmaceuticals

Merrill Lynch
250 Vesey St.
New York, NY 10281
Website: http://www.ml.com
David H. Komansky, Chairman
and CEO
Securities

Metallica
729 7th Ave., #1400
New York, NY 10019
Website: http://
www.Metallica.com/
E-mail: email@metallica.com
Heavy metal group

Metropolitan Life Insurance
1 Madison Ave.
New York, NY 10010
Robert H. Benmosche,
Chairman, President, and
CEO
Life and health insurance (stock)

Meyer, Dina
% UTA
9560 Wilshire Blvd.
Beverly Hills, CA 90212
Actress
Birthday: 6/15/69

Miami Sound Machine
6205 Bird Rd.
Miami, FL 33155
Music group

Midler, Bette
9701 Wilshire Blvd., 10th Floor
Beverly Hills, CA 90212
Actress, singer
Birthday: 12/1/45

**Mighty Morphin Power
    Rangers**
26020-A Avenue Hall
Valencia, CA 91355
TV series

**Mexican American Legal
    Defense and Education
    Fund (MALDEF)**
634 South Spring Street, 1st
    Floor
Los Angeles, CA 90014
Website: http://
www.MALDEF.org/
E-mail: info@maldef.org
Antonia Hernandez
*A national nonprofit organization
    whose mission is to protect
    and promote the civil rights of
    the more than 29 million
    Latinos living in the United
    States*

Mickey Mouse
500 S. Buena Vista St.
Burbank, CA 92521
Website: http://
    www.disney.com/
*Cartoon character, first Mickey
    Mouse, cartoon, Steamboat
    Willie, released 11/18/28*

MicroAge
2400 S. MicroAge Way
Tempe, AZ 85282
Website: http://
    www.microage.com
Jeffrey D. McKeever, Chairman
    and CEO
Computer wholesaler

Micron Technology
8000 S. Federal Way
Boise, ID 83707
Website: http://
    www.micron.com
Steven R. Appleton, Chairman,
    President, and CEO
Electronics, electrical equipment

Microsoft
1 Microsoft Way
Redmond, WA 98052
Website: http://
    www.microsoft.com
William H. Gates III, Chairman
    and Chief Software
    Architect
Steven A. Ballmer, President
    and CEO
Computer software

Mike and the Mechanics
9200 Sunset Blvd., #400
Los Angeles, CA 90069
Music group

Milano, Alyssa
5700 Wilshire Blvd., #575
Los Angeles, CA 90036
Actress
Birthday: 12/19/73

Miles, Vera
Box 1704
Big Bear Lake, CA 92315
Actress
Birthday: 8/23/30

Milius, John
8942 Wilshire Blvd.
Beverly Hills, CA 90211
Director

Millenium Chemicals
230 Half Mile Rd.
Red Bank, NJ 07701
Website:http://
    www.millenniumchem.com
William M. Landuyt, CEO
Chemicals

Miller, Arthur
Tophet Rd.
Box 320
R #1
Roxbury, CT 06783
Playwright

Miller, Bill
% Sherry Halton
1223 17th Ave. S.
Nashville, TN 37212
Singer

Miller, Dennis
7800 Beverly Blvd.
Los Angeles, CA 90036
TV host, comedian, actor
Birthday: 10/5/43

Miller, Glenn Birthplace Society
PO Box 61
Clarinda, IA 51632

Miller, Glenn Orchestra
2250 Lucien Way, #100
Maitland, FL 32751

Miller, Glenn Society
18 Crendon St.
High Wycombe
Bucks
England

Miller, Penelope Ann
9569 Wilshire Blvd., #516
Beverly Hills, CA 90212
Actress
Birthday: 1/13/64

Mills, Donna
253 26th. St., #259
Santa Monica, CA 90402
Actress

Mills, Sir John
Hill House
Denham Village
GB-Buckinghamshire
Actor
Birthday: 2/22/08

Milner. Martin
10100 Santa Monica Blvd.,
    #2490
Los Angeles, CA 90067
Actor

Milsap, Ronnie
PO Box 40665
Nashville, TN 37204
Country music singer

Minghella, Anthony
122 Wigmore St.
London W1H 9FE
England
Film director

Minnelli, Liza
160 Central Park S.
New York, NY 10019
*Actress, singer, Judy Garland's
    oldest daughter*
Birthday: 3/12/46

**Minnesota Mining and
    Manufacturing (3M)**
3M Center
St. Paul, MN 55144
Website: http://www.mmm.com
Livio D. DeSimone, Chairman
    and CEO
*Scientific, photo, control
    equipment, Scotch tape*

Miss America Pageant
1325 Boardwalk
Atlantic City, NJ 08401
Website: www.missamerica.org
Robert Renneisen, Jr.,
    President and CEO
Heather French, Miss America
    2000
*The Miss America competition has
    been broadcast live at one time
    or another by all three of the
    country's major television
    networks and remains one of
    the highest rated annual
    events on national television
    today*

Miss Teen USA
% Dara Arbeiter
Rubenstein Public Relations
1345 Ave. of the Americas
New York, NY 10105
Website: http://
    www.missteenusa.com/
    home.html
Maureen J. Reidy, President
Jillian Parry, Miss Teen USA
    2000

Mistress Marisha
Website: http://
    www.marisha.com/
E-mail: marisha@marisha.com
Dominatrix model

Mitchell, Dennis
% US Olympic Comm.
1750 E. Boulder St.
Colorado Springs, CO 80909
Olympic sprinter

Mister Mr.
PO Box 69343
Los Angeles, CA 90069
Music group

Mitchell, George
8280 Greensboro Dr.
McLean, VA 22102
Former Senator

Mitchell, Waddie
PO Box 268
Elko, NV 89801
or
PO Box 9188
Colorado Springs, CO 80932
Cowboy poet

Moceanu, Dominique
17911 Fall River Circle
Houston, TX 77090
Olympic gymnast

Modernaires, The
11761 E. Speedway Blvd.
Tucson, AZ 85748
Music group

Modine, Mathew
8942 Wilshire Blvd.
Beverly Hills, CA 90211
Actor
Birthday: 3/22/59

Moffat, Donald
151 El Camino Dr.
Beverly Hills, CA 90212
Actor

Moll, Richard
1119 M. Amalfi Dr.
Pacific Palisades, CA 90272
Actor
Birthday: 1/13/43

Molly and the Heymakers
PO Box 1160
Hayward, WI 54843
Music group

Monkees, The
8369A Sausalito Ave.
West Hills, CA 91304
Music group

Monsanto
800 N. Lindbergh Blvd.
St. Louis, MO 63167
Website: http://
    www.monsanto.com
Hendrik A. Verfaillie,
    President and CEO
Chemicals

Montalban, Ricardo
13701 Riverside Dr., #500
Sherman Oaks, CA 91423
Actor

Montana, Joe
21515 Hawthorne Blvd., #1250
Torrance, CA 90503
Former football quarterback

Montana, Patsy
3728 Highway 411
Madisonville, TN 37354
Country music singer

Montanans for Property Rights
PO Box 130399
Coram, MT 59913
Website: http://
     members.spree.com/mfpr/
E-mail: mfpr7@yahoo.com
Russell Crowder, Member
     Board of Directors
*Defends the rights of Montana
     property owners*

Montgomery, George
PO Box 2187
Rancho Mirage, CA 92270
Actor

Montgomery, John Michael
1905 Broadway
Nashville, TN 37203
Country music singer

Moore, Demi
955 S. Carrillo Dr., #200
Los Angeles, CA 90048
E-mail: DemiM2@aol.com
Actress
Birthday: 11/11/62

Moore, Mary Tyler
510 E. 86th St., #21A
New York, NY 10028
or
% William-Morris
1325 Ave. of the Americas
New York, NY 10019
Actress
Birthday: 12/29/36

Moore, Melba
% Hush
231 W. 58th. St.
New York, NY 10019
Actress

Moore, Sir Roger
2-4 Noel St.
London W1V 3RB
United Kingdom
Actor
Birthday: 10/14/27

Moran, Erin
PO Box 3261
Quartz Hill, CA 93586
Actress
Birthday: 10/18/61

**Moreno, Rita (Rosita Dolores
     Alverio)**
160 Gravatt Dr.
Berkeley, CA 94705
Actress
Birthday: 12/11/31

Morgan, Lorrie
1906 Acklen Ave.
Nashville, TN 37212
Country music singer

Morgan Stanley Dean Witter and Co
1585 Broadway
New York, NY 10036
Website: http://www.deanwitter
    discover.com
Philip J. Purcell, CEO
Securities

Morissette, Alanis
75 Rockefeller Plaza, #2100
New York, NY 10019
Singer, songwriter

Morita, Noriuki "Pat"
PO Box 491278
Los Angeles, CA 90049
Actor
Birthday: 6/28/30

Morris, Garret
8436 Third St., #740
Los Angeles, CA 90048
Actor

Morris, Gary
2829 Dogwood Pl.
Nashville, TN 37204
Singer/songwriter

Morrison, Van
1AS
London W1A 1AS
England
Singer, songwriter
Birthday: 8/31/45

Moses, Rick
% The Calder Agency
19919 Redwing St.
Woodland Hills, CA 91364
Actor
Birthday: 9/5/52

Moss, Kate
% Storm Model Mgmt.
1st Floor 5 Jubilee Place
London SW3 3TD
England
Model
Birthday: 1/16/74

Motley Crue
9255 Sunset Blvd., #200
Los Angeles, CA 90069
Music group

Motorola
1303 E. Algonquin Rd.
Schaumburg, IL 60196
Website: http://www.mot.com
Christopher B. Galvin,
    Chairman and CEO
Electronics, electrical equipment

Mowrey, Dude
11 Music Circle S.
Nashville, TN 37203
Musician

MTV
1515 Broadway
New York, NY 10036
Website: http://www.mtv.com/
E-mail: mtvnews@mtv.com
Tom Freston, Chairman and
    CEO
Judy McGrath, Group
    President, MTV Group;
    Chairman, MTVi
Cable TV music network

Mueller-Stahl, Armin
% ZBF-Agentur
Ordensmeisterstr. 15
12099 Berlin
Germany
Actor
Birthday: 12/17/30

Muldaur, Diana
10100 Santa Monica Blvd.,
    #2490
Los Angeles, CA 90067
Actress
Birthday: 8/19/38

Muldoon, Patrick
% Gallin-Morey Assoc.
345 N. Maple Dr., #300
Beverly Hills, CA 90210
Actor

Mulgrew, Kate
612 N. Sepulveda Blvd., #10
Los Angeles, CA 90049
Actress
Birthday: 4/29/45

Mulroney, Dermot
1180 S. Beverly Dr., #618
Los Angeles, CA 90035
Actor
Birthday: 10/31/63

Murphey, David Lee
PO Box 12168
Nashville, TN 37212
Country music singer

Murphey, Michael Martin
PO Box 777
Taos, NM 87571
Country and cowboy singer

Murphy, Eddie
PO Box 1028
Englewood Cliffs, NJ 07632
or
% Int'l Creative Mgmt.
8942 Wilshire Blvd.
Beverly Hills, CA 90211
or
1400 Tower Grove Dr.
Beverly Hills, CA 90210
Actor, comedian
Birthday: 4/3/61

Murray, Anne
4950 Yonge St., #2400
Toronto, Ontario
Canada, M2N 6K1
or
Box 69030
12 St. Clair Ave. East
Toronto, Ontario M4T 1K0
Canada
or
Balmur Entertainment Ltd.
35 Alvin Ave.
Toronto, ON
M4T 2A7
Canada
Website: http://
    www.annemurray.com/
E-mail: anne@annemurray.com
Singer

Murray, Bill
% Creative Artists Agency
9830 Wilshire Blvd.
Beverly Hills, CA 90212
Actor, comedian, writer
Birthday: 9/21/50

Muster, Thomas
% AMJ Pro Management
Steinfeldstr. 17
2351 Wiener Neudorf
Austria
Professional tennis player
Birthday: 10/2/67

Mutual of Omaha Insurance
Mutual of Omaha Plaza
Omaha, NE 68175
Website: http://
www.mutualofomaha.com
John William Weekly,
Chairman and CEO
*Life and health insurance
(mutual)*

Myers, Mike
9150 Wilshire Blvd., #350
Beverly Hills, CA 90212
Actor
Birthday: 5/25/63

N

A writer lives in awe of words for they can be cruel or kind, and they can change their meanings right in front of you. They pick up flavors and odors like butter in a refrigerator.

—ANONYMOUS

National Association for the Advancement of Colored People (NAACP)
Washington Bureau
4805 Mt. Hope Dr.
Baltimore, MD 21215
Website: http://www.naacp.org/
Kweisi Mfume, President and CEO
Its primary objective is to ensure the political, educational, social, and economic equality of minority group citizens of the United States

Nabors, Jim
215 Kulamanu Pl
Honolulu, HI 96816
Actor, singer
Birthday: 6/11/33

Nader, Ralph
1600 20th. St. NW
Washington, DC 20009
Green Party presidential candidate

Nakano, Shinji
% Prost Grand Prix
Technopole de la Nièvre
F-58470 Magny Cours
France
Professional Formula-1 driver

Nana
% Booya Music
Marlowring 3
D-22525 Hamburg
Germany
Singer
Birthday: 10/5/71

Nannini, Alessandro
Via del Paradiso 4
53100 Siena
Italy
Race car driver
Birthday: 7/7/59

Narz, Jack
11365 Ventura Blvd., #100
Studio City, CA 91604
TV game show host, Tom Kennedy's Brother
Birthday: 11/13/22

Nash, Graham
14930 Ventura Blvd., #205
Sherman Oaks, CA 91403
Rock musician

Nash Finch
7600 France Ave. S.
Edina, MN 55435
Allister P. Graham, Chairman
Ron Marshall, President and
    CEO
Wholesalers

National Academy of Science
2101 Constitution Ave. NW
Washington, DC 20418
Website: http://www.nas.edu/
E-mail: wwwfdbk@nas.edu
Bruce Alberts, President
A private, nonprofit society of
    scholars engaged in scientific
    and engineering research,
    dedicated to the furtherance of
    science and technology and to
    their use for the general
    welfare

National Alliance for the
    Mentally Ill
Colonial Place Three
2107 Wilson Blvd., Suite 300
Arlington, VA 22201-3042
Website: http://www.nami.org/
E-mail: namiofc@aol.com
Laurie M. Flynn, Executive
    Director
An organization working with and
    for persons with mental
    illnesses and their families

National Association of Home
    Builders
1201 15th St. NW
Washington, DC 20005
Website: http://
    www.nahb.com/
E-mail: info@nahb.com
Robert Mitchell, President
The voice of America's housing
    industry

National Association of
    Manufacturers
1331 Pennsylvania Ave. NW,
    #1500
Washington, DC 20004
Website: http://www.nam.org/
E-mail:
    manufacturing@nam.org
Amy Foscue, Associate Director
E-mail: afoscue@nam.org
Founded in 1895 to advance a
    pro-growth, pro-manufacturing
    policy agenda

National Association of
    Professional Pet Sitters
NAPPS 1030 15th St. NW,
    Suite 870
Washington, DC 20005
Website: http://
    www.petsitters.org/
E-mail: napps@rgminc.com
Ryan Dryden
Promotes the concept of in-home pet
    care, to support the
    professionals engaged in at-
    home pet care, promote the
    welfare of animals, and to
    improve, and expand the
    industry of pet sitting

National Association of
    Realtors
700 11th St. NW
Washington, DC 20001
Website: http://nar.realtor.com/
E-mail:
    infocentral@realtors.org
Steve Cook, Vice President
Composed of residential and
    commercial Realtors®, who
    are brokers, salespeople,
    property managers, appraisers,
    counselors, and others engaged
    in all aspects of the real estate
    industry

National Audubon Society
700 Broadway
New York, NY 10003
Website: http://
    www.audubon.org/
E-mail: jbianchi@audubon.org
Oakes Ames, Board Member
Ruth O. Russell, Board
    Member
*To conserve and restore natural
    ecosystems, focusing on birds
    and other wildlife, for the
    benefit of humanity and the
    earth's biological diversity*

**National Caucus and Center
    on Black Aged, Inc.**
1424 K St. NW, #500
Washington, DC 20005
Website: http://www.ncba-
    blackaged.org/
E-mail: ncba@aol.com
*A national nonprofit organization
    dedicated to improving the
    quality of life for African
    Americans and low-income
    elderly*

**National Center for Law and
    Deafness**
800 Florida Ave. NE
Washington, DC 20002

**National Center for State
    Courts**
300 Newport Ave.
Williamsburg, VA 23185
Website: http://
    www.ncsc.dni.us/
Gerald W. Vandewalle,
    Chairman
E-mail: vandewallej@
    court.state.nd.us

*An independent, nonprofit
    organization dedicated to the
    improvement of justice;
    founded in 1971 at the
    urging of Chief Justice Warren
    E. Burger, NCSC accomplishes
    its mission by providing
    leadership and service to the
    state courts*

**National Center on Institutions
    and Alternatives (NCIA)**
3125 Mt. Vernon Av.
Alexandria, VA 22305
Website: http:
    //www.igc.apc.org/ncia/
E-mail: info@ncianet.org
*Its mission is to help create a
    society in which all persons
    who come into contact with
    the human service or
    correctional systems will be
    provided an environment of
    individual care*

National City Corp.
1900 E. Ninth St.
Cleveland, OH 44114
Website: http://www.national-
    city.com
David A. Daberko, Chairman
    and CEO
Commercial Banks

**National Organization for the
    Reform of Marijuana Laws
    (NORML)**
1001 Connecticut Ave. NW,
    #1010
Washington, DC 20036
Website: http://
    www.norml.org/
E-mail: norml@norml.org
R. Keith Stroup, Executive
    Director and NORML
    founder

*Since its founding in 1970,
NORML has been the
principal national advocate
for legalizing marijuana*

National Organization for Women (NOW)

1000 16th St. NW, #700
Washington, DC 20036
Website: http://www.now.org/
E-mail: now@now.org
Patricia Ireland, President
*It is dedicated to making legal,
political, social, and economic
change in our society in order
to eliminate sexism*

National Republican Congressional Campaign Committee

320 1st St. SE
Washington, DC 20003
Website: www.nrcc.org
Tom Davis, Chairman
*A political committee devoted to
increasing the 223-member
Republican majority in the
U.S. House of Representatives*

National Rifle Association

Website: http://www.nra.org/
E-mail: nra-contact@NRA.org
Tanya K. Metaksa, Executive
Director, NRA-ILA
Wayne La Pierre, Executive
Vice President
Charlton Heston, President
*The NRA was incorporated in
1871 to provide firearms
training and encourage
interest in the shooting sports*

National Taxpayer's Union

108 North Alfred St.
Alexandria, VA 22314
Website: http://www.ntu.org/
E-mail: ntu@ntu.org
John Berthoud, President
*The largest grassroots taxpayer
organization with more than
300,000 members across all
states*

National Trust for Historic Preservation

1785 Massachusetts Ave. NW
Washington, DC 20036
Website: http://www.nthp.org
Richard Moe, President
*Dedicated to showing how
preservation can play an
important role in
strengthening a sense of
community and improving the
quality of life*

National Urban League

500 East 62nd St.
New York, NY 10021
Website: http://www.nul.org/
E-mail: info@nul.org
Jonathan S. Linen, Chairman
*The premier social service and civil
rights organization in America*

National Wildlife Federation

8925 Leesburg Pike
Vienna, VA 22184
Website: http://www.nwf.org/
Mark Van Putten, President
and CEO
*NWF focuses its efforts on five core
issue areas (Endangered
Habitat, Water Quality, Land
Stewardship, Wetlands, and
Sustainable Communities),
and pursues a range of
educational projects, and
activist, advocacy, and
litigation initiatives within
these core areas*

Nationwide Financial Services, Inc.
1 Nationwide Plaza
Columbus, OH 43215
E-mail: http://
    www.boafuture.com
Dimon R. McFerson, CEO
P and C insurance (stock)

Native American Rights Fund
1506 Broadway
Boulder, CO 80302
Website: http://www.narf.org/
E-mail: pereira@narf.org
John E. Echohawk, Executive
    Director
*A nonprofit legal organization
    dedicated to the preservation
    of the rights and culture of
    Native Americans*

Naughton, David
11774-B Moorpark St.
Studio City, CA 91604
Actor
Birthday: 2/13/51

Navistar International
455 N. Cityfront Plaza Dr.
Chicago, IL 60611
Website: http://
    www.navistar.com
John R. Horne, CEO
Motor vehicles and parts

Navratilova, Martina
c/o WTA Tour
1266 E. Main St., #4
Stamford, CT 06902
Professional tennis player
Birthday: 10/18/56

NCR
1700 S. Patterson Blvd.
Dayton, OH 45479
Website: http://www.ncr.com/
    index.asp
Lars Nyberg, Chairman,
    President, and CEO
Computers, office equipment

Neal, Patricia
45 East End Ave., #4C
New York, NY 10028
Actress
Birthday: 1/20/26

Nealon, Kevin
9363 Wilshire Blvd. #212
Beverly Hills, CA 90210
Actor

Needham, Tracey
J.A.G. (US action series)
% Badgley + Connor
9229 Sunset Blvd., #311
Los Angeles, CA 90069
Actress

Neeson, Liam
76 Oxford St.
London W1N 0AX
England
Actor
Birthday: 6/7/52

Neil, Sam
PO Box 153
Noble Park
Victoria 3174
Australia
Actor
Birthday: 9/14/47

Nelligan, Kate
% IA
1999 Ave. of the Stars, #2850
Los Angeles, CA 90067
Actress
Birthday: 3/16/51

Nelson, Willie
Rt #1
Briarcliff TT
Spicewood, TX 78669
Singer/songwriter
Birthday: 4/30/33

Neville, Aaron
Box 750187
New Orleans, LA 70175
Singer
Birthday: 1/24/41

Nevins, Jason
% Sony Music/epic
Stephanstr. 15
60313 Frankfurt
Germany
Member of Run, D.M.C.

New Edition
151 El Camino Dr.
Beverly Hills, CA 90212
Music group

New Grass Revival
PO Box 1288037
Nashville, TN 37212
Music group

New Israel Fund
National Office
1101 14th St. NW, Sixth Floor
Washington, DC 20005
Website: http://www.nif.org/
    home/
E-mail info@nif.org
Mary Ann Stein, North
    American Chair
*Organization for pluralism and
    religious freedom in Israel*

New Radicals
645 Quail Ridge Rd.
Aledo, TX 76008
Music group

New Rascals, The
PO Box 1821
Ojai, CA 93023
Music group

New Riders of the Purple Sage
PO Box 3773
San Rafael, CA 94912
Music group

Newman, Jimmy C.
2804 Opryland Dr.
Nashville, TN 37214
Country music singer

Newman, Paul
40 W. 57th. St.
New York, NY 10019
*Actor, married to Joanne
    Woodward*
Birthday: 1/26/25

Newman, Randy
21241 Ventura Blvd., #241
Woodland Hills, CA 91364
Singer
Birthday: 11/28/43

Newton, Juice
PO Box 3035
Rancho Santa Fe, CA 92067
Singer

Newton-John, Olivia
PO Box 2710
Malibu, CA 90265
Singer, actress
Birthday: 9/26/47

New York Times
229 W. 43rd St.
New York, NY 10036
Website: http://
    www.nytimes.com or http://
    www.nytco.com
Russell T. Lewis, President and
    CEO
Publishing, printing

New York Life Insurance
51 Madison Ave.
New York, NY 10010
Seymour G. Sternberg,
    Chairman, President and
    CEO
*Life and health insurance
    (mutual)*

Newell Rubbermaid, Inc.
29 E. Stephenson St.
Freeport, IL 61032
Website: http://
    www.newellco.com
John J. McDonough, VC and
    CEO
Metal products

**Niagara Mohawk Holdings,
    Inc.**
300 Erie Blvd. W.
Syracuse, NY 13202
Website: http://www.nimo.com
William E. Davis, CEO
Gas and electric utilities

Nichols, Nichelle
22647 Ventura Blvd.
Woodland Hills, CA 91364
Actress, plays Lt. Uhura on Star
    Trek

Nicholson, Jack
11500 W. Olympic Blvd., #510
Los Angeles, CA 90064
Actor
Birthday: 4/22/37

Nicklaus, Jack
11760 US Hwy. #1-6
N. Palm Beach, FL 33408
Professional golfer
Birthday: 1/21/40

Nicollier, Claude
% NASA
Johnson Space Center
Dept. CB
Houston, TX 77058
Astronaut

Nicks, Stevie
PO Box 7855
Alhambra, CA 91802
Singer, member of Fleetwood Mac

Nielsen, Brigitte
PO Box 57593
Sherman Oaks, CA 91403
Actress
Birthday: 7/15/63

Nielsen, Leslie
1622 Viewmont Dr.
Los Angeles, CA 90069
Actor
Birthday: 2/11/26

Nike
1 Bowerman Dr.
Beaverton, OR 97005
Website: http://www.nike.com/
Philip H. Knight, Chairman,
    President, and CEO

Nimoy, Leonard
2300 W. Victory Blvd., #C-384
Burbank, CA 91506
Actor/director
Birthday: 3/26/31

Nine Inch Nails
83 Riverside Dr.
New York, NY 10019
Music group

Nirvana
151 El Camino Dr.
Beverly Hills, CA 90212
Music group

Nitty Gritty Dirt Band
1227 17th. Ave. S.
Nashville, TN 37212
Musical group

Nixons, The
% Rainmaker Artists
PO Box 720195
Dallas, TX 75372
Music group

No Doubt
% Interscope Records
10900 Wilshire Blvd.
Los Angeles, CA 90024
Music group fan club address

Nolte, Nick
% Kingsgate Films
6153 Bonsall Dr.
Malibu, CA 90265
Actor
Birthday: 2/8/40

Nomo, Hideo
% Los Angeles Dodgers
1000 Elysian Park Ave.
Los Angeles, CA 90012
Pitcher

Nordstrom
617 Sixth Ave.
Seattle, WA 98101
Website: http://
    www.nordstrom.com
Bruce Nordstrom, Chairman
Blake W. Nordstrom, President
General Merchandisers

Norfolk Southern
3 Commercial Place
Norfolk, VA 23510
Website: http://
    www.nscorp.com
David R. Goode, Chairman,
    President, and CEO
Railroads

Norris, Chuck (Carlos Ray)
PO Box 872
Navasota, TX 77868
Actor, athlete, producer,
screenwriter, stunt
choreographer
Birthday: 3/10/40

North, Oliver
RR #1
Box 560
Bluemont, VA 22012
Former presidential aide/senatorial
candidate, radio talk show
host

Northeast Utilities
174 Brush Hill Ave.
West Springfield, MA 01090
Website: http://www.nu.com
Michael G. Morris, CEO
Gas and electric utilities

Northup Grumman
1840 Century Park E.
Los Angeles, CA 90067
Website: http://
www.northgrum.com
Kent Kresa, Chairman,
President, and CEO
Aerospace

Northwest Airlines
5101 Northwest Dr.
St. Paul, MN 55111
Website: http://www.nwa.com
Gary L. Wilson, Chairman
John H. Dasburg, President
and CEO
Airlines

Northwestern Mutual Life
Insurance
720 E. Wisconsin Ave.
Milwaukee, WI 53202
Website: http://
www.northwestern
mutual.com
James D. Ericson, Chairman
and CEO
Life and Health insurance
(mutual)

Norwest Venture Capital
3600 IDS Center
80 South 8th St.
Minneapolis, MN 55402
Website: http://
www.norwestvc.com
John E. Lindahl, General
Partner
Kevin G. Hall, Venture
Partner, Palo Alto
Venture capital

Norville, Deborah
Box 426
Mill Neck, NY 11765
TV personality

Norwood, Daron
PO Box 674659
Nashville, TN 37203
Country music singer

Novello, Don
PO Box 245
Fairfax, CA 94930
Comedian known as Father Guido
Sarducci
Birthday: 1/1/43

N'Sync
% Wright Stuff Mgmt.
7380 St. Lake Rd. #350
Orlando, FL 32819
or
7616 Soundland Blvd., #115
Orlando, FL 32809
Music group

Nuclear Energy Institute
1776 I St. NW, #400
Washington, DC 20006
Website: http://www.nei.org/
E-mail: media@nei.org
Scott Peterson, Media
    Relations
The nuclear energy industry's
    Washington-based policy
    organization

Nuclear Information and
    Resource Service
1424 16th St. NW, #601
Washington, DC 20036
Website: http://www.nirs.org/
E-mail: NirsNet@igc.apc.org
Robert Backus, Chairman
Organization concerned with
    nuclear power, radioactive
    waste, radiation, and
    sustainable energy issues

Nucor
2100 Rexford Rd.
Charlotte, NC 28211
Website: http://www.nucor.com
H. David Aycock, Chairman,
    President, and CEO
Metals

Nye, Bill
% KCTS TV
401 Mercer St.
Seattle, WA 98109
The Science Guy

The world did not impact upon me until I got to the post office.

—CHRISTOPHER MORLEY

Oak Ridge Boys
2501 N. Blackwelder
Oklahoma, City, OK 73106
Musical group

Oasis
54 Linhope St.
London NW1 6HL
England
Music group

O'Brien, Conan
30 Rockefeller Plaza
New York, NY 10112
Talk show host
Birthday: 4/18/63

O'Brien, Tim
PO Box 458
Nevada City, CA 95959
Country music singer

Occidental Petroleum
10889 Wilshire Blvd.
Los Angeles, CA 90024
Website: http://www.oxy.com
Ray R. Irani, Chairman and
    CEO
Chemicals

O'Connell, Jerry
151 El Camino Dr.
Beverly Hills, CA 90212
Actor
Birthday: 2/17/74

O'Donnell, Rosie
666 Fifth Ave., #288
New York, NY 10103
Website: http://www.rosieo.com
Comedian, talk show host
Birthday: 1962

O'Connor, Sinead
43 Brook Green
London W6 7EF
England
Musician
Birthday: 12/8/67

O'Donnell, Chris
8912 Burton Way
Beverly Hills, CA 90211
Actor
Birthday: 1970

Office Depot
2200 Old Germantown Rd.
Delray Beach, FL 33445
Website: http://
    www.officedepot.com/
David I. Fuente, Chairman
Irwin Helford, VC
M. Bruce Nelson, CEO
Specialist retailers

Office Max
3605 Warrensville Ctr. Rd.
Shaker Heights, OH 44122
Website: http://
    www.officemax.com
Michael Feuer, Chairman and
    CEO
Gary Peterson, President and
    COO
Specialist retailers

O'Hara, Maureen
Box 1400
Christiansted
St. Croix, VI 00820
Actress
Birthday: 8/17/20

Olajuwon, Akeem Abdul
10 Greenway Plaza East
Houston, TX 77046
Basketball player

Oldman, Gary
% J.C.M.
Oxford House
76 Oxford St.
London W1N 0AX
England
Actor
Birthday: 3/21/58

Olin, Ken
5855 Topanga Canyon, #410
Woodland Hills, CA 91367
Actor
Birthday: 7/30/54

Olin, Lena
40 W. 57th St.
New York, NY 10019
Actress
Birthday: 3/22/55

Olmos, Edward James
2020 Ave. of the Stars, #500
Los Angeles, CA 90067
Actor
Birthday: 2/24/47

Olsen, Ashley
8916 Ashcroft Ave.
Los Angeles, CA 90048
Actress
Birthday: 6/13/86

Olsen, Mary Kate
8916 Ashcroft Ave.
Los Angeles, CA 90048
Actress
Birthday: 6/13/86

Olsten
175 Broad Hollow Rd.
Melville, NY 11747
Website: http://www.olsten.com
Frank N. Liguori, CEO
Temporary Help

OMC
% Polydor Records
PO Box 617
Auckland
New Zealand
Music group

Omnicom
437 Madison Ave.
New York, NY 10022
Bruce Crawford, Chairman
Fred J. Meyer, VC
John D. Wren, President and
    CEO
Advertising, marketing

O'Neale, Shaquille
% Los Angeles Lakers
Staples Center
1111 S. Figueroa St.
Los Angeles, CA 90015
*L.A. Laker center, Ht. 7' 1 ", Wt.
    315 lbs.*
Birthday: 3/6/72

O'Neal, Tatum
300 Central Park W., #16-G
New York, NY 10024
Actress
Birthday: 11/5/63

Oracle
500 Oracle Pkwy.
Redwood City, CA 94065
Website: http://www.oracle.com
Lawrence J. Ellison, Chairman
    and CEO
Computer software

Ormond, Julia
9465 Wilshire Blvd., #517
Beverly Hills, CA 90212
Actress
Birthday: 1/4/65

Orrall, Robert Ellis
PO Box 121274
Nashville, TN 37212
Country music singer

Osborne Brothers
2801 Columbia Pl.
Nashville, TN 37204
Music group

Osbourne, Jeffrey
1325 Ave. of the Americas
New York, NY 10019
Singer

Osborn, Super Dave
10 Universal City Plaza, Suite
    3100
Universal City, CA 91606
Actor

**Osbourne, Ozzy (John Michael
    Osbourne)**
9 Highpoint Dr.
Gulf Breeze, FL 32561
Singer, songwriter
Birthday: 12/3/46

Oslin, K. T.
1102 18th. Ave. S.
Nashville, TN 37212
Singer
Birthday: 5/15/42

**Osmond, Marie (Olive Marie
    Osmond)**
3325 N. University Ave., Suite
    375
Provo, UT 84604
Singer, actress, talk show host
Birthday: 10/13/59

Oteri, Cheri
315 S. Beverly Dr., #216
Beverly Hills, CA 90212
Comedian

O'Toole, Peter
% Veerline Ltd.
8 Baker St.
GB-London WAA 1DA
England
Actor
Birthday: 8/2/32

Overstreet, Paul
PO Box 320
Pregram, TN 37143
Country music singer

Owens, Buck (Alvis Edgar, Jr.)
3223 Sillect Ave.
Bakersfield, CA 93308
Country music singer

Owens, Gary
18034 Ventura Blvd.
Encino, CA 91316
Radio and TV personality

Owens-Corning
1 Owens Corning Pkwy.
Toledo, OH 43659
Website: http://
    www.owenscorning.com
Glen H. Hiner, Chairman and
    CEO
Building materials, glass

Owens-Illinois
1 Sea Gate
Toledo, OH 43666
Joseph H. Lemieux, Chairman
    and CEO
Building materials, glass

Owens & Minor
4800 Cox Rd.
Glen Allen, VA 23060
Website: http://www.owens-
    minor.com
G. Gilmer Minor III, Chairman
    and CEO
Wholesalers

Oxford Health Plans
48 Monroe Turnpike
Trumbull, CT 06611
Website: http://www.oxhp.com
Norman C. Payson, Chairman
    and CEO
Health care

Oz, Frank (Frank Oznovicz)
PO Box 20750
New York, NY 10023
Muppeteer

P

There are no words to express the abyss between isolation and having one ally. It may be conceded to the mathematician that four is twice two. But two is not twice one; two is two thousand times one.

—G. K. Chesterton

PACCAR
PACCAR Bldg.
777 106th Ave. NE, PO Box 1518
Bellevue, WA 98009
Website: http://www.paccar.com
Charles M. Pigott, Chairman Emeritus
Mark C. Pigott, Chairman and CEO
Motor vehicles and parts

PacifiCare Health Systems
3120 W. Lake Center Dr.
Santa Ana, CA 92704
Website: http://www.pacificare.com
David A. Reed, Chairman
Terry O. Hartshorn, VC
Alan R. Hoops, President and CEO
Health Care

PacifiCorp
700 NE Multnomah St.
Portland, OR 97232
Website: http://www.pacificorp.com
Alan Richardson, President and CEO
Gas and electric utilities

Pacific Life Insurance
700 Newport Center Dr.
Newport Beach, CA 92660
Website: http://www.pacificlife.com
Thomas C. Sutton, Chairman and CEO
Life and health insurance (mutual)

Pacific Research Institute for Public Policy
755 Sansome St. #450
San Francisco, CA 94111
Website: http://www.pacificresearch.org/
Sally C. Pipes, President and CEO
Promotes the principles of individual freedom and personal responsibility; believes these principles are best encouraged through policies that emphasize a free economy, private initiative, and limited government

Pacific Rocket Society
Rod and Randa Milliron
PO Box 662
Mojave, CA 93502
Website: http://www.translunar.org/prs/

Organization dedicated to the promotion of rocketry, space travel, and off-world colonization

Pacino, Al (Alfredo James Pacino)
301 W. 57th St., #16-C
New York, NY 10017
Actor
Birthday: 4/25/40

Paine Webber Group
1285 Ave. of the Americas
New York, NY 10019
Website: http://
    www.painewebber.com
Donald B. Marron, Chairman
    and CEO
Securities

Palance, Jack
PO Box 6201
Tehachapi, CA 93561
Actor, director
Birthday: 2/18/20

Palin, Michael
68A Delancey St.
London NW1 7RY
England
Actor, writer
Birthday: 5/5/43

Palmer, Arnold
9000 Bay Hill Blvd.
Orlando, FL 32819
Golfer

Palmer, Robert
% Dera Associates
584 Broadway, #1201
New York, NY 10012
Singer, songwriter
Birthday: 1/19/49

Palminteri, Chazz
375 Greenwich St.
New York, NY 10013
Actor
Birthday: 5/15/51

Palomino Road
818 18th Ave. S.
Nashville, TN 37203
Music Group

Paltrow, Gwyneth
% Creative Artists Agency
9830 Wilshire Blvd.
Beverly Hills, CA 90212
Actress

Panis, Olivier
% Prost Grand Prix
Technopole de la Nièvre
F-58470 Magny Cours
Professional Formula-1 driver

Parazynski, Scott
Astronaut Office
Mail Code CB
NASA, Johnson Space Center
Houston, TX 77058
Astronaut

Parker, Andrea
% Susan Smith + Associates
121 N. San Vicente Blvd.
Beverly Hills, CA 90211
Actress

Parker, Mary Louise
151 El Camino Dr.
Beverly Hills, CA 90212
Actress
Birthday: 8/2/64

Parker, Ray, Jr.
1025 N. Roxbury Dr.
Beverly Hills, CA 90210
Musician, songwriter

Parker, Sarah Jessica
PO 69646
Los Angeles, CA 90069
Actress
Birthday: 3/25/65

Parker, Hannifin
6035 Parkland Blvd.
Cleveland, OH 44124
Website: http://
 www.parker.com
Duane E. Collins, Chairman,
 President, and CEO
Industrial and farm equipment

Parnell, Lee Roy
PO Box 120073
Nashville, TN 37212
Country music singer

Parrish, Julie
PO Box 247
Santa Monica, CA 90406
Actress
Birthday: 10/21/40

Parsons, Karyn
104–106 Bedford St., #4D
New York, NY 10014
Actress

Partnership for the Homeless
305 7th Ave., 13th Floor
New York, NY 10001
Website: http://
 www.partnership
forhomeless.org/

E-mail: tpfth@partnership
 forhomeless.org
*Organization that coordinates
 shelters and assists homeless
 and formerly homeless
 individuals and families
 obtain housing and other
 basic needs*

Parton, Dolly
PO Box 15037
Nashville, TN 37215
Country music singer/actress
Birthday: 1/19/46

Parton, Stella
PO Box 120295
Nashville, TN 37212
Country music singer

Party of Five
High Productions
10202 W. Washington Blvd.
Gable Bldg., Room 210
Attn: *Party of Five*
Culver City, CA 90232

Patkin, Max
211 Mitchell Rd.
Exton, PA 19341
Actor

**Patric, Jason (Jason Patrick
 Miller)**
℅ Dolores Robinson Ent.
10683 Santa Monica Blvd.
Los Angeles, CA 90025-4807
Actor
Birthday: 6/17/66

Patterson, Floyd
Box 336
New Paltz, NY 12561
Former boxer

Patty, Sandi
PO Box 2940
Anderson, IN 46018
Singer of religious music

Pavarotti, Luciano
Via Giardini
I-41040 Saliceto Panaro
Italy
Opera singer and member of the
*   Three Tenors*
Birthday: 10/12/35

Paxton, Bill
8000 Sunset Blvd., #300
Los Angeles, CA 90046
Actor, director, musician,
*   producer, screenwriter*
Birthday: 5/17/55

Paycheck, Johnny
PO Box 916
Hendersonville, TN 37077
Country music singer

Payne, John
Hoogstraat 161
3131 BB Vlaardingen
The Netherlands
Website: http://
    www.spiritweb.org/Spirit/
    omni.html
Trance Channeller

Payton, Walter
300 N. Martingale Rd., #340
Schaumburg, IL 60173
Former football player
Birthday: 6/25/54

Pearce, Guy
Box 4778
Kings Cross
NSW 2011
Australia
Actor
Birthday: 10/5/67

Pearl Jam
417 Denny Way, #200
Seattle, WA 98109
Rock group

Pearl River
PO Box 150803
Nashville, TN 37215
Music Group

Peck, Gregory
PO Box 837
Beverly Hills, CA 90213
Actor
Birthday: 4/5/16

PECO Energy
2301 Market St.
Philadelphia, PA 19103
Website: http://www.peco.com
Corbin A. McNeill, Jr.,
    Chairman, President and
    CEO
Gas and electric utilities

Peeples, Nia
7800 Beverly Blvd.
Los Angeles, CA 90036
Actress

Pei, I. M.
600 Madison Ave.
New York, NY 10022
Architect

Pele
% Minist. Extraordinario de
    Esporte
Praca dos Tres Poderes
70150-900 Brasilia D.F.
Brasilia
Former soccer player
Birthday: 10/21/40

Penguins, The
708 W. 137th St.
Gardena, CA 90247
Music group

Penn, Sean
2049 Century Park E., #2500
Los Angeles, CA 90067
Actor

Penn and Teller
4132 S. Rainbow Blvd., #377
Las Vegas, NV 89103
Website: http://
    www.sincity.com/
Magicians

Penn Traffic
1200 State Fair Blvd.
Syracuse, NY 13221
Peter L. Zirkow, Chairman
Joseph V. Fisher, President and
    CEO
Food and drug stores

Penthouse Pets
277 Park Ave.
New York, NY 10172

People for the American Way
2000 M St. NW, #400
Washington, DC 20036
Website: http://www.pfaw.org/
E-mail: pfaw@pfaw.org
Ralph G. Neas, President
*Founded by a group of civic and
    religious leaders who were
    concerned by the rising tide of
    intolerance against lesbians
    and gays sweeping the nation,
    produces monthly updates of
    anti-gay activity around the
    U.S.*

**People for the Ethical
Treatment of Animals
(PETA)**
501 Front St.
Norfolk, VA 23510
Website: http://www.peta-
    online.org/
E-mail: info@peta-online.org
Alex Pacheco, Co-Founder
*Believes that animals have the
    same rights as humans: they
    are not ours to eat, wear,
    experiment on, or use for
    entertainment*

PepsiCo
700 Anderson Hill Rd.
Purchase, NY 10577
Website: http://
    www.pepsico.com
Roger A. Enrico, Chairman &
    CEO
Beverages

Peres, Shimon
10 Hayarkon St., #3263
Tel Aviv 63571
Israel
Former Prime Minister of Israel

Perfect Stranger
PO Box 330
Carthage, TX 75633
Music Group

Perkins, Elizabeth
9150 Wilshire Blvd., #340
Beverly Hills, CA 90212
Actress
Birthday: 11/18/60

Perlman, Rhea
PO Box 491246
Los Angeles, CA 90049
Actress
Birthday: 3/31/?

Perlman, Ron
275 S. Beverly Dr., #215
Beverly Hills, CA 90212
Actor
Birthday: 4/13/50

Perot, Ross
1700 Lakeside Square
Dallas, TX 75251
*Businessman, former presidential
    candidate*

Perrine, Valerie
% Soli + Associati
Via Toscana 1
I-00187 Roma
Italy
Actress
Birthday: 9/3/43

Perry, Luke (Coy Perry III)
1122 S. Robertson Blvd., #15
Los Angeles, CA 90035
Actor
Birthday: 10/11/66

Persuaders, The
225 W. 57th St., #500
New York, NY 10019
Music group

Pesci, Joe
PO Box 6
Lavallette, NJ 08735
Actor
Birthday: 2/9/43

Pestova, Daniela
% Next Models
23 Watts St.
New York, NY 10013
Model

Peter Kiewit Sons
1000 Kiewit Plaza
Omaha, NE 68131
Kenneth E. Stinson, Chairman
    and CEO
Engineering, construction

**Peters, Bernadette (Bernadette
    Lazzara)**
323 W. 80th St.
New York, NY 10024
Actress
Birthday: 2/28/48

Petersen, William L.
3330 Cahuenga Blvd. W., #400
Los Angeles, CA 90068
Actor

Petersen, Wolfgang
% C.A.A.
9830 Wilshire Blvd.
Beverly Hills, CA 90212
Director
Birthday: 3/14/41

Pet Shop Boys
27A Pembridge Way, #8
London WII 3EP
England
Music group

Petty, Lori
400 W. Alameda Ave., #301
Burbank, CA 91505
Actress

Petty, Richard
1028 E. 22nd St.
Kannapolis, NC 28083
Race car driver

Pfizer
235 E. 42nd St.
New York, NY 10017
Website: http://www.pfizer.com
William C. Steere, Jr.,
    Chairman and CEO
Pharmaceuticals

PG & E
1 Market Street.
Spear Tower, Suite 2400
San Francisco, CA 94105
Website: http://www.pge.com
Robert D. Glynn, Jr.,
    Chairman, President, and
    CEO
Gas and electric utilities

Phair, Liz
811 Broadway, #730
New York, NY 10012
Singer, songwriter
Birthday: 4/17/67

Pharmacia Corporation
100 Rt. 206 N.
Peapack, NJ 07977
Website: http://www.pnu.com
Fred Hassan, President and
    CEO
Pharmaceuticals

Phelps Dodge
2600 N. Central Ave.
Phoenix, AZ 85004
Website: http://
    www.phelpsdodge.com
Douglas C. Yearley, Chairman
J. Steven Whisler, President
    and CEO
Metals

Philbin, Regis
101 W. 67th St. #51A
New York, NY 10023
Talk show host, game show host
Birthday: 8/25/34

Philip Morris U.S.A.
120 Park Ave.
New York, NY 10017–5592
Website: http://
    www.philipmorrisusa.com
Michael Szymanczyk, President
    and CEO
Tobacco company

Phillips, Ethan
4212 McFarlane Ave.
Burbank, CA 91505
Actor, plays Neelix on Star Trek:
    Voyager

Phillips, Julianne
1999 Ave. of the Stars, #2850
Los Angeles, CA 90067
Actress, model

Phillips, Lou Diamond (Lou Upchurch)
1122 S. Robertson Blvd., #15
Los Angeles, CA 90035
Actor
Birthday: 2/17/62

Phillips, Stone
30 Rockefeller Plaza
New York, NY 10122
News show host

Phillips Petroleum
Phillips Building
Bartlesville, OK 74004
Website: http://
    www.phillips66.com
Jim J. Mulva, Chairman and
    CEO
Petroleum refining

Phoenix Home Life Mutual Insurance
1 American Row
Hartford, CT 06115
Robert W. Fiondella, Chairman
    and CEO
Life and health insurance (stock)

Physicians Committee for Responsible Medicine
5100 Wisconsin Ave., #404
Washington, DC 20016
Website: http://www.pcrm.org/
E-mail: pcrm@pcrm.org
Neal Barnard, M.D., President
*Promotes preventive medicine
    through innovative programs,
    encourages higher standards
    for ethics and effectiveness in
    research, and advocates
    broader access to medical
    services*

Picardo, Robert
PO Box 5617
Beverly Hills, CA 90210
Actor, plays The Doctor on Star
    Trek: Voyager

Pierce, David Hyde
8730 Sunset Blvd., #480
Los Angeles, CA 90069
Actor

Pietz, Amy
PO Box 81
Oak Creek, WI 53134
Actress

Pinkard and Bowden
% Network, Inc.
1101 18th Ave. So.
Nashville, TN 37212
Musical duo

Pinkett, Jada
% United Talent Agency
9560 Wilshire Blvd., #516
Beverly Hills, CA 90212
Actress

Piraro, Dan
% Bizzaro
1119 N. Edgefield Ave.
Dallas, TX 75208
or
% Universal Press Syndicate
4520 Main St.
Kansas City, MO 64111
Cartoonist

Pirates of the Mississippi
PO Box 17087
Nashville, TN 37217
Country music group

Pitney Bowes
1 Elmcroft Rd.
Stamford, CT 06926
Website: http://
    www.pitneybowes.com
Michael J. Critelli, Chairman
Computers, office equipment

Pitt, Brad
% Creative Artists Agency
9830 Wilshire Blvd.
Beverly Hills, CA 90212
Actor
Birthday: 12/18/64

Pittston Minerals Group
448 NE Main St.
Lebanon, VA 24266
Website: http://
    www.pittstonminerals.com
Thomas W. Garges, President
    and CEO, Pittston Coal
    Company and Mineral
    Ventures
Mining

**Planned Parenthood
    Federation of America**
810 Seventh Ave.
New York, NY 10019
Website: http://
www.plannedparenthood.org/
E-mail: communications
    @ppfa.org
Gloria Feldt, President
*Offers extensive information on all
    aspects of sexual and
    reproductive health*

Plant, Robert
46 Kensington C. ST.
London W85DP
England
Singer/songwriter
Birthday: 8/20/48

Platt, Oliver
29 E. 9th. St.
New York, NY 10003
Actor

Playboy Mansion
10235 Charing Cross Rd.
Holmby Hills, CA 90024

Any Playboy Playmate
Playmate Name
% Playmate Promotions
2112 Broadway
Santa Monica, CA 90404

Pleasant Company
The American Girl Collection
8400 Fairway Place
PO Box 620190
Middleton, WI 53562
Website: http://
    www.americangirl.com/
Pleasant Rowland, Founder,
    Chairman, and CEO
Makers of American Girl Dolls

Pleshette, Suzanne
PO Box 1492
Beverly Hills, CA 90210
Actress

Plumb, Eve
5757 Wilshire Blvd., #510
Los Angeles, CA 90036
Actress

Plummer, Amanda
1925 Century Park E., #2320
Los Angeles, CA 90067
Actress
Birthday: 3/23/57

The PNC Financial Services Group, Inc.
1 PNC Plaza, 249 5th Ave.
Pittsburgh, PA 15222
Website: http://
www.pncbank.com
Thomas H. O'Brien, Chairman
James E. Rohr, President and
CEO
Commercial bank

Points of Light Foundation
400 I St., NW, Suite 800
Washington, DC 20005
Website: http://
www.pointsoflight.org/
Robert K. Goodwin, President
and Chief Executive
Officer
E-mail: rgoodwin@pointsof
light.org
*A nonpartisan organization whose
mission is to engage more
people more effectively in
volunteer community service;
offers a hotline for volunteer
opportunity information*

Poitier, Sidney
9255 Doheny Rd.
Los Angeles, CA 90069
Actor, writer, producer
Birthday: 2/20/27

Pollack, Kevin
8942 Wilshire Blvd.
Beverly Hills, CA 90211
Actor

Popcorn, Faith
% BrainReserve
59 E. 64th St.
New York, NY 10021–7003
Website: http://
www.faithpopcorn.com/
E-mail: Webmistress@
faithpopcorn.com
Futurist and author of The
Popcorn Report *and*
Clicking

Official Popeye Fan Club
1001 State St.
Chester, IL 62233

**Population Reference Bureau,
Inc.**
1875 Connecticut Ave., NW,
Suite 520
Washington, DC 20009
Website: http://www.prb.org/
prb/
E-mail: ecarnevale@prb
Michael P. Bentzen, Chairman
of the Board
*Dedicated to providing timely and
objective information on U.S.
and international population
trends*

Porizkova, Paulina
% IMG
304 Park Ave South, 12th floor
New York, NY 10010
Model

Portman, Natalie
8942 Wilshire Blvd.
Beverly Hills, CA 90211
Actress

Post, Markie
10153 1/2 Riverside Dr., #333
Toluca Lake, CA 90049
Actress
Birthday: 11/4/50

Poston, Tom
1 North Venice Blvd., #106
Venice, CA 90291
or
% International Creative
    Management
8942 Wilshire Blvd.
Beverly Hills, CA 90211
Actor
Birthday: 10/17/?

Potts, Annie
PO Box 29400
Los Angeles, CA 90027
Actress
Birthday: 10/27/52

Potts, M. C.
818 18th Ave. S.
Nashville, TN 37203
E-mail: mcfanclub@aol.com

Powell, General Colin
909 N. Washington St., Suite
    767
Alexandria, VA 22314
Military leader, author
Birthday: 4/5/37

Powers, Stefanie (Jennifer Hart)
15821 Ventura Blvd., #235
Encino, CA 91436
Actress
Birthday: 11/2/42

PPG Industries
1 PPG Place
Pittsburgh, PA 15272
Website: http://www.ppg.com
Raymond W. LeBoeuf, CEO
Chemicals

PP & L Industries
2 N. Ninth St.
Allentown, PA 18101
Website: http://www.papl.com
William F. Hecht, Chairman,
    President, and CEO
Gas and electric utilities

Praxair
39 Old Ridgebury Rd.
Danbury, CT 06810
Website: http://
    www.praxair.com
H. William Lichtenberger,
    Chairman
Dennis H. Reilley, President
    and CEO
Chemicals

Presley, Lisa-Marie
1167 Summit Dr.
Beverly Hills, CA 90210
*Daughter of Elvis and Priscilla
    Presley*
Birthday: 2/1/68

Presley, Priscilla
1167 Summit Dr.
Beverly Hills, CA 90210
Actress
Birthday: 5/24/45

Preston, Kelly
15020 Ventura Blvd., #710
Sherman Oaks, CA 91403
Actress
Birthday: 10/13/62

Pretenders, The
28 Kensington Church St.
London W8 4EP
England
Rock band

Price, Ray
10–31 Battlefield St., #224
Springfield, MO 65807
Singer

Pride, Charley
PO Box 670507
Dallas, TX 75367
Country music singer

Priestley, Jason
11766 Wilshire Blvd., #1610
Los Angeles, CA 90025
Actor
Birthday: 8/28/69

Prince Charles
Highgrove House
Tetbury
Gloucestershire
England
Birthday: 11/14/48

Princess Margaret
Kensington Palace
GB-London N5
England
Birthday: 8/21/30

Principal, Victoria
120 S. Spalding Dr., #205
Beverly Hills, CA 90212
Actress
Birthday: 1/3/50

The Principal Financial Group
711 High St.
Des Moines, IA 50392
Website: http://
       www.principal.com
David J. Drury, Chairman
J. Barry Griswell, President and
       CEO
Life and health insurance (stock)

Princz, Freddie, Jr.
9830 Wilshire Blvd.
Beverly Hills, CA 90212
Actor

Procter & Gamble
1 P&G Plaza
Cincinnati, OH 45202
Website: http://www.pg.com
John E. Pepper, Chairman
Alan G. "A. G." Lafley,
       President and CEO
Soaps, cosmetics

The Progressive Corporation
6300 Wilson Mills Rd.
Mayfield Village, OH 44143
Website: http://
       www.progressive.com
Peter B. Lewis, Chairman,
       President, and CEO
P and C insurance (stock)

Prosky, Robert
306 9th Ave.
Washington, DC 20003
Actor

Provident Financial Group, Inc.
1 E. 4th St.
Cincinnati, OH 45202
Website: http://www.provident-financial.com
Robert L. Hoverso, Chairman, President, and CEO
Commercial bank

Prowse, David "Dave"
7 Leicester Ct.
London, WC2H 7BP
England
Actor who played Darth Vader, in Star Wars

Prudential Insurance Company of America
751 Broad St.
Newark, NJ 07102
Website: http://www.prudential.com
Arthur F. Ryan, Chairman and CEO
Life and health insurance (stock)

Prudhomme, Chef Paul
2424 Chartres
New Orleans, LA 70117
Website: http://www.chefpaul.com/
Louisiana chef

Prussia, Guido
Guido Prussia Res.
Campo 602
Milano 2
Segrate Milano
Italy
Italian TV journalist

Pruett, Jeanne
1906 Chet Atkins Pl., #502
Nashville, TN 37212
Country music singer

Public Enemy
298 Elizabeth St.
New York, NY 10012
Rap group

Public Service Enterprise Group
80 Park Plaza
Newark, NJ 07101
Website: http://www.pseg.com
E. James Ferland, Chairman, President, and CEO
Gas and electric utilities

Publix Super Markets
1936 George Jenkins Blvd.
Lakeland, FL 33815
Howard M. Jenkins, Chairman and CEO
Food and drug stores

Puckett, Kirby
% Minnesota Twins
501 Chicago Ave. S.
Minneapolis, MN 55415
Former baseball player

Puff Daddy (Sean Combs)
% Arista Records
9975 Santa Monica Blvd.
Beverly Hills, CA 90212
Rap artist

Pullman, Bill
1122 S. Robertson Blvd., #15
Los Angeles, CA 90035
Actor, producer
Birthday: 12/17/54

Public Service Research Council
320-D Maple Ave. E
Vienna, VA 22180
Website: http://www.psrf.org/
E-mail: info@psrf.org
David Y. Denholm, President
Studying the impact of unionism in government on government

Putin, President Putin
Krasnopresenskaya 2
Moscow
Russia

Real letter-writing makes writing into a different process because the letter is to somebody—a significant other—and not just a pronouncement to an imaginary world, a generalized other.

—ED POWELL, *The Letter Exchange*

Quaid, Dennis
8942 Wilshire Blvd.
Beverly Hills, CA 90211
or
PO Box 742625
Houston, TX 77274
Actor, Randy's brother
Birthday: 4/9/54

Quaid, Randy
PO Box 17572
Beverly Hills, CA 90209
Actor
Birthday: 10/1/50

The Quaker Oats Company
Quaker Tower
321 N. Clark St.
Chicago, IL 60610
Website: http://
    www.quakeroats.com
Robert S. Morrison, Chairman,
    President, and CEO
Food producer

Quantum
500 McCarthy Blvd.
Milpitas, CA 95035
Website: http://
    www.quantum.com
Michael A. Brown, Chairman
    and CEO
Computer peripherals

Quayle, Dan
2929 E. Camelback Rd., #124
Phoenix, AZ 85016
Former vice president of the
    United States
Birthday: 2/4/47

Queen Latifah
155 Morgan St.
Jersey City, NJ 07302
Website: http://latifahshow.
    warnerbros.com/
Actress, musician, talk show host
Birthday: 3/18/70

Queen Mary Hotel
PO Box 8
1126 Queens Hwy.
Long Beach, CA 90802
Website: http://
    www.queenmary.com
E-mail: queenmry@gte.net
*Former cruise ship turned hotel &
    tourist attraction*

Quiet Riot
PO Box 24455
New Orleans, LA 70184
Rock band

Quinn, Aidan
9830 Wilshire Blvd.
Beverly Hills, CA 90212
Actress
Birthday: 3/8/59

Quinn, Anthony
420 Poppasquash Rd.
Bristol, RI 02809
Actor

Quivers, Robin
WXRK-FM
600 Madison Ave.
New York, NY 10022
Radio personality

An intention to write never turns into a letter. A letter must happen to one like a surprise, and one may not know where in the day there was room for it to come into being. So it is that my daily intentions have nothing to do with this fulfillment of today.

—RAINER MARIA RILKE, letter to F. von Bülow

Rachins, Alan
1274 Capri Dr.
Pacific Palisades, CA 90272
Actor

Rae, Cassidy
1801 Ave. of the Stars, #902
Los Angeles, CA 90067
Actress

Rae, Charlotte
10790 Wilshire Blvd., #903
Los Angeles, CA 90024-4448
Actress
Birthday: 4/22/26

Radio-Television News Directors Association (RTNDA)
1000 Connecticut Ave. NW, #615
Washington, DC 20036
Website: http://www.rtnda.org/
E-mail: rtnda@rtnda.org
Barbara Cochran, RTNDA President
E-mail: barbarac@rtnda.org

The world's largest professional organization devoted exclusively to electronic journalism, RTNDA represents local and network news executives in broadcasting, cable, and other electronic media in more than 30 countries

Ted Raimi International Fan Club
Club Ted
2032 Hickory Hill
Argyle, TX 76226
Website: http://
www.tedraimifan.com/
clubmain.html

The Rainbow/Push Coalition
930 East 50th St.
Chicago, IL 60615-2702
Website: http://
www.rainbowpush.org/
aboutrpc/index.html
E-mail: info@rainbowpush.org
Reverend Jesse L. Jackson, Sr. President and CEO
A multiracial, multi-issue, international membership organization founded by Rev. Jesse L. Jackson, Sr.

Ralston Purina
Checkerboard Square
St. Louis, MO 63164
Website: http://
    www.ralston.com
W. Partick McGinnis, President
    and CEO
Food and pet food producer

Rampling, Charlotte
1 av. Emile Augier
78290 Croissy-sur-Seine
France
Actress
Birthday: 2/4/46

Ramsay, Bruce
% Brillstein-Grey Ent.
9150 Wilshire Blvd., #350
Beverly Hills, CA 90212
Actor

Rand
1700 Main St., PO Box 2138
Santa Monica, CA 90407
Website: http://www.rand.org
E-mail:
    correspondence@rand.org
Paul H. O'Neill, Chairman
*A nonprofit institution that helps
    improve policy and decision-
    making through research and
    analysis*

Randall, Bobby
PO Box 208
Unicoi, TN 37692
Country music singer

**Randall, Tony (Leonard
    Rosenberg)**
1 W. 81st St., #6D
New York, NY 10024
Actor, director
Birthday: 2/26/20

Randolph, Boots
541 Richmar Dr.
Nashville, TN 37211
Musician

Rapaport, Michael
1610 Broadway
Santa Monica, CA 90404
Actor

Rather, Dan
524 W. 57th St.
New York, NY 10019
Anchor, correspondent, editor
Birthday: 10/31/31

Ratzenberger, John
13563 Ventura Blvd., #200
Sherman Oaks, CA 91423
Actor
Birthday: 4/16/47

Ratzinger, Joseph Cardinal
00120 Vatican City State
Vatican

Raven, Eddy
1071 Bradley Rd.
Gallatin, TN 37066
Country music singer

Ray, Jimmy
% Sony Music
10 Great Marlborough St.
London W1V 2LP
England
Singer

Raye, Collin
612 Humboldt St.
Reno, NV 89509
Country music singer

Read, James
9229 Sunset Blvd., Suite 315
Los Angeles, CA 90069
Actor
Birthday: 7/3/54

Reader's Digest Association
Reader's Digest Rd.
Pleasantville, NY 10570
Website: http://
    www.readersdigest.com
Thomas O. Ryder, Chairman
    and CEO
Publishing, printing

Reagan, Nancy
668 St. Cloud Rd.
Los Angeles, CA 90077
Former first lady, actress
Birthday: 7/6/21

Reagan, Ronald
668 St. Cloud Rd.
Los Angeles, CA 90077
*Former president of the United
    States, actor*
Birthday: 2/6/11

Reason Foundation
3415 S. Sepulveda Blvd., #400
Los Angeles, CA 90034
Website: http://
    www.reason.org/
E-mail: gpassantino@reason.org
George Passantino
*A national research and
    educational organization that
    explores and promotes the twin
    values of rationality and
    freedom as the basic
    underpinnings of a good
    society*

Red Hot Chilli Peppers
11116 Aqua Vista, #39
North Hollywood, CA 91693
Rock band

Redford, Robert
1101 East Montana Ave.
Santa Monica, CA 90403
Actor, director, producer
Birthday: 3/8/43

Rednex
% ZYX Music
Benzstraße
Industriegebiet
D-35797 Merenberg
Germany
Music group

Reebock
100 Technology Center Dr.
Stoughton, MA 02072
Website: http://
    www.reebok.com
Paul B. Fireman, Chairman,
    President, and CEO
Angel Martinez, Chief
    Marketing Officer
Apparel

Reece, Gabrielle
5111 Ocean Front Walk, #4
Marina del Rey, CA 90291
Model

Reed, Jerry
153 Rue De Grande
Brentwood, TN 37027
Musician

Reed, Pamela
10390 Santa Monica Blvd.,
    #300
Los Angeles, CA 90025
Actress

Reed, Willis
% Basketball Hall of Fame
1150 W. Columbus Ave.
Springfield, MA 01101
Former basketball player

Reef
% Sony Music
1 Red Place
London W1Y 3RE
Music group

Reese, Della
55 West 900 South
Salt Lake City, CA 84101
Actress

Reeve, Christopher
RR #2
Bedford, NY 10506
Actor
Birthday: 9/25/52

Reeves, Del
1300 Division St., #102
Nashville, TN 37203
Country music singer

Reeves, Keanu
9460 Wilshire Blvd., #700
Beverly Hills, CA 90212
Actor
Birthday: 9/4/64

Reeves, Ronna
PO Box 80424
Midland, TX 79709
Country music singer

Regalbuto, Joe
724 24th. St.
Santa Monica, CA 90402
Actor

Regina Regina Fan Club
PO Box 428
Marshville, NC 28103

Reid, Mike
PO Box 218142
Nashville, TN 37203
Country music singer

Reich, Dr. Robert
Brandeis University
The Heller School
MS 035
Brandeis University
PO Box 9110
Waltham, MA 02454
E-mail: reich@brandeis.edu
*Former Secretary of Labor, founder
    and national editor of The
    American Prospect*

Reilly, Charles Nelson
11365 Ventura Blvd., #100
Studio City, CA 91604
Actor
Birthday: 1/13/31

Reiner, Carl
714 North Rodeo Dr.
Beverly Hills, CA 90210
Actor, writer, director, Rob's dad
Birthday: 3/20/22

Reiner, Rob
335 Maple Dr., #135
Beverly Hills, CA 90212
Actor, director, producer
Birthday: 3/16/45

Reinhold, Judge
626 Santa Monica Blvd., #113
Santa Monica, CA 90405
Actor
Birthday: 5/21/56

Reiser, Paul
% Culver Studios
9336 W. Washington
Culver City, CA 90232
Actor
Birthday: 3/30/57

Reitman, Ivan
% Creative Artists Agency
Attn: Rand Holston
9830 Wilshire Blvd.
Beverly Hills, CA 90212
Director
Birthday: 10/27/46

Reliance Group Holdings
Park Avenue Plaza
55 E. 52nd St.
New York, NY 10055
Website: http://www.rgh.com
Saul P. Steinberg, Chairman
George R. Baker, President
    and CEO
P and C insurance (stock)

R.E.M.
170 College Ave.
Athens, GA 30601
Rock band

The Remingtons
% 3 Amigos
25 Paulson Dr.
Burlington, MA 01803
Music group

Renfro, Brad
PO Box 53454
Knoxville, TN 37950
Actor
Birthday: 7/25/82

Republican Liberty Caucus
611 Pennsylvania Ave. SE, #370
Washington, DC 20003
Website: http://www.rlc.org/
Clifford Thies, Chairman
E-mail: cthies@su.edu
Thomas D. Walls, Executive
    Director
E-mail: afn18566@afn.org
*The primary objective of the RLC
    is to help elect libertarian-
    leaning Republicans to public
    office at all levels*

**Republican National
    Committee**
310 1st St. SE
Washington, DC 20003
Website: http://www.rnc.org
E-mail: info@rnc.org
Jim Nicholson, Chairman

Restless Heart
PO Box 156
Littlestown, PA 17340
or
% Fitzgerald Hartley Co.
1908 Wedgewood Ave.
Nashville, TN 37212
Music group

Reubens, Paul
PO Box 29373
Los Angeles, CA 90029
Actor who played Pee-Wee Herman

Reynolds, Burt
PO Box 3288
Tequesta, FL 33469
Actor
Birthday: 2/11/36

Reynolds, Debbie
6415 Lankershim Blvd.
North Hollywood, CA 91606
Actress, Carrie Fisher's mom
Birthday: 4/1/32

Reynolds Metals
6601 W. Broad St.
Richmond, VA 23230
Website: http://www.rmc.com
Jeremiah J. Sheehan,
    Chairman and CEO
Metals

Rhys-Davies, John
8033 Sunset Blvd., #29
Los Angeles, CA 90046
Actor

Ricci, Christina
% ICM
8942 Wilshire Blvd.
Beverly Hills, CA 90211
Actress

Anne Rice
1239 First St.
New Orleans, LA 70130
Website: http://
    www.annerice.com/
Author
Birthday: 10/14/41

Rich, Katie
10100 Santa Monica Blvd.,
    #2490
Los Angeles, CA 90067
Actress

**Richard, Sir Cliff (Harry
    Webb)**
Queen Ann House
Weybridge, Surrey
England
Singer
Birthday: 10/14/40

Richards, Ariana
5918 Van Nuys Blvd.
Van Nuys, CA 91401
Actress

Richards, Denise
PO Box 4590
Oceanside, CA 92052
Actress

Richardson, Joely
Oxford House
76 Oxford St.
London WIN 0AX
England
Actress

Richardson, Patricia
253 26th St., #A-312
Santa Monica, CA 90402
Actress

Richfood Holdings
4860 Cox Rd., Suite 300
Glen Allen, VA 23060
Website: http://
    www.richfood.com
John E. Stokely, Chairman,
    President, and CEO
Wholesalers

Richie, Lionel
PO Box 9055
Calabasas, CA 91372
or
5750 Wilshire Blvd., Suite 590
Los Angeles, CA 90039
Singer

Rickles, Don
Premier Artist Services
℅ Eliot Weisman
1401 University Dr., Suite #305
Coral Springs, FL 33071
Website: http://
    www.thehockeypuck.com/
E-mail: dj@hifrontier.com
Comedian
Birthday: 5/8/26

Richter, Jason James
10683 Santa Monica Blvd.
Los Angeles, CA 90025
Actor
Birthday: 1/29/80

Rickman, Alan
76 Oxford St.
London W1N 0AX
United Kingdom
Actor
Birthday: 2/21/46

Riders in the Sky
38 Music Square E., #300
Nashville, TN 37203
Music group

Riley, Jeannie C.
906 Granville Rd.
Franklin, TN 37064
Country music singer

Rimes, LeAnn
2945 Fondren Dr., #816
Dallas, TX 75205
Country music singer

Ringwald, Molly
1999 Ave. of the Stars, #850
Los Angeles, CA 90067
Actress
Birthday: 2/28/68

Ripa, Molly
7800 Beverly Blvd., #3305
Los Angeles, CA 90036
Actress

Ripkin, Cal, Jr.
2330 W. Juppa Rd., #333
Lutherville, MD 21093
or
Camden Yards at Oriole Park
333 W. Camden St.
Baltimore, MD 21201
Baseball player

Ripon Society
501 Capitol Court NE, #300
Washington, DC 22000
Website: http://
    www.riponsoc.org/
The Honorable Bill Frenzel,
    President
Michael D. Gill, Executive
    Director
*A moderate Republican research
    and policy organization
    dedicated to a commonsense,
    pragmatic system of
    governance*

Rite Aid
30 Hunter Lane
Camp Hill, PA 17011
Website: http://
    www.riteaid.com
Alex Grass, Honorary
    Chairman
Robert G. Miller, Chairman
    and CEO
Mary Sammons, President and
    COO
Food and drug stores

Ritter, John
15030 Ventura Blvd., #806
Sherman Oaks, CA 91403
Actor
Birthday: 9/17/48

Tex Ritter Fan Club
% Sharon L. Sweeting,
    President
15326 73rd Ave. SE
Snohomish, WA 98290

Rivera, Geraldo
524 W. 57th St., #1100
New York, NY 10019
TV show host
Birthday: 7/4/43

**Rivers, Joan (Joan Alexandra
    Molinsky)**
1 E. 62nd St.
New York, NY 10021
or
PO Box 49774
Los Angeles, CA 90049
Comedienne
Birthday: 11/7/37

Rizzuto, Phil
12 Westminster Ave.
Hillside, NJ 07205
Former baseball player

RJR Nabisco
7 Campus Dr.
Parsippany, NJ 07054
Website: http://
    www.rjrnabisco.com
Steven F. Goldstone, Chairman
James M. Kilts, President and
    CEO
Food producer

RMB
% Motor Music
Holzdamm 57
D-20099 Hamburg
Germany
Music group

Robbins, Tim
% I.C.M.
40 W. 57th St.
New York, NY 10019
Actor
Birthday: 10/16/58

Roberts, Eric
132 S. Rodeo Dr., #300
Beverly Hills, CA 90212
Actor, Julia's brother
Birthday: 4/18/56

**Roberts, Julia (Julie Fiona
    Roberts)**
% ICM
8942 Wilshire Blvd.
Beverly Hills, CA 90211
Actress
Birthday: 10/28/67

Roberts, Tanya
1122 S. Robertson Blvd., #15
Los Angeles, CA 90035
Actress

Robinson, Brooks
36 S. Charles St., #2000
Baltimore, MD 21201
Actor

Robinson, David
% San Antonio Spurs
600 E. Market St., Suite 102
San Antonio, TX 78205
Basketball player

Robinson, Holly
% Dolores Robinson
  Entertainment
10683 Santa Monica Blvd.
Los Angeles, CA 90025
Actress
Birthday: 9/18/64

Rock, Chris
527 N. Azusa Ave., #231
Covina, CA 91722
or
ML Management Associates,
  Inc.
1740 Broadway, 15th Floor
New York, NY 10019
Comedian

Rockefeller Foundation, The
420 Fifth Ave.
New York, NY 10018
Website: www.rockfound.org
Alice Stone Ilchman, Chair
Grant organization for arts, the
  humanities, equal opportunity,
  school reform, and
  international science-based
  development

Rockwell International
777 E. Wisconsin Ave., Suite
  1400
Milwaukee, WI 53202
Website: http://
  www.rockwell.com
Don H. Davis, Jr., Chairman
  and CEO
Electronics, electrical equipment

Rockers, The
PO Box 3859
Stamford, CT 06905
Music group

Rocky Horror Fan Club
220 W. 19th St.
New York, NY 10011

Rodgers, Jimmie
PO Box 685
Forsyth, MO 65653
Singer

Rodrique, George
721 Royal St.
New Orleans, LA 70016
Artist known for "The Blue Dog"
  paintings

Rodriguez, Chi Chi
1720 Merriman Rd.
PO Box 5118
Akron, OH 44313
Golfer

Rodriguez, Johnny
PO Box 23162
Nashville, TN 37202
Country music singer

Roe, Tommy
PO Box 26037
Minneapolis, MN 55426
Singer, songwriter

Rogers, Fred
% Family Communications,
Inc.
4802 Fifth Ave.
Pittsburgh, PA 15213
*Children's TV show host,
Presbyterian minister*

Rogers, Kenny
9 Music Square S., #99
Nashville, TN 37203
Singer, songwriter
Birthday: 8/21/38

Kenny Rogers Int'l Fan Club
PO Box 769
Hendersonville, TN 37077

Rogers, Mimi
11693 San Vicente Blvd., Suite
241
Los Angeles, CA 90049
Actress
Birthday: 1/27/56

Roggin, Fred
3000 W. Alameda Ave.
Burbank, CA 91505
TV show host

Rohm and Haas
100 Independence Mall W.
Philadelphia, PA 19106
Website: http://
www.rohmhaas.com
Rajiv L. Gupta, Chairman and
CEO
J. Michael Fitzpatrick,
President and COO
Chemicals

Rohner, Clayton
8271 Melrose Ave., #110
Los Angeles, CA 90046
Actor

Roker, Al
E-mail: mailbag@roker.com
Today Show *weatherman*

Rolling Stones, The
110 W. 57th St., #300
New York, NY 10019
Rock group

Roman, George
270 N. Canon Dr., #1374
Beverly Hills, CA 90210
Website: http://
www.georgeroman.com/
E-Mail:
george@georgeroman.com
Beverly Hills love guru

Roman, LuLu
PO Box 8178
Hermitage, TN 37076
Country music singer

**Ronald Reagan Presidential
Library**
40 Presidential Dr.
Simi Valley, CA 93065
Website: http://
www.reaganlibrary.net/
lobby.html
E-mail: library@reagan.nara.gov
Mark Burson, Executive
Director

Roper Center for Public Opinion Research
University of Connecticut
U-164 Montieth Building
341 Mansfield Rd., Room 421
Storrs, CT 06269
Website: http://www.roper
center.uconn.edu/
Lois Timms-Ferrara, Associate
Director
E-mail:
lois@opinion.isi.uconn.edu
*The leading nonprofit center for
the study of public opinion
maintaining the world's
largest archive of public
opinion data*

Rose, Charlie
524 W. 57th. St.
New York, NY 10019
Television host, journalist

**Roseanne (formerly Barr,
formerly Arnold)**
5664 Cahuenga Blvd., #433
North Hollywoood, CA 91601
Actress, comedienne
Birthday: 11/3/52

Ross, Diana
PO Box 11059
Glenville Stadion
Greenwich, CT 06831
Singer, actress
Birthday: 3/26/44

Ross, Marion
20929 Ventura Blvd., #47
Woodland Hills, CA 91364
Birthday: 10/25/38

Ross, Natanya
1000 Universal Studios Plaza
Blvd.
Bldg. 22
Orlando, FL 32819
Actress

Rossellini, Isabella
575 Lexington Ave., #2000
New York, NY 10022
Actress
Birthday: 6/18/42

Rothrock, Cynthia
2633 Lincoln Blvd., #103
Santa Monica, CA 90405
Actress

Rourke, Mickey
9150 Wilshire Blvd., #350
Beverly Hills, CA 90212
Actor
Birthday: 7/16/53

Rowland, Rodney
PO Box 5617
Beverly Hills, CA 90210
Actor

Roxette
% EMI Svenska AB
Box 1289
17125 Solna
Sweden
Music group

Royal, Billy Joe
PO Box 50572
Nashville, TN 37205
Singer

R. R. Donnelly and Sons
77 W. Wacker Dr.
Chicago, IL 60601
Website: http://
    www.rrdonnelley.com
William L. Davis, Chairman
    and CEO
Publishing, printing

Ruehl, Mercedes
Box 178
Old Chelsea Station
New York, NY 10011
Actress
Birthday: 2/28/48

Ruini, Camillo Cardinal
00120 Vatican City State
Vatican

Run-D.M.C.
160 Varick St.
New York, NY 10013
Music group

RuPaul
902 Broadway, #1200
New York, NY 10010
Entertainer

Rush
189 Carlton St.
Toronto, Ontario M5A 2K7
Canada
Music group

Rush, Geoffrey
% Creative Artists Agency
9830 Wilshire Blvd.
Beverly Hills, CA 90212
Actor

Rushdie, Salman
% Gillon Aitken
29 Fernshaw Rd.
London SW10 OTG
England
Author

Russell, Johnny
PO Drawer 37
Hendersonville, TN 37077
Country music singer

Russell, Kurt
1900 Ave. of the Stars, #1240
Los Angeles, CA 90067
Actor
Birthday: 3/17/51

Russell, Nipsey
1650 Broadway, #1410
New York, NY 10019
Comedian, writer, director
Birthday: 10/13/24

Rutherford, Kelly
PO Box 492266
Los Angeles, CA 90049
Actress

Ryan, Jeri
% Paramount Pictures—*Star
    Trek Voyager*
5555 Melrose Ave.
Los Angeles, CA 90038
Actress

Ryan, Nolan
200 W. South St., #B
Alvin, TX 77511
Baseball great

Ryan, Tim
335 N. Maple Dr., #360
Beverly Hills, CA 90210
Country music singer

Ryder, Winona (Winona Laura Horowitz)
350 Park Ave., #900
New York, NY 10022
Actress
Birthday: 10/29/71

Ryder Systems
3600 N.W. 82nd Ave.
Miami, FL 33166
Website: http://www.ryder.com
M. Anthony Burns, Chairman
and CEO
Truck leasing

S

Probably the disembodied abstractness of a letter permits the reader to impute to the writer whatever qualities the reader is already listening for. . . .

—SHANA ALEXANDER, *The Feminine Eye*

Sabatini, Gabriella
217 E. Redwood St., #1800
Baltimore, MD 21202
Former professional tennis player

Sabato, Antonio, Jr.
PO Box 480012
Los Angeles, CA 90048
Actor

Safeco
Safeco Plaza
Seattle, WA 98185
Website: http://www.safeco.com
Roger H. Eigsti, Chairman and
    CEO
P and C insurance (stock)

Safeway
5918 Stoneridge Mall Rd.
Pleasanton, CA 94588
Website: http://
    www.safeway.com
Steven A. Burd, Chairman,
    President, and CEO
Food and drug stores

Sagal, Katey
7095 Hollywood Blvd., #792
Hollywood, CA 90028
Actress
Birthday: 1956

Saget, Bob
1122 S. Robertson Blvd., #15
Los Angeles, CA 90035
Actor/TV host
Birthday: 5/17/56

Saint Patrick's Cathedral
460 Madison Ave.
New York, NY 10022
Msgr. Anthony Dalla Villa
*The largest Roman Catholic
    church in the United States*

Sajak, Pat
10202 W. Washington Blvd.
Culver City, CA 90232
TV game show host
Birthday 10/26/46

Salt'n'Pepa
250 W. 57th. St., #821
New York, NY 10107
Musical group

Sambora, Richie
248 W. 17th. St., #501
New York, NY 10011
*Musician, married to Heather
    Locklear*
Birthday: 7/11/59

252

Samms, Emma
2934 1/2 N. Beverly Glen Cir.,
    Suite 417
Los Angeles, CA 90077
Actress
Birthday: 8/28/60

Sandler, Adam
9701 Wilshire Blvd., 10th Floor
Beverly Hills, CA 90212
Actor, comedian
Birthday: 9/9/66

Santana, Carlos
121 Jordon St.
San Rafael, CA 94901
or
PO Box 881630
San Francisco, CA 94188
Musician

Sara, Mia
PO Box 5617
Beverly Hills, CA 90210
Actress

Sara, Duchess of York
Birch Hall
Windlesham, Surrey GU2O6BN
England

**Sarandon, Susan (Susan Abigail
    Tomalin)**
40 W. 57th St.
New York, NY 10019
Actress
Birthday: 10/4/46

Sara Lee
3 First National Plaza
Chicago, IL 60602
Website: http://
    www.saralee.com
John H. Bryan, Chairman
C. Steven McMillan, President
    and CEO
Food producer

Sash
% Mighty Records/Polydor
Glockengießerwall 3
20095 Hamburg
Germany
Music group

Savage, Fred
1122 S. Robertson Blvd., #15
Los Angeles, CA 90035
Actor
Birthday: 7/9/76

Sawa, Devon
101-1001 W. Broadway, #148
Vancouver BC V6H 4B1
Canada
Actor
Birthday: 9/7/78

Sawyer Brown
5200 Old Harding Rd.
Franklin, TN 37064
Rock band

Saxon, John
PO Box 492480
Los Angeles, CA 90049
Actor, writer
Birthday: 8/5/35

SBC Communications
175 E. Houston
San Antonio, TX 78205
Website: http://www.sbc.com
Edward E. Whitacre, Jr.,
    Chairman and CEO
Telecommunications

Scacchi, Greta
18–21 Jermyn St., #300
London SW1Y 6HP
England
Birthday: 2/18/60

Scarabelli, Michele
4720 Vineland Ave., #216
North Hollywood, CA 91602
Actress

Scatman, John
% RCA Records
1133 Ave. of the Americas
New York, NY 10036
Singer

Schaech, Jonathon
1122 S. Roxbury Dr.
Los Angeles, CA 90035
Actor
Birthday: 9/10/69

Scheider, Roy
PO Box 364
Sagaponack, NY 11962
Actor
Birthday: 11/10/35

Schell, Maria
A-9451
Preitenegg
Austria
Actress
Birthday: 1/15/26

Schering-Plough
1 Giralda Farms
Madison, NJ 07940
Website: http://www.sch-
    plough.com
Richard Jay Kogan, Chairman
    and CEO
Pharmaceuticals

Schiffer, Claudia
342 Madison Ave., #1900
New York, NY 10173
Supermodel, actress
Birthday: 8/24/71

Schlessinger, Dr. Laura
% Premiere Radio Network
15260 Ventura Blvd., #500
Sherman Oaks, CA 91403
or
PO Box 8120
Van Nuys, CA 91409
Website: drlaura.com
Advice columnist, radio, and
    television talk show host

Schneider, John
8436 W. 3rd St., #740
Los Angeles, CA 90048
Singer, actor

Schroeder, Rick
9560 Wilshire Blvd., #500
Beverly Hills, CA 90212
Actor
Birthday: 4/13/70

Schumacher, Joel
4000 Warner Blvd., Bldg 81,
    #117
Burbank, CA 91522
Director

Schumacher, Michael
Forthausstr.
92 Kepen/Manheim
Germany
Professional Formula-1 driver
Birthday: 1/3/69

Schwartz, Sherwood
The Sherwood Schwartz Co.
1865 Carla Ridge Dr.
Beverly Hills, CA 90210
Creator of Gilligan's Island

Schwarzenegger, Arnold
3110 Main St., #300
Santa Monica, CA 90039
*Actor, author, director,
    restaurateur*
Birthday: 7/30/47

SCI Systems
2101 W. Clinton Ave.
Huntsville, AL 35807
Olin B. King, Chairman
A. Eugene Sapp, Jr., President
    and CEO
Electronics, electrical equipment

Scott, Gini Graham
Creative Communications and
    Research
6114 La Salle Avenue, #358
Oakland, CA 94611
Website: http://
    www.giniscott.com/
    cbkwpb.htm
E-mail: GiniGrahamScott@
    giniscott.com
*Gini Graham Scott is the author of
    over 30 books, host of the
    internationally aired radio
    show* Changemakers, *a
    speaker and seminar leader,
    and the director of
    Changemakers and Creative
    Communications and
    Research. She specializes in the
    area of social issues, criminal
    justice, and lifestyles*

Scott, Ridley
% CAA
9830 Wilshire Blvd.
Beverly Hills, CA 90021
or
632 N. La Peer Dr.
Los Angeles, CA 90014
Director
Birthday: 11/30/37

Scott, Tom Everett
% UTA
9560 Wilshire Blvd., #516
Beverly Hills, CA 90212
Actor

Scully, Vin
% Los Angeles Dodgers
1000 Elysian Park Ave.
Los Angeles, CA 90012
Sportscaster

Seal
% Beethoven Street
    Management
56 Beethoven St.
GB-London W10 4LG
England
Singer
Birthday: 2/19/63

Seals, Brady
2100 West End Ave., #1000
Nashville, TN 37203
Singer

Seals, Dan
153 Saunders Ferry Rd.
Hendersonville, TN 37075
Singer

Sears Roebuck
3333 Beverly Rd.
Hoffman Estates, IL 60179
Website: http://www.sears.com
Arthur C. Martinez, Chairman,
    President, and CEO
General merchandisers

Second Amendment Sisters
18484 Preston Rd., Suite 102,
    #141
Dallas, TX 75252
Website: http://
    www.sas-aim.org/
E-mail: inquire@sas-aim.org
Juli Bednarzyk, Director
*Women's advocacy group dedicated
    to promoting the human right
    to self-defense, as recognized by
    the Second Amendment.*

Sedaka, Neil
201 E. 66th St., #3N
New York, NY 10021
Singer, songwriter
Birthday: 3/13/39

Seagate Technology
920 Disc Dr.
Scotts Valley, CA 95066
Website: http://
    www.seagate.com
Gary Filler, Co-Chairman
Lawrence Perlman, Co-
    Chairman
Stephen J. Luczo, CEO,
    Chairman, Seagate
    Software
William D. Watkins, President
    and COO
Computer peripherals, software

Seinfeld, Jerry
211 Central Park West
New York, NY 10024
Actor, comedian
Birthday: 4/29/54

Selleca, Connie
15030 Ventura Blvd., #355
Sherman Oaks, CA 91403
Actress, married to John Tesh
Birthday: 5/25/55

Selleck, Tom
331 Sage Ln.
Santa Monica, CA 90402
Actor

Semmelrogge, Martin
Terhallest II
D-81545 Munich
Germany
Actor, director of Das Boot

ServiceMaster
1 ServiceMaster Way
Downers Grove, IL 60515
Website: http://www.svm.com
C. William Pollard, Chairman
    and CEO
Diversified outsourcing services

Service Merchandise
7100 Service Merchandise Dr.
Brentwood, TN 37027
Website: http://www.service
    merchandise.com
Raymond Zimmerman,
    Chairman
Sam Cusano, CEO
Charles Septer, President and
    COO
Specialist retailers

Sesame Street
1 Lincoln Plaza
New York, NY 10022

Setzer, Brian
10900 Wilshire Blvd., #1230
Los Angeles, CA 90024
Musician

Severance, Joan
9200 Sunset Blvd., #900
Los Angeles, CA 90069
Actress

Sex Pistols, The
100 Wilshire Blvd., #1830
Santa Monica, CA 90401
Music group

**Seymour, Jane (Joyce
    Frankenberger)**
PO Box 548
Agoura, CA 91376
Actress
Birthday: 2/15/51

Seymour, Stephanie
% IT Model Management
526 N. Larchmont Blvd.
Los Angeles, CA 90004
or
5415 Oberlin Dr.
San Diego, CA 92121
Model

Shaffer, Paul
1697 Broadway
New York, NY 10019
Musical director of The David
    Lettterman Show
Birthday: 11/28/49

Shaggy
% Virgin Records
338 N. Foothill Rd.
Beverly Hills, CA 90212
Singer
Birthday: 10/26/68

Shandling, Garry
9590 Wilshire Blvd., #516
Beverly Hills, CA 90212
Actor, comedian
Birthday: 11/29/49

Shapiro, Joshua and Vera
VJ Enterprises
Attn: Joshua "Illinois" Shapiro
PO Box 295
Morton Grove, IL 60053
Website: http://www.v-j-
    enterprises.com/
E-mail:
    rjoshua@sprintmail.com
*Metaphysical tours to sacred sites,
    etc.*

**Sharif, Omar (Michael
    Shaloub)**
% Anne Alvares Correa
18 rue Troyon
75017 Paris
France
Actor
Birthday: 4/10/32

Sharp, Kevin
PO Box 22105
Nashville, TN 37202
Country music singer

Shatner, William
11288 Ventura Blvd., #725
Studio City, CA 91604
Actor
Birthday: 3/22/31

Shaugnessy, Charles
1999 Ave. of the Stars, #2850
Los Angeles, CA 90067
Actor
Birthday: 2/9/55

Shaw Industries
616 E. Walnut Ave.
Dalton, GA 30720
Website: http://
    www.shawinds.com
J. C. "Bud" Shaw, Chairman
    Emeritus
Robert E. Shaw, Chairman and
    CEO
Textiles

Shearer, Harry
119 Ocean Park Blvd.
Santa Monica, CA 90405
Comedian, writer, director
Birthday: 12/23/43

Sheedy, Ali
132 S. Rodeo Dr., #300
Beverly Hills, CA 90212
Actress
Birthday: 6/13/62

**Sheen, Charlie (Carlos Irwin
    Estevez)**
10580 Wilshire Blvd.
Los Angeles, CA 90024
Actor
Birthday: 9/3/65

Sheldrake, Dr. Rupert
20 Willow Rd.
London NW3 1TJ
England
Website: http://
    www.sheldrake.org/
Biochemist

Shelton, Ricky Van
PO Box 683
Lebannon, TN 37087
Website: http://
    www.rickyvanshelton.com/
Country music singer

Shenandoah
1028-B 18th Ave. So.
Nashville, TN 37212
Music group

Shepard, Jean
PO 428
Portland, TN 37148
Country music singer

Sheperd, Cybill
% Studio Fan Mail
1122 S. Robertson Blvd., #15
Los Angeles, CA 90035
Actress, model
Birthday: 2/18/50

Sheppard, T. G.
PO Box 510
Dundee, IL 60118
Country music singer

Sheridan, Jamey
% ICM
8942 Wilshire Blvd.
Beverly Hills, CA 90211
Actor

Sherwin-Williams
101 Prospect Ave. NW
Cleveland, OH 44115
Website: http://www.sherwin-
    williams.com
John G. Breen, Chairman
Christopher M. Connor, VC
    and CEO
Chemicals

Shields, Brooke
10061 Riverside Dr., #1013
Toluca Lake, CA 91602
Actress
Birthday: 5/31/65

Shimerman, Armin
1999 Ave. of the Stars, #2850
Los Angeles, CA 90067
Actor, plays Quark on Star Trek: Deep Space Nine

Shirley, Mariah
% Cinema Talent Agency
2609 W. Wyoming Ave., Suite. A,
Burbank, CA 91505
Actress

Shore, Pauly
8491 Sunset Blvd., #700
West Hollywood, CA 90069
Actor

Short, Martin
760 N. La Cienega Blvd., #200
Los Angeles, CA 90069
Actor
Birthday: 3/26/50

Shriver, Maria
3110 Main St., #300
Santa Monica, CA 90405
Broadcast journalist, wife of Arnold Schwarzenneger
Birthday: 11/6/55

Shriver, Pam
401 Washington Ave., #902
Baltimore, MD 21204
Tennis player

Shue, Elisabeth
PO Box 464
South Orange, NJ 07079
Actress
Birthday: 10/6/63

Sierra Club National Office
85 Second St., 2nd Floor
San Francisco, CA 94105
Website: http://www.sierraclub.org
E-mail: information@sierraclub.org
A nonprofit organization that promotes conservation

Siegfried and Roy
1639 N. Valley Dr.
Las Vegas, NV 89109
Circus act

Silicon Graphics
1600 Amphitheatre Pkwy.
Mountain View, CA 94043
Website: http://www.sgi.com
Robert R. Bishop, Chairman and CEO
Computers, office equipment

Silver, Ron
955 S. Carillo Dr., #300
Los Angeles, CA 90048
Actor
Birthday: 7/2/46

Silverman, Fred
12400 Wilshire Blvd., #920
Los Angeles, CA 90025
Television producer

Silverman, Jonathan
7920 Sunset Blvd., #401
Los Angeles, CA 90046
or
4024 Radford Ave., Bldg. 6
Studio City, CA 91604
Actor
Birthday: 8/5/66

Silverstone, Alicia
1122 S. Robertson Blvd., #15
Los Angeles, CA 90035
Actress
Birthday: 1/4/76

Simmons, Gene (Chaim Witz)
8730 Sunset Blvd., #175
Los Angeles, CA 90069
Singer, bassist for KISS
Birthday: 8/25/49

Simon, Paul
1619 Broadway, #500
New York, NY 10019
Singer, songwriter
Birthday: 10/13/41

Simple Minds
% Schoolhouse Management
63 Frederic St.
GB-Edinburgh EH1 1LH
England
Music group

Simply Red
48 Princess St.
GB-Manchester M1 6HR
England
Music group

Simpson, O. J.
11661 San Vicente Blvd., #600
Los Angeles, CA 90049
Former football player, actor

Sin, Jaime Cardinal
PO Box 132
10099 Manila
Philippines

Sinatra, Nancy
1121 N. Beverly Dr.
Beverly Hills, CA 90210
Singer, Frank's daughter
Birthday: 6/8/40

Sinbad
21704 Devonshire, #13
Chatsworth, CA 91311
Actor, comedian

Sinise, Gary
% CAA
9830 Wilshire Blvd.
Beverly Hills, CA 90212
Actor
Birthday: 3/17/55

Singer, Lori
1465 Linda Crest Dr.
Beverly Hills, CA 90210
Actress
Birthday: 5/6/62

Singletary, Daryle
1610 16th Ave. Sl
Nashville, TN 37212
Country music singer

Sirhan, Sirhan
#B21014
Corcoran State Prison
Box 8800
Corcoran, CA 93212
Assassinated Robert Kennedy

Sirtis, Marina
4526 Wilshire Blvd.
Los Angeles, CA 90010
Actress

Sista Sledge
236 West 26th St., Suite #702
New York, NY 10001
Music group

Sisters with Voices
35 Hart St.
Brooklyn, NY 11206
Music group

Six Shooter
PO Box 53
Portland, TN 37148
Music group

Sizemore, Tom
9830 Wilshire Blvd.
Beverly Hills, CA 90212
Actor

Skaggs, Ricky
PO Box 150871
Nashville, TN 37215
Country music singer

Skerritt, Tom
1122 S. Robertson Blvd., #15
Los Angeles, CA 90035
Actor
Birthday: 8/25/33

Slash (Sol Hudson)
PO Box 93909
Los Angeles, CA 90093
Guns 'n Roses guitar player

Slater, Christian (Christian Hawkins)
9150 Wilshire Blvd., #350
Beverly Hills, CA 90210
Actor
Birthday: 8/18/69

Slater, Kelly
% The Baywatch Production Company
5433 Beethoven St.
Los Angeles, CA 90066
Actress
Birthday: 11/2/72

Sledge, Percy
% Artists Int. Mgmt.
9850 Sandalfoot Blvd., #458
Boca Raton, FL 33428
Singer
Birthday: 11/25/40

Smalley, Richard E.
Dept. of Chemistry, Rice University
6100 Main St.
Houston, TX 77005
Website: http://cnst.rice.edu/reshome.html
1996 Nobel Prize winner in chemistry

Smart, Jean
151 El Camino Dr.
Beverly Hills, CA 90212
Actress

Smashing Pumpkins
9830 Wilshire Blvd.
Beverly Hills, CA 90212
Music group

Smith and Wesson
2100 Roosevelt Ave.
Springfield, MA 01102
Ed Schultz, CEO and President
Website: www.smith-wesson.com
E-mail: eshultz@smith-wesson.com
Firearms

Smith, Anna Nicole
10927 Santa Monica Blvd.,
    #136
Los Angeles, CA 90025
Model

Smith, Connie
PO Box 428
Portland, TN 37148
Country music singer

Smith, Jaclyn
10398 Sunset Blvd.
Los Angeles, CA 90077
Actress
Birthday: 10/26/47

Smith, Kevin
Box 90–409
Auckland Mail Center
Auckland NZL
New Zealand
Actor

Smith, Lou
11365 Ventura Blvd., #100
Studio City, CA 91604
Widow of Wolfman Jack

Smith, Shawnee
Innovative Artists
1999 Ave. of the Stars, Suite
    #2850
Los Angeles, CA 90069
Actress
Birthday: 7/3/70

Smith, Will
% Creative Artists
    Management
9830 Wilshire Blvd.
Beverly Hills, CA 90212
or
303 Bob Hope Dr.
Burbank, CA 91523
Actor
Birthday: 9/25/68

Smithfield Foods
200 Commerce St.
Smithfield, VA 23430
Joseph W. Luter III, Chairman,
    President, and CEO
Food company

Smithsonian Institution
1000 Jefferson Dr. SW
Washington, DC 20560
Website: http://www.si.edu/
E-mail: webmaster@si.edu/
Larry Small, Secretary of the
    Smithsonian Institution
*The Institution is as an
    independent trust
    instrumentality of the United
    States holding more than 140
    million artifacts and
    specimens in its trust for "the
    increase and diffusion of
    knowledge"*

Smits, Jimmy
PO Box 49922
Barrington Station
Los Angeles, CA 90049
Actor
Birthday: 7/9/55

Smurfit-Stone Container Corporation
150 N. Michigan Ave.
Chicago, IL 60601
Website: http://www.smurfit.ie
Michael W. J. Smurfit,
    Chairman
Ray Curran, President and
    CEO
The world's top maker of
containerboard and corrugated
containers and a leading
wastepaper recycler

Snider, Mike
PO Box 140710
Nashville, TN 37214
Country music singer

Snipes, Wesley
1888 Century Park East, #500
Los Angeles, CA 90067
Actor

Snow
% S. L. Feldman
1505 W. 2nd Ave., #200
Vancouver, BC V6H 3Y4
Canada
Singer
Birthday: 10/30/69

Sodano, Angelo Cardinal
00120 Vatican City State
Vatican

Sojourners
2401 15th St. NW
Washington, DC 20009
E-mail: sojourners@sojo.net
Ryan Beiler, Web Editor
E-mail: rbeiler@sojo.net
Christian ministry whose mission
is to proclaim and practice the
biblical call to integrate
spiritual renewal and social
justice

Solar Energy Industries Association
1616 H Street, NW 8th Floor
Washington, DC 20006
Website: http://www.seia.org/
E-mail: seiaopps@digex.com
Peter Lowenthal,
E-mail: plowenth@seia.org
A national trade association for
all solar businesses and
enterprises in the fields of
photovoltaics, solar electric
power, solar thermal power,
and solar building products

Solectron
777 Gibraltar Dr.
Milpitas, CA 95035
Website: http://
    www.solectron.com
Koichi Nishimura, Chairman,
    President, and CEO
Electronics, electrical equipment

Somers, Suzanne
23852 Pacific Coast Hwy., #916
Malibu, CA 90265
Actress
Birthday: 11/5/40

Sonoco
1 N. Second St.
Hartsville, SC 29550
Website: http://
    www.sonoco.com
Charles W. Coker, Chairman
Harris E. DeLoach, Jr., CEO
    and President
Forest and paper products

Sonnier, Joel
PO Box 120845
Nashville, TN 37212
Singer

Sorbo, Kevin
PO Box 410
Buffalo Center, IA 50424
or
5664 Cahuegna Blvd., Suite
    #437
North Hollywood, CA 91601
Actor

Soros Foundation Network
Open Society Institute
888 Seventh Ave.
New York, NY 10606
Website: http://www.soros.org
George Soros, Founder
*Grant organization that supports
    research that promotes an
    "open society"*

Soraya
% Mercury Records
11150 Santa Monica Blvd.,
    10th Floor
Los Angeles, CA 90025
Singer
Birthday: 3/11/69

Sorenson, Heidi
% Pierce and Shelly
612 Lighthouse Ave., #275
Pacific Grove, CA 93951
E-mail: HeidSoren@aol.com
Model

Sorvino, Mira
110 E. 87th St.
New York, NY 10128
Actress

Sorvino, Paul
110 E. 87th St.
New York, NY 10128
Actor
Birthday: 4/13/49

Sothern, Ann
Box 2285
Ketchum, ID 83340
Actress
Birthday: 1/22/09

Soto, Talisa
9200 Sunset Blvd., #900
Los Angeles, CA 90069
Model

Soul Asylum
955 S. Carrill Dr., #300
Los Angeles, CA 90048
Music group

Soul, David
8306 Wilshire Blvd., #438
Beverly Hills, CA 90211
Actor

Soundgarden
% Curtis Mgmt.
207½ First Ave. S., #300
Seattle, WA 98104
Music group

Southern Energy, Inc.
900 Ashwood Pkwy., Suite. 500
Atlanta, GA 30338
Website: http://
    www.southernco.com/site/
    soenergy
A. W. Dahlberg, Chairman and
    CEO
Gas and electric utilities

Southwest Airlines
2702 Love Field Dr.
Dallas, TX 75235
Website: http://
    www.iflyswa.com
Herbert D. Kelleher,
    Chairman, President, and
    CEO
Airlines

**Spacek, Sissy (Mary Elizbeth
    Spacek)**
Rt. 2, #640
Cobham, VA 22929
Actress
Birthday: 12/25/49

Spacey, Kevin
151 El Camino Dr.
Beverly Hills, CA 90212
Actor
Birthday: 7/26/49

Spade, David
9150 Wilshire Blvd., #350
Beverly Hills, CA 90212
or
% Jonas PR
240 26th St., Suite 3
Santa Monica, CA 90402
Actor

Sparks
106 N. Buffalo St., #200
Warsaw, IN 46580
Music group

Spears, Billie Jo
2802 Columbine Place
Nashville, TN 37204
Country music singer

Spears, Britney
137 W. 25th St.
New York, NY 10001
E-mail: britney@britney.com
Singer, actress
Birthday: 12/2/81

Special Olympics International
1325 G St. NW, Suite 500
Washington, DC 20005
Website: http://
    www.specialolympics.org/
Sargent Shriver, Chairman of
    the Board
*An international program of year-
    round sports training and
    athletic competition for more
    than one million children and
    adults with mental retardation*

Spelling, Aaron
5700 Wilshire Blvd.
Los Angeles, CA 90036
Television producer

Spelling, Tori
5700 Wilshire Blvd.
Los Angeles, CA 90036
or
% SFM
1122 S. Robertson Blvd., #15
Los Angeles, CA 90035
*Actress, daughter of Aaron
    Spelling*
Birthday: 5/16/73

Spencer, Bud
Via Cortina d'Apezzo 156
00191 Rome
Italy
Actor

Spice Girls
35-37 Parkgate Rd., Unit 32
Ransomes Dock
London SW11 4NP
England
Singing group

Spielberg, Steven
PO Box 8520
Universal City, CA 91608
Producer/director
Birthday: 12/18/47

Spinal Tap
4268 Hazeltine Ave.
Sherman Oaks, CA 91423
Music group

Spiner, Brent
PO Box 5617
Beverly Hills, CA 90209
Actor
Birthday: 2/2/55

Spinks, Leon
PO Box 88771
Carol Stream, IL 60188
Boxer

Springer, Jerry
454 N. Columbus Dr., #200
Chicago, IL 60611
*Talk show host, former mayor of
    Cincinnati*

Springfield, Rick
9200 Sunset Blvd., #900
Los Angeles, CA 90069
Singer, actor
Birthday: 8/23/49

Sprint
2330 Shawnee Mission Pwy.
Westwood, KS 66205
Website: http://www.sprint.com
William T. Esrey, CEO
Telecommunications

Spyro Gyro
926 Horseshoe Rd.
Suffern, NY 10301
Music group

Squier, Billy
PO Box 1251
New York, NY 10023
Singer, musician
Birthday: 5/12/50

Squirrel Nut Zippers
9056 Santa Monica Blvd., #203
Los Angeles, CA 90069
Music group

Stack, Robert
415 N. Camden Dr., #121
Beverly Hills, CA 90210
Actor
Birthday: 1/13/19

Stafford, Jim
PO Box 6366
Branson, MO 65616
Country music singer

Stahl, Lisa
% Shelly and Pierce
612 Lighthouse Ave., #275
Pacific Grove, CA 93951
E-mail: lisastahl1@aol.com
Actress

Stallone, Sylvester
9150 Wilshire Blvd., #340
Beverly Hills, CA 90212
Actor, writer, director
Birthday: 7/6/46

Stamos, John
270 N. Canon Dr., #1064
Beverly Hills, CA 90210
Actor, musician
Birthday: 8/19/63

Staples
500 Staples Dr.
Framingham, MA 01702
Website: http://
www.staples.com
Thomas G. Stemberg,
Chairman and CEO
Specialist retailers

Stapleton, Jean
% Bauman, Hiller, and
Associates
5757 Wilshire Blvd., 5th Floor
Los Angeles, CA 90036
Actress

Starr, Ringo (Richard Starkey)
1541 Ocean Ave., #200
Santa Monica, CA 90401
Drummer, actor
Birthday: 7/7/40

**State Farm Insurance
Companie**
1 State Farm Plaza
Bloomington, IL 61710
Edward B. Rust, Jr., Chairman
and CEO
P and C insurance (mutual)

State Street Corp.
225 Franklin St.
Boston, MA 02110
Website: http://
www.statestreet.com
Marshall N. Carter, Chairman
David A. Spina, CEO
Commercial bank

Statler Brothers
PO Box 492
Hernando, MS 68632
Music group

Staubach, Roger
6912 Edelweiss Cr.
Dallas, TX 75240
Football player

Steel, Danielle
PO Box 1637
Murray Hill Station
New York, NY 10156
Author

Steen, Jessica
% Somers Teitelbaum David
(Chris Henze)
1925 Century Park East, #2320
Los Angeles, CA 90067
Web page: http://
www.jessicasteen.com/
Actress

Steinbrenner, George
PO Box 25077
Tampa, FL 33622
Baseball executive

Stern, Daniel
PO Box 6788
Malibu, CA 90264
Actor
Birthday: 8/28/57

Stern, Howard
40 W. 57th. St., #1400
New York, NY 10019
Radio personality

Stevens, Brinke
P.M.B. #556
8033 Sunset Blvd.
Hollywood, CA 90046
Actress

Stevens, Connie (Concetta Ann Ingolia)
426 S. Robertson Blvd.
Los Angeles, CA 90048
Actress, singer
Birthday: 8/8/38

Stevens, Ray (Ray Ragsdale)
1708 Grand Ave.
Nashville, TN 37212
Singer, songwriter
Birthday: 1/24/39

Stevens, Stella (Estelle Eggleston)
2180 Coldwater Canyon
Beverly Hills, CA 90210
Actress
Birthday: 10/1/36

Stevenson, Parker
% Metropolitan Talent Agency
4526 Wilshire Blvd.
Los Angeles, CA 90010
Actor
Birthday: 6/4/51

Stewart, Martha
19 Newton Turnpike
Westport, CT 06880
TV personality, lifestyle consultant, writer, publisher
Birthday: 8/3/41

Stewart, Patrick
PO Box 93999
Los Angeles, CA 90093
Actor, writer
Birthday: 7/13/40

Stewart, Rod
1122 S. Robertson Blvd., #15
Los Angeles, CA 90035
Singer, songwriter
Birthday: 1/10/45

Stich, Michael
Bayerstr 383
A-5071
Salzburg/Wals-Siezenheim
Austria
Professional tennis player

Stiers, David Ogden
121 N. San Vicente Blvd.
Beverly Hills, CA 90211
Actor
Birthday: 10/31/42

Sting (Gordon Matthew Sumner)
2 The Grove
Highgate Village
London N6
England
Singer, songwriter, actor
Birthday: 10/2/51

Stockwell, Dean
PO Box 6248
Malibu, CA 90264
Birthday: 3/5/35

Stone, Cliffie
PO Box 710
Los Angeles, CA 90078
Country music singer

Stone, Doug
PO Box 943
Springfield, TN 37172
Country music singer

Stone, Sharon
PO Box 7304
North Hollywood, CA 91603
Actress

Stone, Sly
6467 Sunset Blvd., #110
Hollywood, CA 90028
Musician

Storch, Larry
330 West End Ave.
New York, NY 10023
Actor
Birthday: 1/8/23

Stowe, Madeleine
9560 Wilshire Blvd., #516
Beverly Hills, CA 90212
Actress
Birthday: 1958

The St. Paul Companies, Inc.
385 Washington St.
St. Paul, MN 55102
Website: http://www.stpaul.com
Douglas W. Leatherdale,
    Chairman and CEO
P and C insurance (stock)

Strait, George
1000 18th Ave. S.
Nashville, TN 37212
Country music singer

Strange, Curtis
% Kingsman Golf Club
100 Golf Club Rd.
Williamsburg, VA 23185
Golfer

Stray Cats
113 Wardour St.
GB-London W1
England
Music group

Streep, Meryl (Mary Louise Streep)
% Creative Artists Agency
9830 Wilshire Blvd.
Beverly Hills, CA 90212
Actress
Birthday: 4/22/49

Streisand, Barbra (Barbara Joan)
320 Central Park West
New York, NY 10025
Singer, actress, director
Birthday: 4/24/42

Stringfield, Sherry
9560 Wilshire Blvd., #516
Beverly Hills, CA 90212
Actress

Stroker, Dr. Carol
Ames, Moffett
Field, CA 94035
*NASA scientist with the Mars
    Mission*

Strugg, Kerry
1122 S. Robertson Blvd., #14
Los Angeles, CA 90035
Gymnast

Struthers, Sally
8721 Sunset Blvd.
Los Angeles, CA 90046
Actress
Birthday: 7/28/48

Stuart, Marty
119 17th Ave. S.
Nashville, TN 37203
Singer, songwriter

Marty Stuart Fan Club
PO Box 24180
Nashville, TN 37202

Sun Microsystems
901 San Antonio Rd.
Palo Alto, CA 94303
Website: http://www.sun.com
Scott G. McNealy, Chairman
    and CEO
Computers, office equipment

Sunny
% WWF
PO Box 3859
Stamford, CT 06905
Professional wrestler

Sun Trust Bank
303 Peachtree St. NE
Atlanta, GA 30308
Website: http://
    www.suntrust.com/
    index.html
L. Phillip Humann, Chairman,
    President, and CEO
Commercial bank

Supernaw, Doug
56 Lindsey Ave.
Nashville, TN 37210
Country music singer

Supertramp
16530 Ventura Blvd., #201
Encino, CA 91436
Music group

Supervalu
11840 Valley View Rd.
Eden Prairie, MN 55344
Website: http://
    www.supervalu.com
Michael W. Wright, Chairman
    and CEO
Wholesaler

Survivor
9850 Sandlefoot Blvd., #458
Boca Raton, FL 33428
Music group

Sutherland, Donald
760 N. La Cienega Blvd., #300
Los Angeles, CA 90069
Actor
Birthday: 7/17/36

Sutherland, Kiefer
132 S. Rodeo Dr., #300
Beverly Hills, CA 90212
Actor, Donald's son
Birthday: 12/18/66

Swanson, Kristy
2934 N. Beverly Glen Circle,
   #416
Los Angeles, CA 90077
Actress
Birthday: 12/19/69

Swayze, Patrick
% Wolf/Kasteler, Inc.
132 S. Rodeo Dr. #300
Beverly Hills, CA 90212
Actor
Birthday: 8/18/52

Sweethearts of the Rodeo
5101 Overton Rd.
Nashville, TN 37220
Music group

Swing Out Sister
132 Liverpool Rd.
Islington
GB-London N1
England
Music group

Sysco
1390 Enclave Pkwy.
Houston, TX 77077
Website: http://www.sysco.com
John F. Woodhouse, Senior
   Chairman
Charles H. Cotros, Chairman
   and CEO
Richard J. Schnieders,
   President and COO
Food wholesalers

T

> Letters blur the lines between two separate lives.
>
> —VICKI RENTZ

Tabuchi, Shoji
HCR Rt. #1
Box 755
Branson, MO 65616
Musician

Takei, George
419 N. Larchmont Blvd., #41
Los Angeles, CA 90004
*Actor, plays Lt. Sulu on Original
    Star Trek*

Talk Talk
121 A Revelstone N.
Wimbledon Place
GB-London W15
England
Music group

Tandy Brands Accessories, Inc.
90 E. Lamar Blvd., Suite 200
Arlington, TX 76011
Website: http://
    www.tandybrands.com
James F. Gaertner, Chairman,
J. S. Britt Jenkins, President
    and CEO
Leather goods manufacturer

Tangerine Dream
PO Box 29242
Oakland, CA 94604
Music group

Tarantino, Quentin
7966 Beverly Blvd., #300
Los Angeles, CA 90048
Director, actor, writer
Birthday: 3/27/63

Taupin, Bernie
450 N. Maple Dr., #501
Beverly Hills, CA 90210
Songwriter

Taylor, Elizabeth
PO Box 55995
Sherman Oaks, CA 91413
Actress
Birthday: 2/27/32

Taylor, James
1250 6th. St., #401
Santa Monica, CA 90401
Singer, songwriter, musician
Birthday: 3/12/48

Taylor, Niki
8326 Pines Blvd., #334
Hollywood, FL 33024
Model

Taylor-Young, Leigh
6500 Wilshire Blvd., #2200
Los Angeles, CA 90048
Actress

Taylor, Les
177 Northwood Dr.
Lexington, KY 40505
Country music singer

Tears For Fears
2100 Colorado Ave.
Santa Monica, CA 90404
Rock band

Tech-Data
5350 Tech Data Dr.
Clearwater, FL 33760
Website: http://
    www.techdata.com
Edward C. Raymund,
    Chairman Emeritus
Steven A. Raymund, Chairman
    and CEO
Wholesalers

Teller, Dr. Edward
Box 808
Livermore, CA 94550
*During World War II he was a
    member of the Manhattan
    Project for the development of
    the atomic bomb*
Birthday: 1/18/08

Temple-Inland
303 S. Temple Dr.
Diboll, TX 75941
Website: http://
    www.templeinland.com
Kenneth M. Jastrow II,
    Chairman and CEO
Forest and paper products

Tenet Healthcare
3820 State St.
Santa Barbara, CA 93105
Website: http://
    www.tenethealth.com
Jeffrey C. Barbakow, Chairman
    and CEO
Health care

Tennant, Victoria
% Metropolitan Talent Agency
4526 Wilshire Blvd.
Los Angeles, CA 90010
Actress
Birthday: 9/30/53

Tenneco Automotive, Inc.
500 North Field Dr.
Lake Forest, IL 60045
Website: http://www.tenneco-
    automotive.com/
Mark P. Frissora, Chairman
    and CEO
Motor vehicles and parts

Texaco
2000 Westchester Ave.
White Plains, NY 10650
Website: http://
    www.texaco.com
Peter I. Bijur, CEO
Petroleum refining

Texas Instruments
12500 TI Blvd.
Dallas, TX 75243
Website: http://www.ti.com
Thomas J. Engibous,
    Chairman, President and
    CEO
Electronics, semiconductors

Texas Tornados
PO Box 530
Bellaire, OH 43906
Musical group

Textron
40 Westminster St.
Providence, RI 02903
Website: http://
    www.textron.com
Lewis B. Campbell, Chairman
    and CEO
Aerospace

Tenney, Jon
1122 S. Roxbury Dr.
Los Angeles, CA 90035
Actor

Tesh, John
PO Box 6010
Sherman Oaks, CA 91413
Musician
Birthday: 7/1/53

Thermo Electron
81 Wyman St.
Waltham, MA 02254
Website: http://
    www.thermo.com
Richard F. Syron, Chairman,
    President, and CEO
Scientific, photo, control equipment

Theismann, Joe
% ESPN
ESPN Plaza
Bristol, CT 06010
Sportscaster

Thiessen, Tiffani-Amber
3500 W. Olive Ave., #1400
Burbank, CA 91505
Actress
Birthday: 1/23/74

Thomas, B. J.
PO Box 120003
Arlington, TX 76012
Singer

Thomas, Dave
429 Santa Monica Blvd., #500
Santa Monica, CA 90401
Comedian, actor

Thomas, Fred Dalton
401 Church St., 12th Floor
Nashville, TN 37219
Actor

Thomas, Heather
1122 S. Robertson Blvd., #15
Los Angeles, CA 90035
Actress
Birthday: 9/8/57

Thomas, Irma
PO Box 26126
New Orleans, LA 70186
Musician

Thomas, Jay
6500 Wilshire Blvd., #2200
Los Angeles, CA 90048
Actor, radio personality
Birthday: 7/12/48

Thomas, Jonathan Taylor
PO Box 64846
Los Angeles, CA 90064
Actor
Birthday: 9/8/81

Thomas, Kristin Scott
9830 Wilshire Blvd.
Beverly Hills, CA 90210
Actress

Thomas, Michael Phillip
PO Box 611222
Miami, FL 33261
Actor
Birthday: 5/26/49

Thompson, Andrea
14431 Ventura Blvd., #260
Sherman Oaks, CA 91423
Actress

Thompson, Emma
31/32 Soho Sq.
London W1V 5DG
England
Actress

Thompson, Fred
United States Senate
Washington, DC 20510
E-mail: senator_thompson@
thompson.senate.gov
Senator from Tennessee and actor

Thompson, Hank
5 Rushing Creek Court
Roanoke, TX 76262
Country music singer

Thompson, Lea
PO Box 5617
Beverly Hills, CA 90210
Actress
Birthday: 5/31/62

Thompson, Sada
PO Box 490
Southebury, CT 06488
Actress
Birthday: 9/27/29

Thorne-Smith Courtney
11693 San Vicente Blvd., #266
Los Angeles, CA 90049
Actress

Thornton, Billy Bob
11777 San Vicente Blvd., #880
Los Angeles, CA 90049
Actor

Thurman, Uma
% Creative Artists Agency
9830 Wilshire Blvd.
Beverly Hills, CA 90212
Actress

**TIAA-CREF (Teachers
    Insurance and Annuity
    Association-College
    Retirement Equities Fund)**
730 Third Ave.
New York, NY 10017
John H. Biggs, Chairman,
    President, and CEO
*Life and health insurance
    (mutual)*

Tiegs, Cheryl
15 E. Putnam Ave., #3260
Greenwich, CT 06830
Model

Tighe, Kevin
PO Box 453
Sedro Woolley, WA 98284
Actor
Birthday: 8/13/44

Tillis, Mell
2527 State Hwy., #248
Box 1630
Branson, MO 65615
Country music singer

Tilly, Jennifer
270 N. Canon Dr., #1582
Beverly Hills, CA 9021
or
% ICM
8942 Wilshire Blvd.
Beverly Hills, CA 90211
Actress, Meg's sister
Birthday: 9/10/58

Tilly, Meg
321 S. Beverly Dr., #M
Beverly Hills, CA 90212
Actress
Birthday: 2/14/60

Tillis, Pam
PO Box 128575
Nashville, TN 37212
Country music singer

Tilton, Charlene
PO Box 1309
Studio City, CA 91614
Actress

Time Warner
75 Rockefeller Plaza
New York, NY 10019
Website: http://
    www.timewarner.com
Gerald M. Levin, Chairman
    and CEO
Entertainment, publishing

Tippin, Aaron
PO Box 121709
Nashville, TN 37212
Country music singer

TJX
770 Cochituate Rd.
Framingham, MA 01701
Website: http://
    tjx.stage.utopia.com
Bernard Cammarata, Chairman
Edmond J. "Ted" English,
    President and CEO
Specialist retailers

Toblowsky, Stephen
% William Morris Agency
151 El Camino Dr.
Beverly Hills, CA 90212
Actor

Today Show
30 Rockefeller Plaza, Rm. 374E
New York, NY 10112
E-mail: today@nbc.com

Tomei, Marissa
120 W. 45th St., #3600
New York, NY 10036
Actress
Birthday: 12/4/64

Tomlin, Lily
PO Box 27700
Los Angeles, CA 90027
Comedian, actress
Birthday: 9/1/39

**Tomas Rivera Policy Institute,
    The**
1050 North Mills Ave.
Pitzer College, Scott Hall
Claremont, CA 91711
Website: http://www.trpi.org/
Harry P. Pachon, President
*A freestanding, nonprofit, policy
    research organization which
    has attained a reputation as
    the nation's 'premier Latino
    think tank'*

**Tom Petty and the
Heartbreakers**
PO Box 260159
Encino, CA 91426
Music group

Tork, Peter
1551 S. Robertson Blvd.
Los Angeles, CA 90035
Musician, actor
Birthday: 2/13/42

Tosco
72 Cummings Point Rd.
Stamford, CT 06902
Website: http://www.tosco.com
Thomas D. O'Malley,
    Chairman and CEO
Petroleum refining

Toys "R" Us
461 From Rd.
Paramus, NJ 07652
Website: http://
    www.toysrus.com
Michael Goldstein, Chairman
John H. Eyler, Jr., President
    and CEO
Specialist retailers

Tractors, The
PO Box 5034
Tulsa, OK 74150
Music Group

Tracy, Paul
% Penske Motorsports
Penske Plaza
Reading, PA 19603
Race car driver

Trans World Airline
One City Center
515 N. Sixth St.
St. Louis, MO 63101
Website: http://www.twa.com
Gerald Gitner, Chairman
William F. Compton, President
    and CEO
Airlines

Transamerica
600 Montgomery St.
San Francisco, CA 94111
Website: http://
    www.transamerica.com
Frank C. Herringer, Chairman
Donald Shepard, President and
    CEO
Life and health insurance (stock)

**Travis, Randy (Randy
    Traywick)**
PO Box 121137
Nashville, TN 37212
Country music singer
Birthday: 5/4/59

**Travelers Property Casualty
    Corp.**
1 Tower Sq.
Hartford, CT 06183
Robert I. Lipp, Chairman
Jay S. Fishman, President and
    CEO; CEO
Commercial Lines
Insurance

Travanti, Daniel J.
1077 Melody Rd.
Lake Forest, IL 60045
Actor
Birthday: 3/7/40

Travolta, John
15821 Ventura Blvd., #460
Studio City, CA 91436
Actor
Birthday 2/18/54

Trebek, Alex
10210 W. Washington
Culver City, CA 90232
Game show host

Tritt, Travis
PO Box 2044
Hiram, GA 40141
Singer, songwriter
Birthday: 2/9/63

Travis Tritt Country Club
Attn: Liz
PO Box 2044
Hiram, GA 30141

Thomas Jefferson Center for the Protection of Free Expression
400 Peter Jefferson Place
Charlottesville, VA 22911
Website: http://
www.tjcenter.org/
E-mail:
freespeech@tjcenter.org
Robert M. O'Neil, Director
Judith G. Clabes, President and CEO
A unique organization devoted solely to the defense of free expression in all its forms. While its charge is sharply focused, the Center's mission is broad. It is as concerned with the musician as with the mass media, with the painter as with the publisher, and as much with the sculptor as the editor.

Trends Research Institute
PO Box 660
Rhinebeck, NY 12572-0660
Website: http://
www.trendsresearch.com/
E-mail: webmaster@
trendsresearch.com
Gerald Celente, Director
E-mail: celente@trends
research.com
Combines unique resources with its own trademarked methodology to help companies profit from trends

Tribune Company
435 N. Michigan Ave.
Chicago, IL 60611
Website: http://
www.tribune.com
John W. Madigan, Chairman, President, and CEO
Newspapers, publishing, owns the Chicago Cubs

Truck Stop
% Lucius B. Rechlng
Quellental 14
D-22609 Hamburg
Germany
Country music group

**Trudeau, Garry (Garretson
    Beckman Trudeau)**
% United Press Media
200 Madison Ave.
New York, NY 10016
Cartoonist, married to Jane Pauley
Birthday: 1948

Trulli, Jarno
% Minardi Team S.p.A.
Via Spellanzani 21
I-48018 Faenza/RA
Professional Formula-1 driver

Trump, Donald
721 5th Ave.
New York, NY 10022
Real estate executive
Birthday: 6/14/46

TruServe
8600 W. Bryn Mawr Ave.
Chicago, IL 60631
Website: http://
    www.truserv.com
E-mail: email@truserv.com
Donald Hoye, President and
    CEO
Specialist retailers

Turner Corp.
Bank of America Plaza
901 Main St., Suite 4900
Dallas, TX 75202
Website: http://www.turner
    construction.com
Thomas C. Leppert, Chairman
    and CEO
Engineering, construction

TRW
1900 Richmond Rd.
Cleveland, OH 44124
Website: http://www.trw.com
Joseph T. Gorman, Chairman
    and CEO
Motor vehicles and parts

Tubb, Justin
PO Box 500
Nashville, TN 37202
Country music singer

Tucker, Tanya
109 Westpark Dr., #400
Brentwood, TN 37027
Country music singer
Birthday: 10/10/58

Tudor, Tasha
PO Box 503
Marlboro, VT 05344
Website: http://www.tashatudor
    andfamily.com/
E-mail: ensingm@together.net
*One of America's most beloved
    author/illustrators, she has
    written, illustrated, or been the
    subject of over 90 books
    spanning more than half a
    century. Her 91st book,* The
    Great Corgiville
    Kidnapping, *was published
    in 1997.*

Tune, Tommy
50 E. 89th St.
New York, NY 10128
Dancer, director, actor
Birthday: 2/28/39

Turlington, Christy
% United Talent Agency
9560 Wilshire Blvd.
Beverly Hills, CA 90212
or
% Celebrity Merchandise
PMB 710
15030 Ventura Blvd.
Sherman Oaks, CA 91403
Model, actress

Turner, Grant
PO Box 414
Brentwood, TN 37027
Country music singer

Turner, Ted (Robert Edward Turner III)
1050 Techwood Dr., NW
Atlanta, GA 30318
Media executive, owner of Atlanta Braves and Atlanta Hawks
Birthday: 11/26/39

Turner Broadcasting Systems
1 CNN Center, Box 105366
Atlanta, GA 30348
Website: http://www.turner.com/
Ted Turner, President
Operator of cable TV networks

Tutu, Archbishop Desmond
7981 Orlando West
Box 1131
Johannesburg
Rep. of South Africa

Twain, Shania
410 W. Elm St.
Greenwich, CT 06830
Country music singer

Tweed, Shannon
9300 Wilshire Blvd., #410
Beverly Hills, CA 90212
Actress

Twiggy (Leslie Hornby)
4 St. George's House
15 Hanover Square
GB-London W1R 9AJ
England
Model, actress
Birthday: 9/19/49

Twister Alley
Rt. 2, Box 138
Lake City, AR 72437
Music group

TXU Corp
Energy Plaza
1601 Bryan St.
Dallas, TX 75201
Website: http://www.txu.com
Erle Nye, Chairman and CEO
Gas and electric utilities

Tyco International
1 Tyco Park
Exeter, NH 03833
Website: http://www.tycoint.com
L. Dennis Kozlowski, Chairman, President, and CEO
Metal products

Tyler, Liv
233 Park Ave. S., 10th Floor
New York, NY 10003
or
1999 Ave. of the Stars, Suite
    2850
Los Angeles, CA 90067
*Actress, daughter of Steven Tyler,
    lead singer of Aerosmith*

**Tyler, Steven (Steven
    Tallarico)**
584 Broadway, #1009
New York, NY 10012
or
% Monterey Pennisula Artists
509 Hartnell St.
Monterey, CA 93940
Lead singer of Aerosmith
Birthday: 3/26/48

Tylo, Hunter
11684 Ventura Blvd., #910
Studio City, CA 91604
Actress

Tyson, Cicely
315 W. 70th St.
New York, NY 10023
Actress
Birthday: 12/19/33

Tyson, Mike
10100 Santa Monica Blvd.,
    #1300
Los Angeles, CA 90067
Boxer
Birthday: 7/1/66

Tyson Foods
2210 W. Oaklawn Dr.
Springdale, AR 72762
Website: http://www.tyson.com
Don Tyson, Senior Chairman
John H. Tyson, Chairman,
    President, and CEO
Food producer

It gives me the greatest pleasure to realize I have one more invisible friend at the other end of the post office. Nearly every week a new one turns up, and I feel like I am having a party, and the postman is a sort of a Santa Claus every day, with letters from my new friends.

—VACHEL LINDSAY to Alice Henderson, 1913

U2
119 Rockland Cntr., #350
Nanuet, NY 10954
Rock band

U96
Bernstorffstr. 123
D-22767 Hamburg
Germany
Rock group

UB40
533-579 Harrow Rd.
London W10 4RN
England
Music group

UAL
1200 E. Algonquin Rd.
Elk Grove Township, IL 60007
Website: http://www.ual.com
James E. Goodwin, Chairman
    and CEO
Airlines

UFO
10 Sutherland
GB-London W9 24Q
England
Music group

Ullrich, Jan
% Team Deutsche Telekom
Königstr. 97
53115 Bonn
Germany
*Winner of the 1997 Tour de
    France*
Birthday: 11/2/73

**Ulrich, Skeet (Brian Ray
    Ulrich)**
8942 Wilshire Blvd.
Beverly Hills, CA 90211
Actor
Birthday: 1/20/69

Ultramor Diamond Shamrock
6000 N. Loop 1604 W.
San Antonio, TX 78249
Website: http://
    www.diasham.com
Jean R. Gaulin, Chairman,
    President, and CEO
Petroleum refining

Underwood, Blair
4116 N. Magnolia Blvd., #101
Burbank, CA 91505
Actor
Birthday: 8/25/64

Unicom
10 S. Dearborn St.
Chicago, IL 60603
Website: http://www.ceco.com
John W. Rowe, Chairman,
    President & CEO
Gas and electric utilities

Union Carbide
39 Old Ridgebury Rd.
Danbury, CT 06817
Website: http://
    www.unioncarbide.com
William H. Joyce, Chairman,
    President, and CEO
Chemicals

Union Pacific
1416 Dodge St., Rm. 1230
Omaha, NE 68179
Website: http://www.up.com
Richard K. Davidson,
    Chairman, President, and
    CEO
Railroad

Unisource
6600 Governors Lake Pkwy.
Norcross, GA 30071
Website: http://
    www.unisourcelink.com
Charles C. Tufano, President
Matthew C. Tyser, VP and CFO
Wholesalers

Unisys
Unisys Way
Blue Bell, PA 19424
Website: http://www.unisys.com
Lawrence A. Weinbach,
    Chairman, President and
    CEO
Computer and data services

Unitas, Johnny
% Pro Football Hall of Fame
2121 George Halas Dr. NW
Canton, OH 44708
Former football player

Union of Concerned Scientists
2 Brattle Square
Cambridge, MA 02238
Website: http://
    www.ucsusa.org/
E-mail: ucs@ucsusa.org
Howard Ris, Executive Director
*A nonprofit alliance of scientists
    and citizens working for a
    healthy environment and a
    safe world, UCS researches
    and promotes clean energy
    and transportation
    technologies*

United Health Care
9900 Bren Rd. E.
Minnetonka, MN 55343
Website: http://
    www.unitedhealthcare.com
William W. McGuire, CEO
Health care

United Parcel Service
55 Glenlake Pkwy. N.E.
Atlanta, GA 30328
Website: http://www.ups.com
James P. Kelly, Chairman and
    CEO
Mail, package, freight delivery

**United Services Automobile
    Association (USAA)**
9800 Fredericksburg Rd.,
    USAA Bldg.
San Antonio, TX 78288
Website: http://www.usaa.com
Robert G. Davis, Chairman,
    President, and CEO
P & C insurance (stock)

United States Olympic Committee
One Olympic Plaza
Colorado Springs, CO 80909
Website: http://www.usoc.org
William Hybl, Chairman,
    President, internationally
Norman P. Blake, Jr., CEO and
    Secretary General

United States Martial Arts Association, The
011 Mariposa Ave.
Citrus Heights, CA 95610
Website: http://
    www.mararts.org
E-mail: psp4@flash.net
Mr. Charles Matza, Chairman
    of the Board of Directors

United Technologies
1 Financial Plaza
Hartford, CT 06101
Website: http://www.utc.com
George David, Chairman and
    CEO
Aerospace

United We Stand America
7616 LBJ Freeway, #727
Dallas, TX 75221
Website: http://www.uwsa.com/
E-mail: uw-bill@uwsa.com

Universal Tobacco
1501 N. Hamilton St.
Richmond, VA 23230
Website: http://
    www.universalcorp.com
Henry H. Harrell, Chairman
    and CEO
Tobacco producer

Unocal
2141 Rosecrans Ave., Suite.
    4000
El Segundo, CA 90505
Website: http://
    www.unocal.com
Roger C. Beach, Chairman and
    CEO
Mining, crude-oil production

Unser, Al, Jr.
PO Box 25047
Albuquerque, NM 87125
Race car driver

Upshaw, Gene
% Pro Football Hall of Fame
2121 George Halas Dr. NW
Canton, OH 44708
Professional football player

Urban Institute
2100 M St., NW
Washington, DC 20037
Website: http://www.urban.org
Robert D. Reischauer,
    President
*A nonprofit economic, social, and
    policy research organization*

Urich, Robert
10061 Riverside Dr., #1026
Toluca Lake, CA 91602
Actor
Birthday: 12/19/47

US Airways Group
2345 Crystal Dr.
Arlington, VA 22227
Website: http://
    www.usairways.com
Stephen M. Wolf, Chairman
Rakesh Gangwal, President and
    CEO
Airline

U.S. Bancorp
601 Second Ave. S.
Minneapolis, MN 55402
Website: http://www.fbs.com/
    home.html
John F. Grundhofer, Chairman
    and CEO
Commercial bank

USF Worldwide, Inc.
1100 Arlington Heights Rd.,
    Suite. 600
Itasca, IL 60143
Website: http://
    www.usfreightways.com/
    structure/seko/index.html
Dan Pera, President
Transportation

USG
125 S. Franklin St. PO Box
    6721
Chicago, IL 60606
Website: http://www.usg.com
William C. Foote, Chairman,
    President, and CEO
Building materials, glass

U.S. Office Products
1025 T. Jefferson St. NW
Washington, DC 20007
Website: http://www.usop.com
Charles P. Pieper, Chairman
Warren D. Feldberg, CEO
Wholesalers

U.S. Term Limits
10 G St., N.W., Suite 410
Washington, DC 20002
Website: http://
    www.termlimits.org/
E-mail: admin@termlimits.org
Howard Rich, President
Jon Lerner, Executive Director
*Organization devoted to setting
    term limits for elected officials*

USX
600 Grant St.
Pittsburgh, PA 15219
Website: http://www.usx.com
Thomas J. Usher, Chairman
    and CEO
Petroleum refining

UtiliCorp United, Inc.
20 W. Ninth St.
Kansas City, MO 64105
Website: http://
    www.utilicorp.com
Richard C. Green, Jr.,
    Chairman and CEO
Gas and electric utilities

La Lettre, l'epitre, qui n'est pas un genre mais tous les genres, la littérature même.
The letter, the epistle, which is not a genre but all the genres, literature itself.

—JACQUES DERRIDA, *"La Carte Postale"*

Valasquez, Patricia
% Ford Model Management
344 E. 59th St.
New York, NY 10022
Model

Van Buren, Abigail
PO Box 69440
Los Angeles, CA 90069
Dear Abby

Van Buren, Steve
% Pro Football Hall of Fame
2121 George Halas Dr. NW
Canton, OH 44708
Football player

Vance, Courtney B.
9171 Wilshire Blvd., #406
Beverly Hills, CA 90210
Actress

Van Damme, Jean-Claude
1122 S. Robertson Blvd., #15
Los Angeles, CA 90035
Actor, martial arts expert
Birthday: 10/18/60

Van Dien, Casper
11837 Courtleigh Dr., #5
Los Angeles, CA 90066
Actor, grandson of Robert Mitchum
Birthday: 1/18/68

Vandross, Luther
PO Box 5542
Beverly Hills, CA 90209
Singer

Van Dyke, Dick
% William Morris Agency
151 El Camino Dr.
Beverly Hills, CA 90212
Actor
Birthday: 12/13/25

Van Dyke, Jerry
PO Box 2130
Benton, AR 72018
Actor, Dick's brother
Birthday: 7/27/31

Van Dyke, Leroy
Rt. 1, Box 271
Smithton, MO 65350
Country music singer

Vangelis
195 Queensgate
GB-London W1
England
Music group

Van Halen
10100 Santa Monica Blvd.,
    Suite 2460
Los Angeles, CA 90067
Rock group

Van Horn, Patrick
9200 Sunset Blvd., #1130
Los Angeles, CA 90069
Actor

Van Houten, Leslie
#W13378
Bed #1B314U
California Inst. for Women
16756 Chino Corona
Frontera, CA 91720
*Member of the Manson "Family,"
    convicted murderer*

Vanilla Ice
250 W. 57th. St., #821
New York, NY 10107
Rapper

Van Peebles, Mario
853 7th Ave., #3E
New York, NY 10019
Actor, writer, director
Birthday: 1/15/57

Van Shelton, Ricky
6424 Bresslyn Rd.
Nashville, TN 37205
Country, music singer

Vargas, Elizabeth
% ABC-TV News Dept.
77 W. 66th St.
New York, NY 10023
Journalist

Vedder, Eddie
1423 34th. Ave.
Seattle, WA 98122
Singer, songwriter
Birthday: 12/23/64

Vencor
1 Vencor Place, 680 S. 4th St.
Louisville, KY 40202-2412
Website: http://
    www.vencor.com
Edward L. Kuntz, Chairman,
    President, and CEO
Health care

Ventura, Gov. Jesse
75 Constitution Ave., #130
St. Paul, MN 55155
*Governor, former Navy Seal,
    former wrestler*

Vereen, Ben
9255 Sunset Blvd., #804
Los Angeles, CA 90069
Actor
Birthday: 1/13/25

Verstappen, Jos
% Tyrrell Racing Organization
    Ltd.
Long Reach
Ockham
Woking
GB-Surrey GU23 6PE
Professional Formula-1 driver

Veterans of Foreign Wars (VFW) Political Action Committee
406 W. 34th. St.
Kansas City, MO 64111
Website: http://www.vfw.org/
E-mail: info@vfw.org
Organization dedicated to securing the rights and benefits of veterans

VF
628 Green Valley Rd., Suite. 500
Greensboro, NC 27408
Website: http://www.vfc.com
Mackey J. McDonald, Chairman, President, and CEO
Apparel

Victoria's Secret
Intimate Brands
3 Limited Pkwy.
Columbus, OH 43216
Leslie H. Wexner, Chairman, President, and CEO
Website: www.victoriassecret.com
Lingerie

Vietnam Veterans of America
8605 Cameron St., Suite 400
Silver Spring, MD 20910
Website: http://www.vva.org
E-mail: membership@vva.org
George C. Duggins, President
National veterans service organization

Vigoda, Abe
8500 Melrose Ave., #208
West Hollywood, CA 90069
Actor
Birthday: 2/24/21

Vila, Bob
Box 749
Marstons Mills, MA 02648
TV Host

Village People
165 W. 46th. St., #13008
New York, NY 10036
Music group

Villeneuve, Jaques
% Williams GP Engineering Ltd.
Grove
Wantage
GB Oxfordshire OX12 0DQ
Professional Formula-1 driver, 1997 World Cup winner

Vincent, Jan Michael
27856 Pacific Coast Hwy.
Malibu, CA 90265
Actor

Vincent, Rhonda
PO Box #31
Greentop, MO 63546
Country music singer

Vincent, Rick
Box #323
1336 North Moorpark Rd.
Thousand Oaks, CA 91360
Country music singer

Vince Shute Wildlife Sanctuary
PO Box 77
Orr, MN 55711
Klari Lee, Co-Founder
360-acre refuge and black bear sanctuary which experts regard as one of the best places in North America to view wild bears and their behavior

Vinton, Bobby
PO Box 6010
Branson, MO 65615
Singer
Birthday: 4/16/35

Visitor, Nana
% *Star Trek: Deep Space 9*
5555 Melrose Ave.
Los Angeles, CA 90036
or
9016 Wilshire Blvd., #363
Beverly Hills, CA 90211
Actress, plays Major Kira on Star
  Trek: Deep Space Nine
Birthday: 2/26/57

Vitale, Dick
% ESPN Plaza
935 Middlestreet
Bristol, CT 06010
Sportscaster

Vodafone Group PLC
The Courtyard, 2-4 London
  Rd.
Newbury, Berkshire RG14 1JX
United Kingdom
Website: http://www.vodafone-
  airtouch-plc.com
Lord MacLaurin of Knebworth,
  Chairman
Christopher C. Gent, CEO
Telecommunications

Vonnegut, Kurt Jr.
Box 27
Sagaponack, NY 11962
Author

Voorhies, Lark
10635 Santa Monica Blvd.,
  Suite 130
Los Angeles, CA 90025
Actress
Birthday: 3/25/74

Dear Pamela, the value of a letter can't be measured quantitatively. If you haven't time to write what you call a "real" letter, then write a few lines. I don't expect anyone to compose longwinded epistles, as I sometimes do. I write letters because I enjoy doing it. It doesn't matter too much whether the recipient takes pleasure in reading what I write; I've had my pleasure.

—"In Absentia"

Wachovia
100 N. Main St.
Winston-Salem, NC 27150
Website: http://
    www.wachovia.com
Leslie M. Baker, Jr., Chairman
    and CEO
Commercial bank

Wade, Virginia
Sharstead Ct.
Sittingbourne, Kent
England
Tennis player

Wagner, Lindsay
PO Box 5002
Sherman Oaks, CA 91403
Actress
Birthday: 6/22/49

Wagoner, Porter
PO Box 290785
Nashville, TN 37229
Country music singer

Wagner, Robert
1500 Old Oak Rd.
Los Angeles, CA 90049
Actor
Birthday: 2/10/30

Wai-hing, Emily Lau
Suite 602, Citibank Tower
3 Garden
Road, Central
Hong Kong
or
No. 12–13, g/f
Hok Sam House
Lung Hang Estatne
Shatin, New Territories
Hong Kong
Website: http://
    www.emilylau.org.hk/
E-mail: Elau@hknet.com
*Hong Kong legislator and
    democracy advocate*
Birthday: 1/2/52

Waits, Tom
PO Box 498
Valley Ford, CA 94972
Singer, songwriter, actor
Birthday: 12/7/49

Walgreens
200 Wilmot Rd.
Deerfield, IL 60015
Website: http://
    www.walgreens.com
L. Daniel Jorndt, Chairman
    and CEO
Food and drug stores

Walker, Ally
10390 Santa Monica Blvd.,
    #300
Los Angeles, CA 90025
Actress

Walker, Billy
PO Box 618
Hendersonville, TN 37077
Country music singer

Walker, Charles,
National Space Society
600 Pennsylvania Ave., #201
Washington, DC 20003
Astronaut

Walker, Charlie
Grand Ole Opry
2804 Opryland Dr.
Nashville, TN 37214
Country music singer

Walker, Clay
PO Box 8125
Gallatin, TN 37066
Country music singer

Walker, Jerry Jeff
PO Box 39
Austin, TX 78767
Country music singer, songwriter

Walker, Marcy
9107 Wilshire Blvd., #700
Beverly Hills, CA 90210
Birthday: 11/26/61

Walker, Mort
% King Features
235 E. 45th St.
New York, NY 10017
Cartoonist

Wallach, Eli
200 W. 57th St., #900
New York, NY 10019
Actor
Birthday: 12/7/15

Wallendas, The Great
138 Frog Hollow Rd.
Churchville, PA 18966
*The most famous highwire family
    in history*

Wallflowers, The
9200 Wilshire Blvd., #1
Los Angeles, CA 90069
Music group

Wal-Mart
702 SW Eighth St.
Bentonville, AR 72716
Website: http://www.wal-
    mart.com
S. Robson Walton, Chairman
David D. Glass, Chairman of
    the Executive Committee
H. Lee Scott, Jr., President and
    CEO
General merchandisers

Walston, Ray
423 S. Rexford Dr., #205
Beverly Hills, CA 90212
Actor
Birthday: 11/2/24

Walt Disney
500 S. Buena Vista St.
Burbank, CA 91521
Website: http://
    www.disney.com
Michael D. Eisner, Chairman
    and CEO
Entertainment

Walters, Barbara
33 W. 60th. St.
New York, NY 10023
TV hostess
Birthday: 9/25/31

Wang, Garret
1440 Veteran Ave., #212
Los Angeles, CA 90024
Actor, plays Ensign Harry Kim on
    Star Trek: Voyager

Ward, Megan
PO Box 481210
Los Angeles, CA 90036
Actress
Birthday: 9/24/69

Ward, Rachel
PO Box 5617
Beverly Hills, CA 90210
Actress
Birthday: 9/12/57

Wariner, Steve
PO Box 1647
Franklin, TN 37065
Country music singer

Warlock, Billy
9229 Sunset Blvd., #315
Los Angeles, CA 90069
Actor
Birthday: 3/26/60

Waste Management
1001 Fannin, Suite 4000
Houston, TX 77002
Website: http://www.wm.com
A. Maurice Myers, Chairman,
    President, and CEO
Waste Management

Waters, John
1018 N. Charles St.
Baltimore, MD 21201
Actor, director, writer
Birthday: 4/22/49

Waters, Roger
% Ten Tenth Management
106 Gifford St.
GB-London N1 0DF
England
Actor
Birthday: 9/6/44

Waterson, Sam
RR1 Box 232
West Cornwall, CT 06796
Actor
Birthday: 11/15/40

Watson, Gene
PO Box 2210
Nashville, TN 37202
Country music singer

Weathers, Carl
10960 Wilshire Blvd., #826
Los Angeles, CA 90024
Actor
Birthday: 1/14/48

Weaver, Dennis
PO Box 257
Ridgeway, CO 81432
Actor
Birthday: 6/4/25

Weaver, Sigourney
200 W. 57th St.
New York, NY 10019
Actress

Webber, Andrew Lloyd
725 Fifth Ave.
New York, NY 10022
Composer, producer
Birthday: 3/22/48

Weber, Steven
% ICM
8942 Wilshire Blvd.
Beverly Hills, CA 90211
Actor

Weinger, Scott
9255 Sunset Blvd., #1010
West Hollywood, CA 90069
Actor

Weir, Peter
Post Office
Palm Beach 2108
Australia
Director

Welch, Kevin
Warner Bros.
1815 Division
Nashville, TN 37212
Country music singer

Welch, Rachquel (Racquel Tejada)
9903 Santa Monica Blvd., #514
Beverly Hills, CA 90212
Actress
Birthday: 9/5/40

Weld, Tuesday
711 West End Ave., #5k-N
New York, NY 10025
Actress

WellPoint Health Networks
1 WellPoint Way
Thousand Oaks, CA 91362
Website: http://www.wellpoint.com
Leonard D. Schaeffer, Chairman and CEO
Health care

Wells, Dawn
11684 Ventura Blvd., #985
Studio City, CA 91604
TV actress (Marianne on Gilligan's Island)

Wells, Kitty
240 Old Hickory Blvd.
Madison, TN 37115
Country music singer

Wells Fargo and Co.
420 Montgomery St.
San Francisco, CA 94163
Website: http://www.wellsfargo.com
Paul Hazen, CEO
Commercial banks

Wenders, Wim
% Wim Wenders Produktion
Segitzdamm 2
10969 Berlin
Germany
Director
Birthday: 8/14/45

Wendt, George
9150 Wilshire Blvd.
Beverly Hills, CA 90212
Actor
Birthday: 10/17/48

West, Adam
PO Box 3477
Ketchum, ID 83340
TV actor (Batman)
Birthday: 9/19/29

West, Jerry
% Basketball Hall of Fame
1150 W. Columbia Ave.
Springfield, MA 01101
Basketball player

Western Digital
8105 Irvine Center Dr.
Irvine, CA 92618
Website: http://
    www.westerndigital.com
Thomas E. Pardun, Chairman
Matthew H. Massengill,
    President and CEO
Computer Peripherals

Westvaco
299 Park Ave.
New York, NY 10171
Website: http://
    www.westvaco.com
John A. Luke, Jr., Chairman,
    President and CEO
Forest and paper products

Wet Wet Wet
% Precius Organisation
Pet Sound Studio
24 Gairbraid Ave., #6-B
Maryhill
GB-Glasgow G20 1XX
England
Music group

Weyerhaeuser
33663 Weyerhaeuser. Way S.
PO Box 2999
Federal Way, WA 98003
Website: http://
    www.weyerhaeuser.com
Steven R. Rogel, Chairman,
    President and CEO
Forest and paper products

Whalley, Joanne
9830 Wilshire Blvd.
Beverly Hills, CA 90212
Actress
Birthday: 8/25/64

Wheaton, Wil
2820 Honolulu, #255
Verdugo City, CA 91403
Actor

Whirlpool
2000 N. M-63
Benton Harbor, MI 49022
Website: http://
    www.whirlpool.com
David R. Whitwam, Chairman
    and CEO
Electronics, electrical equipment

Whites, The
15 Music Square West
Nashville, TN 37203
Music group

White, Barry
% WMA
1325 Ave. of the Americas
New York, NY 10019
Musican

White, Betty
PO Box 491965
Los Angeles, CA 90049
Actress
Birthday: 1/17/22

White, Bryan
2100 West End Ave., #1000
Nashville, TN 37203
Country music singer

White, Jaleel
1122 S. Robertson Blvd., #15
Los Angeles, CA 90035
Actor
Birthday: 1/26/76

White, Joy Lynn
1101 17th Ave. So.
Nashville, TN 37212
Country music singer

White, Lari
1028-B 18th Ave. S.
Nashville, TN 37212
Country music singer

White, Michael
5420 Camelot Rd.
Brentwood, TN 37027
Country music singer

White, Reggie
% Green Bay Packers
PO Box 10628
Green Bay, WI 54307
Football player

White, Vanna (Vanna Rosich)
10202 W. Washington Blvd.
Culver City, CA 90232
TV personality
Birthday: 2/8/57

White House for Kids
Website: http://
www.whitehouse.gov/WH/
kids/html/home.html

Whitman
3501 Algonquin Rd.
Rolling Meadows, IL 60008
Website: http://
www.whitmancorp.com
Bruce S. Chelberg, Chairman
and CEO
Beverages

Whitman, Slim
505 Canton Pass
Madison, TN 37115
Singer

Wilburn, Teddy
Grand Ole Opry
2804 Opryland Dr.
Nashville, TN 37214
Country music singer

Wilder, Gene (Jerome Silberman)
1511 Sawtelle Blvd., #155
Los Angeles, CA 90025
Actor, writer, director, married to the late Gilda Radner
Birthday: 6/11/35

Wilderness Society, The
1615 M St., NW
Washington, DC 20036
Website: http://
www.wilderness.org/
Bill Meadows, President
Devoted primarly to public lands protection and management issues

Wild Rose
PO Box 121705
Nashville, TN 37212
Music group

HRH Prince William
Highgrove House
Gloucestershire
England

Willamette Industries
1300 SW Fifth Ave.
Portland, OR 97201
Website: http://www.wii.com
William Swindells, Chairman
Duane C. McDougall,
     President and CEO
Forest and paper products

The Williams Companies, Inc.
1 Williams Center
Tulsa, OK 74172
Website: http://www.twc.com
Keith E. Bailey, Chairman,
     President, and CEO
Pipelines, communications

Williams, Andy
2500 W. Hwy. 76
Branson, MO 65616
Singer
Birthday: 12/30/30

Williams, Hank, Jr.
PO Box 850
Paris, TN 38242
*Country singer, son of Hank
     Williams, Sr.*

Williams Hank, III
PO Box 121736
Nashville, TN 37212
Country music singer

Williams, Jason D.
819 18th Ave. S.
Nashville, TN 37203
Country music singer

Williams, Jett
PO Box 177
Hartsville, TN 37074
Country music singer

Williams, Jobeth
9465 Wilshire Blvd., #430
Beverly Hills, CA 90212
Actress
Birthday: 1953

Williams, John
Boston Symphony Orchestra
Symphony Hall
301 Massachusetts Ave.
Boston, MA 02115
Composer, conducter
Birthday: 2/8/32

Williams, Robin
9465 Wilshire Blvd., #419
Beverly Hills, CA 90212
Actor, comedian
Birthday: 7/21/52

Williams, Serena
US Tennis Association
70 W. Red Oaks Lane
White Plains, NY 10604
Tennis player

**Williams, Treat (Richard
     Williams)**
% Gladys-Marie Hart
1244 11th St., #A
Santa Monica, CA 90401
Actor
Birthday: 12/1/51

Williams, Vanessa
4526 Wilshire Blvd.
Los Angeles, CA 90010
Actress

Williams, Vanessa
Box 858
Chappaqua, NY 10514
Singer

Williams, Venus
US Tennis Association
70 W. Red Oaks Lane
White Plains, NY 10604
Tennis player

Williams, Walter E.
George Mason University
4400 University Dr.
Fairfax, VA 22030-4444
Website: http://www.gmu.edu/
    departments/economics/
    wew/index.html
Email: wwilliam@gmu.edu
Walter E. Williams, John M.
    Olin Distinguished
    Professor of Economics
Author of Do the Right Thing:
    The People's Economist
    Speaks

Williams and Ree
24 Music Square West
Nashville, TN 37203
Music group

**Willis, Bruce (Walter Bruce
    Willis)**
1122 S. Robertson Blvd., #15
Los Angeles, CA 90035
Actor
Birthday: 3/19/55

Wilson, Carnie
13601 Ventura Blvd., #286
Sherman Oaks, CA 91423
Singer
Birthday: 4/29/68

Wilson, Katharina
% Puzzle Publishing
PO Box 230023
Portland, OR 97281
Website: http://
    www.alienjigsaw.com/
    index.html
Author of The Alien Jigsaw, *a
    book about alien abduction*

Wilson, Mara
3500 W. Olive Ave., #1400
Burbank, CA 91506
Actress

Wilson, Rita
PO Box 900
Beverly Hills, CA 90213
Actress

Windom, William
PO Box 1067
Woodacre, CA 94973
Actor
Birthday: 9/28/23

Winfrey, Oprah
PO Box 909715
Chicago, IL 60690
Talk show host, actress
Birthday: 1/29/54

**Winger, Debra (May Debra
    Winger)**
PO Box 9078
Van Nuys, CA 91409
Actress
Birthday: 5/17/55

Winkler, Henry
1122 S. Robertson Blvd., #15
Los Angeles, CA 90035
Actor, director, played The Fonz on
    Happy Days
Birthday: 10/30/45

Winn-Dixie
5050 Edgewood Court
Jacksonville, FL 32254
A. Dano Davis, Chairman and
    CEO
Allen R. Rowland, President
    and CEO
Food and drug stores

Winslet, Kate
503/504 Lotts Rd.
The Chambers
Chelsea Harbour
London SWIO OXF
England
Actress

Winwood, Steve
PO Box 261640
Encino, CA 91426
Musician

Witt, Katarina
Reichenhaner Str.
D-09023
Chemnitz
Germany
Actress
Birthday: 12/3/65

Wolf, Scott
1122 S. Robertson Blvd., #15
Los Angeles, CA 90035
Actor

Wonder, Stevie
4616 Magnolia Blvd.
Burbank, CA 91505
Singer, songwriter

Wong, B. D.
% Innovative Artists
1999 Ave. of the Stars, #2850
Los Angeles, CA 90067
Actor

Woo, John
450 Roxbury Dr., #800
Beverly Hills, CA 90210
Director

Wood, Elijah
2300 W. Victroy Blvd., #384
Burbank, CA 91506
Actor
Birthday: 1/28/81

Woods, James
760 N. La Cienega Blvd.
Los Angeles, CA 90069
Actor
Birthday: 4/18/47

Woods, Tiger
4281 Katella Ave., #111
Los Alamitos, CA 90720
Website: http://
    www.clubtiger.com/
Professional golfer

Woodward, Joanne
1120 5th. Ave., #1C
New York, NY 10128
Actress, married to Paul Newman
Birthday: 10/27/30

Wooley, Sheb
123 Walton Ferry Rd., 2nd
    Floor
Hendersonville, TN 37075
Singer

Woodard, Alfre
% ICM
8942 Wilshire Blvd.
Beverly Hills, CA 90211
Actor

Wopat, Tom
PO Box 128031
Nashville, TN 37212
Website: http://
    www.wopat.com/
Actor, singer

WorldCom
500 Clinton Center Dr.
Clinton, MS 39056
Website: http://www.wcom.com
Bernard J. Ebbers, President
    and CEO
Telecommunications

World Future Society
7910 Woodmont Ave., #450
Bethesda, MD 20814
Website: http://www.wfs.org/
E-mail: schley@wfs.org
Clement Bezold, Executive
    Director
*A nonprofit educational and
    scientific organization for
    people interested in how social
    and technological
    developments are shaping the
    future*

Worley, Joanne
PO Box 2054
Toluca Lake, CA 91610
Actress

W. R. Grace
7500 Grace Dr.
Columbia, MD 21044
Website: http://www.grace.com
Paul J. Norris, Chairman,
    President, and CEO
Chemical products

Wright, Bobby
PO Box 477
Madison, TN 37116
Country music singer

Wright, Johnny
PO Box 477
Madison, TN 37116
Country music singer

Wright, Michelle
PO Box 152
Morpeth, Ontario NOP 1X0
Canada
Country music singer

Wu-Tang Clan
% BMG Music
1540 Broadway, #9-FL
New York, NY 10039
Music group

**WWF (World Wrestling
    Federation)**
Titan Tower
1241 East Main St.
PO Box 3857
Stamford, CT 06902

W. W. Grainger
100 Grainger Pkwy.
Lake Forest, IL 60045
Website: http://
    www.grainger.com
David W. Grainger, Senior
    Chairman
Richard L. Keyser, Chairman
    and CEO
Wholesalers

Wyman, Bill
344 Kings Rd.
Chelsea
London SW3 5UR
England
Bass player of The Rolling Stones
Birthday: 10/24/36

Wynonna
325 Bridge St.
Franklin, TN 37064
Musician

I see you understand the pleasure that can be got from writing letters. In other centuries this was taken for granted. Not any longer. Only a few people carry on true correspondences. No time, the rest will tell you. Quicker to telephone. Like saying a photograph is more satisfying than a painting. There wasn't all that much time for writing letters in the past, either, but time was found, as it generally can be for whatever gives pleasure.

—Anonymous

**Official Xena: Warrior Princess
  Fan Club**
100 W. Broadway, Suite 1200
Glendale, CA 91210

Xerox
800 Long Ridge Rd.
Stamford, CT 06904
Website: http://www.xerox.com
Paul A. Allaire, Chairman and
  CEO
*Computers, copiers, office
  equipment*

The X-Files
% Studio Fan Mail
1122 S. Robertson Blvd., #15
Los Angeles, CA 90035
or
10201 W. Pico Blvd.
Bldg. 41, Suite 100
Attn: *The X-Files*
Los Angeles, CA 90035
TV series

X-Perience
% WEA Records
Postfach 761260
D-22062 Hamburg
Germany
Music group

But I want music and intellectual companionships and affection. Well, perhaps I'll get all that one day. And in the meantime there are little things to look forward to, letters and the unexpected.

—Anonymous

Yankovic, "Weird Al"
℅ Close Personal Friends of Al
8033 Sunset Blvd.
Los Angeles, CA 90046
Website: http://
    www.weirdal.com/
Musician

Yasbeck, Amy
2170 Century Park East, #1111
Los Angeles, CA 90067
Actress

Yearwood, Trisha
4836-316 Lebanon Pike
Nashville, TN 37076
Country music singer

Yell4You
℅ Nady
Postfach 303
D-74345 Lauffen/N.
Germany
Music group

Yello
℅ Dieter Meier
Aurastraβe 78
CH-8031 Zürich
Switzerland
Music group

Yellow
10990 Roe Ave.
Overland Park, KS 66211
Website: http://
    www.yellowcorp.com
William D. Zollars, Chairman,
    President, and CEO
Trucking

Yellowjackets
9220 Sunset Blvd., #320
Los Angeles, CA 90069
Music group

Yeltsin, Boris
Ulliza Twerskaya
Jamskayaw
Moscow
Russia
Russian political leader
Birthday: 2/1/31

Yes
9 Hillgate St.
GB-London W8 7SP
England
Music group

Yoakam, Dwight
1250 6th St., #401
Santa Monica, CA 90401
Country music singer

York, Michael
9100 Cardell Dr.
Los Angeles, CA 90069
Actor
Birthday: 3/27/42

York International
631 S. Richland Ave.
York, PA 17403
Website: http://www.york.com
Michael R. Young, President
    and CEO
Industrial and farm equipment

Young, Burt
9300 Wilshire Blvd., #410
Beverly Hills, CA 90022
Actor

Young, Faron
1300 Division
Nashville, TN 37203
Country music singer

Young, Jesse Colin
Box 31
Lancaster, NH 03584
Musician

Young, John
% NASA
Houston, TX 77058
Astronaut
Birthday: 9/24/30

Young, Neil
8501 Wilshire Blvd., #220
Beverly Hills, CA 90211
Singer, songwriter

Young, Nina
% Narrow Road Company
22 Poland St.
London W1V 3DD
England
Actress

Young, Sean
PO Box 20547
Sedona, AZ 86341
Actress
Birthday: 11/20/59

Z

I have now attained the true art of letter writing, which, we are always told, is to express on paper exactly what one would say to the same person by word of mouth; I have been talking to you almost as fast as I could the whole of this letter.

—Jane Austen

Zaca Creek
PO Box 237
Santa Ynez, CA 93460
Music group

Zadora, Pia
9560 Wilshire Blvd.
Beverly Hills, CA 90212
Actress, singer
Birthday: 5/4/56

Zahn, Steve
1964 Westwood Blvd., #400
Los Angeles, CA 90025
Actor

Zane, Billy
450 N. Rossmore Ave., #1001
Los Angeles, CA 90004
or
% Celebrity Merchandise
PMB 710
15030 Ventura Blvd.
Sherman Oaks, CA 91403
Actor
Birthday: 2/24/66

Zappa, Dweezil
PO Box 5265
North Hollywood, CA 91616
Musician, Frank Zappa's son
Birthday: 9/5/69

Zappa, Moon Unit
PO Box 5265
North Hollywood, CA 91616
*Frank Zappa's Daughter, actress,
   singer, Dweezil's sister*
Birthday: 9/28/68

Zeman, Jackie
% *General Hospital*, ABC-TV
4151 Prospect Ave.
Los Angeles, CA 90027
Soap opera actor

Zemeckis, Robert
1880 Century Park E., Suite
   900
Los Angeles, CA 90067
Director, producer, screenwriter
Birthday: 5/14/51

Zero Population Growth (ZPG)
1400 16th St. NW, #320
Washington, DC 20036
Website: http://www.zpg.org
Dr. Nafis Sadik, Executive
   Director
*The nation's largest grassroots
   organization concerned with
   the impacts of rapid
   population growth and
   wasteful consumption*

Zero To Three
National Center for Clinical
    Infant Programs
734 15th St., NW, Suite 1000
Washington, DC 20005
Website: http://
    www.zerotothree.org/
E-mail:
    webmaster@cyberserv.com
Joy D. Osofsky, Ph.D., Board of
    Directors
A national nonprofit dedicated to
    the healthy development of
    infants, toddlers, and their
    families, with information for
    parents and professionals

Ziering, Ian
1122 S. Robertson Blvd., #15
Los Angeles, CA 90035
Actor

Zimbalist, Stephanie
1925 Century Park E., #2320
Los Angeles, CA 90067
Actress

Zucchero
% Prima Pagina
Via Hayech 41
I-20100 Milano
Italy
Singer

Zuniga, Daphne
% Contellation
PO Box 1249
White River Junction, VT
    05001
Actress

Zydeco, Buckwheat
PO Box 561
Rhinebeck, NY 12572
Musician

ZZ Top
PO Box 163690
Austin, TX 78716
Rock band

U.S. GOVERNORS

Don Siegelman
Alabama
State Capitol, 600 Dexter Ave.
Montgomery, AL 36130

Tony Knowles
Alaska
PO Box 110001
Juneau, AK 99811-0001

Tauese P. F. Sunia
American Samoa
Executive Office Building
Pago Pago, AS 96799

Jane Dee Hull
Arizona
State Capitol, 1700 West
   Washington
Phoenix, AZ 85007

Mike Huckabee
Arkansas
250 State Capitol
Little Rock, AR 72201

Gray Davis
California
State Capitol
Sacramento, CA 95814

Bill Owens
Colorado
136 State Capitol
Denver, CO 80203-1792

John G. Rowland
Connecticut
210 Capitol Ave.
Hartford, CT 06106

Ruth Ann Minner
Delaware
Tatnall Building
William Penn St.
Dover, DE 19901

Jeb Bush
Florida
The Capitol
Tallahassee, FL 32399

Roy Barnes
Georgia
203 State Capitol
Atlanta, GA 30334

Carl T. C. Gutierrez
Guam
Executive Chamber
PO Box 2950
Agana, GU 96932

Benjamin J. Cayetano
Hawaii
State Capitol
Honolulu, HI 96813

Dirk Kempthorne
Idaho
State Capitol
PO Box 83720
Boise, ID 83720

George H. Ryan
Illinois
State Capitol
Springfield, IL 62706

Frank O'Bannon
Indiana
206 State Capitol
Indianapolis, IN 46204

Tom Vilsack
Iowa
State Capitol
Des Moines, IA 50319

Bill Graves
Kansas
Capitol Building, Second Floor
Topeka, KS 66612-1590

Paul E. Patton
Kentucky
State Capitol
700 Capitol Ave.
Frankfort, KY 40601

Mike Foster
Louisiana
PO Box 94004
Baton Rouge, LA 70804

Angus S. King, Jr.
Maine
State House, Station 1
Augusta, ME 04333

Parris N. Glendening
Maryland
State House
100 State Circle
Annapolis, MD 21401

Argeo Paul Cellucci
Massachusetts
State House, Room 360
Boston, MA 02133

John Engler
Michigan
PO Box 30013
Lansing, MI 48909

Jesse Ventura
Minnesota
130 State Capitol
75 Constitution Ave.
St. Paul, MN 55155

Ronnie Musgrove
Mississippi
PO Box 139
Jackson, MS 39205

Bob Holden
Missouri
State Capitol, Room 216
Jefferson City, MO 65101

Judy Martz
Montana
PO Box 0801
Helena, Montana 59620

Mike Johanns
Nebraska
PO Box 94848
Lincoln, NE 68509-4848

Kenny C. Guinn
Nevada
State Capitol
Carson City, NV 89710

Jeanne Shaheen
New Hampshire
State House, Room 208
Concord, NH 03301

Christine T. Whitman
New Jersey
125 West State St.
PO Box 001
Trenton, NJ 08625

Gary E. Johnson
New Mexico
State Capitol, Fourth Floor
Santa Fe, NM 87503

George E. Pataki
New York
State Capitol
Albany, NY 12224

Mike Easley
North Carolina
State Capitol
116 West Jones St.
Raleigh, NC 27603

John Hoeven
North Dakota
600 E. Boulevard Ave.
Bismarck, ND 58505

Pedro P. Tenorio
Northern Mariana Is.
Caller Box 10007
Saipan, M.P. 96950

Bob Taft
Ohio
77 South High St., 30th Floor
Columbus, OH 43266-0601

Frank Keating
Oklahoma
State Capitol Building, Suite
   212
Oklahoma City, OK 73105

John A. Kitzhaber
Oregon
254 State Capitol
Salem, OR 97310

Tom Ridge
Pennsylvania
225 Main Capitol Building
Harrisburg, PA 17120

Sila Calderon
Puerto Rico
La Fortaleza
San Juan, PR 00901

Lincoln Almond
Rhode Island
State House
Providence, RI 02903

Jim Hodges
South Carolina
PO Box 11829
Columbia, SC 29211

William J. Janklow
South Dakota
500 East Capitol
Pierre, SD 57501

Don Sundquist
Tennessee
State Capitol
Nashville, TN 37243-0001

Rick Perry
Texas
PO Box 12428
Austin, TX 78711

Michael O. Leavitt
Utah
210 State Capitol
Salt Lake City, UT 84114

Howard Dean, M.D.
Vermont
Pavilion Office Building, 109
    State St.
Montpelier, VT 05609

James S. Gilmore III
Virginia
State Capitol
Richmond, VA 23219

Charles W. Turnbull
Virgin Islands
Government House, Charlotte
    Amalie
St. Thomas, VI 00802

Gary Locke
Washington
PO Box 40002, Legislative
    Building
Olympia, WA 98504-0002

Robert E. Wise, Jr.
West Virginia
State Capitol Complex
Charleston, WV 25305

Tommy G. Thompson
Wisconsin
State Capitol, PO Box 7863
Madison, WI 53707

Jim Geringer
Wyoming
State Capitol Building, Room
    124
Cheyenne, WY 82002

THE SENATE MAILING ADDRESS

The Honorable (Name of
   Senator
United States Senate
Washington DC 20510

Dear Senator_____

SENATOR E-MAIL ADDRESSES

Stevens, Ted (R-AK)
   Senator_Stevens@
   stevens.senate.gov

Murkowski, Frank (R-AK)
   http://murkowski.senate.gov/
   webmail.html

Sessions, Jeff (R-AL)
   senator@sessions.senate.gov

Shelby, Richard (R-AL)
   senator@shelby.senate.gov

Lincoln, Blanche (D-AR)
   blanche_lincoln@
   lincoln.senate.gov

Hutchinson, Tim (R-AR)
   Senator.Hutchinson@
   hutchinson.senate.gov

Kyl, Jon (R-AZ)
   info@kyl.senate.gov

McCain, John (R-AZ)
   John_McCain@
   mccain.senate.gov

Boxer, Barbara (D-CA)
   senator@boxer.senate.gov

Feinstein, Dianne (D-CA)
   senator@feinstein.senate.gov

Allard, Wayne (R-CO)
   http://www.senate.gov/
   ~allard/webform.html or
   senator_allard@
   exchange.senate.gov

Campbell, Ben (R-CO)
   administrator@
   campbell.senate.gov

Dodd, Christopher (D-CT)
   senator@dodd.senate.gov

Lieberman, Joseph (D-CT)
   http://www.senate.gov/
   member/ct/lieberman/
   general/contact.html

Biden, Joe (D-DE)
   senator@biden.senate.gov

Carper, Thomas (D-MO)

Graham, Bob (D-FL)
   bob_graham@
   graham.senate.gov

Nelson, Bill (D-FL)

Cleland, Max (D-GA)
   http://www.senate.gov/
   cleland/webform.html

Miller, Zell (D-GA)
none

Akaka, Daniel (D-HI)
senator@akaka.senate.gov

Inouye, Daniel (D-HI)
senator@inouye.senate.gov

Harkin, Tom (D-IA)
tom_harkin@
harkin.senate.gov

Grassley, Charles (R-IA)
chuck_grassley@
grassley.senate.gov

Craig, Larry (R-ID)
http://craig.senate.gov/
webform.html

Crapo, Mike (R-ID)
http://crapo.senate.gov/
webform.html

Durbin, Richard (D-IL)
dick@durbin.senate.gov

Fitzgerald, Peter (R-IL)
senator_fitzgerald@
fitzgerald.senate.gov

Bayh, Evan (D-IN)
http://bayh.senate.gov/
WebMail.html

Lugar, Richard (R-IN)
senator_lugar@
lugar.senate.gov

Brownback, Sam (R-KS)
webmail@
brownback.senate.gov

Roberts, Pat (R-KS)
pat_roberts@
roberts.senate.gov

Bunning, Jim (R-KY)
jim_bunning@
bunning.senate.gov

McConnell, Mitch (R-KY)
senator@
mcconnell.senate.gov

Breaux, John (D-LA)
senator@breaux.senate.gov

Landrieu, Mary (D-LA)
senator@
landrieu.senate.gov

Kennedy, Ted (D-MA)
feedback@
kennedy.senate.gov

Kerry, John (D-MA)
john_kerry@
kerry.senate.gov

Mikulski, Barbara (D-MD)
senator@mikulski.senate.gov

Sarbanes, Paul (D-MD)
senator@sarbanes.senate.gov

Collins, Susan (R-ME)
senator@collins.senate.gov

Snowe, Olympia (R-ME)
Olympia@snowe.senate.gov

Levin, Carl (D-MI)
senator@levin.senate.gov

Stabenow, Debbie (D-MI)

Dayton, Mark (D-MN)

Wellstone, Paul (D-MN)
senator@wellstone.senate.gov

Carnahan, Joan (D-MO)

Bond, Christopher (R-MO)
kit_bond@bond.senate.gov

Cochran, Thad (R-MS)
senator@cochran.senate.gov

Lott, Trent (R-MS)
senatorlott@lott.senate.gov

Baucus, Max (D-MT)
http://baucus.senate.gov/
EmailMax.htm

Burns, Conrad (R-MT)
conrad_burns@
burns.senate.gov

Edwards, John (D-NC)
Senator@Edwards.senate.gov

Helms, Jesse (R-NC)
jesse_helms@
helms.senate.gov

Conrad, Kent (D-ND)
senator@conrad.senate.gov

Dorgan, Byron (D-ND)
senator@dorgan.senate.gov

Hagel, Chuck (R-NE)
chuck_hagel@
hagel.senate.gov

Nelson, Ben (D-NE)

Gregg, Judd (R-NH)
mailbox@gregg.senate.gov

Smith, Bob (R-NH)
opinion@smith.senate.gov

Corzine, Jon (D-NY)

Torricelli, Robert (D-NJ)
senator@torricelli.senate.gov

or http://torricelli.senate.
gov/webform.html
(preferred)

Bingaman, Jeff (D-NM)
Senator_Bingaman@
bingaman.senate.gov

Domenici, Pete (R-NM)
senator_domenici@
domenici.senate.gov

Ensign, John (R-NV)

Reid, Harry (D-NV)
senator_reid@
reid.senate.gov

Schumer, Charles (D-NY)
senator@schumer.senate.gov

Clinton, Hillary (D-NY)

Dewine, Michael (R-OH)
senator_dewine@
dewine.senate.gov

Voinovich, George (R-OH)
senator_voinovich@
voinovich.senate.gov or http:/
/voinovich.senate.gov/
contact_form.html

Inhofe, James (R-OK)
jim_inhofe@
inhofe.senate.gov

Nickles, Don (R-OK)
senator@nickles.senate.gov

Smith, Gordon (R-OR)
Oregon@gsmith.senate.gov

Wyden, Ron (D-OR)
senator@wyden.senate.gov

Santorum, Rick (R-PA)
http://santorum.senate.gov/
#email or pennstater@
santorum.senate.gov

Specter, Arlen (R-PA)
senator_specter@
specter.senate.gov

Reed, Jack (D-RI)
jack@reed.senate.gov

Chafee, Lincoln (R-RI)

Thurmond, Strom (R-SC)
senator@
thurmond.senate.gov

Hollings, Ernest (D-SC)
http://hollings.senate.gov/
hollings/webform.html

Daschle, Thomas (D-SD)
tom_daschle@
daschle.senate.gov

Johnson, Tim (D-SD)
tim@johnson.senate.gov

Thompson, Fred (R-TN)
senator_thompson@
thompson.senate.gov

Frist, Bill (R-TN)
senator_frist@
frist.senate.gov

Gramm, Phil (R-TX)
Phil_Gramm@
gramm.senate.gov

Hutchison, Kay (R-TX)
senator@
hutchison.senate.gov

Bennett, Robert (R-UT)
senator@bennett.senate.gov

Hatch, Orrin (R-UT)
senator_hatch@
hatch.senate.gov

Allen, George (R-VA)

Warner, John (R-VA)
senator@warner.senate.gov

Leahy, Patrick (D-VT)
senator_leahy@
leahy.senate.gov

Jeffords, Jim (R-VT)
vermont@jeffords.senate.gov

Murray, Patty (D-WA)
senator_murray@
murray.senate.gov

Cantwell, Maria (D-VA)

Feingold, Russell (D-WI)
russell_feingold@
feingold.senate.gov

Kohl, Herbert (D-WI)
senator_kohl@
kohl.senate.gov

Byrd, Robert (D-WV)
senator_byrd@
byrd.senate.gov

Rockefeller, Jay (D-WV)
senator@
rockefeller.senate.gov

Enzi, Michael (R-WY)
senator@enzi.senate.gov

Thomas, Craig (R-WY)
craig@thomas.senate.gov

**Senate Committee on Energy
and Natural Resources**

webmaster@
energy.senate.gov

Senate Committee on Small Business
committee@
small-bus.senate.gov

HOUSE OF REPRESENTATIVES MAILING ADDRESSES

The Honorable
U.S. House of Representatives
Washington, DC 20515

Dear Representative_____

UNITED STATES HOUSE OF REPRESENTATIVES E-MAIL ADDRESSES

Representatives may also be reached by constituents only through
http://www.house.gov/writerep/.

Callahan, Sonny (R-AL, 1st)
sonny.callahan@
mail.house.gov

Everett, Terry (R-AL, 2nd)
Terry.Everett@
mail.house.gov

Riley, Bob (R-AL, 3rd)
bob.riley@mail.house.gov

Aderholt, Robert (R-AL, 4th)
robert.aderholt@
mail.house.gov

Cramer, Bud (D-AL, 5th)
budmail@mail.house.gov

Bachus, Spencer (R-AL, 6th)
http://www.house.gov/
writerep/

Hilliard, Earl (D-AL, 7th)
http://www.house.gov/
writerep/

Young, Don (R-AK, AL)
Don.Young@mail.
house.gov

Berry, Marion (D-AR, 1st)
http://www.house.gov/
writerep/

Snyder, Vic (D-AR, 2nd)
snyder.congress@
mail.house.gov

Hutchinson, Asa (R-AR, 3rd)
asa.hutchinson@
mail.house.gov

Ross, Mike (D-AR, 4th)
mike.ross@mail.house.gov

Faleomavaega, Eni (D-American Samoa, AL)
faleomavaega@
mail.house.gov

Flake, Jeff (R-AZ, 1st)
jeff.flake@mail.
house.gov

Pastor, Ed (D-AZ, 2nd)
ed.pastor@mail.house.gov

Stump, Robert (R-AZ, 3rd)

Shadegg, John (R-AZ, 4th)
j.shadegg@mail.house.gov

Kolbe, Jim (R-AZ, 5th)
jim.kolbe@mail.house.gov
or http://www.house.gov/
writerep/

Hayworth, J. D. (R-AZ, 6th)
jdhayworth@mail.house.gov

Thompson, Mike (D-CA, 1st)
m.thompson@mail.
house.gov

Herger, Walter (R-CA, 2nd)
http://www.house.gov/
writerep/

Ose, Doug (R-CA, 3rd)
doug.ose@mail.house.gov

Doolittle, John (R-CA, 4th)
doolittle@mail.house.gov

Matsui, Robert (D-CA, 5th)
http://www.house.gov/
writerep/

Woolsey, Lynn (D-CA, 6th)
lynn.woolsey@mail.
house.gov

Miller, George (D-CA, 7th)
George.Miller@
mail.house.gov

Pelosi, Nancy (D-CA, 8th)
sf.nancy@mail.house.gov

Lee, Barbara (D-CA, 9th)
barbara.lee@mail.
house.gov

Tauscher, Ellen (D-CA, 10th)
ellen.tauscher@
mail.house.gov

Pombo, Richard (R-CA, 11th)
rpombo@mail.house.gov

Lantos, Tom (D-CA, 12th)
http://www.house.gov/
writerep/

Stark, Pete (D-CA, 13th)
petemail@stark.house.gov

Eshoo, Anna (D-CA, 14th)
annagram@mail.house.gov
or http://
www.eshoo.house.gov/
ccc.html

Honda, Michael M. (D-CA,
15th)
michael.honda@mail.house.gov

Lofgren, Zoe (D-CA, 16th)
zoe@lofgren.house.gov

Farr, Sam (D-CA, 17th)
samfarr@mail.house.gov

Condit, Gary (D-CA, 18th)
http://www.house.gov/
writerep/

Radanovich, George (R-CA,
19th)
george.radanovich@
mail.house.gov

Dooley, Calvin (R-CA, 20th)
http://www.house.gov/
writerep/

Thomas, Bill (R-CA, 21st)
http://www.house.gov/
writerep/

Capps, Lois (D-CA, 22nd)
http://www.house.gov/
writerep/

Gallegly, Elton (R-CA, 23rd)
http://www.house.gov/
writerep/

Sherman, Brad (D-CA, 24th)
brad.sherman@
mail.house.gov

McKeon, Howard (R-CA, 25th)
tellbuck@mail.house.gov or
http://www.house.gov/
mckeon/opinion.htm

Berman, Howard (D-CA, 26th)
Howard.Berman@
mail.house.gov

Schiff, Adam
http://www.house.gov/
writerep/

Dreier, David (R-CA, 28th)
http://www.house.gov/
dreier/talkto.htm

Waxman, Henry (D-CA, 29th)
http://www.house.gov/
writerep/

Becerra, Xavier (D-CA, 30th)
http://www.house.gov/
writerep/

Solis, Hilda (D-CA, 31st)
http://www.house.gov/
writerep/

Roybal-Allard, Lucille (D-CA, 33rd)
http://www.house.gov/
writerep/

Napolitano, Grace (D-CA, 34th)
grace@mail.house.gov

Waters, Maxine (D-CA, 35th)
http://www.house.gov/
waters/guest.htm

Harman, Jane (D-CA, 36th)
http://www.house.gov/
writerep/

Millender-McDonald, Juanita (D-CA, 37th)
Millender.McDonald@
mail.house.gov

Horn, Steve (R-CA, 38th)
Stephen.Horn@
mail.house.gov

Royce, Edward (R-CA, 39th)
http://www.house.gov/
writerep/

Lewis, Jerry (R-CA, 40th)
http://www.house.gov/
writerep/

Miller, Gary (R-CA, 41st)
PublicCA41@mail.
house.gov

Baca, Joe (D-CA, 42nd)
http://www.house.gov/
writerep/

Calvert, Ken (R-CA, 43rd)
http://www.house.gov/
writerep/

Bono, Mary (R-CA, 44th)
http://www.house.gov/
writerep/

Rohrabacher, Dana (R-CA, 45th)
dana@mail.house.gov

Sanchez, Loretta (D-CA, 46th)
loretta@mail.house.gov

Cox, Christopher (R-CA, 47th)
christopher.cox@
mail.house.gov

Issa, Darrell E. (R-CA, 48th)
http://www.house.gov/
writerep/

Davis, Susan (D-CA, 49th)
http:// www.house.gov/
writerep/

Filner, Bob (D-CA, 50th)
http://www.house.gov/
writerep/

Cunningham, Randy (R-CA, 51st)
http://www.house.gov/
cunningham/IMA/
get_address3.htm

Hunter, Duncan (R-CA, 52nd)
http://www.house.gov/
writerep/

DeGette, Diana (D-CO, 1st)
degette@mail.house.gov

Udall, Mark (D-CO, 2nd)
mark.udall@mail.house.gov

McInnis, Scott (R-CO, 3rd)
http://www.house.gov/
writerep

Schaffer, Bob (R-CO, 4th)
rep.schaffer@mail.house.
gov

Hefley, Joel (R-CO, 5th)
http://www.house.gov/
writerep

Tancredo, Thomas (R-CO, 6th)
tom.tancredo@
mail.house.gov

Larson, John (D-CT, 1st)
http://www.house.gov/
writerep/

Simmons, Rob (R-CT, 2nd)
http://www.house.gov/
writerep

DeLauro, Rosa (D-CT, 3rd)
http://www.house.gov/
writerep/

Shays, Christopher (R-CT, 4th)
rep.shays@mail.house.gov

Maloney, James (D-CT, 5th)
http://www.house.gov/
writerep/

Johnson, Nancy (R-CT, 6th)
http://www.house.gov/
writerep/

Norton, Eleanor (D-DC, AL)
http://www.house.gov/
writerep/

Castle, Michael (R-DE, AL)
Delaware@mail.house.gov

Scarborough, Joe (R-FL, 1st)
fl01@mail.house.gov

Boyd, Allen (D-FL, 2nd)
http://www.house.gov/
writerep/

Brown, Corrine (D-FL, 3rd)
same as above

Crenshaw, Ander
http://www.house.gov/
writerep

Thurman, Karen (D-FL, 5th)
thurman@mail.house.gov

Stearns, Cliff (R-FL, 6th)
cstearns@mail.house.gov

Mica, John (R-FL, 7th)
John.Mica@mail.house.gov

Keller, Ric (R-FL, 8th)
http://www.house.gov/
writerep

Bilirakis, Michael (R-FL, 9th)
http://www.house.gov/
writerep/

Young, C. W., Bill (R-FL, 10th)
same as above

Davis, Jim (D-FL, 11th)
http://www.house.gov/
writerep/

Putnam, Adam (R-FL, 12th)
same as above

Miller, Dan (R-FL, 13th)
http://www.house.gov/
writerep/

Goss, Porter (R-FL, 14th)
porter.goss@mail.house.gov

Weldon, Dave (R-FL, 15th)
http://www.house.gov/
writerep/

Foley, Mark (R-FL, 16th)
mark.foley@mail.house.gov

Meek, Carrie (D-FL, 17th)
cpm@mail.house.gov

Ros-Lehtinen, Ileana (R-FL, 18th)
http://www.house.gov/
writerep/

Wexler, Robert (D-FL, 19th)
http://www.house.gov/
writerep/

Deutsch, Peter (D-FL, 20th)
http://www.house.gov/
writerep/

Diaz-Balart, Lincoln (R-FL, 21st)
http://www.house.gov/
writerep/

Shaw, Clay (R-FL, 22nd)
http://www.house.gov/
writerep/

Hastings, Alcee (D-FL, 23rd)
alcee.pubhastings@
mail.house.gov

Kingston, Jack (R-GA, 1st)
jack.kingston@
mail.house.gov

Bishop, Sanford (D-GA, 2nd)
bishop.email@mail.house.
gov

Collins, Mac (R-GA, 3rd)
mac.collins@mail.house.
gov

McKinney, Cynthia (D-GA, 4th)
cymck@mail.house.gov

Lewis, John (D-GA, 5th)
john.lewis@mail.house.gov

Isakson, Johnny (R-GA, 6th)
ga06@mail.house.gov

Barr, Bob (R-GA, 7th)
http://www.house.gov/barr/
guestlog.htm or
barr.ga@mail.house.gov

Chambliss, Saxby (R-GA, 8th)
saxby.chambliss@
mail.house.gov

Deal, Nathan (R-GA, 9th)
http://www.house.gov/
writerep/

Norwood, Charles (R-GA, 10th)
http://www.house.gov/
writerep/

Linder, John (R-GA, 11th)
john.linder@mail.house.
gov

Underwood, Robert (D-Guam)
guamtodc@mail.house.gov

Abercrombie, Neil (D-HI, 1st)
neil.abercrombie@
mail.house.gov

Mink, Patsy (D-HI, 2nd)
http://www.house.gov/
writerep/

Leach, Jim (R-IA, 1st)
talk2jim@mail.house.gov

Nussle, James (R-IA, 2nd)
nussleia@mail.house.gov or
http://www.house.gov/
writerep/

Boswell, Leonard (D-IA, 3rd)
rep.boswell.ia03@
mail.house.gov

Ganske, Greg (R-IA, 4th)
Rep.Ganske@mail.house.
gov

Latham, Tom (R-IA, 5th)
latham.ia05@mail.house.
gov

Otter, C. L. "Butch" (R-ID, 1st)
http://www.house.gov/
writerep

Simpson, Mike (R-ID, 2nd)
mike.simpson@
mail.house.gov

Rush, Bobby (D-IL, 1st)
bobby.rush@mail.house.gov

Jackson, Jesse, Jr. (D-IL, 2nd)
comments@jessejacksonjr.
org

Lipinski, William (D-IL, 3rd)
http://www.house.gov/
lipinski/

Gutierrez, Luis (D-IL, 4th)
luis.gutierrez@
mail.house.gov

Blagojevich, Rod (D-IL, 5th)
Rod.Blagojevich@
mail.house.gov

Hyde, Henry (R-IL, 6th)
judiciary@mail.house.gov

or http://www.house.gov/
writerep/

Davis, Danny (D-IL, 7th)
http://www.house.gov/
writerep/

Crane, Philip (R-IL, 8th)
none

Schakowsky, Jan (D-IL, 9th)
jan.schakowsky@
mail.house.gov

Kirk, Mark (R-IL, 10th)
http://www.house.gov/
writerep/

Weller, Jerry (R-IL, 11th)
http://www.house.gov/
writerep/

Costello, Jerry (D-IL, 12th)
jfc.il12@mail.house.gov

Biggert, Judy (R-IL, 13th)
http://www.house.gov/
writerep/

Hastert, Dennis (R-IL, 14th)
speaker@mail.house.gov

Johnson, Tim (R-IL, 15th)
http://www.house.gov/
writerep/

Manzullo, Donald (R-IL, 16th)
http://www.house.gov/
writerep/

Evans, Lane (D-IL, 17th)
lane.evans@mail.house.gov

LaHood, Ray (R-IL, 18th)
http://www.house.gov/
writerep/

Phelps, David (D-IL, 19th)
http://www.house.gov/
writerep/

Shimkus, John (R-IL, 20th)
http://www.house.gov/
writerep/

Visclosky, Peter (D-IN, 1st)
http://www.house.gov/
writerep/

Pence, Mike (R-IN, 2nd)
http://www.house.gov/
writerep/

Roemer, Tim (D-IN, 3rd)
tim.roemer@mail.house.
gov

Souder, Mark (R-IN, 4th)
souder@mail.house.gov

Buyer, Steve (R-IN, 5th)
http://www.house.gov/
writerep

Burton, Dan (R-IN, 6th)
http://www.house.gov/
writerep

Kerns, Brian (R-IN, 7th)
http://www.house.gov/
writerep

Hostettler, John (R-IN, 8th)
John.Hostettler@
mail.house.gov

Hill, Baron (D-IN, 9th)
http://www.house.gov/
writerep/

Carson, Julia (D-IN, 10th)
rep.carson@mail.house.gov

Moran, Jerry (R-KS, 1st)
jerry.moran@mail.house.
gov

Ryun, Jim (R-KS, 2nd)
http://www.house.gov/
writerep/

Moore, Dennis (D-KS, 3rd)
dennis.moore@
mail.house.gov

Tiahrt, Todd (R-KS, 4th)
tiahrt@mail.house.gov or
http://www.house.gov/
tiahrt/guestbook.html

Whitfield, Ed (R-KY, 1st)
ed.whitfield@mail.house.
gov

Lewis, Ron (R-KY, 2nd)
ron.lewis@mail.house.gov

Northup, Anne (R-KY, 3rd)
rep.northup@mail.house.
gov

Lucas, Ken (D-KY, 4th)
write.kenlucas@
mail.house.gov

Rogers, Harold (R-KY, 5th)
http://www.house.gov/
writerep/

Fletcher, Ernest (R-KY, 6th)
http://www.house.gov/
writerep/

Vitter, David (R-LA, 1st)
http://www.house.gov/
writerep/

Jefferson, William (D-LA, 2nd)
http://www.house.gov/
writerep/

Tauzin, Billy (R-LA, 3rd)
http://www.house.gov/
writerep/

McCrery, Jim (R-LA, 4th)
jim.mccrery@mail.house.
gov

Cooksey, John (R-LA, 5th)
congressman.cooksey@
mail.house.gov

Baker, Richard (R-LA, 6th)
http://www.house.gov/
writerep/

John, Christopher (D-LA, 7th)
christopher.john@
mail.house.gov

Olver, John (D-MA, 1st)
http://www.house.gov/
writerep/

Neal, Richard (D-MA, 2nd)
http://www.house.gov/
writerep/

McGovern, Jim (D-MA, 3rd)
jim.mcgovern@
mail.house.gov

Frank, Barney (D-MA, 4th)
http://www.house.gov/
writerep

Meehan, Martin (D-MA, 5th)
martin.meehan@
mail.house.gov

Tierney, John (D-MA, 6th)
http://www.house.gov/
writerep/

Markey, Edward (D-MA, 7th)
http://www.house.gov/
writerep/

Capuano, Mike (D-MA, 8th)
http://www.house.gov/
writerep/

Moakley, Joe (D-MA, 9th)
joe.moakley@mail.house.
gov

Delahunt, William (D-MA, 10th)
william.delahunt@
mail.house.gov

Gilchrest, Wayne (R-MD, 1st)
http://www.house.gov/
writerep/

Ehrlich, Robert (R-MD, 2nd)
ehrlich@mail.house.gov

Cardin, Ben (D-MD, 3rd)
rep.cardin
@mail.house.gov

Wynn, Albert (D-MD, 4th)
http://www.house.gov/
writerep/

Hoyer, Steny (D-MD, 5th)
http://www.house.gov/
writerep/

Bartlett, Roscoe (R-MD, 6th)
http://www.house.gov/
writerep/

Cummings, Elijah (D-MD, 7th)
Rep.Cummings@
mail.house.gov

Morella, Constance (R-MD, 8th)
rep.morella@mail.house.
gov

Allen, Thomas (D-ME, 1st)
rep.tomallen@mail.house.
gov

Baldacci, John (D-ME, 2nd)
baldacci@me02.house.gov

Stupak, Bart (D-MI, 1st)
stupak@mail.house.gov

Hoekstra, Peter (R-MI, 2nd)
tellhoek@mail.house.gov

Ehlers, Vernon (R-MI, 3rd)
rep.ehlers@mail.house.gov

Camp, Dave (R-MI, 4th)
http://www.house.gov/
writerep/

Barcia, James (D-MI, 5th)
jim.barcia-
pub@mail.house.gov

Upton, Fred (R-MI, 6th)
talk2.fsu@mail.house.gov

Smith, Nick (R-MI, 7th)
rep.smith@mail.house.gov

Rogers, Mike (R-MI, 8th)
http://www.house.gov/
writerep

Kildee, Dale (D-MI, 9th)
dkildee@mail.house.gov

Bonior, David (D-MI, 10th)
david.bonior@mail.house.
gov

Knollenberg, Joe (R-MI, 11th)
rep.knollenberg@
mail.house.gov

Levin, Sander (D-MI, 12th)
slevin@mail.house.gov

Rivers, Lynn (D-MI, 13th)
http://www.house.gov/
writerep/ or
lynn.rivers@mail.house.gov

Conyers, John (D-MI, 14th)
john.conyers@
mail.house.gov

Kilpatrick, Carolyn (D-MI, 15th)
http://www.house.gov/
writerep/

Dingell, John (D-MI, 16th)
http://www.house.gov/
writerep/ or
public.dingell@
mail.house.gov

Gutknecht, Gil (R-MN, 1st)
gil.gutknecht@
mail.house.gov

Kennedy, Mark (R-MN, 2nd)
http://www.house.gov/
writerep/

Ramstad, Jim (R-MN, 3rd)
mn03@mail.house.gov

McCollum, Betty (D-MN, 4th)
http://www.house.gov/
writerep

Sabo, Martin (D-MN, 5th)
martin.sabo@mail.house.
gov

Luther, Bill (D-MN, 6th)
tell.bill@mail.house.gov

Peterson, Collin (D-MN, 7th)
http://www.house.gov/
writerep/

Oberstar, James (D-MN, 8th)
http://www.house.gov/
writerep/

Clay, William (D-MO, 1st)
http://www.house.gov/
writerep

Akin, W. Todd (R-MO, 2nd)
http://www.house.gov/
writerep

Gephardt, Richard (D-MO, 3rd)
gephardt@mail.house.gov

Skelton, Ike (D-MO, 4th)
ike.skelton@mail.house.gov

McCarthy, Karen (D-MO, 5th)
http://www.house.gov/
writerep/

Graves, Sam (R-MO, 6th)
http://www.house.gov/
writerep/

Blunt, Roy (R-MO, 7th)
blunt@mail.house.gov

Emerson, JoAnn (R-MO, 8th)
joann.emerson@
mail.house.gov

Hulshof, Kenny (R-MO, 9th)
rep.hulshof@mail.house.
gov

Wicker, Roger (R-MS, 1st)
http://www.house.gov/
wicker/guestbook.htm or
roger.wicker@mail.house.
gov

Thompson, Bennie (D-MS, 2nd)
thompsonms2nd@
mail.house.gov

Pickering, Charles (R-MS, 3rd)
http://www.house.gov/
writerep/

Shows, Ronnie (D-MS, 4th)
ronnie.shows@
mail.house.gov

Taylor, Gene (D-MS, 5th)
http://www.house.gov/
writerep/

Rehberg, Dennis (R-MT, AL)

Clayton, Eva (D-NC, 1st)
EClayton1@mail.house.gov

Etheridge, Bob (D-NC, 2nd)
http://www.house.gov/
writerep/

Jones, Walter (R-NC, 3rd)
congjones@mail.house.gov

Price, David (D-NC, 4th)
david.price@mail.house.gov

Burr, Richard (R-NC, 5th)
Richard.BurrNC05@
mail.house.gov

Coble, Howard (R-NC, 6th)
howard.coble@
mail.house.gov

McIntyre, Mike (D-NC, 7th)
CongMcIntyre@
mail.house.gov

Hayes, Robin (R-NC, 8th)
http://www.house.gov/
writerep/

Myrick, Sue (R-NC, 9th)
myrick@mail.house.gov or
http://www.house.gov/
myrick/guest.htm

Ballenger, Cass (R-NC, 10th)
cass.ballenger@
mail.house.gov

Taylor, Charles (R-NC, 11th)
repcharles.taylor@
mail.house.gov

Watt, Mel (D-NC, 12th)
nc12.public@mail.house.
gov

Pomeroy, Earl (D-ND, AL)
Rep.Earl.Pomeroy@
mail.house.gov

Bereuter, Douglas (R-NE, 1st)
http://www.house.gov/
writerep

Terry, Lee (R-NE, 2nd)
talk2lee@mail.house.gov

Osborne, Tom (R-NE, 3rd)
http://www.house.gov/
writerep/

Sununu, John (R-NH, 1st)
Rep.Sununu@mail.house.
gov

Bass, Charlie (R-NH, 2nd)
cbass@mail.house.gov or
http://www.house.gov/
writerep/

Andrews, Robert (D-NJ, 1st)
rob.andrews@mail.house.
gov

LoBiondo, Frank (R-NJ, 2nd)
lobiondo@mail.house.gov

Saxton, James (R-NJ, 3rd)
http://www.house.gov/
writerep/

Smith, Christopher (R-NJ, 4th)
http://www.house.gov/
writerep/

Roukema, Marge (R-NJ, 5th)
http://www.house.gov/
writerep/ or
rep.roukema@mail.house.
gov

Pallone, Frank (D-NJ, 6th)
frank.pallone@
mail.house.gov

Ferguson, Mike (R-NJ, 7th)
http://www.house.gov/
writerep

Pascrell, William (D-NJ, 8th)
bill.pascrell@mail.house.
gov

Rothman, Steven (D-NJ, 9th)
steven.rothman@
mail.house.gov

Payne, Donald (D-NJ, 10th)
donald.payne@
mail.house.gov

Frelinghuysen, Rodney (R-NJ, 11th)
rodney.frelinghuysen@
mail.house.gov

Holt, Rush (D-NJ, 12th)
rush.holt@mail.house.gov

Menendez, Robert (D-NJ, 13th)
menendez@mail.house.gov

Wilson, Heather (R-NM, 1st)
ask.heather@mail.house.
gov

Skeen, Joe (R-NM, 2nd)
joe.skeen@mail.house.gov

Udall, Tom (D-NM, 3rd)
http://www.house.gov/
writerep/

Berkley, Shelley (D-NV, 1st)
shelley.berkley@
mail.house.gov

Gibbons, Jim (R-NV, 2nd)
mail.gibbons@mail.house.
gov

Grucci, Felix Jr. (R-NY, 1st)
http://www.house.gov/
writerep

Israel, Steve (D-NY, 2nd)
http://www.house.gov/
writerep

King, Peter (R-NY, 3rd)
peter.king@mail.house.gov

McCarthy, Carolyn (D-NY, 4th)
http://www.house.gov/
writerep/

Ackerman, Gary (D-NY, 5th)
http://www.house.gov/
writerep/

Meeks, Gregory (D-NY, 6th)
congmeeks@mail.house.
gov

Crowley, Joseph (D-NY, 7th)
write2joecrowley@
mail.house.gov

Nadler, Jerrold (D-NY, 8th)
jerrold.nadler@
mail.house.gov

Weiner, Anthony (D-NY, 9th)
http://www.house.gov/
writerep/

Towns, Edolphus (D-NY, 10th)
none

Owens, Major (D-NY, 11th)
major.owens@mail.house.gov

Velazquez, Nydia (D-NY, 12th)
none

Fossella, Vito (R-NY, 13th)
vito.fossella@mail.house.gov

Maloney, Carolyn (D-NY, 14th)
rep.carolyn.maloney@mail.house.gov

Rangel, Charles (D-NY, 15th)
http://www.house.gov/writerep/

Serrano, Jose (D-NY, 16th)
jserrano@mail.house.gov

Engel, Eliot (D-NY, 17th)
http://www.house.gov/writerep/

Lowey, Nita (D-NY, 18th)
nita.lowey@mail.house.gov

Kelly, Sue (R-NY, 19th)
dearsue@mail.house.gov

Gilman, Benjamin (R-NY, 20th)
http://www.house.gov/writerep/

McNulty, Michael (D-NY, 21st)
mike.mcnulty@mail.house.gov

Sweeney, John (R-NY, 22nd)
http://www.house.gov/writerep/

Boehlert, Sherwood (R-NY, 23rd)
Rep.Boehlert@mail.house.gov

McHugh, John (R-NY, 24th)
http://www.house.gov/writerep/

Walsh, James (R-NY, 25th)
rep.james.walsh@mail.house.gov

Hinchey, Maurice (D-NY, 26th)
mhinchey@mail.house.gov

Reynolds, Tom (R-NY, 27th)
http://www.house.gov/writerep/

Slaughter, Louise (D-NY, 28th)
louiseny@mail.house.gov

LaFalce, John (D-NY, 29th)
http://www.house.gov/writerep/

Quinn, Jack (R-NY, 30th)
http://www.house.gov/writerep

Houghton, Amory (R-NY, 31st)
http://www.house.gov/writerep/

Chabot, Steve (R-OH, 1st)
http://www.house.gov/writerep/

Portman, Rob (R-OH, 2nd)
portmail@mail.house.gov

Hall, Tony (D-OH, 3rd)
http://www.house.gov/writerep/

Oxley, Michael (R-OH, 4th)
mike.oxley@mail.house.gov

Gillmor, Paul (R-OH, 5th)
http://www.house.gov/
writerep/

Strickland, Ted (D-OH, 6th)
http://www.house.gov/
writerep/

Hobson, David (R-OH, 7th)
http://www.house.gov/
hobson/formmail.htm

Boehner, John (R-OH, 8th)
john.boehner@
mail.house.gov

Kaptur, Marcy (D-OH, 9th)
rep.kaptur@mail.house.gov

Kucinich, Dennis (D-OH, 10th)
http://www.house.gov/
writerep/

Jones, Stephanie (D-OH, 11th)
stephanie.tubbs.jones@
mail.house.gov

Tiberi, Patrick (R-OH, 12th)
http://www.house.gov/
writerep

Brown, Sherrod (D-OH, 13th)
sherrod@mail.house.gov

Sawyer, Thomas (D-OH, 14th)
none

Pryce, Deborah (R-OH, 15th)
pryce.oh15@mail.house.gov

Regula, Ralph (R-OH, 16th)
http://www.house.gov/
writerep/

Traficant, James (D-OH, 17th)
telljim@mail.house.gov

Ney, Bob (R-OH, 18th)
bobney@mail.house.gov

LaTourette, Steven (R-OH, 19th)
http://www.house.gov/
writerep/steve.latourette@
mail.house.gov

Largent, Steve (R-OK, 1st)
ok01.largent@mail.house.
gov

Carson, Brad (R-OK, 2nd)
http://www.house.gov/
writerep

Watkins, Wes (R-OK, 3rd)
wes.watkins@mail.house.
gov

Watts, J. C. (R-OK, 4th)
rep.jcwatts@mail.house.gov

Istook, Ernest, Jr. (R-OK, 5th)
istook@mail.house.gov or
http://www.house.gov/
istook/guest.htm

Lucas, Frank (R-OK, 6th)
http://www.house.gov/
writerep/ or
replucas@mail.house.gov

Wu, David (D-OR, 1st)
david.wu@mail.house.gov

Walden, Gregory (R-OR, 2nd)
greg.walden@mail.house.
gov

Blumenauer, Earl (D-OR, 3rd)
write.earl@mail.house.gov

DeFazio, Pete (D-OR, 4th)
http://www.house.gov/
writerep/

Hooley, Darlene (D-OR, 5th)
darlene@mail.house.gov

Brady, Robert (D-PA, 1st)
robert.a.brady@
mail.house.gov

Fattah, Chaka (D-PA, 2nd)
http://www.house.gov/
writerep/

Borski, Robert (R-PA, 3rd)
robert.borski@
mail.house.gov

Hart, Melissa (R-PA, 4th)
http://www.house.gov/
writerep

Peterson, John (R-PA, 5th)
http://www.house.gov/
writerep/

Holden, Tim (D-PA, 6th)
http://www.house.gov/
writerep/

Weldon, Curt (R-PA, 7th)
curtpa07@mail.house.gov

Greenwood, Jim (R-PA, 8th)
http://www.house.gov/
writerep/
pawizard@mail.house.gov

Shuster, Bud (R-PA, 9th)
http://www.house.gov/
writerep

Sherwood, Donald (R-PA, 10th)
http://www.house.gov/
writerep/

Kanjorski, Paul (D-PA, 11th)
paul.kanjorski@
mail.house.gov

Murtha, John (D-PA, 12th)
murtha@mail.house.gov

Hoeffel, Joseph (D-PA, 13th)
http://www.house.gov/
writerep/

Coyne, William (D-PA, 14th)
http://www.house.gov/
writerep

Toomey, Patrick (R-PA, 15th)
rep.toomey.pa15@
mail.house.gov

Pitts, Joseph (R-PA, 16th)
pitts.pa16@mail.house.gov
or http://www.house.gov/
writerep/

Gekas, George (R-PA, 17th)
http://www.house.gov/
gekas/district/survey.html

Doyle, Mike (D-PA, 18th)
rep.doyle@mail.house.gov

Platts, Todd Russell (R-PA, 19th)
http://www.house.gov/
writerep/

Mascara, Frank (D-PA, 20th)
http://www.house.gov/
writerep/

English, Phil (R-PA, 21st)
http://www.house.gov/
writerep/

Acevedo-Vilá, Aníbal (D-Puerto Rico, AL)

Kennedy, Patrick (D-RI, 1st)
patrick.kennedy@
mail.house.gov

Langevin, James (D-RI, 2nd)
http://www.house.gov/
writerep

Brown, Henry Jr. (R-SC, 1st)
http://www.house.gov/
writerep
or
sanford@mail.house.gov
http://www.house.gov/
sanford/guest.htm

Spence, Floyd (R-SC, 2nd)
http://www.house.gov/
writerep/

Graham, Lindsey (R-SC, 3rd)
http://www.house.gov/
graham/Opinions/
opinions.htm

DeMint, James (R-SC, 4th)
jim.demint@mail.house.gov
or http://www.house.gov/
writerep/

Spratt, John (D-SC, 5th)
Rep.Spratt@mail.house.gov

Clyburn, James (D-SC, 6th)
jclyburn@mail.house.gov

Thune, John (R-SD, AL)
jthune@mail.house.gov

Jenkins, Bill (R-TN, 1st)
http://www.house.gov/
writerep/

Duncan, John (R-TN, 2nd)
http://www.house.gov/
writerep/

Wamp, Zach (R-TN, 3rd)
http://www.house.gov/
writerep/

Hilleary, Van (R-TN, 4th)
http://www.house.gov/
writerep/

Clement, Bob (D-TN, 5th)
bob.clement@mail.house.
gov

Gordon, Bart (D-TN, 6th)
bart.gordon@mail.house.
gov

Bryant, Ed (R-TN, 7th)
http://www.house.gov/
writerep/

Tanner, John (D-TN, 8th)
john.tanner@mail.house.
gov

Ford, Harold, Jr. (D-TN, 9th)
rep.harold.ford.jr@
mail.house.gov or http://
www.house.gov/writerep/

Sandlin, Max (D-TX, 1st)
http://www.house.gov/
writerep/

Turner, Jim (D-TX, 2nd)
http://www.house.gov/
writerep/ or
tx02wyr@mail.house.gov

Johnson, Sam (R-TX, 3rd)
http://www.house.gov/
samjohnson/ or IMA/
get_address.htm

Hall, Ralph (D-TX, 4th)
rmhall@mail.house.gov

Sessions, Pete (R-TX, 5th)
petes@mail.house.gov

Barton, Joe (R-TX, 6th)
http://www.house.gov/
barton/get_address.htm

Culberson, John (R-TX, 7th)
http://www.house.gov/
writerep/

Brady, Kevin (R-TX, 8th)
rep.brady@mail.house.gov

Lampson, Nick (D-TX, 9th)
nlmail@mail.house.gov

Doggett, Lloyd (D-TX, 10th)
lloyd.doggett@
mail.house.gov

Edwards, Chet (D-TX, 11th)
none

Granger, Kay (R-TX, 12th)
texas.granger@
mail.house.gov

Thornberry, Mac (R-TX, 13th)
http://www.house.gov/
writerep/

Paul, Ron (R-TX, 14th)
rep.paul@mail.house.gov

Hinojosa, Ruben (D-TX, 15th)
Rep.Hinojosa@
mail.house.gov

Reyes, Silvestre (D-TX, 16th)
http://www.house.gov/
writerep/

Stenholm, Charles (D-TX,
17th)
http://www.house.gov/
writerep/

Jackson-Lee, Sheila (D-TX,
18th)
http://www.house.gov/
writerep/

Combest, Larry (R-TX, 19th)
http://www.house.gov/
writerep/

Gonzalez, Charlie (D-TX, 20th)
http://www.house.gov/
writerep/

Smith, Lamar (R-TX, 21st)
http://www.house.gov/
writerep/

DeLay, Tom (R-TX, 22nd)
thewhip@mail.house.gov

Bonilla, Henry (R-TX, 23rd)
http://www.house.gov/
writerep/

Frost, Martin (D-TX, 24th)
martin.frost@mail.house.
gov

Bentsen, Ken (D-TX, 25th)
http://www.house.gov/
writerep/

Armey, Dick (R-TX, 26th)
http://www.house.gov/
writerep

Ortiz, Solomon (D-TX, 27th)
http://www.house.gov/
writerep

Rodriguez, Ciro (D-TX, 28th)
http://www.house.gov/
writerep/

Green, Gene (D-TX, 29th)
ask.gene@mail.house.gov

Johnson, Eddie Bernice (D-TX, 30th)
rep.e.b.johnson@
mail.house.gov

Hansen, James (R-UT, 1st)
http://www.house.gov/
writerep/

Matheson, Jim (D-UT, 2nd)
http://www.house.gov/
writerep

Cannon, Chris (R-UT, 3rd)
cannon.ut03@mail.house.
gov

Davis, Jo Ann (R-VA, 1st)
http://www.house.gov/
writerep/

Schrock, Edward (R-VA, 2nd)
http://www.house.gov/
writerep

Scott, Robert (D-VA, 3rd)
http://www.house.gov/
writerep/

Sisisky, Norman (D-VA, 4th)
http://www.house.gov/
writerep/

Goode, Virgil (I-VA, 5th)
rep.goode@mail.house.gov

Goodlatte, Bob (R-VA, 6th)
talk2bob@mail.house.gov

Cantor, Eric (R-VA, 7th)
http://www.house.gov/
writerep

Moran, Jim (D-VA, 8th)
jim.moran@mail.house.gov

Boucher, Rick (D-VA, 9th)
ninthnet@mail.house.gov

Wolf, Frank (R-VA, 10th)
http://www.house.gov/
writerep/

Davis, Tom (R-VA, 11th)
tom.davis@mail.house.gov

Christensen, Donna (D-VI, AL)
http://www.house.gov/
writerep/

Sanders, Bernie (I-VT, AL)
bernie@mail.house.gov

Inslee, Jay (D-WA, 1st)
jay.inslee@mail.house.gov

Larsen, Rick (R-WA, 2nd)
http://www.house.gov/
writerep

Baird, Brian (D-WA, 3rd)
brian.baird@mail.house.
gov

Hastings, Doc (R-WA, 4th)
http://www.house.gov/
writerep/

Nethercutt, George (R-WA, 5th)
george.nethercutt-
pub@mail.house.gov

Dicks, Norman (D-WA, 6th)
http://www.house.gov/
writerep/

McDermott, James (D-WA, 7th)
http://www.house.gov/
writerep/

Dunn, Jennifer (R-WA, 8th)
dunnwa08@mail.house.gov

Smith, Adam (D-WA, 9th)
adam.smith@mail.house.
gov

Ryan, Paul (R-WI, 1st)
pryan@mail.house.gov

Baldwin, Tammy (D-WI, 2nd)
tammy.baldwin@
mail.house.gov

Kind, Ron (D-WI, 3rd)
ron.kind@mail.house.gov

Kleczka, Gerald (D-WI, 4th)
http://www.house.gov/
writerep/

Barrett, Tom (D-WI, 5th)
telltom@mail.house.gov

Petri, Tom (R-WI, 6th)
http://www.house.gov/
writerep/

Obey, David (D-WI, 7th)
http://www.house.gov/
writerep/

Green, Mark (R-WI, 8th)
mark.green@mail.house.
gov

Sensenbrenner, James (R-WI, 9th)
sensen09@mail.house.gov

Mollohan, Alan (D-WV, 1st)
http://www.house.gov/
writerep

Capito, Shelley Moore (R-WV, 2nd)
http://www.house.gov/
writerep

Rahall, Nick (D-WV, 3rd)
nrahall@mail.house.gov

Cubin, Barbara (R-WY, AL)
http://www.house.gov/
writerep/ or
cubin.webmaster@
mail.house.gov

HOUSE OF REPRESENTATIVES COMMITTEE WEBSITES

House Web Site
http://www.house.gov/

House Agriculture
http://www.house.gov/
agriculture/

House Appropriations
http://www.house.gov/
appropriations/

House Banking (All)
http://www.house.gov/
banking/

House Banking (Democrats)
http://www.house.gov/
banking_democrats/

House Banking/Subcommittee
on Domestic and
International
http://www.house.gov/
castle/banking/

Monetary House Budget
(Republicans)
http://www.house.gov/
budget/

House Budget (Democrats)
http://www.house.gov/
budget_democrats/
mainmenu.htm

House Commerce
http://www.house.gov/
commerce/

**House Economics and
Educational Opportunity**
http://www.house.gov/eeo/

**House Government Reform
and Oversight**
http://www.house.gov/
reform/

House International Relations
http://www.house.gov/
international_relations/

House Oversight
http://www.house.gov/cho/

House Judiciary
http://www.house.gov/
judiciary/

House National Security
http://www.house.gov/nsc/

House Resources
http://www.house.gov/
resources/

House Rules
http://www.house.gov/rules/

**House Rules Subcommittee on
Rules**
http://www.house.gov/
rules_org/21home.html

House Science
http://www.house.gov/
science/

House Science (Democrats)
http://www.house.gov/
science_democrats/

House Small Business
http://www.house.gov/
smbiz/

**House Standards of Official
Conduct**
http://www.house.gov/
ethics/ethics_memos.html

House Transportation
http://www.house.gov/
transportation/

House Veterans
http://www.house.gov/va/

House Ways and Means
http://www.house.gov/
ways_means/

Clerk of the House
http://clerkweb.house.gov/

House Democratic Caucus
http://www.house.gov/
demcaucus/

House Democratic Leadership
http://www.house.gov/
democrats/

**House GPO Freshmen/104th
Congress**
http://www.house.gov/
gop_ freshmen/

House Leadership
http://www.house.gov/
orgs_pub_hse_ldr
www.html

House Majority Whip
http://www.house.gov/
majoritywhip/

House Republican Conference
http://hillsource.house.gov/

House Republican Policy Committee
http://www.house.gov/
republican-policy/

Office of the Speaker
http://
speakersnews.house.gov/

JOINT COMMITTEE WEB SITES

Congressional Budget Office
http://gopher.cbo.gov:7100/

Joint Committee on Printing
http://www.access.gpo.gov/
demo/jcp.html

Joint Economic Committee
http://www.town.hall.org:80/
places/jec or http://
www.senate.gov/~jec/, or
http://www.house.gov/jec/

Congressional Black Caucus
http://drum.ncsc.org/
~carter/CBC.html

Congressional Budget Office
http://gopher.cbo.gov:7100/

U.S. Supreme Court
U.S. Supreme Court Bldg.
Washington, DC 20543

Yugoslavia

Mirko Marjanovic
Prime Minister
Office of the Prime Minister
Belgrade, Republic of Serbia
Yugoslavia

Milo Djukanovic
President
Office of the President
Cetinje, Republic Montenegro
Yugoslavia

Filip Vujanovic
Prime Minister
Office of the Prime Minister
Podgorica, Republic of
    Montenegro
Yugoslavia
Website: http://
    www.vlada.cg.yu/drugi.htm
E-mail: vlada@cg.yu

Zambia (Republic of)
Frederick Chiluba
President
Office of the President, State
    House
Cabinet Office, Box 30208
Lusaka
Zambia
Website: http://
    www.statehouse.gov.zm
E-mail: state@zamnet.zm

Zimbabwe (Republic of)
Robert Mugabe
Executive President
Office of the President
Private Bag 7700, Causeway
Harare
Zimbabwe
Website: http://
    www.gta.gov.zw/
E-mail: http://www.gta.gov.zw/
    feedback.htm

CONSULATES GENERAL

Argentina
5055 Wilshire Blvd., Suite 210
Los Angeles, CA 90036

Australia
2049 Century Park East, 19th
    Floor
Century City, CA 90067

Austria
11859 Wilshire Blvd., Suite 501
West Los Angeles, CA 90025

Barbados
3440 Wilshire Blvd., Suite 1215
Los Angeles, CA 90010

Belgium
6100 Wilshire Blvd., Suite 1200
Los Angeles, CA 90048

Botswana
333 S. Hope St., 38th Floor
Los Angeles, CA 90071

Brazil
8484 Wilshire Blvd., Suite 730
Beverly Hills, CA 90211

Canada
300 S. Grand Ave., Suite 1000
Los Angeles, CA 90071

Chile
1900 Ave. of the Stars, Suite
    2450
Century City, CA 90067

China
44 Shatto Pl.
Los Angeles, CA 90020

Costa Rica
3540 Wilshire Blvd., Suite 404
Los Angeles, CA 90010

Denmark
10877 Wilshire Blvd., Suite
    1105
Westwood, CA 90024

Finland
1900 Ave. of the Stars, Suite
    1025
Century City, CA 90067

France
10990 Wilshire Blvd., Suite 300
Westwood, CA 90024

Germany
6222 Wilshire Blvd., Suite 500
Los Angeles, CA 90048

Great Britain
11766 Wilshire Blvd., Suite 400
West Los Angeles, CA 90025

Greece
12424 Wilshire Blvd., Suite 800
West Los Angeles, CA 90025

Guatemala
2975 Wilshire Blvd., Suite 101
Los Angeles, CA 90010

Honduras
3450 Wilshire Blvd., Suite 230
Los Angels CA 90010

Indonesia
3457 Wilshire Blvd., 4th. Floor
Los Angeles, CA 90010

Israel
6380 Wilshire Blvd., Suite 1700
Los Angeles, CA 90048

Italy
12400 Wilshire Blvd., Suite 300
West Los Angeles, CA 90025

Japan
350 S. Grand Ave., Suite 1700
Los Angeles, CA 90071

Kenya
9150 Wilshire Blvd., Suite 160
Beverly Hills, CA 90212

Korea
3243 Wilshire Blvd.
Los Angeles, CA 9010

Malaysia
350 S. Figueroa St., Suite 400
Los Angeles, CA 90071

Mexico
2401 W. Sixth St.
Los Angeles, CA 90057

The Netherlands
11766 Wilshire Blvd., Suite
1150
West Los Angeles, CA 90025

New Zealand
12400 Wilshire Blvd., Suite
1150
West Los Angeles, CA 90025

Nicaragua
2500 Wilshire Blvd., Suite 915
Los Angeles, CA 90057

Peru
3460 Wilshire Blvd., Suite 1005
Los Angels, CA 90010

Philippines
3660 Wilshire Blvd., Suite 900
Los Angeles, CA 90010

Russian Federation
2790 Green St.
San Francisco, CA 94123

Saudi Arabia
2045 Sawtelle Blvd.
West Los Angeles, CA 90025

South Africa
50 N. La Cienega Blvd., Suite
300
Beverly Hills, CA 90211

Spain
5055 Wilshire Blvd., Suite 960
Los Angeles, CA 90036

Sweden
530 Broadway Ave., Suite 1106
San Diego, CA 92101

Switzerland
11766 Wilshire Blvd., Suite
    1400
West Los Angeles, CA 9025

Thailand
801 N. La Brea Ave.
Hollywood, CA 90038

Turkey
4801 Wilshire Blvd., Suite 310
Los Angeles, CA 90010

Uruguay
429 Santa Monica Blvd., Suite
    400
Santa Monica, CA 90401

MAJOR LEAGUE BASEBALL ADDRESSES

Office of the Commissioner
350 Park Ave., 17th Floor
New York, NY 10022
Website: http://
   www.MLB@BAT

American League
350 Park Ave., 18th Floor
New York, NY 10022

National League
350 Park Ave.
New York, NY 10022

Anaheim Angels
Office: 2000 Gene Autry Way
Anaheim, CA 92806
Mailing address: PO Box 2000
Anaheim, CA 92803
Website: http://
   www.angelsbaseball.com/

Baltimore Orioles
333 W. Camden St.
Baltimore, MD 21201
Website: http://
   www.theorioles.com/

Boston Red Sox
Fenway Park
4 Yawkey Way
Boston, MA 02215
Website: http://
   www.redsox.com/

Chicago White Sox
333 W 35th St.
Chicago, IL 60616
Website: http://
   www.chisox.com/

Cleveland Indians
Jacobs Field
2401 Ontario St.
Cleveland, OH 44115
Website: http://
   www.indians.com/

Detroit Tigers
Tiger Stadium
2121 Trumbull Ave.
Detroit, MI 48216
Website: http://
   www.detroittigers.com/

Kansas City Royals
Office: One Royal Way
Kansas City, MO 64129
Mailing address: PO Box
   419969
Kansas City, MO 64141
Website: http://
   www.kcroyals.com/

Minnesota Twins
34 Kirby Puckett Place
Minneapolis, MN 55415
Website: http://www.wcco.com/
   sports/twins/

New York Yankees
Yankee Stadium
161st St. and River Ave.
Bronx, NY 10451
Website: http://
   www.yankees.com/

Oakland Athletics
7677 Oakport St., Suite 200
Oakland, CA 94621
Website: http://
   www.oaklandathletics.com/

Seattle Mariners
Office: 83 S. King St.
Seattle, WA 98104
Mailing address: POB 4100
Seattle, WA 98104
Website: http://
   www.mariners.org/

Tampa Bay Devil Rays
Tropicana Field
One Tropicana Dr.
St. Petersburg, FL 33705
Website: http://
   www.devilray.com

Texas Rangers
Office: 1000 Ballpark Way
Arlington, TX 76011
Mailing address: POB 90111
Arlington, TX 76004
Website: http://
   www.texasrangers.com/

Toronto Blue Jays
One Blue Jays Way
Suite 3200, Skydome
Toronto, Ontario M5V 1J1
Canada
Website: http://
   www.bluejays.ca/

Arizona Diamondbacks
Office: 401 East Jefferson St.
Phoenix, AZ 85004
Mailing address: PO Box 2095
Phoenix, AZ 85001
Website: http://
   www.azdiamondbacks.com/

Atlanta Braves
Office: 755 Hank Aaron Dr.
Atlanta, GA 30315
Mailing address: PO Box 4064
Atlanta, GA 30302
Website: http://
   www.atlantabraves.com/

Chicago Cubs
Wrigley Field
1060 West Addison St.
Chicago, IL 60613
Website: http://www.cubs.com/

Cincinnati Reds
100 Cinergy Field
Cincinnati, OH 45202
Website: http://
   www.cincinnatireds.com/

Colorado Rockies
2001 Blake St.
Denver, CO 80205
Website: http://
   www.coloradorockies.com/

Florida Marlins
Pro Player Stadium
2267 NW 199th St.
Miami, FL 33056
Website: http://
   www.flamarlins.com/

Houston Astros
Office: 8400 Kirby Dr.
Houston, TX 77054
Mailing address: PO Box 288
Houston, TX 77001
Website: http://
   www.astros.com/

Los Angeles Dodgers
1000 Elysian Park Ave.
Los Angeles, CA 90012
Website: http://
   www.dodgers.com/

Milwaukee Brewers
Stadium
201 S 46th St.
Milwaukee, WI 53214
Mailing address: PO Box 3099
Milwaukee, WI 53201
Website: http://www.milwaukee
   brewers.com

Montreal Expos
Office: 4549
Pierre-de-Courbertin Avenue
Montreal, Quebec H1V 3N7
Mailing: PO Box 500, Station
   M
Montreal, Quebec H1V 3P2
Canada
Website: http://
   www.montrealexpos.com/

New York Mets
Shea Stadium
123-01 Roosevelt Ave.
Flushing, NY 11368

Philadelphia Phillies
Veterans Stadium
3501 S Broad St.
Philadelphia, PA 19148
Mailing address: PO Box 7575
Philadelphia, PA 19101
Website: http://
   www.phillies.com

Pittsburgh Pirates
600 Stadium Circle
Pittsburgh, PA 15212
Mailing address: PO Box 7000
Pittsburgh, PA 15212
Website: http://
   www.pirateball.com/

St. Louis Cardinals
250 Stadium Plaza
St. Louis, MO 63102
Website: http://
   www.stlcardinals.com/

San Diego Padres
Office: Jack Murphy Stadium
8880 Rio San Diego Dr., Suite
   400
San Diego, CA 92108
Mailing Address: POB 2000
San Diego, CA 92112
Website: http://
   www.padres.org/

San Francisco Giants
3Com Park at Candlestick
   Point
San Francisco, CA 94124
Website: http://
   www.sfgiants.com/

BASEBALL TEAM SPRING TRAINING ADDRESSES

AMERICAN LEAGUE

Anaheim Angels
Tempe Diable Stadium
2200 West Alameda
Tempe, AZ 85282

Baltimore Orioles
Fort Lauderdale Stadium
5301 Northwest 12th Ave.
Ft. Lauderdale, FL 33309

Boston Red Sox
City of Palm Park
2201 Edison Ave.
Fort Myers, FL 33901

Chicago White Sox
Tucson Electric Park
2500 East Ao Way
Tucson, AZ 85713

Cleveland Indians
Chain of Lakes Park
Winter Haven, FL 33880

Detroit Tigers
2125 North Lake Avenue
Lakeland, FL 33805

Kansas City Royals
Baseball City Stadium
300 Stadium Way
Davenport, FL 33837

NATIONAL LEAGUE

Arizona Diamondbacks
Tucson Electric Park
2500 East Ao Way
Tucson, AZ 85713

Minnesota Twins
Hammond Stadium
14100 Six Mile Cypress Pkwy.
Fort Myers, FL 33912

New York Yankees
3802 W. Martin Luther King
  Blvd.
Tampa, FL 33614

Oakland Athletics
Phoenix Municipal Stadium
5999 East Van Buren St.
Phoenix, AZ 85008

Seattle Mariners
Peoria Sports Complex
PO Box 999
Peoria, AZ 85380-0999

Tampa Bay Devil Rays
Al Lang Stadium
180 Second Ave. SE
St. Petersburg, FL 33701

Texas Rangers
Rangers Complex
2300 El Jobean Rd.
Port Charlotte, FL 33948

Toronto Blue Jays
PO Box 957
Dunedin, FL 34697

Atlanta Braves
700 S. Victory Way
Kissimmee, FL 34744

Chicago Cubs
HoHoKam Park
1235 North Center St.
Mesa, AZ 85201

Cincinnati Reds
12th St. and Tuttle Ave.
Sarasota, FL 34237

Colorado Rockies
Hi Corbett Field
3400 E. Camino Campestre
Tucson, AZ 85716

Florida Marlins
Space Coast Stadium
5800 Stadium Pkwy.
Melbourne, FL 32940

Houston Astros
PO Box 422229
Kissimmee, FL 34742-2229

Los Angeles Dodgers
Holman Stadium at
    Dodgertown
PO Box 2887
Vero Beach, FL 32961

Milwaukee Brewers
Maryvale Baseball Park
3600 North 51st Ave.
Phoenix, AZ 85031

Montreal Expos
PO Box 8976
Jupiter, FL 33468

New York Mets
525 Northwest Peacock Blvd.
Port St. Lucie, FL 34986

Philadelphia Phillies
PO Box 10336
Clearwater, FL 34617

Pittsburgh Pirates
Pirate City
PO Box 1359
Bradenton, FL 34206

St. Louis Cardinals
PO Box 8929
Jupiter, FL 33468

San Diego Padres
Peoria Sports Complex
16101 N. 83rd Ave.
Peoria, AZ 85382

San Francisco Giants
Scottsdale Stadium
7408 E. Osborn Road
Scottsdale, AZ 85251

NATIONAL BASKETBALL ASSOCIATION TEAMS

National Basketball Assoc.
Olympic Tower
645 Fifth Ave.
New York, NY 10022
Official Website: http://
    www.nba.com/

Atlanta Hawks
One CNN Center
Suite 405, South Tower
Atlanta, GA 30303

Boston Celtics
151 Merrimac St., 4th Floor
Boston, MA 02114

Charlotte Hornets
100 Hive Dr.
Charlotte, NC 28217

Chicago Bulls
1901 West Madison
Chicago, IL 60612

Cleveland Cavaliers
Gund Arena
One Center Court
Cleveland, OH 44115

Dallas Mavericks
Reunion Arena
777 Sports St.
Dallas, TX 75207

Denver Nuggets
1635 Clay St.
Denver, CO 80204

Detroit Pistons
The Palace of Auburn Hills
Two Championship Dr.
Auburn Hills, MI 48326

Golden State Warriors
Oakland Coliseum Arena
7000 Coliseum Way
Oakland, CA 94621

Houston Rockets
10 Greenway Plaza
Houston, TX 77046

Indiana Pacers
Indianapolis, IN 46204

Los Angeles Clippers
Staples Center
1111 S. Figueroa St.
Los Angeles, CA 90015

Los Angeles Lakers
Staples Center
1111 S. Figueroa St.
Los Angeles, CA 90015

Miami Heat
SunTrust International Center
One Southeast Third Ave.,
   Suite #2300
Miami, FL 33131

Milwaukee Bucks
1001 North Fourth St.
Milwaukee, WI 53203

WOMEN'S NATIONAL BASKETBALL ASSOCIATION TEAMS

EASTERN CONFERENCE

Charlotte Sting
3308 Oak Lake Blvd., Suite B
Charlotte, NC 28208

Cleveland Rockers
Gund Arena
1 Center Court
Cleveland, OH 44115

Detroit Shock
The Palace of Auburn Hills
Two Championship Dr.
Auburn Hills, MI 48326

Indiana Fever
Conseco Fieldhouse
One Conseco Court
125 S. Pennsylvania St.
Indianapolis, IN 46204

New York Liberty
Madison Square Garden
Two Pennsylvania Plaza, 14th
    Floor
New York, NY 10121

Orlando Miracle
P.O. Box 4000
Orlando, FL 32802

Miami Sol
601 Biscayne Blvd.
Miami, FL 33010

Washington Mystics
1 Harry S. Truman Dr.
Landover, MD 20785

WESTERN CONFERENCE

Houston Comets
Two Greenway Plaza, Suite 400
Houston, TX 77046

Portland Fire
The Rose Garden
1 Center Court
Portland, OR 97227

Los Angeles Sparks
PO Box 10
Inglewood, CA 90306
or
555 N. Nash St.
El Segundo, CA 90245

Sacramento Monarchs
One Sports Pkwy.
Sacramento, CA 95834

Minnesota Lynx
Target Center
600 First Avenue North
Minneapolis, MN 55403

Seattle Storm
351 Elliot Avenue, #500
Seattle, WA 98119

Phoenix Mercury
America West Arena
201 East Jefferson
Phoenix, AZ 85004

Utah Starzz
Delta Center
301 West South Temple
Salt Lake City, UT 84101

AMERICAN BASKETBALL LEAGUE TEAMS

American Basketball League
1900 Embarcadero Rd., Suite
    110
Palo Alto, CA 94303
Website: http://

www.ableague.com/
E-mail: hoops@ableague.com

Atlanta Glory
2100 Powers Ferry Rd., Suite
    400
Atlanta, GA 30339
Website: http://
    www.atlantaglory.com
E-mail: info@atlantaglory.com

Colorado Xplosion
800 Grant St., Suite 410
Denver CO 80203
Website: http://
    www.xplosion.com
E-mail: info@xplosion.com

Columbus Quest
7451 State Route 161
Dublin, OH 43016
Website: http://
    www.columbusquest.com

Long Beach Stingrays
One World Trade Center,
    Suite 202
Long Beach, CA 90831
Website: http://
    www.lbstingrays.com

New England Blizzard
179 Allyn St., Suite 403
Hartford, CT 06103
Website: http://
    www.neblizzard.com
E-mail: info@neblizzard.com

Portland Power
439 North Broadway
Portland, OR 97227
Website: http://
    www.portlandpower.com

Philadelphia Rage
123 Chestnut St., 4th Floor
Philadelphia, PA 19106
Website: http://
    www.phillyrage.com/

San Jose Lasers
1530 Parkmoor Ave., Suite A
San Jose, CA 95128
Website: http://
    www.sjlasers.com

Seattle Reign
400 Mercer St., Suite 408
Seattle, WA 98109
Website: http://
    www.seattlereign.com
E-mail: reign@seattlereign.com

CONTINENTAL BASKETBALL ASSOCIATION TEAMS

Continental Basketball Assoc.
Two Arizona Center
400 N. 5th St., Suite 1425
Phoenix, AZ 85004
Website: http://
    www.cbahoops.com/
E-mail: cbagc@netcom.com

Connecticut Pride
#21 Waterville Rd.
Avon, CT 06001

Idaho Stampede
90 South Cole Rd.
Franklin Business Park
Boise, ID 83709

Fort Wayne Fury
1010 Memorial Way, Suite 210
Fort Wayne, IN 46805

Grand Rapids Hoops
190 Monroe NW, Room 222
Grand Rapids, MI 49503

La Crosse Bobcats
200 Main St., Suite 200
PO Box 1717
La Crosse, WI 54602

Quad City Thunder
7800 14th St. West
Rock Island, IL 61201

Rockford Lightning
3660 Publisher's Dr.
Rockford, IL 61109

Sioux Falls Skyforce
330 N Main Ave, #101
Sioux Falls, SD 57102

Yakima Sun Kings
PO Box 2626
Yakima, WA 98907

NATIONAL FOOTBALL LEAGUE TEAMS

National Football League
410 Park Ave.
New York, NY 10022
Website: http://www.nfl.com

Arizona Cardinals
PO Box 888
Phoenix, AZ 85001-0888

Atlanta Falcons
2745 Burnette Rd.
Suwanee, GA 30174

Baltimore Ravens
11001 Owings Mills Blvd.
Owings Mills, MD 21117

Buffalo Bills
One Bills Dr.
Orchard Park, NY 14127

Carolina Panthers
227 West Trade St., Suite 1600
Charlotte, NC 28202

Chicago Bears
250 North Washington Rd.
Lake Forest, IL 60045

Cincinnati Bengals
200 Riverfront Stadium
Cincinnati, OH 45202

Dallas Cowboys
One Cowboys Pkwy.
Irving, TX 75063

Denver Broncos
13655 Broncos Pkwy.
Englewood, CO 80112

Detroit Lions
Pontiac Silverdome
1200 Featherstone Rd.
Pontiac, MI 48342

Green Bay Packers
1265 Lombardi Ave.
Green Bay, WI 54304

Houston Oilers
6910 Fannin St.
Houston, TX 77030

Indianapolis Colts
PO Box 535000
Indianapolis, IN 46253

Jacksonville Jaguars
One Stadium Place
Jacksonville, FL 32202

Kansas City Chiefs
One Arrowhead Dr.
Kansas City, MO 64129

Miami Dolphins
2269 N.W. 199th St.
Miami, FL 33056

Minnesota Vikings
9520 Viking Dr.
Eden Prairie, MN 55344

New England Patriots
60 Washington St.
Foxboro, MA 02035
Website: http://
       www.patriots.com/

New Orleans Saints
6928 Saints Dr.
Metairie, LA 70003

New York Giants
Giants Stadium
East Rutherford, NJ 07073

New York Jets
1000 Fulton Ave.
Hempstead, NY 11550

Oakland Raiders
332 Center St.
El Segundo, CA 90245

Philadelphia Eagles
3501 South Broad St.
Philadelphia, PA 19148

Pittsburgh Steelers
300 Stadium Circle
Pittsburgh, PA 15212

St. Louis Rams
100 North Broadway
St. Louis, MO 63102

San Francisco 49ers
4949 Centennial Blvd.
Santa Clara, CA 95054

San Diego Chargers
PO Box 609609
San Diego, CA 92160

Seattle Seahawks
11220 N.E. 53rd St.
Kirkland, WA 98033

Tampa Bay Buccaneers
One Buccaneer Place
Tampa, FL 33607

Washington Redskins
21300 Redskin Park Dr.
Ashburn, VA 22011

NATIONAL HOCKEY LEAGUE TEAMS

National Hockey League
1251 Ave. of the Americas
New York, NY 10020
Website: http://www.nhl.com/

National Hockey League
Toronto Office
75 International Blvd., Suite
   300
Rexdale, Ontario M9W 6L9

National Hockey League
Montreal Office
1800 McGill College Ave.,
    Suite 2600
Montreal, Quebec H3A 3J6

The Mighty Ducks of Anaheim
2695 E. Katella Ave.
PO Box 61077
Anaheim, CA 92803

Boston Bruins
Fleet Center
Boston, MA 02114

Buffalo Sabres
Marine Midland Arena
One Seymour Knox III Plaza
Buffalo, NY 14203

Calgary Flames
Canadian Airlines Saddledome
PO Box 1540, Station M
Calgary, AB T2P 3B9
Canada

Chicago Blackhawks
United Center
1901 W. Madison St.
Chicago, IL 60612

Colorado Avalanche
McNichols Sports Arena
1635 Clay St.
Denver, CO 80204

Dallas Stars
Star Center
211 Cowboys Pkwy.
Irving, TX 75063

Detroit Red Wings
Joe Louis Arena
600 Civic Center
Detroit, MI 48226

Edmonton Oilers
11230-110 Ave.
Edmonton, AB T5G 3G8
Canada

Florida Panthers
100 N.E. 3rd Ave., 10th Floor
Ft. Lauderdale, FL 33301

Carolina Hurricanes
5000 Aerial Center, Suite 1000
Morrisville, NC 27560

Los Angeles Kings
Staples Center
1111 S. Figueroa St.
Los Angeles, CA 90015

Montreal Canadiens
Molson Centre
1260, rue de la Gauchetiere
Ouest
Monteal, Quebec H3B 5E8
Canada

New Jersey Devils
Continental Airlines Arena
PO Box 504
East Rutherford, NJ 07073

New York Islanders
Nassau Coliseum
Uniondale, NY 11553

New York Rangers
Madison Square Garden
4 Pennsylvania Plaza
New York, NY 10001

Ottawa Senators
Corel Center
1000 Palladium Dr.
Kanata, ON K2V 1A5
Canada

Philadelphia Flyers
CoreStates Center
1 CoreStates Complex
Philadelphia, PA 19148

Phoenix Coyotes
One Renaissance Square
2 North Central, Suite 1930
Phoenix, AZ 85004

Pittsburgh Penguins
Civic Arena
Gate 9
Pittsburgh, PA 15219

St. Louis Blues
Kiel Center
1401 Clark Ave.
St. Louis, MO 63103

San Jose Sharks
San Jose Arena
525 W. Santa Clara St.
San Jose, CA 95113

Tampa Bay Lightning
Ice Palace
401 Channelside Dr.
Tampa, FL 33602

Toronto Maple Leafs
Maple Leaf Gardens
60 Carlton St.
Toronto, ON M5B 1L1
Canada

Vancouver Canucks
General Motors Place
800 Griffiths Way
Vancouver, BC V6B 6G1
Canada

Washington Capitals
US Airways Arena
Landover, MD 20785

AMERICAN HOCKEY LEAGUE TEAMS

American Hockey League
425 Union St.
West Springfield, MA 01089
Website: http://www.canoe.ca/
    AHL/

Portland Pirates
Cumberland County Civic
    Center
85 Free St.
Portland, ME 04101

Providence Bruins
Providence Civic Center
1 LaSalle Square
Providence, RI 02903

Springfield Falcons
PO Box 3190
Springfield, MA 01101

Worcester Ice Cats
303 Main St.
Worcester, MA 01608

Beast of New Haven
275 Orange St.
New Haven, CT 06510

Cincinnati Mighty Ducks
2250 Seymour Ave.
Cincinnati, OH 45212

Hershey Bears
PO Box 866
Hershey, PA 17033

Kentucky Thoroughblades
410 West Vine St.
Lexington, KY 40507

Philadelphia Phantoms
The CoreStates Spectrum
1 CoreStates Complex
Philadelphia, PA 19148

Fredericton Canadiens
Aitken University Centre
PO Box HABS
Fredericton, NB E3B 4Y2

Hamilton Bulldogs
85 York Blvd.
Hamilton Ontario L8R 3L4
Canada

Saint John Flames
PO Box 4040, Station B
Saint John, NB E2M 5E6
Canada

St. John's Maple Leafs
6 Logy Bay Rd.
St. John's, Newfoundland
A1A 1J3 Canada

Adirondack Red Wings
1 Civic Center Plaza
Glens Falls, NY 12801

Albany River Rats
Knickerbocker Arena
51 South Pearl St.
Albany, NY 12207

Hartford Wolf Pack
196 Trumbull St., 3rd Floor
Hartford, CT 06103

Rochester Americans
50 South Ave.
Rochester, NY 14604

Syracuse Crunch
Onondaga County War
    Memorial
800 South State St.
Syracuse, NY 13202

CENTRAL HOCKEY LEAGUE TEAMS

Central Hockey League
5840 S. Memorial Dr., Suite 302
Tulsa, OK 74145

Columbus Cottonmouths
PO Box 1886
Columbus, GA 31902-1886

Huntsville Channel Cats
Von Braun Center
700 Monroe St.
Huntsville, AL 35801
Website: http://
    www.channelcats.com

Macon Whoopee
Macon Centreplex
200 Coliseum Dr.
Macon, GA 31201
Website: http://
    www.maconwhoopee.com

Memphis RiverKings
Mid-South Coliseum
The Fairgrounds
Memphis, TN 38104

Nashville Ice Flyers
PO Box 190595
Nashville, TN 37219

Fort Worth Fire
University Centre
1300 S. University, Suite 515
Fort Worth, TX 76107
Website: http://www.fwfire.
   com/

Oklahoma City Blazers
119 N. Robinson, Suite 230
Oklahoma City, OK 73102
Website: http://
   www.okcblazers.com/

Fayetteville Force
121 E. Mountain Dr., Rm22B
Fayetteville, NC 28306
Website: http://
   www.fayettevilleforce.com

Tulsa Oilers
613 S. Mingo
Tulsa, OK 74133

Wichita Thunder
505 West Maple, Suite 100
Wichita, KS 67213

EAST COAST HOCKEY LEAGUE TEAMS

East Coast Hockey League
125 Village Blvd., Suite 210
Princeton, NJ 08540
Website: http://www.echl.org/

Columbus Chill
7001 Dublin Park Dr.
Dublin, OH 43016

Dayton Bombers
Ervin J. Nutter Center
3640 Colonel Glenn Highway,
   Suite 417
Dayton, OH 45435

Huntington Blizzard
763 Third Ave.
Huntington, WV 25701

Johnstown Chiefs
326 Napoleon St.
Johnstown, PA 15901

Louisville River Frogs
PO Box 36407
Louisville, KY 40233

Peoria Rivermen
201 SW Jefferson
Peoria, IL 61602

Toledo Storm
One Main St.
Toledo, OH 43605

Wheeling Nailers
PO Box 6563
Wheeling, WV 26003-0815

Baton Rouge Kingfish
PO Box 2142
Baton Rouge, LA 70821

Birmingham Bulls
PO Box 1506
Birmingham, AL 35201

Jacksonville Lizard Kings
5569-7 Bowden Rd.
Jacksonville, FL 32216

Louisiana IceGators
444 Cajundome Blvd.
Lafayette, LA 70506

Mississippi Sea Wolves
2350 Beach Blvd.
Biloxi, MS 39531

Mobile Mysticks
PO Box 263
Mobile, AL 36601

Pensacola Ice Pilots
Civic Center/201 E. Gregory
    St., Rear
Pensacola, FL 32501

Tallahassee Tiger Sharks
505 W. Pensacola St., Suite 1
Tallahassee, FL 32301

Charlotte Checkers
2700 E. Independence Blvd.
Charlotte, NC 28205

Hampton Roads Admirals
PO Box 299
Norfolk, VA 23501

Knoxville Cherokees
500 East Church St.
Knoxville, TN 37915

Raleigh Ice Caps
4000 West Chase Blvd, Suite
    110
Raleigh, NC 27607

Richmond Renegades
601 East Leigh St.
Richmond, VA 23219

Roanoke Express
4502 Starkey Rd. SW, Suite 211
Roanoke, VA 24014

South Carolina Stingrays
3107 Firestone Rd.
North Charleston, SC 29418

WESTERN PROFESSIONAL HOCKEY LEAGUE TEAMS

**Western Professional Hockey
    League**
14040 North Cave Creek Rd.,
    Suite #100
Phoenix, AZ
Website: http://
    www.wphlhockey.com
E-mail: wphl@netzone.com

Amarillo Rattlers
320 South Polk St., Suite #800
Amarillo, TX 79101
Website http://www.wphl-
    rattlers.com

Austin Ice Bats
7311 Decker Lane
Austin, TX 78724

Central Texas Stampede
600 Forest Dr.
Belton, TX 76513

El Paso Buzzards
4100 East Paisano Dr.
El Paso, TX 79905

Fort Worth Bramahs
PO Box 470606
Fort Worth, TX 76147

Lake Charles Ice Pirates
900 Lakeshore Dr., 2nd Floor
Lake Charles, LA 70602

Monroe Moccasins
2102 Louisville Ave.
Monroe, LA 71201

San Angelo Outlaws
3260 Sherwood Way
San Angelo, TX 76901

New Mexico Scorpions
1101 Cardenas Plaza, Suite 201
Albuquerque, NM 87110

Shreveport Mudbugs
3701 Hudson St., 2nd Floor
Shreveport, LA 71109

Odessa Jackalopes
PO Box 51187
Midland, TX 79710

Waco Wizards
2040 North Valley Mills Dr.
Waco, TX 76710

MAJOR LEAGUE SOCCER TEAMS

Major League Soccer
110 East 42nd St., 10th Floor
New York, NY 10017
Website: http://
  www.mlsnet.com

Dallas Burn
2602 McKinney, Suite 200
Dallas, TX 75204
Website: http://www.
  burnsoccer.com
E-mail: mail@burnsoccer.com

Chicago Fire
311 West Superior, Suite #444
Chicago, IL 60610
Website: http://www.chicago-
  fire.com

DC United
13832 Redskin Dr.
Herndon, VA 22071
Website: http://
  www.dcunited.com
E-mail: united-fan@mlsnet.com

Colorado Rapids
555 17th St., Suite 3350
Denver, CO 80202
Website: http://
  www.coloradorapids.com
E-mail: Rapids@mlsnet.com

Kansas City Wizards
706 Broadway St., Suite 100
Kansas City, MO 64105
Website: http://
  www.kcwizards.com/
E-mail: ctaylor@mlsnet.com

Columbus Crew
77 East Nationwide Blvd.
Columbus, OH 43215
Website: http://
  www.thecrew.com/
E-mail: crew2739@aol.com

Los Angeles Galaxy
1640 S. Sepulveda Blvd., Suite
  114
Los Angeles, CA 90025

Miami Fusion
2200 Commercial Blvd., Suite
    104
Ft. Lauderdale, FL 33309
Website: http://
    www.miamifusion.com

New England Revolution
Foxboro Stadium
60 Washington St., Route 1
Foxboro, MA 02035
Website: http://
    www.nerevolution.com/

NY/NJ MetroStars
One Harmon Plaza, 8th Floor
Secaucus, NJ 07094
Website: http://
    www.metrostars.com/
E-mail:MetroFan@mlsnet.com

San Jose Clash
1265 El Camino Real, 2nd
    Floor
Santa Clara, CA 95050
Website: http://
    www.clash.com/
E-mail: clash@clash.com

Tampa Bay Mutiny
1408 Westshore Blvd, Suite
    1004
Tampa, FL 33607
Website: http://
    www.tampabaymutiny.com/
E-mail:
    mutinymail@mlsnet.com
National Professional Soccer
    League Teams

**National Professional Soccer
    League**
115 Dewalt Ave., NW, Fifth
    Floor
Canton, Ohio 44702
E-mail: NPSL1@aol.com

Baltimore Spirit
201 West Baltimore St.
Baltimore, MD 21201
Website: http://
    www.baltimorespirit.com
E-mail: spiritsoccer@
baltimorespirit.com

Buffalo Blizzard
Marine Midland Arena
One Seymour Knox III Plaza
Buffalo, NY 14203
Website: http://
    www.buffaloblizzard.com

Cincinnati Silverbacks
537 E. Pete Rose Way, 2nd
    Floor
Cincinnati, OH 45202

Cleveland Crunch
34200 Solon Rd.
Solon, OH 44139

Detroit Rockers
600 Civic Center Dr.
Detroit, MI 48226
E-mail: rockersoc@aol.com

Edmonton Drillers
11230 110th St.
Edmonton, AB
Canada T5G 3G8
Website: http://
    www.edmontondrillers.com
E-mail:
    drillers@compusmart.ab.ca

Harrisburg Heat
PO Box 60123
Harrisburg, PA 17106
Website: http://
    www.heatsoccer.com/
E-mail: heatsoccer@aol.com

Kansas City Attack
1800 Genessee
Kansas City, MO 64102

Milwaukee Wave
10201 N. Port Washington Rd.,
    Suite 200
Mequon, WI 53092
Website: http://
    www.wavesoccer.com

Montreal Impact
8000 Langelier, Suite 104
St. Leonard QUE H1P 3K2
Canada
Website: http://
    www.impactmtl.com
E-mail: Info@impact.usisl.com

Philadelphia Kixx
CoreStates Spectrum
1 CoreStates Complex
Philadelphia, PA 19148-9727
Website: http://
    kixx.phillynews.com
E-mail: kixxsoccer@aol.com

St. Louis Ambush
7547 Ravensridge
St. Louis, MO 63119

Wichita Wings
500 South Broadway
Wichita, KS 67202
Website: http://www.wichita-
    wings.com

THE A-LEAGUE HOCKEY TEAMS

The A-League
14497 N. Dale Mabry, Suite
    211
Tampa FL 33618

Atlanta Ruckus
1131 Alpharetta St.
Roswell, GA 30075

California Jaguars
12 Clay Street
Salinas, CA 93901

Carolina Dynamo
3517 W. Wendover Ave.
Greensboro, NC 27407

Charleston Battery
4401 Belle Oaks Dr., Suite 450
Charleston, SC 29405

Colorado Foxes
6200 Dahlia St.
Commerce City, CO 80022

Connecticut Wolves
PO Box 3196
Veterans Memorial Stadium
New Britain, CT 06050-3196

El Paso Patriots
6941 Industrial
El Paso, TX 79915

Hershey Wildcats
100 W. Hersheypark Dr.
Hershey, PA 17033

Jacksonville Cyclones
9428 Bay Meadows Rd., Suite
    175
Jacksonville, FL 32256

Long Island Rough Riders
1670 Old Country Rd., Suite
    227
Plain View, NY 11803

Milwaukee Rampage
Uihlein Soccer Park
7101 West Good Hope Rd.
Milwaukee, WI 53223

Minnesota Thunder
1700 105th Ave. NE
Elaine, MN 55449

Montreal Impact
8000 Langelier, Suite 104
St. Leonard Quebec H1P 3K2
Canada

Nashville Metros
7115 South Spring Dr.
Franklin, TN 37067-1616

**New Orleans Riverboat
    Gamblers**
5690 Eastover Dr.
New Orleans, LA 70128

Orange County Zodiac
% Unicor
14210 Quail Ridge Dr.
Riverside, CA 92503

Orlando Sandogs
One Citrus Bowl Place
Orlando, FL 32805

Raleigh Flyers
130 Wind Chime Ct.
Raleigh, NC 27615

Richmond Kickers
2320 West Main St.
Richmond, VA 23220

Rochester Raging Rhinos
333 N. Plymouth Ave.
Rochester, NY 14608

Seattle Sounders
10838 Main St.
Bellevue, WA 98004

Toronto Lynx
% HIT Pro Soccer, Inc.
55 University Ave., Suite 506
Toronto Ontario M5J 2H7
Canada

Vancouver 86ers
1126 Douglas Rd.
Burnaby BC V5C 4Z6
Canada

Worcester Wildfire
500 Main St., Suite 515
Worcester, MA 01608

Write to Me

The Address Book is updated every two years, and you can play an active role in this process. If you are notable in any field or know someone who is, send the name, mailing address, and some documentation of the notability (newspaper clippings are effective) for possible inclusion in our next edition.

Also, we are very interested in learning of any success stories resulting from *The Address Book*.

During the last few years, I have received tens of thousands of letters, ranging from loving to vituperative, from owners of *The Address Book*. Despite the overwhelming task of answering this mail, I really enjoy the letters.

But, please, remember a couple of rules if you write:

- Remember to include a *self-addressed stamped envelope*. For reasons of both time and expense, this is the only way I can respond to mail; so, unfortunately, I've had to draw the line—no SASE, no reply.
- I need your comments. While I confess I'm partial to success stories, comments from purchasers of the book have helped me a great deal for updating editions; so fire away.
- Many people have written to request addresses of people not listed in the book. As much as I would like to, I simply can't open up this can of worms. Requests for additional addresses are carefully noted and considered for future editions.

Receiving a photo from someone who writes adds an entirely new dimension to the letter, so feel free. That's right, enclose a photo of yourself. After all, from the photo on the back cover, you know what I look like, and I'm rather eager to see you.

Keep those cards and letters coming.

Michael Levine
5750 Wilshire Blvd., #555
Los Angeles, CA 90036
levinepr@earthlink.net

OTHER BOOKS OF INTEREST

THE ADDRESS BOOK (10th Edition)
by Michael Levine   0-399-52667-6/$13.95

The definitive guide to reaching just about anyone; provides
mailing addresses of over 3,500 VIPs and celebrities in every
field imaginable.
A Perigee Trade Paperback

THE KID'S ADDRESS BOOK (5th Edition)
by Michael Levine   0-399-52688-9/$13.95

Kids can make a difference, make a suggestion, or make a
new pen pal, with more than 2,000 addresses of the most
popular and important people and organizations.
A Perigee Trade Paperback

TAKE IT FROM ME
by Michael Levine   0-399-52217-4/$12.00

Career advice from the brighest stars in entertainment,
business, politics, and sports. From Woody Allen to Donald
Trump, the powerful and celebrated share witty ancedotes
and words of wisdom on following one's dreams, excelling at
work, overcoming setbacks, and reaching the top.
A Perigee Trade Paperback